M000222958

Monte Cassino

Monte Cassino

Opening the Road to Rome

Richard Doherty

Pen & Sword
MILITARY

AN IMPRINT OF PEN & SWORD BOOKS LTD.
YORKSHIRE - PHILADELPHIA

First published in Great Britain in 2018 by
Pen & Sword Military
An imprint of
Pen & Sword Books Ltd
47 Church Street
Barnsley
South Yorkshire
S70 2AS

Copyright © Richard Doherty 2018

ISBN 978 1 52670 329 3

The right of Richard Doherty to be identified as Author of this work has been
asserted by him in accordance with the Copyright, Designs and Patents Act 1988.

A CIP catalogue record for this book is
available from the British Library.

All rights reserved. No part of this book may be reproduced or transmitted in any
form or by any means, electronic or mechanical including photocopying, recording
or by any information storage and retrieval system, without permission from the
Publisher in writing.

Printed and bound in England by TJ International Ltd, Padstow, Cornwall.

Pen & Sword Books Limited incorporates the imprints of Atlas, Archaeology,
Aviation, Discovery, Family History, Fiction, History, Maritime, Military, Military
Classics, Politics, Select, Transport, True Crime, Air World, Frontline Publishing,
Leo Cooper, Remember When, Seaforth Publishing, The Praetorian Press,
Wharncliffe Local History, Wharncliffe Transport, Wharncliffe True Crime and
White Owl.

For a complete list of Pen & Sword titles please contact
PEN & SWORD BOOKS LIMITED
47 Church Street, Barnsley, South Yorkshire, S70 2AS, England
E-mail: enquiries@pen-and-sword.co.uk
Website: www.pen-and-sword.co.uk

By the same author

Wall of Steel: The History of 9th (Londonderry) HAA Regiment, RA (SR) (North-West Books, Limavady, 1988)

The Sons of Ulster: Ulstermen at war from the Somme to Korea (The Appletree Press, Belfast, 1992)

Clear The Way! A History of the 38th (Irish) Brigade, 1941-47 (Irish Academic Press, Dublin, 1993)

Irish Generals: Irish Generals in the British Army in the Second World War (The Appletree Press, Belfast, 1993)

Only the Enemy in Front: The Recce Corps at War, 1940-46 (Tom Donovan Publishing, London, 1994)

Key to Victory: The Maiden City in the Second World War (Greystone Books, Antrim, 1995)

The Williamite War in Ireland, 1688-1691 (Four Courts Press, Dublin, 1998)

A Noble Crusade: The History of Eighth Army, 1941 to 1945 (Spellmount Publishers, Staplehurst, 1999)

Irish Men and Women in the Second World War (Four Courts Press, Dublin, 1999)

Irish Winners of the Victoria Cross (with David Truesdale) (Four Courts Press, Dublin, 2000)

Irish Volunteers in the Second World War (Four Courts Press, Dublin, 2001)

The North Irish Horse (Spellmount Publishers, Staplehurst, 2002)

The Sound of History: El Alamein 1942 (Spellmount, Staplehurst, 2002)

Normandy 1944: The Road to Victory (Spellmount, Staplehurst, 2004)

Ireland's Generals in the Second World War (Four Courts Press, Dublin, 2004)

The Thin Green Line: A History of the Royal Ulster Constabulary GC, 1922-2001 (Pen & Sword, Barnsley, 2004)

None Bolder: A History of 51st (Highland) Division, 1939-1945 (Spellmount, Staplehurst, 2006)

The British Reconnaissance Corps in World War II (Osprey, Oxford, 2007)

Eighth Army in Italy: The Long Hard Slog (Pen & Sword, Barnsley, 2007)

The Siege of Derry 1689: The Military History (Spellmount, Stroud, 2008)

Only the Enemy in Front: The Recce Corps at War, 1940-46 (revised p/bk edn) (Spellmount, Stroud, 2008)

Ubique: The Royal Artillery in the Second World (Spellmount, Stroud, 2008)

Helmand Mission: With the Royal Irish Battlegroup in Afghanistan, 2008 (Pen & Sword, Barnsley, 2009)

In the Ranks of Death: The Irish in the Second World War (Pen & Sword, Barnsley, 2010)

The Humber Light Reconnaissance Car 1941-45 (Osprey, Oxford, 2011)

Hobart's 79th Armoured Division at War: Invention, Innovation and Inspiration (Pen & Sword, Barnsley, 2011)

British Armoured Divisions and Their Commanders 1939-1945 (Pen & Sword, Barnsley, 2013)

Victory in Italy: 15th Army Group's Final Campaign (Pen & Sword, Barnsley, 2014)

Churchill's Greatest Fear: The Battle of the Atlantic 3 September 1939 to 7 May 1945 (Pen & Sword, Barnsley, 2015)

The Somme: 24 June to 19 November 1916 (Northern Ireland War Memorial, Belfast, 2016)

El Alamein 1942: Turning Point in the Desert (Pen & Sword, Barnsley, 2017)

Dedication

To the memory of a dear friend

Danilo Paul Radcliffe

13 April 1952 to 19 April 2016

O body swayed to music, O brightening glance,
How can we know the dancer from the dance?

William Butler Yeats

and his much-loved mother

Lucia Bedeschi Radcliffe
7 November 1924 to 4 October 2017

My 'other mother', a kind, generous and gentle friend

Oft, in the stilly night,
Ere Slumber's chain has bound me,
Fond Memory brings the light
Of other days around me

Thomas Moore

Contents

Dedication   vii

Maps   x

Acknowledgements   xxiii

Glossary and Notes   xxviii

Introduction   xxxvi

Preface   xli

Chapter One   1

Chapter Two   19

Chapter Three   39

Chapter Four   55

Chapter Five   81

Chapter Six   101

Chapter Seven   133

Chapter Eight   158

Chapter Nine   198

Chapter Ten   234

Chapter Eleven   261

Chapter Twelve   297

Chapter Thirteen   328

Chapter Fourteen   350

Endnotes   363

Bibliography   388

Index   405

Maps

Map symbols		xi
Map 1	The Allied advance through Italy from September 1943	xii
Map 2	The first battle, January 1944	xiii
Map 3	The second battle, 15-18 February: the Allied plan of attack	xiv
Map 4	German defences in Cassino, February 1944	xv
Map 5	2nd New Zealand Division's attack on Cassino railway station, 17–18 February.	xvi
Map 6	The third battle: Operation REVENGE: the advance to Albaneta Farm	xvii
Map 7	The fourth battle: 11-17 May	xviii
Map 8	Operation DIADEM: Fifth Army operational plan	xix
Map 9	4th Division's crossing of the Gari river south of Cassino; a panoramic view from Monte Trócchio	xx
Map 10	VI US Corps' break-out from Anzio, 23-31 May	xxi
Map 11	Operation CHESTERFIELD: I Canadian Corps breaks through the Hitler Line and advances to the Melfa, 23-25 May	xxii

Note on maps

It is impossible to represent accurately in a small scale the terrain over which the Cassino battles were fought and so these maps have been simplified and include only spot heights rather than series of contours. The reader may obtain further detail on Touring Club Italiano maps 10 (Lazio) and 12 (Campania e Basilicata), which are 1:200,000 scale, or from Google Earth.

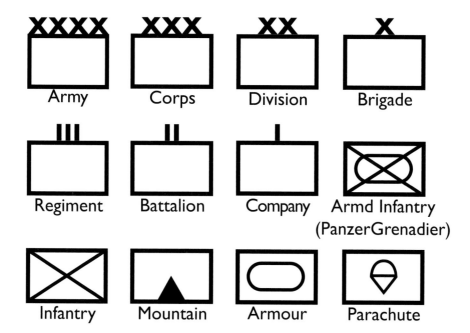

Army   Corps   Division   Brigade

Regiment   Battalion   Company   Armd Infantry
(PanzerGrenadier)

Infantry   Mountain   Armour   Parachute

Key to unit identification

Unit identifier Parent unit

Key to military symbols

Map 1: The Italian Campaign September 1943-May 1944

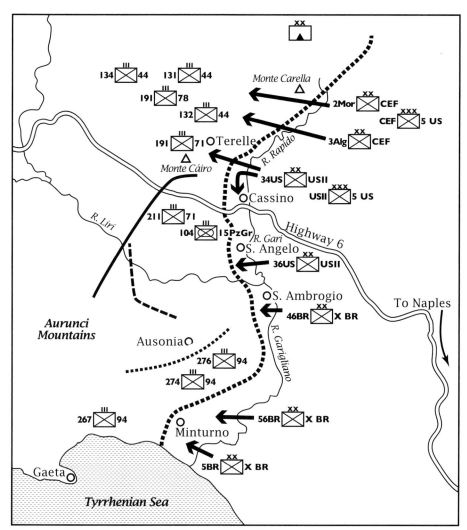

Map 2: The First Battle, January 1944

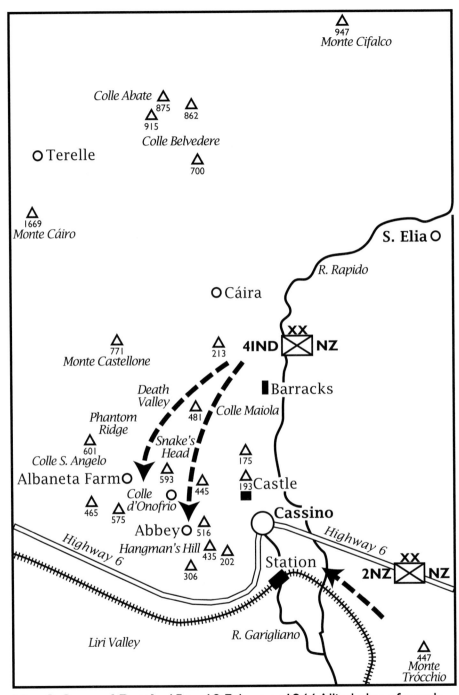

Map 3: Second Battle 15 to 18 February 1944 Allied plan of attack

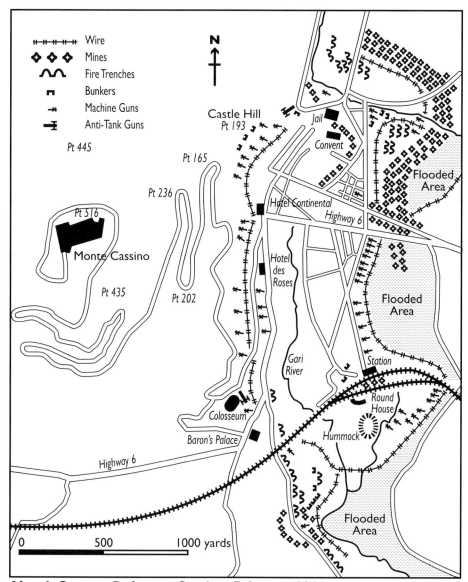

Map 4: German Defences, Cassino, February 1944

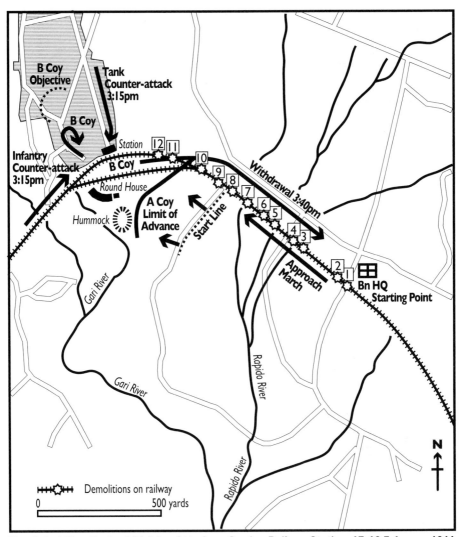

Map 5: 2nd New Zealand Division Attack on Cassino Railway Station, 17-18 February 1944

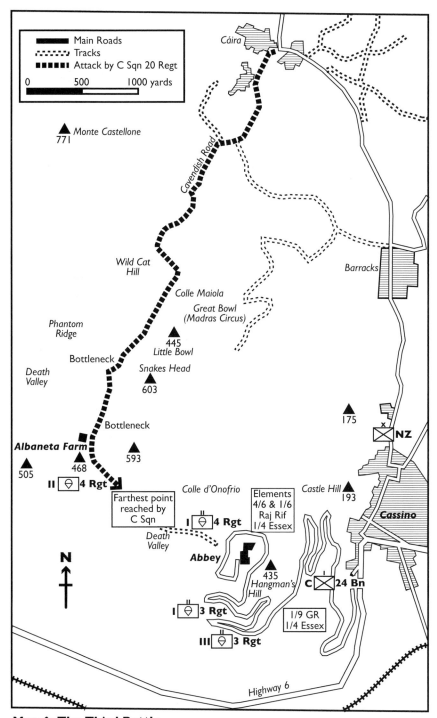

Map 6: The Third Battle
      Operation REVENGE: The advance to Albaneta Farm

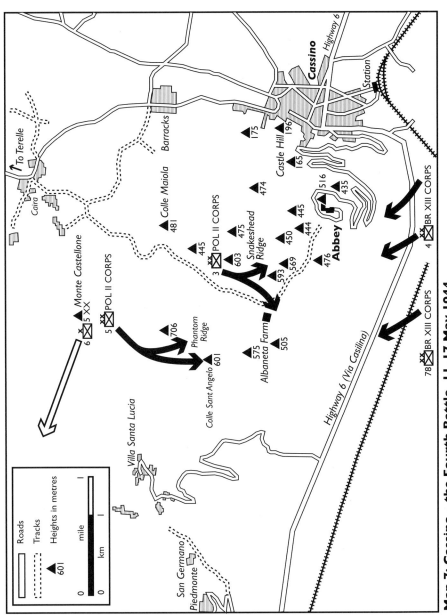

Map 7: Cassino - the Fourth Battle, 11-17 May 1944

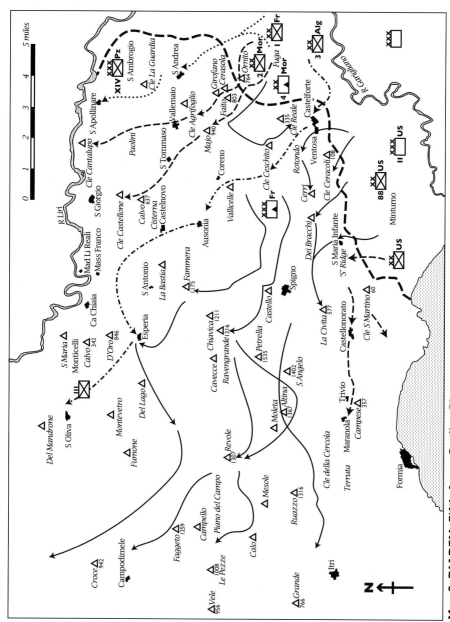

Map 8: DIADEM: Fifth Army Outline Plan

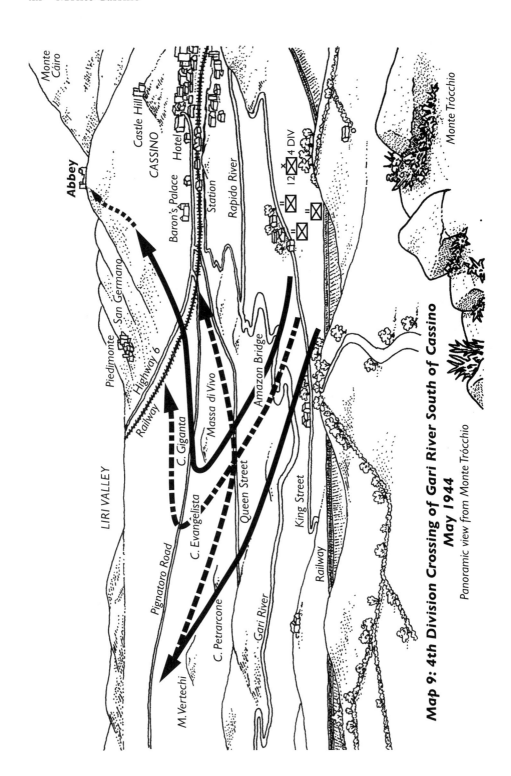

Map 9: 4th Division Crossing of Gari River South of Cassino May 1944
Panoramic view from Monte Trócchio

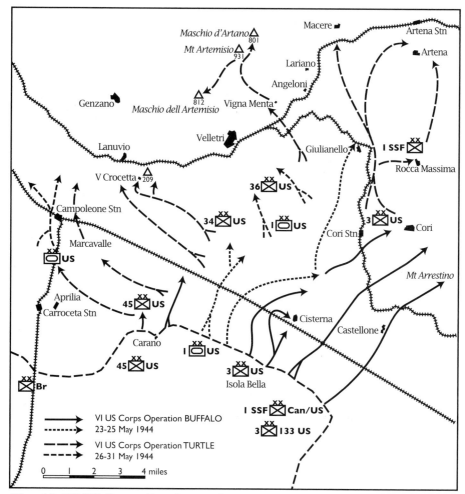

Maschio d'Artano △
801
Mt Artemisio △
931
812 △
Maschio dell'Artemisio
Genzano
Vigna Menta
Lanuvio
Velletri
V Crocetta ▪ 209
Campoleone Stn
Marcavalle
Aprilia
Carroceta Stn
Carano
Isola Bella
Br

Macere ▪
Artena Stn
▪ Artena
Lariano
Angeloni
Giulianello
I SSF ⊠
Rocca Massima
36 ⊠ US
34 ⊠ US
I ◉ US
3 ⊠ US
Cori
Cori Stn
Mt Arrestino
45 ⊠ US
I ◉ US
45 ⊠ US
3 ⊠ US
Cisterna
Castellone
I SSF ⊠ Can/US
3 ⊠ 133 US

→ VI US Corps Operation BUFFALO
⋯▸ 23-25 May 1944
⇢ VI US Corps Operation TURTLE
--▸ 26-31 May 1944

0   1   2   3   4 miles

Map 10: VI US Corps Break-out from Anzio 23-31 May 1944

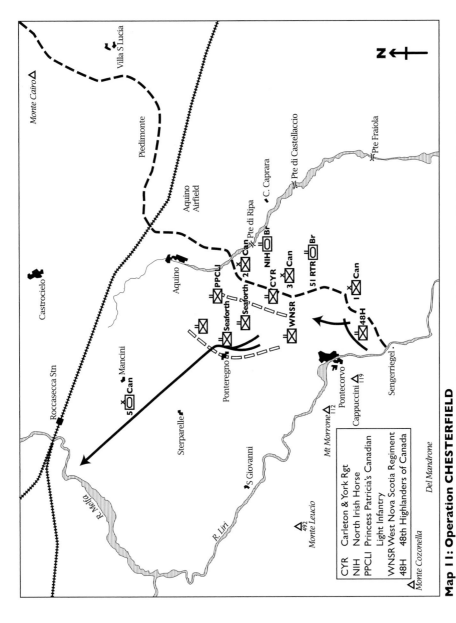

Map 11: Operation CHESTERFIELD
I Canadian Corps breaks through the Hitler Line and advances to the Melfa 23-25 May 1944

CYR   Carleton & York Rgt
NIH   North Irish Horse
PPCLI Princess Patricia's Canadian
       Light Infantry
WNSR West Nova Scotia Regiment
48H   48th Highlanders of Canada

Acknowledgements

As this book approached completion, a friend asked me what I was writing about. When I replied that I was finishing a book on the battles of Monte Cassino he commented that I had been 'working on that for years'. That we had talked about Monte Cassino decades before was an indicator of how long I have been interested in the Cassino battles and in the Italian campaign. I can trace that interest back some sixty years and in the books that I have written over the past three decades Italy has featured in more than half.

The idea of a book on Cassino has germinated for more than a quarter of a century. Having known many who served there, and having studied the Italian campaign and the Cassino battles in some depth, it was inevitable that one day I would write about Cassino. Most of those whom I knew who were there are now dead, but I owe them a great debt for the time that they gave me so willingly and the information that they imparted. In several cases they provided me with written or recorded accounts of their service which have proved invaluable for this book.

Those who served in Italy and knew the blast of war included: Major General H.E.N. 'Bala' Bredin CB DSO** MC*, Major General L.H. Plummer CBE, Brigadier R.C.P. Jeffries CBE, Brigadier E.D. 'Birdie' Smith DSO, Colonel J.H.C. Horsfall DSO MC*, Colonel K.G.F. Chavasse DSO*, Colonel Hugh Holmes TD MA, Colonel Ian Lawrie DSO MC, Colonel M.J.F. Palmer DSO, Colonel P.J.C. Trousdell OBE, Colonel A.D. Woods MC*, Lieutenant Colonel B.D.H. Clark MC GM, Lieutenant Colonel Val ffrench-Blake DSO, Major Neville Chance, Major Geoffrey Cox, Major J.S. Clarke MC*, Major Sir Mervyn Davies MC, Major John Duane MC, Major Desmond Fay MC, Major G.L. Richards MC MM, Captain J.D. Broadbent, Captain Bill Croucher MC, Captain Ian McKee MBE, Captain J. O'Rourke MBE, Captain A.G. Parsons MC, Captain R.J. Robinson DCM, Captain J.A. Stocks, Messrs E.C. Barnett, Bobby Baxter BEM, Les Birch, Sir George Burton OBE DL, James Caddick, T.S. Cox, Fred Corfield, B. Davies, K.R. Drury, Henry Elwood, R.C. Evans, Les Finch BEM, Jack Furnell, Colin Gunner, W. Goldie MM, R.J. Hamilton MM, Bill Hannigan, Sam Henry, F. Herriott, L.G. Jones, J. Jones, Tim Kelly MBE DCM MSM, L. Kennedy, Ron Langford, Bernard Law, Joe Leckey, John Ledwidge, H. Lines MM, John Logue, G.B. Lucas, W. Magowan, P. Manson CBE MC, Ron Mayhew, J. Meehan MM, W.J. McCullagh, John Newton, John J. Ormsby, M.E.R. Pattinson, Barney Phillips, A.S. Pearce,

Bob Pite, Joe Robinson, E. Simmons, John Skellorn, the Revd R.D.St J. Smith TD MA BD, B. Sweeting, Fred Taylor, L. Timperley, Len Trinder, Ken Wakefield, Victor Webb, P.R.D. Wilson, C.W. Woodgate.

In addition to those named above, I have been assisted by many others, including German veterans Hans Teske, Karl Eisenfeller and Rudi Hambuch. All three were *Fallschirmjäger* although they did not serve at Cassino (Karl was captured at El Alamein in 1942 and Hans in Tunisia in 1943), but they gave me an insight into the morale and doughtiness of their fellow 'storming eagles'. I am grateful also to Major Alan Hay, John Mitten MM and P.W. Paver. Others who assisted me included relatives of veterans, among them the late Mrs Biddy Scott, widow of Major General Pat Scott CB CBE DSO, and Mrs Anne Johnson (née Ormsby), daughter of the late J.J. Ormsby. My apologies to anyone I may have omitted.

Researching this book has also taken me to many archives and libraries in both the physical and digital realms. While there is a very real pleasure in working with original documents, feeling the texture of documents and sometimes the dust, there is a tremendous convenience in working with those online. I am grateful to the staffs of the Imperial War Museum's departments of documents and printed books for their friendly assistance over many years, and to the staff of the IWM's photographic archive. Likewise, the National Army Museum, Chelsea, has provided much rich material. Online I have searched the National Archives of the United States, an almost overwhelming source of riches for the historian, Library and Archives Canada and Archives New Zealand/Te Rua Mahara o te Kāwanatanga. My grateful thanks go to all of them for their help.

A special word of thanks is due to my good friend Bob O'Hara and his team of researchers at Kew, particularly Jane and Phil, who have filled in many gaps for me when I have not been able to visit Kew in person. They have also provided friendly and stimulating company over tea or coffee in the café at Kew and we have often been able to help each other on research questions.

In 2014 I had the privilege of meeting Polish veteran Dr Tomasz Piesakowski who served in 13th Rifle Battalion of 5th Kresowa Division. His description of the sufferings of Polish soldiers and civilians as prisoners of the Soviets were harrowing, to put it mildly, and explained clearly why the men, and women, of General Anders' Polish II Corps were so determined in their approach to battle. My thanks are also due to Dr Andrzej Suchcitz of the Polish Institute and Sikorski Museum at Prince's Gate in London, who accompanied Dr Piesakowski, for his advice. Members of the Polish II Corps Facebook community were also helpful in providing information.

Closer to home, I have availed of the services of the Linen Hall Library, Belfast, the only subscription library on the island of Ireland, where the staff have been most helpful, as have those of Derry Central Library, Foyle Street, Londonderry. Librarians are exceptional individuals, thanks to whom I have been able to obtain several long-out-of-print publications.

My friend and fellow historian, and proud US Marine, Pat Mooney, was an always willing researcher across the Atlantic and a fund of authoritative knowledge on the US armed forces of the Second World War. I am grateful to Pat for his enthusiastic advice and assistance with this book (and his guidance on several battlefields of the American Civil War, in which we also share an interest). Semper Fi, Pat.

Also in the United States, Gordon L. Rottman, a US Army veteran and historian, helped with information on the US forces in Italy. John Griffith of California was kind enough to allow me to use two of his photos of Medal of Honor laureates.

In the UK, Ian Blackwell, Richard Mead and Ken Ford have been helpful, Ian with information on Fifth Army and some of the NARA photographs included in this volume and Ken with background information plus other NARA photographs. Richard Mead helped to organize my meeting with Dr Tomasz Piesakowski and Dr Andrzej Suchcitz while his excellent biography of Lieutenant General Sir Richard McCreery was extremely useful in my research.

Andy Shepherd, another good friend over many years, read and commented on the book in draft form, in spite of his very busy life, spotting some errors that have been corrected and suggesting a few changes to the text, which have been incorporated in the final version. Thanks for your critique, Andy.

The Reverend Father Michael Fava CF was kind enough to read, comment upon and correct the first draft of the Preface. I appreciate his advice and help, and his excellent company on a memorable battlefield study in 2015.

The late Bob McCreery, son of Sir Richard McCreery, provided the photograph of his father which appears in this book. I am grateful to the McCreery family for granting permission to use this image of an outstanding commander.

Terence Cuneo painted an impressive image of Royal Engineers bridging the Gari river with Amazon bridge and I am grateful to the Royal Engineers Museum in Gillingham, Kent, for their kind permission to use the image. My thanks are also due to Colonel D.L.D. Bigger, Corps Colonel Royal Engineers, for his assistance in obtaining that permission.

Another painting is reproduced in the book: David Rowlands' image of the O Group of 2nd London Irish Rifles during the final battle. David has faithfully depicted the scene following the deaths of two commanding officers when the original O Group was caught in the blast of a German shell. The late Colonel John Horsfall gave his seal of approval to the painting, stating that it reflected the scene that he remembered all too well from that May day. I am grateful to Regimental Headquarters Royal Irish Regiment for permission to use the image in this account.

Over the past three decades I have amassed many photographs relating to the Second World War, some of which appear in these pages. Most were given to me by ex-servicemen, or their families, and I am grateful to all those who entrusted me with these images.

Lieutenant General Sir Philip Trousdell KBE CB, formerly Colonel of the Royal Irish Regiment, is the son of a Royal Irish Fusiliers' officer who fought in the final battle of Cassino, Lieutenant (later Colonel) P.J.C. Trousdell OBE, some of whose account of his experience is quoted in the book. I am grateful to General Sir Philip for his kind permission to use the quotations.

In Cassino I have enjoyed the advice and support of Damiano Parravano whose encyclopaedic knowledge of the battleground is second to none. Not only has Damiano acted as a guide, but he has also produced many of the photographs that appear in this book, as well as others that I have used in presentations on the Cassino battles. Battlefield studies for both HQ 38 (Irish) Brigade and 2nd Bn Royal Irish were enhanced greatly by Damiano's knowledge of the ground: in both cases and, thanks to Damiano, we were able to visit the heights of Monte Castellone where soldiers of the Irish Brigade spent most of April 1944. Damiano also took us to Casa Sinagoga, an objective of the Irish Brigade, where 2nd London Irish Rifles' H Company suffered heavily. There, thanks are due to Franco Sinagoga and his wife, Clara Perna, as we enjoyed the hospitality of the Sinagoga family and were able to see in detail the buildings that stood there in 1944; the family now live in a modern house along the road. Thanks are also due to Enrico Canini for his informative tour of the Anzio beachhead, especially the caves.

It would be remiss of me not to mention those who took part in the battlefield studies with which I have been involved since the discussions that took place on the many 'stands' of each study were knowledgeable, interesting and enthusiastic. Each study has increased my own understanding of the battles and my appreciation of what those who served at Cassino endured.

A word of thanks is also due to the proprietors and staff of the Hotel Rocca, Via Sferracavalli, Cassino, particularly Angela Rossi for her courteous and efficient service. The hotel is especially welcoming to guests wishing to study the Cassino battles and the comfortable reception area includes a small display of artefacts related to the battles.

As I mentioned in my opening paragraph my interest in the Italian campaign and the Cassino battles goes back some sixty years, to my childhood days when my home was the middle of three bungalows occupied by families of whom the fathers were veterans of the war in Italy. One of those fathers was Joe Radcliffe, who had served in the Royal Signals, and had married an Italian girl, Lucia Bedeschi. On his retirement from the Ministry of Defence, Joe and Lucia chose to live in Rome, where they had met, and Lucia was a wonderful hostess to me on many occasions.

Their children, Marina and Danilo, have been lifelong friends. Sadly, Danilo died in 2016 and I chose to dedicate this book to his memory. Lucia died on 4 October 2017, in her 93rd year, and I thought it fitting that both she and Danilo should be remembered in the Dedication, with thanks for memories that cover many decades.

Dottore Pier Paolo Battistelli and Professore Piero Crociani are leading authorities on the Italian forces and on the war in Italy and I have benefited greatly from their advice and the sharing of their knowledge.

The maps included in this book are the work of Tim Webster who has produced maps for many of my books and whose skills will be obvious to readers. My thanks to Tim for his patience and tolerance over the years we have worked together, as well as his attention to detail.

Needless to say this book could not have come to publication without the excellent team at Pen and Sword. I extend my gratitude to Brigadier Henry Wilson, Publishing Manager, for his encouragement, friendship and support, as well as his patience with this project, Matt Jones, Production Manager, the epitome of professionalism and patience, as well as being good-humoured, and Jon Wilkinson who never fails to produce eye-catching jacket designs.

Finally, Carol, my wife, Joanne, James and Catríona, my children, and Cíaran, Katrina, Josh and Sophie, my grandchildren, have always been strong in their support for my research and writing and tolerant of my absences. Without their support it would have been impossible for me to write this, or any other, book.

Richard Doherty
Co. Londonderry
January 2018

Glossary and Notes

AA	anti-aircraft
AAI	Allied Armies in Italy, one of several titles borne by the army group in the Italian campaign
ACMF	Allied Central Mediterranean Force, another army group title
ADC	*Aide-de-Camp*
ADS	Advanced Dressing Station
AFV	Armoured Fighting Vehicle
AGPA	Army Group Polish Artillery
AGRA	Army Group Royal Artillery
AOP	Air Observation Post
Army Group	Two, or more, field armies
Bangalore torpedo	an explosive device in a metal tube used to destroy barbed-wire entanglements and other obstacles. Created at Bangalore in India in 1912 by an Irishman, Captain Robert McClintock of the Madras Sappers and Miners, and used in both world wars.
Bar	to a decoration, such as the VC etc. More than one Bar may be awarded, indicated by a bar or bars on the medal ribbon.
BAR	Browning automatic rifle. A .30-inch-calibre weapon that, despite its name, was a squad light machine gun used by both the US Army and Marine Corps.
Battle sledge	metal sledges towed behind tanks to carry infantrymen into battle in a prone position
Bren gun	British Army light machine gun of .303-inch calibre; rate of fire 500-520rpm. The name Bren describes its origins as a Czech weapon, designed in Brno, adopted by the UK and manufactured at Enfield.
Brew up	a tank being set on fire by enemy action was said to 'brew up'

Cab-rank	fighter-bombers in the air, ready to provide close air support to ground forces
CCB	Combat Command B, of a US armoured division; a flexible sub-grouping
CCRA	Corps Commander Royal Artillery (British and Commonwealth)
CE	Chief Engineer
CEF	*Corps expéditionnaire français* – French Expeditionary Corps
CIGS	Chief of the Imperial General Staff
Churchill tank	British heavy infantry support, or I, tank
Civitavecchia	the port of Rome
Contrails	condensation trails created by high-flying aircraft
Counter-battery	artillery fire directed on enemy artillery
Counter-mortar	artillery fire directed on enemy mortars
CRA	Commander Royal Artillery (of a division)
CRE	Commander Royal Engineers (of a division)
DAF	Desert Air Force; officially 1st Tactical Air Force (1TAF)
DCM	Distinguished Conduct Medal, the second-tier gallantry award for other ranks
D Day	the day on which an operation was planned to begin
Doughboys	soubriquet for US Army soldiers dating from the Civil War; superseded by GIs
DSO	Distinguished Service Order, an award for such service usually to officers from lieutenant colonel up but also awarded as the second-tier gallantry award for officers
DUKW	pronounced 'duck'; amphibious six-wheeled lorry, developed in the USA
'Factory', the	the town of Aprilia in Lazio; the stark fascist architectural style looked more like factory buildings to Allied troops who dubbed it thus
Faughs	pronounced 'Fogs'; soubriquet of the Royal Irish Fusiliers, from the regimental motto Faugh A Ballagh! – Clear The Way! in Irish Gaelic
Ferdinand	German tank destroyer, or *Panzerjäger*, based on the failed Porsche design for the Tiger I tank; named for

	its designer, Ferdinand Porsche, it was improved and renamed Elefant in 1944
FMC	Field maintenance centre, a store for essentials from ammunition to rations to maintain troops in the field
FOO	Forward Observation Officer, artillery officer attached to infantry/armour to provide detailed and up-to-date information for the guns
FSU	Field Surgical Unit
FTU	Field Transfusion Unit
GI	US Army soldier, said to originate from the term 'Government Issue'
GL radar	gun-laying radar, for AA guns
GOC	General Officer Commanding (a division)
GSOI	General Staff Officer responsible for manpower/personnel
HAA	heavy anti-aircraft (artillery)
Heavy cruiser	warship mounting 8-inch guns
Hejnał	a traditional Polish bugle call, dating to the Middle Ages
H Hour	the time at which an operation was planned to begin
Howitzer:	an artillery piece designed to fire in the 'upper register', i.e. with elevation above 45 degrees. Rounds fired by howitzers have a much higher trajectory than those from guns.
HQ	headquarters
Jawan	a young soldier (Indian Army)
Kampfgruppe	an ad-hoc battle-group
K-ration	a one-day basic ration pack designed for the US Army, intended for short-term needs only; often referred to as a paratrooper's ration
LCA	Landing Craft, Assault
LCT	Landing Craft, Tanks
LI	Light Infantry, as in Somerset LI
LSI	Landing Ship, Infantry

LST	Landing Ship, Tank
Luftwaffe	German Air Force
M1	standard US Army rifle – the Garand .30-inch calibre, bolt action
MAAF	Mediterranean Allied Air Forces
MAC	Mediterranean Air Command
MATAF	Mediterranean Allied Tactical Air Force
MASAF	Mediterranean Allied Strategic Air Force
MBE	Member of the Order of the British Empire
MC	Military Cross, third-tier gallantry award for officers (up to the rank of major) and warrant officers
Medal of Honor	first-tier US gallantry award
Mention in Despatches	fourth-tier gallantry award, but also issued as a service award
MG42	German 7.92mm light machine gun with a rate of fire of over 1,000 rounds per minute
MM	Military Medal, third-tier gallantry award for other ranks, excluding warrant officers, until 1993
M7 Priest	a 105mm howitzer mounted on the hull of an M3 Grant tank. A howitzer motor carriage in US parlance, it was dubbed Priest in British service as the machine-gun mounting resembled a pulpit; an earlier British SPG was named Bishop and an improvised, lightly-armoured, lorry-mounted anti-tank gun received the name Deacon.
M10	a US tank-destroyer, a 3-inch (76.2mm) anti-tank gun on the hull of an M3 Lee/Grant. In British service it was up-gunned with the 17-pounder anti-tank gun and later renamed Achilles.
NCO	non-commissioned officer
Nebelwerfer	literally 'smoke thrower', German multi-barrelled rocket weapon
OBE	Officer of the Order of the British Empire
O Group	Orders Group
OKW	*Oberkommando der Wehrmacht* or Supreme Command of the Armed Forces, a token combined services command as the *Heer*, *Kriegsmarine* and *Luftwaffe* retained separate command and control and inter-service rivalry continued

OP	Observation Post, usually for artillery spotters
Panther	German medium tank, armed with a 75mm gun; also known as the Panzer V
Panzer	common name for German tanks and armoured units and formations, an abbreviation of *Schützengraben-vernichtungspanzerkraftwagen* (trench-destroying armoured fighting vehicle), the original name, which provides the origin of the designations of German tanks as *Panzer* or *PzKw*
Panzerfaust	a one-use infantry anti-tank weapon, fired from the shoulder
Panzerjäger	literally tank-hunter, a separate branch of the army that manned specialist AFVs
Panzer Mark IV	The most common German tank of the war. Originally fitted with a short 75mm gun and intended to support infantry, it was re-armed with a long-barrelled 75mm.
Pfc	Private, First Class in the US Army, equivalent to the British lance corporal.
PIAT	Projector, Infantry, Anti-tank. Man-portable, spigot-launched
PoW	Prisoner of War.
Purple Heart	US award for wounded service personnel dating back to the era of George Washington.
RAF	Royal Air Force.
RAMC	Royal Army Medical Corps.
RASC	Royal Army Service Corps.
Red Bulls	soubriquet for the US 34th Division from its divisional badge of a red bull's head.
RHQ	regimental headquarters.
RM	Royal Marines.
Rover David	ground control unit for Cab-rank close support aircraft
RSM	regimental sergeant major; a warrant officer, first class
Sangar	originally used in India for small temporary fortified positions built from stone, it was also used in the Italian campaign

Section	in 1944 ten infantrymen commanded by a corporal, with six privates armed with rifles forming a rifle group and a lance corporal and two privates forming a light-machine-gun (LMG) group, armed with a Bren LMG.
Sherman	the standard Allied medium tank from late-1942 until the end of the war. At the time of the Cassino battles it was usually fitted with a 75mm gun.
Skins	soubriquet for the Royal Inniskilling Fusiliers
SMG	sub-machine gun.
Snake	a variation of the Bangalore torpedo, pushed into place by a tank.
SPG	self-propelled gun, an artillery piece mounted on a tracked hull.
Squad	US infantry equivalent of the British section
StuG	*Sturmgeschütz*; a self-propelled gun
Tank destroyer	a self-propelled anti-tank gun on a tank chassis. US designs usually had turrets; other nations, including Germany and the UK, deployed versions with fixed guns.
Tiger	or Panzer VI, a heavy German tank mounting an 88mm gun
Todt Organization	established by Fritz Todd, a senior engineer and prominent Nazi Party member, this was a civil and military engineering group that carried out a wide range of works and used forced labour. In 1943 it became part of the Ministry of Armaments and War Production under Albert Speer.
Tommy gun	US-produced .45-inch SMG
Ultra	codename for intelligence gleaned from intercepting and decoding German Enigma signals by the staff of Bletchley Park
USAAF	United States Army Air Forces; an independent air arm, the US Air Force, was not created until 1947.
USSR	Union of Soviet Socialist Republics
VC	Victoria Cross, the first-tier British (and Commonwealth/Empire) gallantry award

Volkswagen	or *Kübelwagen*, German light general-purpose military car, equivalent to the jeep
Werfer	mortar
William target	the ranging of all the guns of a field army on a single target.
WOI	warrant officer, first class, e.g. regimental sergeant major

Formation and Unit Designations

Throughout this book the designations of higher formations have been standardized with German formations referred to in the British style, i.e. Tenth Army, 90th Division, rather than AOK 10 and 90. Division. However, designations of lower formations are unaltered so that American and German divisions' subordinate formations are described as regiments and their battalions in the appropriate manner, i.e. 3rd/133rd Regiment or III/44th Division.

In the Italian campaign most British armour fought in armoured brigades and armoured divisions but some was to be found in tank brigades. The distinction was that 'armoured' brigades deployed cruiser tanks (which included the Sherman) with a motorized infantry battalion, while 'tank' brigades were equipped with infantry tanks (I-tanks; by this stage of the war the Churchill) but included no infantry, since their role was to support infantry units/formations. Later in the campaign a tank brigade could deploy both types of tank.

British regimental and battalion designations have caused some confusion for authors and historians not familiar with the British regimental system. Cavalry, by this time all armour-equipped, was usually grouped in regiments within the Royal Armoured Corps. Traditionally, regiments had had designations such as dragoon guards, dragoons, hussars and lancers. After the First World War the number of cavalry regiments had been reduced by amalgamating some of the more junior units, creating 'new' regiments with titles such as 13th/18th Hussars and 17th/21st Lancers. Such 'vulgar fraction' designations denoted a single regiment with dual heritage; thus 17th/21st Lancers was the result of amalgamating the 17th Lancers and 21st Lancers rather than the 17th Battalion of the 21st Lancers.

Being new to the *Army List*, the Royal Tank Regiment (RTR) was different and so was divided into battalions. In part, this was because the RTR had been the Royal Tank Corps until becoming part of the Royal Armoured Corps. Regular Army RTR battalions were numbered from 1st to 8th while 9th, 10th, 11th and

12th Battalions were formed during the war as 'hostilities only' units. In the Territorial Army there were battalions numbered from 40th to 51st, most of them re-roled former TA infantry battalions. After the war the RTR was reduced and the designation 'battalion' dropped. Until 1992 there were four regiments but these were reduced to 1st and 2nd Royal Tank Regiment which amalgamated as the Royal Tank Regiment in 2014.

The reader will notice an apparent inconsistency in infantry battalion designations with some described as 2/4th and others as 1st/9th. Such styles denote the units' origins. In 1939 Territorial Army (now Reserve Army) infantry units were ordered to create duplicates. As a result the original battalion had '1/' prefixed to its title while the duplicate became '2/'. Thus 4th Bn Essex Regiment became 1/4th Essex and 2/4th Essex, the former achieving fame in the Cassino battles. The author is aware of 5th/7th Gordon Highlanders, a title that is not an exception to the rule but the result of the amalgamation of 5th and 7th Battalions of the Gordons.

The example of the Gordons would suggest that 1st/9th Gurkhas was the result of the amalgamation of two battalions of Gurkha Rifles, 1st and 9th, but this was not the case. Since the Gurkhas were Indian Army, another set of rules applied. In this case 1st/9th Gurkhas indicates the 1st Battalion of the 9th Gurkha Rifles, a regiment that included five battalions in the course of the war. Likewise 4th/16th Punjab Regiment was the 4th Battalion of 16th Punjab Regiment, which deployed twelve battalions during the war.

Introduction

When the Royal British Legion organized a pilgrimage to Cassino in May 1993, one of those present was my friend Lieutenant Colonel Brian Clark MC GM, Chairman of the Legion in the Republic of Ireland, a veteran of the battle and of the Italian campaign, during which he was the adjutant of 1st Royal Irish Fusiliers, the Faughs. At the Memorial Service in Cassino War Cemetery, the retired officer who was to lay the official wreath at the Cross of Sacrifice froze and the pilgrimage organizer asked Brian if he would take over. In his own words, 'the Irish infantry once more filled the gap'. After the service Brian was approached by a German veteran who asked if he would come to the German Cemetery at Cáira and lay the official wreath there alongside a German veteran. He was pleased to do so. From that simple and dignified gesture was born a friendship between the Faugh and *Fallschirm-pionier* veteran Oberstleutnant Jupp Klein which led to the creation of an international Monte Cassino veterans' organization.

The body created by Clark and Klein was a clear expression of respect between former foes, men who knew that they had endured and survived a very hard battle. Sadly, some British veterans, including the secretary of one UK veterans' group, took exception to the concept of reconciliation with that secretary even attempting to blacken the name of Brian Clark. Fortunately, the majority of veterans saw themselves as a brotherhood irrespective of national allegiances and such is the essence of commemorative events at Cassino today.

Whether a German defender or an Allied attacker, those who fought at Cassino experienced the hardest battle fought in western Europe during the Second World War, in conditions ranging from the bleak winter weather of January along the Gari, Rapido and Garigliano rivers and in the mountains above Cassino to the increasing heat of early summer in which the fourth and final battle was fought and the army group broke through to Rome. Nowhere else did the western Allies fight in one area for over 140 days. The Soviets fought at Stalingrad for 156 days while the siege of Leningrad lasted almost two-and-a-half years. While the battles at Leningrad and Stalingrad are identified as sieges, it is not generally appreciated that the Cassino battles were also a form of siege warfare, fought in linear fashion more akin to the trench siege warfare of the First World War.

Walking the ground at Cassino, or more accurately, in the mountains above the town gives the visitor a much better appreciation of the obstacles facing the Allies and the assistance the Germans had from the topography of the land. Winston Churchill failed to appreciate what the Allied generals faced in 1944, believing that it should have been possible to force a passage through the gap in the mountains that is the entrance to the Liri valley. Even looking down from the heights, either in the Cassino massif or the Aurunci, it is also easy to believe that the land in the valley is flat. It *looks* flat but on the ground it becomes clear that there are many undulations from which an effective defence could be mounted, as well as rivers and streams that reduce the manoeuvrability of tanks and other vehicles. Everywhere along the front was difficult. A breakthrough required a preponderance of strength as well as clever and detailed planning to overcome the excellent defences, manned by very determined soldiers with a great conceit of their abilities and professionalism.

The first battle was intended to draw German forces away from the landings at Anzio but failed in its objective. One RASC veteran, who landed at Anzio with 1st British Division on D Day, 22 January, told me that they were briefed before landing that they would be there only forty-eight hours before being relieved by troops who had broken through the Gustav Line. He was wounded at Anzio on 9 March, evacuated to Naples in time to see Vesuvius erupt, and had returned to his unit in Anzio long before the bridgehead was relieved. That first attack was a three-pronged effort by General Juin's *Corps expéditionnaire français* on Fifth Army's right flank, Lieutenant General McCreery's British X Corps on the left and the US II Corps in the centre. For Mark Clark, the army commander, the main effort was in the centre. However, that was where the German defences were strongest. The soldiers of 36th (Texas) Division had to cross flat, wet land before crossing the fast-flowing Gari river (not the Rapido as most accounts claim) under the machine guns, mortars, artillery and small-arms fire of defenders on higher ground. The attack had to be called off. II Corps' other assaulting formation, 34th Division, crossed the Rapido north of Cassino before attacking into the town and onto the mountains. That task proved almost impossible, even with the division reinforced by a regiment of 36th. Yet the Red Bulls of the 34th persevered, making gains on which those who relieved them would build. When finally relieved, many soldiers of 34th Division had to be carried out, frozen, cramped and unable to move, yet still manning their weapons. In the annals of the Second World War there are few feats to equal the commitment and endurance of 34th Division in the first battle of Cassino.

X British Corps also enjoyed success: two divisions created a bridgehead across the Garigliano, prompting German commanders to deploy reinforcements in that sector. Thus Clark had two sectors where he had the opportunity to exploit success. Instead, he ordered the French to change their axis of advance, thereby losing the opportunity of breaking into the Liri valley behind the defenders. General von Senger und Etterlin was so concerned about the French advance that he moved his headquarters from Roccasecca where it had been threatened by the French; he also deployed reinforcements in front of X Corps.

With the need to keep as many German troops as possible away from the Anzio beach-head, now threatened by a German build up, Clark used reinforcements transferred by the army group commander, Alexander, to renew his offensive. Those reinforcements constituted the ad hoc New Zealand Corps of 2nd New Zealand and 4th Indian Divisions; 78th British Division was also transferred to the corps to be held in reserve for the breakthrough. Unfortunately, New Zealand Corps had to rely on headquarters staff who were acting in the same roles in 2nd New Zealand Division, while the corps commander, Sir Bernard Freyberg, was not an effective commander at that level, which he demonstrated by refusing to have a 'soviet' of divisional commanders make demands of him.

New Zealand Corps continued the advance of II Corps but Freyberg demanded the bombing of the Abbey before launching his infantry, the first occasion on which strategic bombers deployed tactically to support ground troops. All that the bombing achieved was to provide the Germans with defensive positions while the timing meant that an immediate infantry follow up was impossible, a situation created by the airmen not appreciating all the operational aspects of the mission. The second battle, really a continuation of the efforts of II Corps, was called off and preparations began for a fresh assault. Once again strategic bombers were to be called upon, on this occasion to destroy the town of Cassino.

Bombing Cassino made it almost impossible for armour to support the New Zealand infantry who advanced into the town and German troops maintained control of the heart of the town. Freyberg had failed to learn from the Canadian operations in Ortona only months earlier and all-arms co-operation proved impossible in a town that had been reduced to rubble. The British 78th Division was sucked into the battle in its final phase but operations ended before its units deployed on offensive tasks. This third battle had seen the enterprise of the Gurkhas who took and held Hangman's Hill until ordered to withdraw, the defence of Castle Hill by the Essex and the daring but doomed Operation REVENGE by Indian, New Zealand and American tankmen along Cavendish Road.

Neither the second nor third battles had led to a breakthrough, and Alexander decided to regroup for a fourth assault. With more manpower and resources, the plan drawn up by John Harding, Alexander's chief of staff, was detailed and yet simple. It included an elaborate deception plan to mislead the Germans about the timing of the attack and the deployment of Allied troops, especially the French and Poles. With both Fifth and Eighth Armies on the western side of the Apennines, there would be assaults by four corps (actually five as the French corps created a discrete mountain corps): from left to right these were US II Corps, Juin's *Corps expéditionnaire français* and the *Corps de montagne*, British XIII Corps and Polish II

Corps. X Corps protected the left flank while VI US Corps prepared to break out of the Anzio beachhead. Allied intelligence on enemy dispositions was excellent and mostly accurate, largely due to Allied air supremacy. Axis intelligence was lacking in most respects as the Luftwaffe in Italy was greatly reduced in strength.

The final operation was a success, although the Germans fought hard, as was their wont. Polish attempts to seize Monastery Hill and the ruined Abbey were rebuffed and only when the Germans withdrew did 3rd Carpathian Division claim the objective. German withdrawal was prompted by the pressure exerted by XIII Corps in the Liri valley (aided by their Polish comrades) but more especially by the French attack through the mountains threatening the Hitler Line, the fall-back position for the Gustav Line defenders. Considering the Aurunci mountains too difficult for the Allies to attack through, the Germans had defended only lightly; French North African soldiers, at ease in mountainous terrain, moved quickly through the defences, often taking German troops by surprise. Sadly, the achievements of Juin's men were stained by the atrocities committed around Esperia by soldiers under his command, a crime the French government has never acknowledged fully.

In the breakout from Anzio, Lucian Truscott's VI Corps made good progress but the possibility of destroying German Tenth Army was thrown away by Clark's desire to be first in Rome and his order to Truscott to change the axis of his advance. Although Clark had his day of fame in Rome, his disobedience played a major part in ensuring that the Italian campaign would last through another winter.

The Cassino battles lasted from 12 January until the liberation of Rome on 5 June, but have been overshadowed by the battles fought in north-west Europe and are, especially, less well known in the United States. Indeed there are relatively few US visitors to the battlefields today. That Fifth Army included many men of other nations – British, French, Italian and, later, Brazilian – may explain this, but so also may Clark's keenness to portray the army as his, denying publicity to his corps commanders and divisional commanders.

Although the role of the French, and the quality of their leaders, is often overlooked, and even ignored, there is no doubt that excellent leadership and a fast operational tempo were more likely to be found in the French divisions than in most others. It is interesting to speculate what might have happened, for example, had the New Zealand Corps had a Juin at its head. In XIII Corps vastly improved all-arms co-operation meant a level of teamwork not been seen before in Italy. The creation of battle-groups within 4th and 78th Divisions especially, marrying armour of 6th Armoured Division and 1 Canadian Armoured Brigade with infantry down to company level, predated the introduction of such tactics in Normandy, while the engineers of both Fifth and Eighth Armies had reached a high pitch of efficiency and effectiveness; further operational innovation would continue to the end of the campaign in Italy.

At army group, army and corps levels leadership was generally competent but varied from the lacklustre performance of Freyberg through the workmanlike Keyes of II US Corps and Anders of II Polish Corps, the battle-hardened Keightley of XIII British Corps, to the energetic and thrusting Truscott of VI US Corps and Juin of the *Corps expéditionnaire français.* Alexander, commanding a multinational coalition force, was the best man for that role; the only alternative was Eisenhower, who was engaged elsewhere. While Oliver Leese was a competent, but not outstanding, commander of Eighth Army, Mark Clark was a less than inspiring commander of Fifth Army, failing to recognize opportunities that his corps commanders had opened up in the first battle and not listening to either his divisional and corps commander on the plan for 36th Division to cross the Gari in January. The courageous soldiers of 36th and 34th Divisions in January and February 1944 deserved better leadership than that shown by Clark.

In the pages that follow I have attempted to show how those soldiers, their opponents and their commanders fought the Cassino battles, collectively the longest and toughest 'battle' fought by the Western Allies in the Second World War.

Preface

❬ Icon' and 'iconic' are words used promiscuously nowadays to describe the mundane and the mediocre. Indeed it is rare to find them used in their correct context, but describing the abbey sitting atop Monte Cassino as an icon or as iconic would be using those words in their correct context and suffusing them with their true meaning.

For the Abbey of Saint Benedict of Nursia, or *San Benedetto da Norcia*, is an icon. As the *OED* defines the word, it is 'a representative symbol of a culture, movement, etc.; … something afforded great admiration or respect'. Thus it is *iconic*, 'of the nature of an icon'. It had long been iconic of the monastic tradition, founded by Benedict of Nursia, and in the past century has also become iconic of one of the bloodiest and fiercest battles of the bloodiest and most costly war in history. Rather it was the destruction of the historic building that symbolized so much of the horror and futility of the Second World War, as well as the pain and loss inflicted on the people of Italy through the folly and vainglory of national leaders.

1: The Abbey in the 1930s. (Author's collection)

The Abbey, or monastery as it is also known, was seen as one of the great symbols of European civilization, a haven of peace and learning, and a centre of Christian devotion. To appreciate fully its importance, a brief look at the life of Saint Benedict is helpful. The son of a Roman noble, Benedict was born in Nursia, near Spoleto, in about AD 480, but his boyhood was spent with his parents in Rome where he attended school until he was about 19 or 20. At that stage he seems to have become disillusioned with the way in which his contemporaries were living their lives and 'giving over his books, and forsaking his father's house and wealth, with a mind only to serve God, he sought for some place where he might attain to the desire of his holy purpose' and thus quit Rome 'instructed with learned ignorance and furnished with unlearned wisdom'.[1]

Accompanied by his old nurse, Benedict moved to live in Enfide, close to a church dedicated to Saint Peter. They appear to have been associated with a group of 'virtuous men' whose views on life reflected those of Benedict. (Enfide, now in ruins, is near present-day Affile and was built on a ridge, as are so many Italian towns and villages.) Having performed his first miracle, by restoring a *capisterium*, or earthenware wheat sifter, which his servant had broken unintentionally, Benedict achieved a fame that he disliked, perhaps even viewing it as notoriety. He thus sought to distance himself from that reputation by moving to the more isolated area of Subiaco. This time he moved alone, 'determined to be poor and to live by his own work', choosing 'the hardships of life and the weariness of labour'.

During this time Benedict came in contact with a monk called Romanus who had a monastery on a nearby mountain. Romanus talked with Benedict about why he had come to Subiaco and gave him the monk's habit. He also suggested that Benedict should become a hermit, advice that he accepted and followed by taking up residence in a cave above a lake. That cave, with a 'large triangular-shaped opening' is about ten-feet deep and overhung by a cliff below the mountain on which Romanus had his monastery. For three years, 'unknown to men', Benedict lived there and, apart from regular visits by Romanus, who brought food on specific days, had only occasional contact with the world outside. That occasional contact, however, was sufficient for the community of another monastery in the area to invite Benedict to become their abbot following the death of the previous incumbent.

Benedict seems to have had doubts about accepting the invitation since he knew that the monks' standards differed from his own and they 'would never agree together'. However, he eventually agreed to their pleas and became their abbot. His earlier doubts proved prophetic as the community and Benedict did not gel harmoniously. In fact the monks attempted to poison their new abbot who abandoned the monastery and returned to his previous existence in the cave.

As before Benedict was not left alone. His reputation was increasing, as were reports of miracles attributed to him. Many sought him out for his advice and spiritual guidance. His holiness and character were held in such regard that he became a focus for pilgrimage and found that many of those who came to him for guidance wanted to become his followers. Such were their numbers that Benedict established no fewer than thirteen monasteries in the valley. Twelve of these each housed a dozen monks under a superior designated by Benedict while he was the superior in the other house in which he was joined by 'a few, such as he thought would more profit and be better instructed by his own presence'. Benedict was the abbot, or father, of all thirteen houses and with their establishment he also started schools for children. Among the first to join him were Maurus and Placidus, or Placid, both of whom subsequently helped spread the Benedictine Rule. Saint Maurus later left Italy for Gaul and established the first Benedictine community in what is now France. Of Saint Placidus little is known, other than that he was rescued from drowning by Maurus on Benedict's orders and seems to have accompanied Benedict when the latter moved from Subiaco to Monte Cassino in about AD 529.[2]

***

Benedict's *Rule* was written initially to enable people who were technically lay to live their domestic lives by a set of guidelines that allowed them to follow as far as possible the message of the gospels: 'My words are addressed to thee, whoever thou art, that, renouncing thine own will, dost put on the strong and bright armour of obedience in order to fight for the Lord Christ, our true King.' These lay people were not ordained clergy in the modern sense but were professed members of a religious order who would today be considered clergy since they had taken vows. The *Rule* was designed for people who had adopted a cenobitic lifestyle, i.e. monks who lived a communal settled life in one location while making their own living. It was a life characterized by strict discipline, regular worship, and manual work. Saint Pachomius was the author of the first cenobitic rule, which was later developed by Saint Basil the Great. However, it was Benedict who introduced the cenobitic rule into Western monasticism and it became the norm for the Benedictines, the Cistercians (a development of the Benedictines) and the many other monastic orders that followed.

A distinctive aspect of the Benedictine and other cenobitic orders is the concept of 'tertiaries', lay members, or a third order, known as 'oblates' in the Benedictines, living either in communities as regular tertiaries, or in the world as secular tertiaries. In the following account of the battles for Monte Cassino it will be noticed that the German commander in the Cassino sector, Lieutenant General Fridolin von

Senger und Etterlin, was a secular oblate of the Benedictines while the commander of the US Fifth Army's II Corps, Geoffrey Keyes, a devout Roman Catholic, lived a life, even as a soldier on campaign, that mirrored the fundamental precepts of the Benedictines: pray and work.

Benedict laid great stress on the importance of work in the task of bringing people 'back to God by the labour of obedience, from whom they had departed by the idleness of disobedience'. He saw work as being essential to men, but did not prescribe the type of work his followers should undertake; it could be farming, as was the case at Monte Cassino in its early days, or any of a variety of endeavours. Moreover, he advocated community life through a group living, working, eating and praying together; his form of prayer he called the 'first degree of humility'. The golden rule adopted by Benedict for his followers, which remains the Benedictine motto, or mission statement in modern parlance, was 'Ora et Labora' – Pray and Work. Following Benedict's golden rule, the monks devoted eight hours of each day to prayer, another eight hours to sleep and the remaining eight to work, spiritual reading or performing charitable acts.

The *Rule* is divided into seventy-three short chapters, the wisdom of which is binary: spiritual guidance on living a Christ-centred life in this world; and administrative guidance on the efficient running of a monastic community. Emphasis is laid on how to be obedient and humble, and how to deal with a member of a community who fails to be obedient and humble. A quarter of the chapters govern the way in which the work of God is carried out and a tenth provide guidance on how a monastery should be managed, including who should be responsible for that management.

***

When Benedict moved to the Monte Cassino area he found the remains of an older settlement, Casinum Acropolis, on the mountain, with another settlement in the valley below. It was on the mountain that Benedict founded his monastery. Some parts of a Roman temple of Apollo survived, as did part of a tower, but Benedict destroyed the image of Apollo and the remaining pagan altars before dedicating the site for his monastery which he blessed in the name of Saint John the Baptist. The tower was incorporated into the new monastery. Benedict was never to leave his new home, spending the remaining years of his life in it and writing his *Rule* there. A village soon grew up around it. In spite of the passage of so many centuries, and the ravages of nature and man, some of the original monastery survives. The visitor approaching the Abbey from the coach or car park will notice the Latin word PAX – peace – writ large above a closed gate. This corner of the modern building is the remnant of the original monastery founded by Benedict and has survived earthquake, attacks by Lombards, Saracens and Normans, and bombing by the Allies.

Benedict's *Rule* was to have a major effect on European civilization as it became a guide for celibate asceticism and for monasticism in the western world. Many other orders were to follow Benedict's example over the centuries, although some, such as the Dominicans, would eschew the communal monastic life for a mendicant preaching lifestyle. However, Monte Cassino may truly be described as the wellspring of western monasticism.

According to Benedictine tradition, Benedict's sister Scholastica lived in the first Benedictine convent at Piumarola, some five miles from Monte Cassino, although she may have lived in a hermitage in a small female community housed at the base of Monte Cassino; an ancient church there is named for her. One writer, Ruth Clifford Engs, notes that, since Gregory the Great's *Dialogues* indicate that Scholastica was dedicated to God at an early age, it is possible that she lived with other religious women in her father's house until his death, after which she and her community moved nearer to Benedict.

Benedict died on 21 March 547, not long after Scholastica. They were buried together. At this time Italy was racked by war between the Eastern, or Byzantine, Roman Empire and the Ostrogoths. The Goths were eventually absorbed into the Lombards, a Germanic people, who established a kingdom in Italy in 568. This survived for about two centuries, during which the Lombards, who were either pagans or Arian Christians, converted partially to orthodox Christian beliefs. Early in the Lombard era, probably in 581, Benedict's monastery on Monte Cassino was stormed by them. It was pillaged and the community fled, not returning for over a century. However, the monastery's precious copy of the *Rule* was taken to Rome for safety.

Almost three centuries later the monastery was again stormed, this time by Saracens in 884 when the monastery was attacked and burned, and Abbot Bertharius killed. Although the monastery was rebuilt and continued its work, the town was renamed San Germano and a defensive castle was built on Rocca Janula, which overlooks the town. An eleventh-century abbot, Desiderius, whose period in office lasted over three decades, became Pope Victor III, but Monte Cassino suffered another attack during that century, this time by the Normans. During his time as abbot, Desiderius commissioned new bronze doors for the abbey; these were cast in Constantinople.

Among the many names associated with Monte Cassino is that of Constantine the African, a scholar and monk who died in 1087. Constantine's translations of ancient Greek documents gave western civilization its first systematic account of medicine in the classical age. Better known than Constantine was Thomas of Aquino, a town not far from Cassino, who joined the monastery for spiritual education in 1230. He was to become the famed theologian, and patron saint of scholars, Saint Thomas Aquinas.

***

In 1349 the monastery suffered severe damage from an earthquake. Repair was not completed until 1600, although the buildings were also extended. By then the monastery church had been declared a cathedral by Pope John XXII. Yet another attack and pillaging occurred in 1799 with Napoleon Bonaparte's troops targeting the monastery. A major battle occurred in the shadow of Monte Cassino in May 1815, a month before the Battle of Waterloo. This final battle of the Neapolitan war was fought between an Austrian army under the Irish-born Laval Graf Nugent von Westmeath and a Neapolitan army under Joachim Murat, king of Naples. Westmeath's army took victory in the Battle of San Germano.

There was a period of relative calm in the nineteenth century, although this was the century during which Italy was united as a nation state and so saw considerable upheaval and change. In 1863 the town was allowed to revert to its original name of Cassino and in that year also it was linked to the new Italian railway system. However, in 1866 the Italian government dissolved the monasteries and Monte Cassino became a national monument while the work of the monks became that of curators of Italian national archives.

In late-1943 the town became an important element of the German defences against the Allied armies and its citizens were evacuated as Cassino was fortified; on the initiative of a German medical officer, many of the Abbey's treasures were also moved to Rome for safekeeping.[3] On 14 February 1944 Allied guns fired leaflets warning that the Abbey was to be bombed since it was believed to be occupied by German troops. In the bombing attack next day the Abbey was destroyed. (After the war it was rebuilt and re-dedicated by Pope Paul VI in 1964. Although most of the decorative detail of the basilica and the Abbey had been lost, some elements survived, including the great bronze doors which were recovered and now stand in their proper place.)

In 2008 Pope Benedict XVI delivered a homily on Saint Benedict during a general audience in Saint Peter's Square, in which he stated that 'with his life and work Saint Benedict exercised a fundamental influence on the development of European civilization and culture' and had helped the continent to emerge from the 'dark night of history' after the collapse of the Roman empire. Saint Benedict certainly contributed more than any other person to the rise of monasticism in the West with his *Rule* providing the foundation for countless mediaeval religious communities.

2: The Abbey today. (© Damiano Parravano, Chairman, Associazione Linea Gustav)

3: The author (left) and Danilo Radcliffe, to whom this book is dedicated, on the Abbey balcony overlooking the Liri Valley. (Author's collection)

That *Rule* remains the most common and influential code for monasteries and monks over fourteen centuries after Benedict wrote it. Saint Benedict inspired 'a true spiritual ferment' in Europe with his followers spreading across the continent and establishing a new cultural unity based on Christian faith. It is because of the importance of Benedict to the development of European civilization that the destruction of the Abbey in 1944 chimed to such an extent not only with the Christians of Europe but across the globe. No other battle of the Second World War was fought on ground that was quite so steeped in history.

Debate over the bombing will continue for many years with arguments both for and against it. Perhaps one of the best comments on the destruction of the Abbey was made, appropriately enough, by the Benedictine oblate Lieutenant General Fridolin von Senger und Etterlin:

> As a tactical prelude the destruction of the Abbey appeared to have no significance. We felt sad at the failure of our efforts to preserve the Abbey in the midst of the battlefield. The prototype of all western religious Orders, the venerable mother of monasteries, lay in ruins.[4]

Chapter One

CASSINO. The name almost encapsulates the Italian campaign. Probably only Anzio is a name as recognizable from that campaign today. There is a general perception that Cassino was a hard-fought battle, but perhaps not a realization that it was arguably the hardest-fought of the Second World War in western Europe. It was not a single battle but a series of clashes beginning in January 1944, or even December 1943 if one considers the prelude to those actions, and not ending until early June 1944. More accurately, in the words of one participant who later produced a vibrant account, 'Operations, though formal and abstract, is a more appropriate term' than 'battle'. Major Fred Majdalany, Lancashire Fusiliers, described the word 'battle' as misleading, suggesting 'a coherent clash between orderly formations of men and machines'. In his view the word belonged 'to the past'.

> A modern battle is not an isolated event existing in a vacuum. It is a phase in a continuous integrated process. It develops logically from what has gone before, and relates to what follows. The beginning is often hard to pinpoint, the end is seldom final – unless it is the last battle of a campaign. It is convenient to speak of this or that battle, but what is really meant is operations between this date and that. A battle is generally without identity until it is viewed retrospectively within the context of a campaign.[1]

Accepting Majdalany's definition, this book attempts to place the battles of Cassino in their rightful place in a 'continuous integrated process'. The term 'battles of Cassino' is used since the Allies identified four distinct battles although the Germans saw only three; to them the Allied first and second battles were but one.

Where therefore should the story begin? Since the Cassino battles symbolize the Italian campaign, the origins of that campaign provide a logical starting point. The campaign followed the North African campaign which had raged from June 1940 until May 1943 when Allied forces overcame Axis armies in Tunisia and General Sir Harold Alexander, commanding 18 Army Group, signalled to Winston Churchill: 'It is my duty to report that the Tunisian Campaign is over. We are masters of the North African shores.' That victory had been foreseen during the Casablanca, or

SYMBOL, conference in January 1943 when Churchill and President Roosevelt, with the Allied Combined Chiefs of Staff, met to decide future strategy. Stalin, the Soviet leader, was to have attended but did not do so due to the continuing battle for Stalingrad.

The anticipated Axis defeat in Tunisia meant that major Allied forces would be left in North Africa. A decision on their deployment had to be made. The British Chiefs of Staff suggested that the Allies invade Sicily or Sardinia after Tunisia. This was no new idea: British planners had deliberated over it in late 1941 but had abandoned it before drawing up similar plans in November 1942. There was a strategic logic to seizing Sicily, the Mediterranean's largest island and part of Italy: this would re-open the Mediterranean sea routes, allow use of the Suez canal and reduce the time spent by convoys then routed around the Cape of Good Hope. The time thus saved would free valuable merchant shipping tonnage for the build-up in the UK of Allied forces to liberate north-west Europe.

Any operation to seize Sicily or Sardinia could be executed with forces already in the Mediterranean without diverting formations from the planned landings in France. This, and the benefits for Allied shipping, won American support for the plan. Sicily, rather than Sardinia, was chosen, the Americans considering it more important, both militarily and politically. However, they considered other British reasons for such a strategy as being 'irrelevant to an integrated plan to win the war'. Those reasons included knocking Italy out of the war and persuading Turkey to join the Allies, a dream long pursued by Churchill. General George Marshall, the US Army's Chief of Staff, was adamant that American commitment to the Sicilian operation was not to be seen as applying to any further operations in the Mediterranean.[2]

Once Churchill and Roosevelt had agreed the plans for Sicily the Combined Chiefs of Staff appointed General Dwight D. Eisenhower, the Allied Commander-in-Chief North Africa, to command Operation HUSKY, the invasion of Sicily, scheduled for the July moon. Eisenhower's appointment was announced on 23 January, the day Eighth Army took Libya's capital, Tripoli, as Axis forces continued retreating westward.[3]

Allied forces landed in Sicily on 10 July 1943, having first secured the small Italian island of Pantelleria, some sixty miles off the Sicilian coast. The ensuing campaign, involving General Bernard Montgomery's Eighth Army and General George S. Patton's Seventh US Army, was concluded in less than six weeks but the Germans evacuated much of their manpower and equipment across the Strait of Messina to mainland Italy. One of the architects of that evacuation, General Fridolin von Senger und Etterlin, would play a crucial role in the battles in the Cassino sector some months later.

The occupation of Pantelleria and Sicily should have ended the Mediterranean war since the agreed objective, securing the sea lanes, had been achieved. Marshall had not foreseen any further operations in the region, other than a possible landing in Sardinia. Churchill had other ideas and believed that Sicily should be followed by Allied forces landing in mainland Italy. Such operations were not in Marshall's plans but had been broached with Roosevelt by Churchill at the TRIDENT conference in Washington in May. Although Churchill had pressed Roosevelt for a commitment to operations in Italy the Americans had demurred.[4] Events in Italy conspired to moderate American attitudes. During the Sicilian campaign, Benito Mussolini, *Duce* since 1922, was deposed by King Victor Emmanuel III on 25 July and replaced by Marshal Pietro Badoglio. On 4 August Badoglio's government began secret negotiations with the Allies for an armistice.

Badoglio's approach raised several questions for the Allies and suggested some possibilities. Even if agreement was reached with the new Italian government, it was uncertain that Allied forces would be welcome in Italy since Italian forces had spent over three years fighting them. There might be a defiant defence of the homeland which the Germans might reinforce. Even if Italy collapsed there was the possibility of the Germans occupying the country, although Allied planners thought this unlikely because such an undertaking would require considerable manpower while Italian forces fighting elsewhere for the Axis would also have to be replaced. The latter included Italian Eighth Army on the Eastern Front, four divisions in southern France and no fewer than thirty divisions in Yugoslavia, Greece, Albania and the Greek islands. Allied planners mistakenly concluded that replacing those formations, and maintaining their front against the Red Army, would place such a burden on German manpower as to rule out occupation of Italy.[5]

General, later Field Marshal, Alexander noted that although the landings in Italy followed close on the conquest of Sicily and could be seen, 'both historically and strategically, as a sequel to it', in terms of the grand strategy of the war there was 'a great cleavage between the two' with the Sicilian campaign marking the final stage of operations that began in North Africa, whereas operations in Italy would be 'part of the next period in European strategy … destined to culminate in the invasion of the West and the destruction of the German armies'.[6]

Alexander played an important role in the Italian campaign, as commander of 15 Army Group and, later, Supreme Allied Commander, Mediterranean. One of the best-known British generals of the war, Sir Harold Alexander, son of the Earl of Caledon, was commissioned in the Irish Guards in 1911. During the First World War, 'Alex', as he was known popularly, earned an outstanding reputation for courage and rose to command a brigade. Later he saw active service in several theatres and in 1939 took 1st Division to France in the British Expeditionary Force.

4: General Sir Harold Alexander (later Field Marshal The Earl Alexander of Tunis and Errigal) commanded Allied Armies in Italy during the Cassino battles. (9th HAA Regiment Archive)

Promoted to command I Corps in the final days of the campaign, his reputation was probably sealed in Churchill's eyes when he ensured that he was the last man of I Corps to leave the beaches at Dunkirk, even cruising off those beaches and through the harbour in a small motorboat calling through a loudspeaker 'Is anyone there?' in English and French. Alex became a national hero, and subsequently GOC.-in-C., Southern Command before Churchill sent him to Burma to oversee the retreat into India. In August 1942 Churchill selected him to succeed Auchinleck as Commander-in-Chief in North Africa.

Alex had critical roles in the second (known as Alam el Halfa) and third battles of El Alamein and in the Tunisian campaign. In Tunisia he commanded 18 Army Group and continued as an army group commander with 15 Army Group in Sicily where he had two highly egotistical subordinates as army commanders: Montgomery and Patton. Alexander was the army group commander in Italy until late 1944 with, again, two powerful egos as army commanders, Montgomery until 31 December 1943 and Clark, commanding Fifth Army. Although Alex supported Clark when the latter appeared to lose his confidence at Salerno, the American disobeyed Alexander's orders as the Allies ruptured the Gustav Line and broke out of the Anzio bridgehead by making Rome his objective rather than the destruction of one or both of the German armies. Clark continued testing Alexander's undoubted skills of diplomacy and patience until the end of the campaign. Such skills were necessary when commanding a coalition force with personnel from over twenty different nations. In this, Alexander found his métier and was arguably the finest man for that role.[7]

***

With attention turning to possible operations on the Italian mainland, the strategic advantages that might accrue were also considered. The first, of course, was the detachment of Italy from its Axis partner and its removal from the war. Should Hitler deploy troops into Italy, Italian forces could help contain them. The large Italian fleet would no longer present a threat, allowing significant Allied naval forces to leave the Mediterranean. Deploying Allied strategic bombers to Italy would also be feasible; they could operate against targets in southern Germany as well as the Romanian oilfields. From Italy it might also be possible to attack the Balkans, while the British Chiefs considered that operations in Italy would help the Soviets by drawing off German forces from the Eastern Front.

Initial Allied thinking on operations in Italy was centred on limited objectives. Fighting from the toe of the country to the Lombardy Plain was neither necessary nor desirable, due to the terrain. Strategic objectives could be achieved by limited operations in the south, aimed at securing a good port, such as Naples, and the airfields of the Foggia plain.[8]

Clearly the planners were considering the nature of possible operations in Italy. Eisenhower, the Supreme Allied Commander, and Admiral Cunningham, the naval C.-in-C., were agreed on landings on the toe and heel of Italy to take Naples; they also agreed to seize Sardinia and Corsica. However, the air C.-in-C., Air

Marshal Tedder, did not agree. He believed that his colleagues did not appreciate the strategic bounty arising from taking the Foggia airfields whence bombing operations against southern Germany and the Balkans might be launched against less opposition than faced bombers from Britain; the Luftwaffe, unable to replicate their air defence system to counter a southern threat, would have to spread existing arrangements more thinly. Tedder was no advocate of seizing Sardinia.[9]

A slight change in Marshall's attitude was discernible when, in May, he and Eisenhower met Churchill, Alexander, Cunningham, Tedder and Montgomery, commanding Eighth Army, in Algiers to discuss future operations. A consensus was reached on operations in Italy: Eisenhower was favourably disposed; Alexander and Cunningham felt that, provided the Sicilian campaign was successful, landings in Italy should follow. Since Marshall agreed with that proviso, Eisenhower was told to plan for operations in Italy itself.[10]

Operations to seize Sardinia and Corsica were still being considered, as well as landings in the toe of Italy. All were to be executed by forces not committed to the Sicilian campaign: Fifth US Army was to seize Sardinia with Free French Forces liberating Corsica and the British V and X Corps operating on the Italian mainland.[11] However, by 3 July, a week before HUSKY, the British Chiefs concluded that:

> The full exploitation of Husky [Sicily] would best be secured if offensive action be prosecuted on the mainland of Italy with all the means at our disposal towards the final elimination of Italy from the war.[12]

With the Germans deciding to evacuate Sardinia and Corsica, Fifth Army was freed for operations on the mainland, thereby increasing 'the means at our disposal'. American enthusiasm for a campaign in Italy also increased only days into the Sicilian campaign. Major General George V. Strong, the US Army G-2, possibly influenced by the launch of a major German offensive in the Soviet Union on 5 July, considered that 'the time was right for bold action and the assumption of great risks in conducting the war in Europe' and felt that the Allies had sufficient resources for an operation into mainland Italy in the vicinity of Naples. On 15 July Strong recommended 'that planners investigate at once the feasibility of an amphibious assault to capture Naples as the first step toward securing Rome'.[13]

Marshall considered Strong's proposal favourably and put it to the Combined Chiefs on the 16th, recommending that they advise Eisenhower to study the idea. With the low losses in shipping and landing craft during HUSKY, and the expectation that Sicily's ports might be secured sooner than anticipated, Marshall believed that such an operation 'might be mounted before the onset of winter weather … without unreasonably great risks'. Admiral Ernest King, the US Navy chief, a strong advocate of operations in the Pacific, 'commented that an invasion at Naples might serve in lieu of a landing on Sardinia' and supported Marshall's suggestion, which was adopted by the Combined Chiefs.[14]

Committing Allied forces to the Italian motherland was the best means of eliminating Italy from the war in Alexander's opinion since it would also increase the manpower strain on Germany. The decision that Allied forces would land in France in 1944, probably in the early summer, suggested two powerful arguments for an Italian campaign: eliminating Italy from the war, as already noted, and 'the containing of the maximum number of German divisions, from its very nature indefinable'.[15] As Alexander noted, these were the only *desiderata* for the campaign: no geographical objectives were defined.

The HUSKY planning team had almost six months to prepare, whereas those involved in planning the landings in Italy had much less time to plan a far more complex operation. Some work had already been done for possible operations in Calabria, Italy's toe, and Sardinia, but consideration had to be given to the state of Allied forces after the Sicilian campaign. Since fresh formations were preferred, the British V and X Corps HQs were ordered to plan operations to be mounted from North Africa, one against Reggio di Calabria by X Corps and the second by V Corps against Crotone. Other operations were planned, including that against Sardinia involving Fifth Army, should those on the mainland be unsuccessful. A landing in Corsica was considered, and an airborne assault near Rome, but, finally, on 16 August, with the Sicilian campaign almost ended, final decisions were taken on the landings in Italy. Eighth Army's XIII Corps was to land in Calabria in Operation BAYTOWN between 1 and 4 September (the actual date was 3 September) with Fifth Army's X (British) Corps and VI US Corps landing at Salerno in Operation AVALANCHE on the 9th. In a further operation, SLAPSTICK, V Corps would land at Taranto.[16] (Fifth Army replaced Seventh US Army in 15 Army Group, under Alexander's command.)

With Mussolini's fall it was known that German troops were 'pouring into Italy, mainly re-formed divisions from the old Sixth Army destroyed at Stalingrad'. By the end of August there were 'as many as eighteen German divisions in Italy'.[17] The German forces were under two commanders, Field Marshals Erwin Rommel and Albrecht Kesselring. Although the latter was Commander-in-Chief, South (*Oberbefehlshaber Süd*, or *OB Süd*), Hitler had decided in May that Rommel would command *all* German troops in Italy should Germany take control, a decision not revealed to Kesselring.

At first Rommel's HQ was given the cover name *Arbeitsstab Rommel* (Rommel's Planning Staff), later changed to *OKW Auffrischungstab München* (OKW Refitting

HQ Munich); at this time, May to July 1943, Rommel was recuperating from the ill-health that had forced his departure from North Africa. The Desert Fox was also involved in planning for Operation ALARICH, the defence of Italy against Allied landings, and the linked Operation ACHSE, neutralizing Italian forces should the Allies land in Italy and the country quit the Axis.[18]

Most of Rommel's skeleton staff had served with him in North Africa, including Major General Alfred Gause, Colonel von Bonin, Captain Aldinger and Corporal Böttcher. Both Gause and von Bonin had served in *Panzerarmee Afrika*, Aldinger had been Rommel's adjutant and Böttcher his secretary. Hitler then had another change of mind, appointing Rommel to command German forces in Greece, Crete and the Aegean islands but able to move to Italy later with his HQ redesignated Army Group B (*Heeresgruppe B*). No sooner had Rommel arrived in Greece, on 23 July, than Mussolini was deposed. Rommel was ordered to meet Hitler again: his role in Italy would take priority and his undercover HQ in Munich would become that of Army Group B, responsible for northern Italy and the Alpine passes.[19]

While Rommel's HQ commanded all German formations in northern Italy, Kesselring's *OB Süd* commanded those in the south.[20] On 22 August Kesselring formed an army HQ to take direct control of southern-based formations. Tenth Army, or *Armeeoberkommando 10* (AOK 10), was commanded by General Heinrich von Vietinghoff-Scheel, 'an old Prussian infantryman of the Guards, competent, sure of himself and adaptable'.[21] Vietinghoff came from the traditional German military class, to which neither Kesselring nor Rommel belonged; this made Hitler more likely to take advice from them. However, they differed considerably in their strategic views: Rommel advised that Allied air superiority made withdrawal behind the Pisa-Rimini line the best option; Kesselring counselled that the peninsula be defended in the south. Hitler, always loath to concede ground, found Kesselring's advice more to his taste and accepted *OB Süd's* plans. Rommel remained as Army Group B commander with a diminished role before being transferred to France with responsibility for defending against Allied landings. Under Kesselring's command Army Group C was formed in southern Italy in November 1943.

Kesselring decided that Calabria would not be held but anticipated an Allied attack near Naples. He began concentrating forces to meet such a threat, including 26th Panzer and 29th Panzergrenadier Divisions, both part of *General der Panzertruppen* Traugott Herr's LXXVI Panzerkorps, which also included 1st *Fallschirmjäger* (Parachute) Division; the corps had been responsible for Puglia and Calabria. None of the formations was at full strength: elements of 1st *Fallschirmjäger* were deployed around Rome on security duties while 26th Panzer disposed only two companies of tanks; 29th Panzergrenadier had very few tanks. The rugged landscape of Calabria and Puglia was considered unsuitable for armoured operations.[22] An Eighth Army HQ intelligence summary dated

2 September concluded that there was 'no evidence of any [enemy] intention to make a real stand even at the Catanzaro narrows'.[23] Vietinghoff's command also included XIV Panzerkorps, commanded by Lieutenant General Hans-Valentin Hube, with 16th Panzer, 15th Panzergrenadier and the Hermann Göring Divisions. The formations under Hube were also preparing to meet any Allied landing near Naples.

Kesselring had identified a strong natural defensive line across Italy which his engineers could reinforce, given time. That line ran from the mouth of the Garigliano river, on the Tyrrhenian coast, through the town of Cassino and along the Sangro river to the Adriatic. Thus, before either Eighth or Fifth Armies landed in Italy, Kesselring was planning and preparing a series of fortifications to put a brake on any Allied advance. Referred to by the Allies as the Winter Line, the fortifications comprised a series of interlocked lines, the most important being the Gustav Line. On 10 September, during the Salerno battle, Kesselring drew on a map

> our successive defence positions in the event of a retirement from southern Italy; they were more or less kept to when we later withdrew. … it might still be possible to go over to the defensive south of Rome, perhaps on a line running through Monte Mignano (the later Reinhard Line) or on the Garigliano-Cassino Line (later the Gustav Line). If there were to be any hope of halting the enemy these positions must be consolidated and fresh construction and fighting units brought up. It was up to von Vietinghoff and his Tenth Army to gain us the time we needed.[24]

Thus, while Kesselring was preparing to fight the Allies as they landed, he was also prepared to cede ground to them, falling back through the series of defensive lines under preparation. As Allied soldiers prepared and trained for landing in Italy, their foes were ensuring that there would be no easy victories; every foot of ground would be contested. In the ensuing struggles the name of Monte Cassino would become prominent with the majestic Benedictine abbey on its summit assuming a worldwide importance that the monks of Saint Benedict could never have anticipated.

***

Generalfeldmarschall Albrecht Kesselring, a Bavarian, joined the Royal Bavarian Army as an artillery officer cadet in 1904 and served in the artillery on both Western and Eastern Fronts in the First World War, being appointed to the staff in spite of not attending the Bavarian War Academy.[25] After the war he remained in the army at the behest of his 'politically-minded GOC'. Appointed to the

5: Field Marshal Albrecht Kesselring, Axis commander in Italy. (NARA)

Reichswehr Ministry in Berlin in 1922, he served in the Reichswehr until 1933 when he was transferred to the Luftwaffe as a commodore.[26] Learning to fly at the age of 48, he flew operationally, being shot down five times.[27] By September 1939 he was commanding *Luftflotte I* (Air Fleet I), based in Berlin, which supported Bock's Army Group North in the invasion of Poland. Subsequently, Kesselring commanded *Luftflotte II* with 'considerable success in the Low Countries and France (1940), Russia (1941), and the Mediterranean and North Africa (1942-43)' but was 'less successful' in the Battle of Britain.[28]

Promoted to field marshal in 1940 he became responsible for the Mediterranean theatre from November 1941, quickly learning some of the problems inherent in coalition warfare as he sought to ensure the most effective organization of German and Italian forces. The organization in Libya seemed ideal on paper but was 'foredoomed to failure in practice because Rommel and [Marshal] Bastico [governor of Libya] were continually at loggerheads ... . Rommel's great reputation, then at its zenith, was an obstacle to the introduction of any change, but at the same time it helped to smooth over certain delicate situations'.[29]

Kesselring remained in the Mediterranean but, with defeat in North Africa, found himself in an unclear situation when Rommel, also a field marshal, was appointed to command Army Group B in Italy. However, as we have seen, this situation was resolved when Hitler chose to support Kesselring's plan to defend south of Rome and Rommel's HQ was reduced and moved to France. 'Uncle Albert', as he was known to German servicemen (the Allies called him 'Smiling Albert') proved a very effective opponent to the Allied armies.

***

Eighth Army's Operation BAYTOWN, on 3 September, saw two divisions of XIII Corps land in Calabria supported by a massive artillery bombardment across the Strait of Messina, fire from naval vessels and air cover. The landing was seen as a 'prerequisite for AVALANCHE', to secure 'a bridgehead on the Calabrian toe' and secure the Strait of Messina for Allied shipping.[30] Rather than facing resistance, XIII Corps' soldiers were welcomed ashore. Strictly speaking, Eighth Army was invading Italy, but war-weary Italians saw them as liberators. Reggio was under Canadian control before the morning was out. Both 1st Canadian and 5th British Divisions then advanced through the Calabrian countryside. Both 26th Panzer and 29th Panzergrenadier Divisions, with orders not to engage in heavy fighting, started withdrawing before Eighth Army's soldiers landed. However, they blew up roads, demolished bridges and cut down trees in this most heavily-wooded region of Italy to slow the Allies. There were some skirmishes but no major engagements.[31]

Meanwhile V Corps was preparing to embark for Taranto. The first element, 1st Airborne Division, did so on four ships of the Royal Navy's 12th Cruiser Squadron, the fast cruiser-minelayer HMS *Abdiel*, and the US Navy's cruiser USS *Boise*. Their landing, on 9 September, was almost uneventful but next day *Abdiel* struck a mine while swinging at anchor with heavy loss of life, including 120 men of 6th Parachute Battalion. Nonetheless, V Corps was soon on the advance: 1st Airborne secured Taranto and pushed out northwards and eastwards. Again there was little fighting, although in a skirmish on the 11th the GOC, Major General Hopkinson, was wounded, later succumbing to his injuries.[32]

6: Eighth Army soldiers coming ashore at Reggia in Calabria during Operation BAYTOWN, to be welcomed as liberators rather than invaders. (Author's collection)

By now the Italian armistice had been announced and Hitler had ordered German forces to seize control. The signal '*Ernte Einbringe*', 'bring in the harvest', was the order for action against Italian forces, which were disarmed, sometimes brutally in Operation ACHSE, originally ALARICH. Eisenhower had announced the armistice by radio on the 8th, hoping to galvanize Italian personnel into organized co-operation with the Allies but instead the Italian army was neutralized. Eisenhower's broadcast was made as Fifth Army was sailing towards the Gulf of Salerno for Operation AVALANCHE.[33] The approach of the armada did not go unobserved. Luftwaffe aircraft spotted British taskforce ships south of Capri and launched attacks. Knowledge of the ships' approach did not give Kesselring any clear indication of where the Allies would land and he lacked sufficient troops to

7: LCT 222 discharges US Army tanks and equipment during Operation AVALANCHE, the Salerno landings. Fifth US Army's landings met stern opposition and a major counter-attack threatened the Allied beachhead. (9th HAA Regiment Archive)

cover every possible site. Clark estimated that the Germans could have as many as 39,000 troops in the landing area on D Day, a figure that could rise to 100,000 by D + 3.[34] Fifth Army was landing 125,000 men of VI US Corps, under Major General Ernest Dawley, and X British Corps, under Lieutenant General Richard McCreery.[35]

The first troops were US Rangers, followed by British Commandos, the Rangers pushing inland while the Commandos secured Salerno town. X Corps (46th and 56th Divisions) began landing in the northern sector of the bay while VI Corps deployed 36th (Texas) Division farther south, at Paestum, with 45th Division as a floating reserve. Unlike BAYTOWN, the landings were opposed and casualties occurred. However, American and British forces established lodgements and, in some cases, pushed inland. For Kesselring the landings confirmed the Allies' intentions and, although he maintained forces around Rome, he began concentrating formations against the beachhead.

As more German units and formations reached the battle area, pressure on the Allied forces increased with Kesselring determined to drive them back into the sea. Fighting continued for a week before Allied strength prevailed and the Germans began withdrawing. Clark was unsure of himself during the battle and, at one point, wanted to evacuate VI Corps, a suggestion rejected by his superiors.

Alexander released 82nd Airborne Division from reserve to strengthen Fifth Army, which helped stabilize the situation. Subsequently, Clark's report to Eisenhower on Dawley's performance led to the corps commander being relieved and replaced by Major General John P. Lucas.[36]

A difficult battle, it provided a taste of what lay ahead as the Allies advanced from Salerno on the Tyrrhenian side of Italy and from Calabria through Puglia on the Adriatic side. Neither army was at full strength, nor were their logistic support systems operating at their best. Moreover, four American and three British divisions were to return to the United Kingdom by 1 November with another two British divisions 'to be held in readiness to fulfil our commitments to Turkey'.[37] (The divisions due to leave were 50th (Northumbrian), 51st (Highland), 1st Airborne, 2nd (US) Armored, 1st (US) Infantry, 9th (US) Infantry and 82nd (US) Airborne; 7th Armoured Division, the Desert Rats, joined the list subsequently.)[38]

Naples was liberated by Fifth Army on 1 October but the port had suffered heavy damage from Allied bombing and German demolitions, while civilians remaining in the city were racked by hunger, having had little to eat for ten days.[39] It would take time to create a logistical support base in the city, but this had to be done to allow Fifth Army to advance towards Rome. In the meantime, Eighth Army had secured Bari and the Foggia airfields and was advancing against stiffening resistance. The weather had also come to the aid of Kesselring's forces.

239 NAPOLI - Panorama

8: Naples with the bay in the foreground and Vesuvius in the background. The port was essential to Allied plans for operations in Italy. (Author's collection)

An eighteen-hour downpour on 3 October raised levels in rivers and streams, making roads impassable; such heavy rain had not been expected until the end of the month.[40] Adverse weather remained a problem with bridges washed away and roads damaged. The resources of the Royal Engineers were stretched considerably. Montgomery had planned to advance to Pescara, unleash the New Zealanders in a right hook towards Rome and then, since he would be exhausted, take some leave and 'probably write a book "Alamein to Rome"'.[41]

By this stage both armies had encountered the 'Winter Line'. In fact, they had penetrated elements of it, only to find that it was not simply a line but a complex defensive system that would frustrate many breakthrough efforts. Having identified a natural line across Italy from the mouth of the Garigliano on the west coast to the mouth of the Sangro on the east, Kesselring deployed engineers, under Major General Hans Bessel, his Chief Engineer, to reinforce with concrete, steel and weaponry what Italy's topography had already provided.

> [The line] was to follow the general line Garigliano-Mignano-course of the Volturno-Maiella massif-Sangro, being strongest below the Cassino valley, in the Garigliano, at the southern spurs of the Maiella range and on the Adriatic plain. It was not to be a single line but a system of positions organized in depth which would allow possible enemy penetrations to be sealed off.[42]

This defensive system included interlocking lines that Kesselring hoped would pin down 15 Army Group until at least spring 1944. He intended delaying Alexander's advance for a prolonged period at the peninsula's narrowest point, the 'waist' of Italy. Here stood the Gustav Line, which followed the courses of three rivers, the Garigliano, Gari and Rapido (the Gari is often wrongly called the Rapido) and then, from the Rapido's upper waters, rejoined the Bernhardt Line. However, the hard core of the system was the Gustav Line, protecting the Liri valley, some six miles wide, with its twin sentinels of Monte Cassino, to the north, and Monte Maio, to the south; the former stands 1,600 feet high (516 metres) and the latter about 3,000 feet high (940 metres). (Since the Italian peninsula runs north-westerly from its 'foot' to the Alps, the German defensive positions generally faced east rather than south.) Soaring above Monte Cassino is Monte Cáiro at some 5,400 feet (1,669 metres). Cáiro allowed German observers a view of the entire battlefield; from its summit on a clear day it is possible to see as far as the Bay of Naples. The British official history provides an excellent description.

> The most important of the switch positions [was] ... the Gustav Line. The Gustav took final shape in early 1944 after continual alterations. It

broke off from the Bernhardt Line at the 'Garigliano sluice' near [Monte] Valle Martina (Pt 321), and then ran west of the Garigliano, Gari and Rapido rivers. It incorporated the Cassino massif including the town of Cassino, and ran on across [Colle] Belvedere (Pt 721) and east of San Biagio to Alfedena. Here it merged again in the Bernhardt Line.[43]

In front of the Gustav Line on the Tyrrhenian sector lay the Bernhardt, or Reinhard, Line which crossed to the Adriatic sector and was as strong as the Gustav. (Some accounts, including that of Rudolf Böhmler, a *Fallschirmjäger* officer involved in the defence of Cassino, describe the continuation of the Bernhardt Line from its junction with the Gustav Line as being the latter.) That section of the Bernhardt Line bulging forward of the Gustav Line was itself a daunting barrier: a wide defensive belt, anchored at Minturno, near the Garigliano's mouth, it included 'the forbidding masses of Monte Camino, Monte La Difensa, Monte Maggiore, and … the hulking height of Monte Sammucro'.[44] It was also mined heavily, both within the line and on its approaches. From its junction with the Gustav, the Bernhardt Line crossed the Abruzzi mountains to Castel di Sangro whence, on the Adriatic sector, it took in the Maiella massif and the Sangro's lower waters. At first intended

9: Monte Cáiro from Cáira village. The mountain dominates the area in which much of the battle was fought; from its summit the Bay of Naples is visible on a clear day. (Author's photo)

as a delaying line with early work on it consisting only of light field defences, that changed when Hitler ordered Kesselring to defend the Gaeta-Ortona line. Since the Bernhardt Line looked best suited as the position on which to do battle, the task of strengthening began. With time needed to carry out that work, the Viktor and Barbara Lines were defended more staunchly than originally intended. As autumn slipped into winter there was savage fighting on the Bernhardt Line and 'as the forward bastions fell to Allied attacks the Bernhardt was constantly strengthened and deepened by fresh positions. The whole system became known to the Allies as the Winter Line'.[45]

Testifying to the Bernhardt Line's effectiveness is the fact that, although Fifth Army made first contact with it at the start of December 1943, it took until mid-January 1944 to battle through and come up against the Gustav Line. The US Army official history notes that, while the Barbara and Bernhardt Lines would be defended 'stubbornly enough', the Germans 'would try to hold the Gustav position'.[46] According to the commander of XIV Panzerkorps during the Cassino battles, Lieutenant General Fridolin von Senger und Etterlin, the Bernhardt Line had been selected by his predecessor, Hube.[47]

The Barbara Line, lying before the Bernhardt, was less of an obstacle, being more a line of fortified outposts from Mondragone on the west coast via the 2,667-foot-high (813 metres) Monte Massico, near the coast, through Teano and Presenzano into the Matese mountains and then following the Trigno river to San Salvo on the east coast. Hastily constructed, it was not well defined and was intended only to slow the Allied advance, although the Allies initially expected it to be stronger.[48]

By the time they encountered the Barbara Line, Fifth Army's soldiers had already fought through the southernmost of the German defensive lines, the Viktor, or Volturno, Line on the line of the Volturno river in the west before crossing the Apennines to follow the Biferno river to Termoli on the east coast; like the Barbara Line it was intended only to delay. The Viktor Line lay about forty miles south of Cassino and some twenty miles north of Naples. A week after liberating Naples, elements of Fifth Army had reached the Volturno, establishing a secure zone for Naples and bringing Operation AVALANCHE to a close.[49] The cost had been high: between D Day for AVALANCHE and the Volturno the soldiers of Fifth Army had suffered about 2,000 dead, 7,000 wounded and 3,500 missing, a brutal foretaste of what lay ahead. From the German viewpoint, von Senger summed up the tactical situation.

> Our task was to put up so tough a resistance on the Volturno that there would be time to prepare the Bernhardt Line. Some sections of the troops fighting in the immediate front were already being withdrawn into this

line to link up with advanced detachments that were falling back more quickly than planned, and to help in preparing the new positions.[50]

The delaying task was carried out effectively and it was a very tired Fifth Army that closed on the Barbara Line. Ahead lay a daunting task: break through the Barbara Line, close with and break through the Bernhardt Line and then repeat that feat with the Gustav Line. And Kesselring's engineers had not finished their work on the Gustav Line. In December 1943 they began building another switch line some eight miles behind the Gustav. To this was given the title Hitler Line, although it was renamed the Senger Line in late January 1944, lest it be broken by the Allies: it would never do to have the Führer's name associated with defeat. On the western end of the Hitler Line was the Dora Line and finally there lay yet another line, the Caesar Line, some fifty miles to the north of Cassino, and south of Rome. As Allied forces pushed towards Rome this last line was hardly noticed.

Chapter Two

For Fifth and Eighth Armies the battles fought to reach the Gustav Line were hard and bitter. Assisted by rain, mud and mountains, von Vietinghoff's men displayed exemplary skill in slowing the Allied advance. On the Tyrrhenian sector Fifth Army pushed through the Barbara Line, only to come up against the Bernhardt defences. The Viktor and Barbara Lines had already cost many casualties. The Bernhardt Line would add greatly to that toll.

Both sides knew that the options for approaching Rome were limited by topography. With the Apennines forming a central spine with many peaks over 5,000 feet (1,560 metres) above sea level, movement across Italy is difficult and so from Naples there were only two possible routes to Rome. Highway 7, the Via

10: General Heinrich von Vietinghoff-Scheel, commander Tenth Army. He succeeded Kesselring as the overall commander in Italy and surrendered to the Allies on 2 May 1945. (Deutsches Bundesarchiv (German Federal Archive), Bild 101I-313-1019-14)

Appia of old, hugged the coast, leaving no manoeuvre room for major formations, especially where the Aurunci mountains drop down into the sea at Gaeta and Terracina and the road is carved into those mountains. Even had the attackers been able to overcome such difficulties, there remained the Pontine marshes in Lazio which the Germans had flooded (Mussolini's government had drained the marshes and reclaimed much land, settling many people from northern Italy there). The alternative was the Via Casilina, Highway 6, a road of major significance in Italy's history. Majdalany called it 'one of the great roads of history', noting that, three centuries before Christ, Roman legions had marched along it to fight the Samnites near Cassino while Fabius used it in his campaign against Hannibal. In the sixth century AD, Belisarius, in his advance to liberate Rome from the Goths, took his army along the route, which was also used by the Gallic leader Totila, or Baduila, who recaptured Rome some years later before striking out along the road to seize additional territory. In 1503 the Spanish General Gonzalo Fernández de Córdoba, the 'father of trench warfare', used it in his campaign against the French.[1] As 1943 became 1944 the Via Casilina was about to feature in yet another war, the bloodiest in its history. The road takes the traveller from Naples to Rome through a series of river valleys of varying widths, the widest being the Liri, of about six miles, or nearly ten kilometres, across. Although the valleys were overlooked by higher ground on either side, Highway 6 offered a more suitable route for an army heading for Rome than did Highway 7. While it also presented major problems, especially those heights to its flanks, Highway 6 was really the Allied commanders' only choice. That this was the case was also clear to Kesselring and his commanders. Thus there could be no element of surprise as far as the axis of the Allied advance was concerned.

***

As Eighth Army fought its way up the leg of Italy on the Adriatic sector and into the mountains, Fifth Army was doing likewise from Naples on the western sector. Although an American formation, Fifth Army included a substantial British component and, throughout its existence, was to include nationalities other than American. These included British, French, Italian, Brazilian and South African soldiers and, since the British and French were both imperial powers, soldiers from India and Nepal, and from France's North African territories. The Brazilians and South Africans came into Fifth Army later but at this period in its history the British were already there, the Italians were arriving and the French about to arrive. American reinforcements were also arriving, which makes this a useful point at which to consider Fifth Army and its commander, Lieutenant General Mark Wayne Clark.

Fifth Army came into being at Oujda in French Morocco on 4 January 1943, the first American field army formed outside the continental United States, while the Tunisian campaign was underway. It was under the command of Clark who, in part at least, was responsible for its creation, having urged the formation of a field army to command US ground forces under 18 Army Group in Tunisia. Although the army was established, Clark's concept of an American field army fighting alongside British First Army in Tunisia did not come to pass since Marshall wanted Fifth Army to be ready to act against Spanish Morocco.[2]

Lieutenant General Mark Wayne Clark, the youngest man ever to hold that rank in the US Army, had been born into the Army, in which his father was an officer.[3] Entering West Point in 1913, he was commissioned four years later. Deployed to France with 11th Infantry Regiment of 5th Division, he was wounded seriously while supervising a hand-over from French troops on his first day in the line and, during surgery, suffered further injury when a hot-water bottle fell over, scalding his left leg. Clark recovered but, being unfit for infantry duties, saw no action. For an ambitious officer this was a setback, but he remained a soldier after the war, building a solid reputation for efficient administration and sound judgement. Following the Command and General Staff College course at Fort Leavenworth, he was marked out for advancement should the United States go to war; the rapid

11: Lieutenant General Mark Wayne Clark, commander Fifth US Army. Clark's plans for the first battle led to heavy losses in 36th Division on the Gari river in January 1944. His name is unpopular in Texas to this day. (NARA)

expansion required in such a situation needed officers with Clark's staff training. And so it was. As a staff officer in 3rd Infantry Division HQ, Clark was noticed by the commander of 5 Brigade, Brigadier General George Marshall, later to become US Army Chief of Staff.[4]

When the Japanese attacked Pearl Harbor, thrusting America into the war, Clark was a brigadier general, having leapfrogged officers with longer service. Further promotion followed in 1942 with advancement to major general, command of II Corps and then appointment as Deputy Supreme Commander, Allied Force Headquarters (AFHQ), London.[5] However, General Sir Charles Richardson noted that Clark 'had never commanded a division', which, in the British Army, 'would have been regarded as an essential qualification' for an army commander.[6]

As Deputy Supreme Commander AFHQ, Clark undertook a secret mission by submarine to Algeria to discuss the planned Allied invasion of French North-West Africa and continued negotiating with the Vichy French after the TORCH landings on 8 November 1942. Promoted to lieutenant general on 11 November, on the 22nd he signed an agreement with Admiral François Darlan, whom the Allies recognized as political head of French North-West Africa.[7] (On Christmas Eve 1942, Darlan, who had served the Vichy government, was assassinated by an anti-Vichy gunman.)[8]

Clark's army did not go into action until September 1943, its headquarters having a training role in the interim. By September Fifth Army included two corps: VI US and X British. Initially X Corps was commanded by Lieutenant General Brian Horrocks, who had considerable combat experience and whom Clark, according to Blumenson, found 'somewhat patronizing', although that probably owed much to Clark's imagination and Anglophobia. Eighth Army would also fight in Italy and thus Clark and Montgomery had to work together under HQ 15 Army Group, commanded by Alexander. Relations between Clark and Montgomery were strained at times, as they later were with Montgomery's successor, Lieutenant General Sir Oliver Leese Bt. Clark also disliked Richard McCreery, who took over command of X Corps after Horrocks had been wounded severely in a Luftwaffe attack on Bizerte.

Comments in letters home to his wife indicate that Clark had an intense dislike and distrust of the British. He was also anxious to promote himself and portray Fifth Army as 'General Clark's Fifth Army'. With the liberation of Rome in June 1944 he would have his best opportunity to display his penchant for publicity. Such was his desire for publicity that he earned the soubriquet 'Marcus Aurelius Clarkus' from some of his staff. Lemnitzer, Alexander's American chief of staff, believed that there were several times during the Italian campaign when Alexander might have relieved Clark.

There was, in fact, ample justification for relieving him, as he had made every mistake in the book [at Salerno] and then heaped the majority of the blame on Dawley, whose performance as beachhead commander was not nearly as inept as Clark portrayed it to Eisenhower. Thus, Dawley's relief was partly a face-saving gesture by the Allied high command, as he became the first of several senior field commanders who would pay a high price for a faulty plan.[9]

As we have seen, Fifth Army at Salerno included Dawley's VI US Corps and McCreery's X British Corps plus two British Commando units and three US Ranger battalions; both Commandos and Rangers came under McCreery's command. VI Corps deployed 36th Division, which made the initial landings in the American sector, and 45th Division, the floating reserve; these were National Guard formations from Texas and Oklahoma respectively. X Corps included 46th and 56th Divisions, both Territorial Army formations, the former from the North Midlands and West Riding of Yorkshire, the latter from London. Follow-up formations included the British 7th Armoured Division, the 'Desert Rats', 1st US Armored Division, 'Old Ironsides', and 34th and 3rd US Infantry Divisions. With the breakout from Salerno, the liberation of Naples and advance to the Volturno, additional formations joined, although some, including the Desert Rats, later left for the UK to prepare for Normandy. As Fifth Army fought through the Barbara Line and first encountered the Bernhardt Line the two original corps were still in action and would remain so for some time.

X Corps' commander, Richard McCreery, was commissioned in 12th (The Prince of Wales's Royal) Lancers in 1915 and earned the Military Cross on 9 November 1918, two days before the Armistice. His achievement was all the more remarkable since he had been wounded so seriously in April 1917 that it was feared he might lose his right leg. Surgeons saved the leg, although not the toes of the foot; thereafter he walked with a pronounced gait. Between the wars, he commanded his regiment, attended Staff College and was an enthusiast for mechanization, becoming familiar with the problems of mechanized warfare in a desert setting when 12th Royal Lancers went to Egypt in 1936.

McCreery crossed to France with the BEF in 1939 as GSO I (chief of staff) of Alexander's 1st Division; his relationship with Alex was good and teamwork in divisional headquarters was excellent. In January 1940 McCreery was promoted to command 2 Armoured Brigade in 1st Armoured Division which was still in Britain and did not reach France until May. Nonetheless, McCreery led 2 Armoured Brigade in action, earning an excellent reputation and the DSO for his leadership of the rearguard action, fought in very difficult circumstances, between the Somme and Seine rivers. Back in Britain and promoted major general, he

12: Lieutenant General Richard McCreery, who commanded X Corps in Fifth Army. His corps created a substantial bridgehead across the Garigliano in January and early February that was invaluable to II US Corps in the final battle. (McCreery family)

became GOC 8th Armoured Division, which he led and trained to a very high standard. Subsequently, he was posted to Egypt and, in March 1942, became General Auchinleck's principal adviser on armoured warfare. Although the two were later not to see eye to eye on the organization of armoured formations, as a result of which Auchinleck removed McCreery, they ensured that Eighth Army had sufficient tanks to meet Rommel's advance after the fall of Tobruk and fight *Panzerarmee Afrika* to a standstill along the El Alamein line in July 1942.

When Alexander succeeded Auchinleck in August 1942 he appointed McCreery as his chief of staff. The team that had inspired 1st Division was again in operation and it was McCreery's suggestion that led to Montgomery recasting his break-in plan for Operation SUPERCHARGE in November, although, typically, Monty claimed it as his own idea. When Brian Horrocks was wounded in June 1943, McCreery succeeded him as commander X Corps, an assault formation of Fifth US Army for Operation AVALANCHE. Throughout the Italian campaign, and despite the friction of working under Clark's command, McCreery's courage and leadership had few equals, so much so that he was chosen to succeed Leese to command Eighth Army.[10] His handling of the aftermath of the Operation OLIVE offensive earned much admiration and was one of the factors inspiring John Strawson, an Italian veteran, to describe McCreery as 'the greatest cavalry soldier of his generation and at the same time that rare coalition of a brilliant staff officer and higher commander'.[11]

***

December 1943 saw Eighth and Fifth Armies fighting in difficult terrain on either side of the Apennines. Eighth Army had crossed the Sangro in late November, breaking through the Bernhardt Line in the east, but in December met the 'Stalingrad of the Abruzzi', Ortona. The advance came to a standstill; although Ortona was liberated, worsening winter conditions impeded further movement. Fifth Army was also fighting through the Bernhardt defences, striking blows at the defenders and gaining some surprise by attacking on the German left when its commanders expected the Allies to use their armour to strike through the centre via the Mignano Gap. However, the Gap was but a mile wide and tanks attempting the passage would have been at the mercy of German artillery on the high ground to either flank. Thus the infantry were faced with the task of securing the Gap and the neighbouring mountains. General von Senger described this fighting, 'that led to the penetration of the Winter Line and heralded the Cassino battles', as being 'characterized by the fact that the enemy held the initiative', not, perhaps, a view with which Fifth Army's soldiers would have concurred.[12] Senger also noted:

> Evidently the Americans were no longer affected by the novelty of battle. In Sicily they had hardly learned how to adapt themselves to the conditions, and their attacks still lacked spirit. Here they showed no such shortcomings. This also held good for their attacks on the centre of the front, which we still regarded as the most threatened.[13]

Eventually Fifth Army broke into the centre and von Senger had to reinforce his defences, admitting that, at the end of November, 'the Bernhardt Line had been dented in the centre and to the north of Venafro'.[14] Fighting continued throughout December with British, American, Canadian and Italian troops operating in desperate conditions as they assaulted mountain positions. This series of battles in November and December was fought for heights such as Monte Camino, Monte Maggiore, Monte La Difensa and Monte Lungo, the last-named seeing Italian combat troops, of 1st Motorized Combat Group (*1º Raggruppamento Motorizzato*), fighting for the Allies for the first time, but in uniforms intended for North Africa rather than an Apennine winter. That clothing caused a problem when a reconnaissance party was 'captured' by American troops of 142nd Infantry Regiment who failed to recognize the Italian uniforms. First Motorized Combat

Group included elements of the former *Legnano*, *Mantova* and *Piceno* Divisions under command of General Vincenzo Dapino.[15]

Monte La Difensa had been taken early in December by 1st Special Service Force, a US-Canadian special forces group that was in action for the first time. The defenders were caught off-balance, having believed that the sheer cliffs on which they were perched could not be scaled, but the men of 1st Special Service Force did so to catch the Germans by surprise and support the main attack on the feature, Operation RAINCOAT. The eviction of the Germans from Monte La Difensa allowed McCreery's X Corps to secure Monte Camino and the US 142nd Infantry to do likewise with Monte Maggiore, thus opening the Mignano Gap from the south and allowing Fifth Army's advance to continue.[16]

The level of Allied success worried von Senger who could foresee significant elements of XIV Panzerkorps being cut off.

13: An Italian civilian guides soldiers of the US/Canadian 1st Special Service Force in the mountains. (NARA)

Prolonged resistance became more pointless in proportion as the enemy gained more ground through single attacks against the [44th] Division in the Abruzzi mountains, which are nearly 2,000 metres high. In the middle of the month a general withdrawal to the Gustav Line was approved. In the centre 29th Panzergrenadier Division was still fighting for every inch of ground and this governed the rate of withdrawal of the whole corps.[17]

By this time Hitler had decided that there would be no more withdrawals in Italy and sent Rommel and the HQ of Army Group B to France 'to inspect the defences of the west and make recommendations'.[18] Rommel left Italy 'without regrets' on 21 November, telling those of his entourage who would remain that the war 'was as good as lost'.[19]

***

Kesselring was left in command in Italy. Although there was another field marshal, he was a Luftwaffe officer: Freiherr Wolfram von Richtofen controlled the dwindling German air assets in the peninsula, *Luftflotte II*, but with no authority over ground forces. (Richtofen, a cousin of the brothers Manfred and Lothar von Richtofen, had also been a fighter 'ace' in the First World War with eight victories.)[20]

On the Allied side Eisenhower and Montgomery were to leave Italy to prepare for the Normandy landings. However, before leaving, Eisenhower had made some significant decisions. In early November he outlined a revised strategy whereby Eighth Army, then on the Sangro, would cross that river, advance the twenty-five miles to Pescara and then continue to Avezzano, fifty miles east of Rome, from where Montgomery could move on and liberate the Eternal City. The threat from Eighth Army would compel the Germans to thin out their forces facing Fifth Army. If, in turn, Clark could then break through the defences of the Bernhardt Line about the Mignano Gap and advance into the Liri valley, a distance of about fifty miles, he would be able to push on to Frosinone, another twenty-five mile bound, from where 'he would be close enough to Anzio to warrant a landing'.[21]

D'Este outlines a broader canvas. With Fifth Army in Naples, Churchill sent Eisenhower a congratulatory telegram, noting his willingness to take risks. However, while Eisenhower was enjoying that praise, Marshall 'took the starch out of Ike' with a telegram reminding him that there could be no resting on laurels for the Allied armies in Italy.

> Ever anxious to dispose of the Italian campaign as quickly as possible, Marshall wanted to know if Eisenhower could hold the line below Naples

and concentrate instead on an amphibious end run behind enemy lines to capture Rome. Eisenhower was shocked by Marshall's no-nonsense bluntness and the absence of even a simple gesture of congratulations. His pride was so deeply wounded by the intimation that he lacked aggressiveness and initiative that he ate neither breakfast [n]or lunch.[22]

It may have been Marshall's spur to his pride that led to Eisenhower proposing the amphibious operation behind German lines that would become Operation SHINGLE in January 1944. (The immediate reaction to Marshall's prompting was the establishment of a Fifth Army planning team at the Royal Palace in Caserta on 12 November; the preferred landing area was at Anzio, about thirty miles from Rome. Alexander was also a proponent of such an operation.)[23] Although the landings had been planned for 20 December that target proved impossible and a new round of planning began which resulted in SHINGLE.[24] The operation had deep and baleful influence on the land-bound operations against the Gustav Line since it created an imperative for those fighting against that line to break through to relieve and join those in the beachhead.

Since SHINGLE was a Fifth Army operation, planning fell to Clark's staff, although it involved many others, especially from both the Royal and US Navies. Landing craft, particularly the large LSTs (Landing Ships, Tank) had to be assembled, no easy task as they were in high demand for the planned landings in France. Warships also had to be available to protect convoys sailing to Anzio and the supply ships that would sustain the landing force once ashore. Fifth Army would have to provide the force to land at Anzio; this would be VI Corps, which had landed at Salerno, now under Major General John P. Lucas.

Fortunately, II US Corps had arrived to join Fifth Army during October and General (later Marshal of France) Alphonse Juin's *Corps expéditionnaire français* (CEF), or French Expeditionary Corps, started arriving in November. The French component of the Allied forces might have caused an embarrassment since the French intended to create an army headquarters, *Détachement d'armée A*, or Detachment of Army A, which would become an army, while Juin, as a *général d'armée*, a full general, outranked Clark, as well as being older and more experienced. Juin proved an extremely diplomatic individual who decided that his command would be known as the *Corps expéditionnaire français* while he would reduce to the rank of *général de corps d'armée*. The first French staff officers arrived on 18 November, followed by their logistical headquarters and the first CEF division, *2e Division d'infanterie Marocaine*, 2nd Moroccan Infantry Division, commanded by Major General André Dody. Until the second French division arrived Dody's formation was to come under Lucas's command in VI Corps. Lucas was concerned that Juin, who 'aspires to command a corps', would be a

14: General Alphonse Juin, commander of the *Corps expéditionnaire français* in Fifth Army. Although underrated by Clark the French came close to success in January when he ordered them to change their axis of advance. It was also the French, advancing through the Aurunci mountains, who put most pressure on the Germans in May. (NARA)

complication in his command but need not have worried. He wrote that the French commander 'turned out to be not only a splendid soldier but a fine and courteous gentleman as well'.[25] Juin's corps would play a major part in the first and fourth battles on the Gustav Line, a part not always fully appreciated. The CEF took over VI Corps' sector in December when its second formation, *3e Division d'infanterie Algérienne*, 3rd Algerian Infantry Division, arrived.[26] The CEF did not have long to wait for its baptism of fire: it would participate in the first battle for Cassino in January 1944, even though the Americans had been unimpressed by the Moroccan Division, who consisted for the most part of native North Africans led by French officers. According to American standards, the training … was somewhat deficient, particularly at the lower echelons. The tactical handling of battalions, for example, left something to be desired. The division, Lucas remarked, would have to learn many lessons from the enemy, 'and he is a tough drillmaster'.[27]

Tough drillmaster the enemy may have been, but Lucas was underestimating the fighting quality of Juin's soldiers.

Critical to the plans for SHINGLE was the availability of LSTs in the Mediterranean. Negotiations involving both Churchill and Roosevelt ensured that sufficient would be retained for the landings, for which a provisional date of 20 January was set. Only the LSTs presented a problem since there were sufficient LCIs (landing craft, infantry), LCTs (landing craft, tanks) and LSIs (landing ships, infantry); Wilson noted that 'There was an adequate number of LCIs to meet any emergency'.[28] Since this 'was to be the first [amphibious operation] to be mounted after my assumption of Command of the Mediterranean Theatre, I took a broad interest in the materialization of the plan as it was presented in broad outline.' Although he agreed with the overall concept of the SHINGLE plan, Wilson stressed the 'importance of putting in a force of sufficient strength at the outset'.[29]

***

The growing momentum of the SHINGLE plan increased the pressure for the main body of Fifth Army to be close enough to permit a speedy junction of both forces. Clark was therefore anxious to ensure that the other corps of Fifth Army could break free of the Bernhardt Line and push through the Gustav Line into the Liri valley. While a positive decision on Anzio was awaited, Clark was distracted to some extent in early December by being called to Sicily for a day where he and several other officers were decorated by President Roosevelt. The president briefed those present on the decisions reached at the Cairo and Tehran conferences, from which he was returning, and informed Clark that he would command the Allied landings in southern France that would coincide with OVERLORD in Normandy. This was to be Operation ANVIL, in which Clark would command Seventh US Army.[30] He ruminated on this, and having toured the two American corps of Fifth Army on Christmas Day, returned to Caserta to learn that the final decision on the Anzio operation had been made and a date set: 22 January 1944.

Spurred by this news, Clark turned to solve the other vital problem. He had to crash through the German Winter Line and get into the Liri valley before that date. He had to get to and across the Garigliano and Rapido [sic] rivers in the shadow of Monte Cassino by the time the Anzio landing was scheduled to go in. He had less than three weeks to do all this. But by superhuman effort, he resolved to make it all work. It was their last chance.[31]

Clark wrote that he felt 'that I had a pistol pointed at my head'[32] as not only had he to plan the Anzio operation but also to initiate a Fifth Army offensive 'which would be started a week or so prior to the Anzio landings in order to draw the Germans away from the beachhead area'.[33] He told Alexander that Fifth Army's offensive would be started off on the right wing near Sant'Elia Fiumerapido by Juin's French corps, which had relieved VI Corps. In the week following the French attack, X Corps, under McCreery, would attack across the Garigliano while II US Corps would strike across the Gari and Rapido. Thus, while VI Corps prepared for Anzio, Clark's other three corps pushed hard and painfully towards the line of the Garigliano, Gari and Rapido rivers.*

***

The French offensive opened on 12 January with Juin's Moroccan and Algerian divisions operating across a wide axis. Their opposition, the German 5th *Gebirgs* (Mountain) Division, commanded by Lieutenant General Julius Ringel, an Austrian, had transferred from the Eastern front where it had suffered heavily. In late December the *Gebirgsjäger* relieved 305th Division but the newcomers did not have all their pack-animal units and found themselves in action soon after arriving; in spite of being mountain troops they had not anticipated the conditions in the Abruzzi mountains, imagining all Italy to be the 'sunny south'.[34] As with many others, both Allied and German, Ringel's mountain soldiers 'were too swift to discount General Juin's virtually untried CEF … now opposite them on the right flank of the Fifth Army front'.[35] Senger had a higher opinion of the French, noting that they were 'led by superbly trained French staff officers, [and] equipped with modern American weapons and accoutrements'. He had been concerned about

---

*   The Rapido, rising in the mountains north-east of Sant'Elia Fiumerapido, flows to the east of Cassino. The Gari's source is in the foothills south of Cassino; it flows to the south before changing direction to the south-east. About two miles south of Cassino the Rapido joins the Gari which then flows across the Liri valley to converge with the Liri; at that point the two rivers become the Garigliano which flows into the Gulf of Gaeta.

15: Soldiers of the *Corps expéditionnaire français* in January. Mostly Algerian, Moroccan and Tunisian, these skilled mountain soldiers were able to outfight their German opponents. (NARA)

their presence facing 5th Division, whose situation was 'already critical' since there was no second line of defended positions; he also described the divisions on his left flank as 'new and largely untried'. However, the Allies had been held off sufficiently to enable Ringel's men to improve the defences.[36]

Ringel's division was in XIV Panzerkorps, commanded by Lieutenant General Fridolin von Senger und Etterlin, he who had conducted the evacuation of German forces from Sicily. Following that, von Senger was appointed as liaison officer to the Italian commander-in-chief in Sardinia with the task of evacuating German troops from Sardinia and Corsica. On 8 October 1943 he was appointed to command XIV Panzerkorps in Tenth Army, succeeding General Hans-Valentin Hube who was promoted to command an army. (Hube was later killed in an air crash.) Senger felt that his new appointment was an acknowledgement of his conduct of the evacuations of Sicily, Sardinia and Corsica.

> I was appreciative of the fact that my new position involved taking over by far the most important part of the Italian land-front – the western

sector, extending more than halfway across the peninsula. Because of its extent and the size of the forces it was the equivalent of an Army. The sector of the front covered by my corps faced the US 5th Army under General Mark Clark.[37]

Senger proved a very capable opponent for Fifth Army. A remarkable individual, he 'differed in many ways from the "Prussian" German general of popular conception'.[38] Born in Waldshut, Baden-Württemberg, in south-west Germany in 1891, he was a Rhodes Scholar at St John's College, Oxford, before the First World War, an experience that created a deep impression, gave him an understanding of the United Kingdom, broadened his outlook and made him an anglophile.

16: Lieutenant General Fridolin von Senger und Etterlin, commander XIV Panzerkorps, which was responsible for the main battle front during the first three battles. An intelligent and very skilled general, von Senger proved a difficult opponent for the Allies. (Author's collection)

Commissioned early in the First World War as a reserve infantry officer, he fought on the Western Front, received a regular commission later in the war and distinguished himself by his courage and leadership.

Among those selected for the postwar *Reichswehr*, von Senger transferred to the cavalry, a choice driven more by his love of horses (he was an international competitor in equestrianism) than by any belief in a future for cavalry. Before the Second World War von Senger had been appointed to a staff post in the high command, although he had not undertaken a general staff course, usually a requirement for such appointments. In September 1939 he commanded 3rd Cavalry Regiment, but saw no action in Poland as his regiment was split between several divisions, and then formed a new cavalry regiment before promotion to command a motorized brigade which fought in the 1940 campaign in western Europe. His brigade was assigned to Panzerkorps Hoth and took part in the breakthrough in France before passing to Rommel's 7th Panzer Division for the assault on Cherbourg.

Following the French capitulation von Senger was sent as a liaison officer to Italy, a country that became his 'second home'; his appointment lasted two years.[39] The attack on the Soviet Union in June 1941 led to his next active posting. After a spell in France, he was promoted to command 17th Panzer Division on the Eastern Front in autumn 1942. The German summer offensive had prompted some optimism amongst German officers but had been followed by the encirclement of Paulus' Sixth Army in Stalingrad. Senger's division was included in a force that attempted to relieve Paulus. Although the mission failed, von Senger's impressive handling of his weakened formation was rewarded with the Knight's Cross. Then, in June 1943, he was posted to the Mediterranean as a lieutenant general where his work in the evacuation of Sicily led to the award of the German Cross in Gold. In October 1943 came his appointment to command XIV Panzerkorps with the task of slowing the advance of Fifth Army so that the Gustav Line works could be completed. His defence of the Gustav Line would see him awarded Oak Leaves to his Knight's Cross in April 1944.[40]

As mentioned in the Preface (page xliv) von Senger was a Catholic and a lay member of the Benedictine Order; he was named for Saint Fridolin, a German monk who was believed to have been an Irish missionary. According to Forty, von Senger had trained as a monk and 'hence his great personal interest in safeguarding the monastery at Cassino'.[41] For the first three battles of Cassino the Allies were engaged against von Senger but before the final battle von Vietinghoff had reduced XIV Panzerkorps' area to that between the Tyrrhenian coast and the Liri, with LI Mountain Corps taking responsibility from that river to the junction with the Bernhardt Line.

***

The first contact between the CEF and Ringel's division had occurred as the latter relieved 305th Division in the line although Juin's men had already seen action against the Germans. Dody's 2nd Moroccan Division, under command of Lucas's VI US Corps, had relieved 34th US Division by 12 December, taking over the sector including the Colli-Atina road. On the 15th the Moroccans took the offensive: 4th and 8th Rifle Regiments, each the equivalent of a British brigade, attacked San Biagio Saracinisco in the Gustav Line, but with an outflanking movement rather than a frontal attack. Although they made some progress, reaching Michele, they were rebuffed by a German counter-attack next day. Two days later the Moroccans attacked again. This failed when their ammunition supplies ran out. However, the third Moroccan regiment, 5th Rifle, took the Pantano massif and thrust forward to Monte Casale's northern slopes. During this phase 45th US Division seized Lagone, a mountain village, before continuing towards Monte Cavallo, about midway between Venafro and Sant'Elia. Lucas, unimpressed by Dody's tactics with 4th and 8th Rifle Regiments, called off their flanking move before launching a frontal attack against 305th Division, seemingly inspired by the progress of 5th Moroccan Rifle Regiment and Major General Troy H. Middleton's 45th Division.[42]

Since Ringel's division was moving into the line to relieve 305th Division, its leading units came into contact with the Americans and, before long, the Moroccans. With its units deploying piecemeal, Ringel's division suffered setbacks. On 22 December he assumed responsibility for the sector, against which Dody had been maintaining pressure. That pressure was increased on the 26th as Dody launched 8th Moroccan Regiment against 100th Mountain Regiment on the Mainarde massif. The attack might have had immediate disastrous consequences for 100th Mountain Regiment had they not been saved by a 115th Panzergrenadier Regiment counter-attack. However, this proved only a temporary respite. The Moroccans renewed their assault next day with a supporting artillery programme and took the positions. Although fighting persisted until the end of December, Dody did not reach San Biagio.[43]

Elsewhere on the XIV Panzerkorps' front Middleton's 45th Division had made gains at the expense of the recently-arrived 44th *Hoch-und-Deutschmeister* Division, also known as the Vienna Division. Three days before Christmas this Austrian formation was pushed off the 6,600-foot-plus (2,039 metres) Monte Cavallo by 45th Division which continued advancing towards Viticuso. As 1944 began 36th Division relieved 45th, which was to take part in the Anzio landing. However, heavy snow on 31 December put a temporary end to operations by cutting off roads and positions in the Abruzzi mountains. On 4 January II Corps, now less 3rd Division, commanded by Major General Lucian K. Truscott, also destined for Anzio, re-opened its advance on the axis of the Via Casilina with 1st

Special Service Force moving on the right to take Viticuso and Monte Maio and Major General Charles W. Ryder's 34th Division, the Red Bulls, attacking Cervaro and San Vittore. Behind these formations Major General Ernest Harmon's 1st Armored Division was ready to exploit forward once Monte Trócchio was in American hands.[44]

San Vittore fell to Ryder's 135th Regiment on 5 January, in spite of a defence by 29th Panzergrenadier Division. On the 6th an armoured combat group forced an entry into German positions on Monte Porchia, only to be ejected by a Hermann Göring Division battalion. For the Red Bulls it was a temporary setback. They seized the German positions next day. The first US Army division to deploy to Europe, in January 1942, Ryder's men had become seasoned combat soldiers. In Rudolf Böhmler's words, 'In the Cervaro area, General Ryder made a clean sweep' with 1st Special Service Force driving 132nd Panzergrenadier Regiment from Monte Maio while the Vienna Division was pushed back to the high ground north of Cervaro, only succeeding in its withdrawal 'with the greatest difficulty'.[45] In this prelude to the battles for Cassino a US Army engineer NCO earned the Medal of Honor 'for conspicuous gallantry and intrepidity at risk of life, above and beyond the call of duty'. On the night of 7 January 1944 Sergeant Joe Specker, 48th Combat Engineer Battalion, was advancing up Monte Porchia with his company. Having been sent forward on reconnaissance, he told his company commander that an enemy machine-gun nest and several well-placed snipers were directly in their path. Receiving permission to place a machine gun near the enemy weapon, he climbed the mountain alone with a gun and ammunition. Observed by the enemy, he was wounded severely. Unable to walk, he dragged himself over rough terrain to a suitable position and silenced the enemy machine-gun nest. The snipers withdrew. The platoon took its objective but Specker was found dead at his gun.[46]

The Americans maintained their pressure, chasing 'the Vienna Grenadiers over Monte Aquilone to Monte Capraro and from there back to Cervaro'. What was left of Cervaro was occupied by Ryder's 168th Infantry Regiment on 11 January.[47] Four days later 135th Infantry Regiment took Monte Trócchio from which the defenders had melted away. Monte Trócchio, 'a small ugly feature',[48] was a 'bare, commanding height a mile and a half in front of Cassino'[49] that would play an important role in the subsequent battles. It was abandoned by the Germans since it did not fit into the Gustav Line complex; any garrison left there would have been isolated.

The mountainous territory was difficult country in which to fight or move. Alexander's biographer described it well.

> Imagine a tossing mass of hills of about the same height and same degree of ruggedness as the English Lake District. Their steep slopes

were covered by chutes of small, grey stones, between which you would sometimes find a shy Alpine plant, but more often the rusting splinter of a high-explosive shell. Although it was less than three miles to the front-line trenches from the nearest point approachable on wheels, the steep climb would take a fully laden man as much as four hours. If he were wounded near the summit, the stretcher-bearers could not bring him down to an ambulance in less than five hours, sometimes eight, and many died. The tracks followed the easiest gradients, and though their foundations had been well laid by generations of Italian peasants, and widened and revetted by our engineers, a four-inch covering of liquid mud would overlie the solid stone after every shower of rain. Day and night the stores of food, water and ammunition were carried into these remote mountains, for the first part of the journey by strings of mules and then doggedly handled beyond the point where shellfire made the tracks impassable to every animal but man.[50]

***

17: Monte Trócchio was taken by Fifth Army in the first battle. It was used as an observation post for air and artillery officers. Some of the Allied logistical build-up was hidden from enemy view behind it. (Author's photo)

On the German right flank, again difficult terrain, McCreery's X Corps had also 'jostled the Germans' with a diversionary operation on the night of 29/30 December, in part intended to cover the relief of Walker's 36th Division by Ryder's 34th. With the sea area around the mouth of the Garigliano cleared of mines, No.9 (Army) Commando carried out a seaborne raid while 3rd Coldstream and 2nd Scots Guards of 201 Guards Brigade crossed the river 'to gain prisoners and information'. Both raids were intended to play on German concerns about possible Allied amphibious operations.[51] Kesselring wrote that 'Foreign writers have often charged me with an "invasion-phobia". In view of the Allies' ascendancy both at sea and in the air, however, this fear was clearly justified.'[52] He further commented that in Alexander's position he would have 'at least attempted to shorten the Italian campaign by tactical landings in the rear of Army Group C, which would still have succeeded even allowing for the enemy's barely sufficient tonnage'. Both Kesselring and von Senger emphasized the drawbacks created by this possibility, notably the need to deploy divisions on coastal fronts.[53]

The raids were successful, the commandos going ashore 600 yards north of the Garigliano to gain complete surprise and, under heavy artillery and naval gunfire, range 'at will over the north bank of the Garigliano before withdrawing at dawn with twenty prisoners and precious information on enemy defences'. The Coldstream and Scots Guards had similar results.[54]

Chapter Three

For von Senger it was time to ensure that the Gustav Line was manned fully to meet Fifth Army's attack. Troops were pulled back from the advancing Americans to occupy defensive positions while the exhausted 29th Panzergrenadier Division was withdrawn to rest and re-organize on the coast at Ostia; the *Reichsgrenadier Hoch-und-Deutschmeister* Division held the line against Fifth Army before falling back into the Gustav Line on 13 January.

Senger described Juin's Moroccans' attacks on his left flank as a crisis, especially as there was only a single battle line in the sector. However, that crisis passed and the French attack was held although von Senger confessed to 'moments when the whole thing seemed to hang by a thread'.[1] On the right wing he also had cause for concern: 94th Division, under Lieutenant General Bernard Steinmetz, 'a competent officer, thoroughly grounded in the General Staff, who saw things as they were',[2] was also responsible for coastal defence and a battle in its centre would see it fighting in a back-to-the-wall situation. The lack of depth in 94th Division's positions meant that re-supplying the formation in battle would be impossible; it was also possible that it might be split in two.[3]

On the left flank of 94th was Lieutenant General Eberhard Rodt's 15th Panzergrenadier Division, in von Senger's view his sole formation experienced in 'this theatre of war', but one in need of rest. Rodt's division held the line of the upper Garigliano to Cassino. In the centre, from Cassino to Cáira village, a distance of four miles, were the defensive positions of the Austrian 44th *Hoch-und-Deutschmeister* Division, referred to by Böhmler as the 'High and Mighties', which, like 5th *Gebirgsjäger* on the left, holding an eleven-mile front against the CEF, had yet to prove its ability in battle. Commanding 44th was Lieutenant General Fritz Franek. En route from Trieste to enter the line with 44th Division in the centre was 71st Division, under Lieutenant General Wilhelm Raapke, while 90th Grenadier Division was being transferred from the Eighth Army front to strengthen the line along the Garigliano. Senger could also call on reinforcements from 3rd Panzergrenadier and 29th Panzergrenadier Divisions, as well as the Luftwaffe's Hermann Göring Panzer Parachute Division. Although other divisions were coming down from north of Rome these would be diverted to meet the landing at Anzio.[4]

Added to this, the operational effectiveness of the Gustav position was altogether conjectural. Moreover, in the given organization of the divisions it was questionable how much importance should be attached to defensive positions that were too often assessed by senior officers on the basis of recollections of the First World War.[5]

Senger wrote those words after the war but it seems that he was not convinced that the Gustav Line was as stout a barrier as others believed it to be. However, Kesselring was happy that Major General Bessel's engineers had created a defensive

18: The Aurunci mountains viewed from above the Tyrrhenian coast. Considering the range impossible for a modern army to fight through the Germans defended only lightly in the sector. (NARA)

system that would extract a heavy price from any Allied troops seeking to breach it. In the time bought by the delaying lines along the Volturno, and between there and the Bernhardt Line, Bessel had created a defensive position as strong as any that Europe had witnessed in its recent history. Italy is a country made for defence with its mountain spine, the smaller ranges branching off from the Apennines, and the rivers and streams flowing from the heights of those mountains to make their way to either the Tyrrhenian or Adriatic seas. Bessel's engineers had taken full advantage of what nature had provided and, with explosives, concrete and steel, improved upon the natural barriers. Thus the high mountains provided observation posts with a wide range of vision (one British veteran who commanded

19: Looking down from Monte Cassino, the ruins of the town and castle are visible as are the roads approaching the town. Monte Trócchio is to the right. Allied forces had already fought through the mountains behind Trócchio before encountering the Gustav Line. (NARA)

an infantry battalion in the final battle told the author how he later climbed to the top of Monte Cáiro on a clear day and could see the Bay of Naples, some fifty miles distant), gun positions blasted into the mountainsides, as were machine-gun posts and mortar pits. The low ground leading to the Liri valley was obstructed by anti-tank ditches, barbed-wire entanglements and machine-gun nests while the watercourses cutting their way through that ground were also used as obstacles. One of the best examples of this was to be encountered by US troops in January 1944 when 36th (Texas) Division attempted an assault crossing of the Gari river in the vicinity of the village of Sant'Angelo in Theodice, south of Cassino, and 34th Division crossed the Rapido north of the town. Where nature had not provided something that could be modified or enhanced, German engineers created steel shelters and pillboxes; the latter, factory-made to hold two-man teams with MG34 or MG42 machine guns, were dubbed *Panzernester.*[6]

In the mountains shelters were blasted from the rock, or existing fissures enlarged to create weapon pits or infantry shelters. Surviving houses and other buildings in towns, villages and across the countryside were strengthened and sandbagged with cellars adapted as defensive positions while holes were blown

20: Illustrating how Monte Cáiro overlooks all, this view from the mountain shows the ridges over which Allied soldiers fought from January to May. The Abbey is dwarfed, as is Trócchio (left of and slightly above the Abbey). (© Damiano Parravano, Chairman, Associazione Linea Gustav)

through dividing walls to allow defenders to move quickly under cover. The most common local building material was a stone that is bulletproof; this is travertine limestone, favoured as a building material since Roman times. The old town of Cassino, destroyed in the course of the battle, had most of its buildings constructed of travertine, thereby creating retreats for infantry that were immune to rifle and machine-gun fire. Sant'Angelo in Theodice sits on a spur of travertine rock above the Gari and other local towns and villages are similarly situated. Travertine stone had a major disadvantage as, although it is hardwearing in normal use, it chips easily when struck by shells or bombs, or even bullets, multiplying the effects of a bomb or shell explosion by the addition of chips of rock to fragments of the explosive devices. This added an additional burden for the medical services during the battles.

Extensive minefields were laid, approaches to river lines being sown liberally with anti-personnel and anti-tank devices, integrated with barbed-wire obstacles, as well as being under the sights of machine-gun teams that could bring devastating interlocking fire to bear. Nowhere was this more effective than in the approaches to Sant'Angelo as 36th Division found to its cost.[7] One of those manning the Gustav Line summarized the creation of the defences.

21: A German troop shelter in the shadow of Point 593. Such natural caves were often extended with explosives and provided cover from fire or storage space for ammunition and equipment. (Author's photo)

During the autumn army construction units, the Todt Organization, Italian auxiliaries and labour battalions, under the direction of Pioneer General Bessel ... created a strong network of modern defensive localities. The villages in the forward area were transformed into massive strongpoints with bomb-proof shelters; pneumatic drills carved out caverns in the precipitous mountainsides; minefields protected easily approachable sectors, and the upper Rapido and the lower reaches of the Garigliano were used to flood certain areas. In short, Bessel transformed the Gustav Line into a position upon which the enemy might well break his teeth, provided that it was defended by even moderately good troops.[8]

The US official history confirms Böhmler's evidence, noting the use of *Panzernester*, barbed wire, mortars on reverse slopes, automatic weapons on forward slopes and 'lavish use of the box mine, which was difficult to detect because it had almost no metallic parts' in minefields on the 'few natural avenues of advance'.[9]

***

On the northern flank of XIV Panzerkorps General Juin's Corps HQ had become fully operational and launched the first of Fifth Army's three phased corps attacks on 12 January, designed to 'pin down the Germans and prevent them from transferring troops to Anzio; to attract additional German forces to the Gustav Line, particularly those stationed in the Rome area; and to break through the Gustav Line and speed up the Liri valley to a quick juncture with the Anzio forces'.[10]

Just before the new year Juin's Moroccans had been reinforced by the arrival of 3rd Algerian Division, under General Aimé de Goislard de Monsabert, allowing the CEF to take command of the sector previously held by Lucas' VI Corps. On 1 January Juin had issued a Special Order of the Day to his command expressing appreciation and recalling those who had already fallen in Italy and who were in his thoughts, and those who continued to fight and were prepared to sacrifice themselves for 'la Patrie'. In addition, he personally distributed cigarettes, dates and oranges to his men, surprising those veterans mobilized in 1940 and delighting those of 1942.[11]

On 12 January, at 6.30am, the CEF opened Fifth Army's fresh offensive. While Dody's Moroccans moved off from their start line without any preparatory artillery bombardment, thus gaining surprise that helped them take their objective, Monte Casale, Monsabert's Algerians had the support of a short artillery bombardment. While *5e Regiment de Tirailleurs Marocains* (5 RTM) climbed Point 1029, the guns of Colonel Radiguet de la Bastaïe were lighting up the crests from Monna Casale to

Monna Acquafondata. When the artillery fell silent 7th Algerians charged for their objective, 'les Jumelles' (the Twins), which had eluded 5 RTM on 29 December. Opposition was fierce, with machine-gun fire and mortars added to rifle fire. A mortar round killed Captains Bouscary and Michel as well as Lieutenant Sans, while Commandant Thomazo of the 3rd Battalion had his nose torn off and handed over command to Captain Gobillot, under whom the advance continued.[12] Monna Casale was fought over by the 7th Regiment of Algerian Tirailleurs and 85th *Gebirgsjäger* Regiment for a full day, the position changing hands four times before the attackers finally prevailed.[13]

The CEF objectives were the mountains north and north-west of Cassino and their axes of advance were towards the villages of Atina and Sant'Elia Fiumerapido. German reaction was furious: the Moroccans, Algerians, and Tunisians (who formed a regiment in the Algerian division) found themselves in close fighting during which bayonets and grenades predominated. However, the enemy reaction did not overawe the attackers and by nightfall on the 15th Juin's men had advanced almost four miles to the headwaters of the Rapido and onto Monte Santa Croce. Sant'Elia was in French hands but four days of constant fighting had left the men exhausted, forcing Juin to pause.[14]

Next day, the 16th, it was the turn of II US Corps. The corps faced the entrance to the Liri valley and elements of both 34th and 36th Divisions had prepared an assault on Monte Trócchio but, as already noted on p.36, the attackers found the feature abandoned. An air strike by forty-eight USAAF P-40 fighter-bombers had been arranged but the aircraft were diverted to 'bomb and strafe German positions along the west bank of the Rapido'. When darkness fell, few Germans remained east of the river. Once Monte Porchia had fallen Trócchio had become too isolated and von Vietinghoff decided that it should be abandoned. Although Fifth Army was clearly intent on pushing into the Liri valley the defences along the river and on the high ground dominating it were much superior. Much of XIV Panzerkorps' centre was re-arranged to ensure 'first, a strong defence at the river line and, second, a pool of locally available reserves'.[15]

The advances by the CEF and II Corps meant that Fifth Army was 'firmly up against the main defences of the Gustav Line, with French, American and British patrols operating to the river line and beyond'. McCreery's X Corps, having already 'jostled the Germans' over two weeks before, was poised for a major strike to breach the German defences along the lower Garigliano.[16]

As it nears the Tyrrhenian sea the Garigliano flows through a wide flood plain, most of it east of the river. Close to Highway 7 and the Rome-Naples railway line, west of the river, the plain is nearly two miles wide. Flat land then gives way to undulations and low hills which gave the defenders command over the lower reaches of the Ausente river and Highway 7 as it hugs the coast to

22: On the German right flank coastal defences were also manned in case of a landing in the Gulf of Gaeta. Looking down from the mountains the short stretch of waterway meeting the coast is the canalized section of the Garigliano as it flows into the gulf. Between there and the high ground are the main road (Highway 7, the old Via Appia) and the railway. (Author's photo)

Formia. The western plain narrows to less than half that width between the river and Point 413 while the hills again provided 'excellent observation posts' for the enemy as well as serving as the local outer defences of the Gustav Line. Farther inland Castelforte sits on high ground in the Monte Maio massif, which was incorporated firmly into the German defensive plan. In mid-November a plan for a crossing in the Castelforte area had been developed but cancelled. However, X Corps was being reinforced by the arrival of 5th Division, under Major General Philip Gregson-Ellis, from Eighth Army, leading to a revival of the plan to cross near Castelforte. McCreery's corps also included 46th Division, commanded by Major General John Hawkesworth, and Major General Gerald Templer's 56th (London) Division, plus 23 Armoured Brigade, commanded by Brigadier R.H.E. Arkwright. The Garigliano crossing, Operation PANTHER, was to be executed by 5th Division, on the left, and 56th, on the right, their first objective being to establish a bridgehead between the sea and Castelforte. Thereafter, 5th Division was to strike north towards the Liri on the Minturno-Ausonia-San Giorgio road, expecting to reach Ausonia on D + 1. Overall, it was

23: A panoramic shot in the same sector. The Garigliano meeting the Gulf of Gaeta may be seen and the narrowness of the flat coastal strip appreciated. (© Damiano Parravano, Chairman, Associazione Linea Gustav)

intended that X Corps should envelop the German right and distract attention from II Corps' crossing.[17]

Also under 5th Division's command was 201 Guards Brigade while 40 (RM) Commando was attached to 56th; tanks of 40th Royal Tank Regiment supported both divisions. Two days after the initial attack, Hawkesworth's 46th Division would cross the upper Garigliano to create a bridgehead in the area of Sant'Ambrogio sul Garigliano. This second bridgehead had a dual purpose: to support the right flank of X Corps and the left flank of II Corps.[18] Although naval gunfire (for the operations close to the mouth of the Garigliano) and air support were available, the air forces' attempts to cut off the bridgehead area on 16/17 January failed to destroy bridges over the Liri at Pontecorvo and San Giorgio.[19]

D Day for X Corps was 17 January and 5th Division, which had moved up secretly the previous night, was ready to cross the Garigliano at H Hour, 9.00pm. Three battalions made the initial assault, 6th Seaforth Highlanders of 17 Brigade and 2nd Royal Inniskilling Fusiliers and 2nd Wiltshires of 13 Brigade. The Seaforth crossed at Puntafiume, the Inniskillings and Wiltshires to either side of the two railway bridges, north of Highway 7. In addition 2nd Royal Scots Fusiliers, also of 17 Brigade, made an amphibious assault from DUKWs and LCTs, debarking near the low prominence of Monte d'Argento, some 2,000 yards west of the Garigliano near present-day Marina di Minturno.[20] Once ashore, the Scots Fusiliers had to negotiate minefields; but only DUKWs had arrived at the correct beach, the LCTs having beached on the near shore. Finding no evidence of the DUKWs, the LCTs returned to Mondragone with artillery and tanks still aboard. Only A Company had arrived at the intended destination, diminishing the role the battalion could play: their intended assault towards Minturno with the Seaforth and 2nd Northamptons was not made. Both Royal Scots Fusiliers and Royal Inniskilling Fusiliers had suffered some of the worst frustrations that can beset an operation. The former had 'enjoyed' a strange encounter when a DUKW strayed so far out to sea that it closed on a cruiser shelling German positions. As the Jocks were about to hail the cruiser to seek navigational assistance, a submarine surfaced alongside them. Concerned that this might be a U-boat, one fusilier took aim with a PIAT ready to fire on the vessel when a head appeared over the rim of the conning tower and shouted 'Who the hell are you?' The answer 'Royal Scots Fusiliers' brought the blistering response 'Never heard of you', at which point the hatch closed and the submarine dived, possibly saving itself from the wrath of several angry Scots.[21]

Although the Inniskillings were held up by the non-appearance of the boats intended to ferry them across the river, the Seaforth and Wiltshires made good initial progress. When the Inniskillings finally crossed, the artillery bombardment for 56th Division had begun and German observers became aware of the Irishmen preparing their crossing. The 'Skins' lost heavily but eventually assaulted the enemy positions, breaking into the German line and preparing to meet counter-attacks. Their position was precarious, however, since they had created a deep salient in 94th Division's defences and, although the Wiltshires were farther to the left in Tufo, south of the Minturno ridge, the assaults to right and left of the Inniskillings had not made much progress.[22] Nonetheless, the BBC was able to announce that 'In a new attack by British troops in Italy, the crossing of the Garigliano river has been made, an entry in the main defences of the Gustav Line'.[23]

German counter-attacks succeeded in retaking Tufo but it was back in 5th Division's hands after an attack by 1st King's Own Yorkshire Light Infantry while 1st Green Howards advanced towards Minturno, pushing the Germans out. By the end of the day on 19 January 17 Brigade had taken Monte d'Argento and pushed forward to the railway line a mile south of Minturno. Next day 15 Brigade moved out to Monte Natale, Tremensuoli and the high ground above Capo d'Acqua stream; 201 Guards Brigade concentrated near Minturno for an attack on Monte Scauri.[24]

24: British troops of X Corps cross the Garigliano under cover of darkness in Operation PANTHER. (Author's collection)

25: A daylight crossing of the Garigliano by Royal Engineers. (IWM TR1522)

Templer's 56th Division had also made progress against strong resistance from 94th Division. Assaulting with 167 Brigade on the left and 169 on the right, the 'Black Cats', so named because the divisional emblem was Dick Whittington's cat, made for the Point 413-Castelforte area and the high ground of Monte Valle Martina. Although 9th Royal Fusiliers were rebuffed on the extreme left, their sister battalion, 8th Royal Fusiliers, had captured Salvatito Hill and part of Point 413 by the end of the day on the 18th. Following 8th Royal Fusiliers, 7th Oxfordshire and Buckinghamshire Light Infantry moved on to Ventosa, west of Castelforte, on the 19th. On that day also 1st London Irish Rifles entered the fray, advancing to Castelforte where their progress was arrested. Next day the London Irish moved on to the west of Castelforte while 10th Royal Berkshires entered Lorenzo and the Ox and Bucks took Point 411 on Monte Damiano.[25]

Meanwhile 169 Brigade had achieved considerable success with 2/7th Queen's Royal Regiment taking Suio and moving onto the high ground east of Castelforte while 2/6th Queen's, 2/5th Queen's and Force II (A, P and X Troops of 40 Commando)[26] created a bridgehead between one and two miles wide overlooking the Garigliano. During the night of the 20th/21st there was a re-organization within the bridgehead in which 46th Division's 138 Brigade relieved most of 169 Brigade while 168 Brigade took over the area around Point 413.[27]

While 5th and 56th Divisions were in the opening phase of their assaults, 46th Division took Vandra and Campofiore, improving the divisional position prior to launching the planned attack. The first element of that attack was launched by 128 (Hampshire) Brigade, under Brigadier Douglas 'Joe' Kendrew, late Leicestershire Regiment and one of the most decorated British officers of the war (he earned the DSO and two Bars, adding a third Bar in the Korean War), but their attempts to cross the Garigliano near Sant'Ambrogio were unsuccessful. The speed of the current swept away assault boats on the first attempt. At the next, using a cable, the line broke after only five men had crossed. A third attempt saw about thirty men of 2nd Hampshires cross at the mouth of the Peccia stream but the swift current made it impossible for the boats to return and the isolated platoon was overrun. Dense fog hindered operations, forcing the assaulting battalions to return to their former positions. The failure of the Hampshire Brigade to cross meant that the left flank of II US Corps would be exposed as it made its subsequent efforts to cross the Gari to the north.[28]

However, Operation PANTHER's opening attacks had taken the Germans by surprise and X Corps had ten battalions across the Garigliano in the first twenty-four hours. Senger wrote that it was this attack that he first identified as a major operation; the French attack had been 'counted as one of the battles on the immediate front, because it had come to a halt before reaching the main battle line'.[29] Even after the American attacks on the Gari and Rapido by 36th and 34th Divisions, the Germans continued to identify X Corps' attack as the major effort. Senger confirmed that it was a surprise: the overrunning of 94th Division's battle outposts and capturing the 'division's lengthy fortified position on the slope' had caused Steinmetz and him concern.[30] Thus, while visiting Steinmetz at his battle HQ, von Senger telephoned Kesselring and asked that two divisions behind the right wing of XIV Panzerkorps, as an operational reserve, be released to him 'as a prerequisite for a success that I felt I could guarantee with some assurance'.[31] Interestingly, von Senger also noted that, in Kesselring's position, he would not have released the two formations. However, Kesselring was

> determined that a stand should be made. Being firmly convinced of the value of so-called built-up positions, he looked to the Gustav Line for the eventual stabilization of the Italian front. And so he played his trump card: the two Panzergrenadier Divisions stationed south of Rome as Army Group reserves, the 29th and the 90th, were allocated to the corps.[32]

As the German reinforcements entered the line, principally in the Castelforte and Minturno areas, a series of counter-attacks was begun to halt X Corps. On its front 56th Division repelled attacks between the river and Point 413 as well as Salvatito Hill as the Germans made a determined attempt to create a wedge between 138 Brigade of 46th Division and 168 Brigade of 56th Division. The deployment of three troops of 40 (RM) Commando to reinforce 8th Royal Fusiliers stopped the German attack and the line remained intact. Monte Natale was lost on the 22nd but 1st Green Howards stopped the inherent threat to Minturno. On that day, and the next, Point 201, north of Tufo, changed hands four times but 2nd Cameronians finally secured it.[33]

> By nightfall on 23 January the enemy had lost heavily in these counter-attacks and had recovered very little ground, mostly in the Minturno area. After a renewal of his counter effort on the 24th against Point 413, he went on the defensive, content for the time being to hold Monte Rotondo (Point 342), the north slopes of Point 413, and Castelforte.[34]

During the fighting on the 23rd the first Victoria Cross of the Cassino and Anzio campaigns was earned by Private George Allan Mitchell of 1st London Scottish in 168 Brigade. During the night of the 23rd/24th a company of London Scottish had been ordered to restore the situation on part of the main Damiano ridge. Two platoons made the assault with one section making a right-flanking movement against enemy machine guns that were holding up the advance. The officer who gave the order was killed almost immediately and, with no platoon sergeant, command devolved on a lance corporal who had only three men. However, they were shortly joined by Private Mitchell, the 2-inch mortarmen from platoon headquarters, and another private.

When the Germans opened up heavy machine-gun fire at close range, Mitchell dropped the 2-inch mortar he was carrying, seized a rifle and bayonet, and charged uphill through intense fire. Reaching the machine gun, he silenced it by shooting one gunner and bayoneting the other. The platoon advance continued but, shortly afterwards, the leading section was again delayed by strongly-entrenched German sections. Mitchell charged again, firing from the hip, followed by the remainder of his section. The German position was taken, with twelve prisoners, but another

26: Pte George Allan Mitchell of the London Scottish earned the VC on the Damiano ridge during X Corps' operations across the Garigliano. He was shot dead by a German soldier who had already surrendered. (Public domain)

machine gun opened up, prompting another successful attack by Private Mitchell. A further attack, under Mitchell's leadership, saw the Germans on the ridge crest forced to surrender. Minutes later a prisoner picked up a rifle and shot Private Mitchell through the head.[35]

***

Although German counter-attacks temporarily halted the British offensive against von Senger's right flank there was no relief for X Corps. To the north II US Corps had gone into action with 36th Division along the Gari river on the 20th and had suffered heavily while 34th Division attacked farther north across the Rapido on the 21st. To assist II Corps, McCreery regrouped between the 23rd and 27th, shortening 56th Division's front by moving 46th Division into the Castelforte area and deploying 23 Armoured Brigade with 2/5th Leicesters in the former 46th Division area east of the Garigliano as a screening force.[36]

The re-organization complete, McCreery resumed his offensive on the 27th with 5th Division directed on Monte Natale and 46th driving north for Monte Fuga. Three days later 17 Brigade recaptured Monte Natale while 138 Brigade, having reached Monte Fuga on the 29th, reached Monte Purgatorio on the last day

27: Soldiers of 5th Reconnaissance Regiment RAC freshen up and do some laundry near Minturno. Formed from 3rd Tower Hamlets Rifles, 5 Recce maintained Rifles' distinctions, including black buttons. (Author's collection)

of January. Other attacks failed, including 16th Durham Light Infantry's attempt to get behind the German defences at Castelforte and 56th Division's attack on Point 413. An attempt to take Monte Faito on 2 February also failed. This had been carried out by 2 Special Service Brigade (9 (Army), 10 (Army) and 43 (RM) Commandos), withdrawn from Anzio on 24 January).[37] By 8 February X Corps had exhausted its resources and the Garigliano bridgehead could be extended no further. However, the Gustav Line had been breached and 46th Division had taken some six square miles north-east of Castelforte, the only area in which the corps had not only taken all its original objectives but had exploited northward. X Corps lost 56th Division when the Black Cats were withdrawn to join VI US Corps at Anzio. Thus plans to advance through the Ausonia valley had to be abandoned and X Corps moved over to the defensive. Between the opening of Operation PANTHER and 31 January, McCreery's forces had suffered 4,152 casualties and had taken 1,035 prisoners. Although its bridgehead across the Garigliano seemed of little significance in Fifth Army's plan to break through the Gustav Line at the time, it would prove important to Clark's army in the final battle in May.[38] Blumenson described X Corps' bridgehead as an 'enormous achievement'.[39]

Chapter Four

Clark considered II Corps' attack the most important element of the offensive as it aimed to open the Liri valley by establishing a bridgehead over the Gari in the area of Sant'Angelo and pushing as far as Pignataro. Through that bridgehead Combat Command B of 1st Armored Division (the remainder of the division was en route by sea to Anzio) would advance towards Aquino and Piedimonte, with 91st Cavalry Reconnaissance Squadron protecting its left flank, to 'make contact with Lucas', who was to land at Anzio on 22 January.[1] Leading the attack would be two regiments (141st and 143rd) of 36th (Texas) Division crossing the Gari (wrongly called the Rapido in American records) close to Sant'Angelo with 34th Division attacking on the right flank to hold the Germans in the area of Cassino and north of the town, along the Rapido. II Corps' third division, 45th,

28: The waters of the Gari close to Sant'Angelo in Theodice where 36th (Texas) Division attempted to cross in January. Although relatively narrow, the river is deep and fast flowing. (Author's photo)

was to prepare to pass through 36th's bridgehead and reinforce Combat Command B to take Cassino from the south-west, or seize Piedimonte and Aquino. The same mission was assigned to 142nd Regiment of 36th Division, which was to assemble close to Monte Trócchio, an apparent duplication of effort prompted by the possibility that 45th Division could be withdrawn to join VI Corps at Anzio.

The Texans were committed to an opposed river crossing in an area where topography favoured the defenders. Although the Gari is narrow, between twenty-five and fifty-feet across, it is fast-flowing and up to twelve feet deep in January, when the flow is even faster. Its banks are steep and between three and six feet high but higher on the defenders' side than the attackers'. Sant'Angelo stands some forty feet above the west bank on a rocky outcrop which slopes down both north and south of the village. Sant'Angelo therefore gave the Germans observation over the river, its east bank and the approaches from the east. Defending along the Gari were 104th Panzergrenadier Regiment, deployed from Highway 6 to just south of Sant'Angelo, 115th Reconnaissance Battalion, on the right of 104th and opposite the mouth of the Cesa Martino stream; 1st Battalion, 129th Panzergrenadier

29: Sant'Angelo sits above the Gari on a small promontory of rock and it is easy to see how the German defenders rebuffed the attack. A sign on the bridge tells visitors that the Gari is the river of the four battles. (Author's photo)

Regiment (I/129th) was situated between the Gari and Liri rivers. In reserve close to Piedimonte was 211th Grenadier Regiment.[2] All held well-prepared positions.

> On the west bank, about 200–1,000 yards inland, was a belt of dugouts, machine-gun positions, slit trenches and concrete bunkers behind hedgerows. All trees had been cut to clear fields of fire. Double-apron fences, booby-trapped with mines, lay in front of these positions. Machine-gun emplacements with interlocking fields of fire extended west in depth for hundreds of yards. Portable steel pillboxes, connected by communication trenches to well-constructed bunkers, were impregnable to all but direct artillery hits. Sant'Angelo itself, reduced to rubble and shattered walls by demolitions, bombs and artillery fire, contained prepared machine-gun emplacements.[3]

Add to this the minefields on the east side of the river, through which any attacker would have to approach, and the task facing 36th Division may be appreciated. Of course the locations and strength of the defences were known to 36th Division and plans had been made accordingly.

Heavy artillery support was provided for the attackers: 8-inch howitzers featured in a range of weaponry that included the anti-tank weapons of the attacking regiments, field artillery battalions (twelve corps units in addition to those of the assaulting divisions) and two tank-destroyer battalions; a chemical battalion laid smoke to cover the attackers. During the 20th XII Air Support Command flew 124 sorties in preparation for the attack. Continuing support for X Corps and preparation for SHINGLE restricted the air effort to A-20 Havoc light bombers and P-40 Warhawk fighter-bombers striking at roads, strongpoints and gunsites.[4]

Final preparations were made on the night of the 19th/20th. Patrols checked the locations and strength of enemy defensive positions, crossing sites were reconnoitred, lanes cleared through the minefields on the east side of the river, and wooden and rubber assault boats brought up, as well as fifty sections of catwalk to serve as floating footbridges by laying them on the rubber boats. The engineers who had cleared the minefield paths had to check that those remained clear as 15th Panzergrenadier Division soldiers were re-laying them as quickly as possible.[5]

North of Sant'Angelo 141st Regiment was to cross at the S-bend in the river while 143rd Regiment had two crossing sites south of the village, one some 1,000 yards below the mouth of the Cesa Martino and the second a further 500 yards south. What followed was described later as 'perhaps a little emotionally, as "the biggest disaster to American arms since Pearl Harbor"'.[6] That disaster was to haunt Clark but had been foreseen by others. When Gruenther and Richardson

30: A Curtiss P-40 Warhawk of the USAAF. Improved versions, adapted for the fighter-bomber, or close air support, role served the Allied air forces in Italy in significant numbers. In US service the aircraft retained the name Warhawk while British and Commonwealth air forces' versions were called Kittyhawk and Tomahawk. (NARA)

discussed the offensive with McCreery, telling him that the main effort would be II Corps' crossing of the Gari, Richardson recorded his reaction.

> As we left, Dick McCreery's voice, still a whisper but *choked with emotion* [author's italics] followed us to our jeep: 'It's not on! Tell your Army Commander he will have a disaster.' And for the Americans it was; their casualties were appalling, leading eventually to a Congressional investigation.[7]

Richardson's point about McCreery speaking in a whisper was significant as the quietly-spoken general was known to lower his voice thus when 'deeply concerned'. Clearly, he was concerned about 36th Division's planned assault crossing. Alexander, also concerned about the difficulties of II Corps' operations, offered Clark reinforcements from Eighth Army, now commanded by Lieutenant General Sir Oliver Leese, stalled across the Apennines by the winter weather. Alexander offered to transfer 2nd New Zealand Division to Fifth Army so that, when II Corps entered the Liri valley, Lieutenant General Sir Bernard Freyberg's division would advance to Frosinone, whence the Kiwis could push on to Anzio.

Clark demurred. He judged Harmon's tanks able to drive more quickly up the valley. Moving the New Zealanders across the Apennines and inserting them into battle positions would take too much time and delay the schedule.

Alexander did not insist.[8]

The only way in which 36th Division's planned assault could have any chance of success was to attack at night. However, on the night of 20/21 January a heavy fog descended as darkness fell, adding to the many difficulties of a night crossing. As they assembled and collected their boats, the attackers came under fire from across the river. Artillery and mortar fire struck, including rounds from the German *Nebelwerfer* (literally smoke-thrower) multi-barrelled rocket launchers, before they reached the riverbank. Men seeking cover ran into the minefields, leading to even more casualties. The crossings were made under intense fire with some who reached the far bank becoming isolated. Engineers threw four footbridges across, but all were quickly damaged by enemy fire. However, the engineers persevered, constructing a single bridge from the wreckage, allowing two and a half companies of 1st/141st Regiment to cross but the assistant divisional commander stopped the operation as dawn broke and crossing became much too dangerous. Farther south, a company of 1st/143rd Regiment crossed before all the boats were destroyed. Replacements were eventually obtained, and the remainder of the battalion crossed by dawn but heavy German attacks forced the commanding officer to order a withdrawal to the home bank. Elsewhere 3rd/143rd Regiment did not cross at all, such was the combined effect of shellfire, mines and fog.[9]

The first crossings had failed. Major General Fred L. Walker, the divisional commander, ordered a second attempt on the night of the 21st. He was overruled by Keyes, the corps commander, who ordered an immediate attack. This proved impossible but 143rd Regiment was ready to cross by 4.30pm. Using footbridges and boats, 3rd/143rd crossed with two battalions of 2nd/143rd following and then two companies of 1st/143rd.

Despite this success, the situation of the 143rd Infantry was unenviable. The Germans poured fire upon them and upon the eastern bank. The engineers were unable to build bridges heavier than footbridges, and the American artillery could not observe its supporting fire because of the thick haze of fog and smoke. On the morning of the 22nd the regimental commander withdrew his men, except for a few unlucky groups, to the east bank.[10]

Disaster met 141st Regiment in its second crossing attempt. Most of their rifle companies of two battalions had crossed but, under heavy enemy fire, footbridges

31: Major General Fred L. Walker, commander 36th Division. A competent commander, Walker was unable to convince Clark and Keyes that the Gari crossing should be attempted farther upriver. The oldest US Army divisional commander, he was transferred back to the United States in July 1944 to command the Infantry School at Fort Benning, Georgia. (NARA)

were destroyed, boats sunk and signal cables cut. Haze prevented American artillery observers directing accurate supporting fire. As the day wore on 'the noise of combat on the far bank died down, and here and there a swimmer returned'. The attempt to cross the Gari was over with 36th Division suffering 1,681 casualties: 143 were dead, 663 wounded and 875 missing. Most losses had fallen on the infantry. II Corps' artillery had not been able to provide maximum support either before or during the attack. Counter-battery fire was very difficult as the enemy artillery generally remained silent before H Hour and when it did fire it was almost impossible to observe through the smoke wreathing the battleground. With corps and divisional artilleries firing, sound-ranging was unreliable. The Germans could move their artillery and Nebelwerfer units almost with impunity under cover of the smoke. Likewise, smoke and poor communications prevented artillery support for the infantry against counter-attacks. Even so, II Corps' artillery fired 112,303 rounds between 20 and 24 January, mostly to support the Gari crossings.[11]

The Germans considered that they had had only a local success, not realizing that they had defeated Clark's main effort.[12] Senger wrote that neither 15th Panzergrenadier Division nor XIV Panzerkorps 'fully realized the extent of the enemy's costly failure'. It was not until the US Congressional enquiry into the attack was held 'that the facts came to light' for the Germans.

> The German Command paid little attention to this offensive for the simple reason that it caused no particular anxiety. The repulse of the attack did not even call for reserves of 15th Panzergrenadier, still less the reserves from other parts of the front, and it proved unnecessary to postpone the relief of 19th Panzergrenadier Division, which duly took place after the battle. I am unable to say whether the higher Allied

32: Polish Army officers pay tribute to the dead of 36th Division during a ceremony in Sant'Angelo to mark the 65th anniversary of the fourth battle in 2009. Monte Trócchio is behind the officer on the right. (Author's photo)

33: Each May, during a poignant service, local schoolchildren throw baskets of red flowers into the waters of the Gari from the bridge (photo on page 55), representing the blood shed along the river in 1944. In January yellow roses, denoting Texas, are also cast onto the waters. (Author's photo)

commanders had ordered the plan of attack in such detail as to leave their local commanders no scope for initiative.[13]

The action had cost the Americans dearly. Engineers and infantrymen had demonstrated tremendous courage, perhaps none more so than Staff Sergeant Thomas E. McCall, 143rd Regiment, who earned the Medal of Honor 'for conspicuous gallantry and intrepidity … beyond the call of duty'. Company F was to cross and attack German positions to the west with McCall's machine-gun section providing fire support. Under intense enemy fire, Company F crossed an ice-covered bridge before re-organizing, having suffered many casualties. Exposing himself to deadly fire, Thomas McCall encouraged his men before leading them across muddy, exposed terrain through barbed-wire entanglements to a road where he deployed his weapons to cover the battalion front. When a shell exploded close to one position, wounding the gunner, killing his assistant, and destroying the weapon, McCall crawled forward to treat the wounded man and, helped by another soldier, dragged him into cover. The second machine-gun team had been wounded by shell fragments, leaving Staff Sergeant McCall as the only member of his section.

he ran forward with the weapon on his hip, reaching a point thirty yards from the enemy, where he fired two bursts …, killing or wounding all of the crew and putting the gun out of action. A second machine gun now opened fire upon him and he rushed its position … killing four of the gun crew. A third machine gun, fifty yards in rear of the first two, was delivering a tremendous volume of fire upon our troops.

McCall also attacked that gun in spite of overwhelming enemy fire. He was not seen again by his comrades, having been captured by the Germans.[14]

Harold L. Bond arrived as a replacement officer in 3rd/141st as the battle raged but was not sent into action. Recounting that 141st Regiment lost almost 1,000 men in the two nights of battle,[15] he noted:

> The entire attack seemed to have been conceived in haste and improperly planned. Preliminary reconnaissance had been inadequate. The men had barely more than a day to prepare …. All of the complicated operations of the division were rushed forward without enough time for anyone to do his job thoroughly. The engineers got mixed up about their orders and left some of the assault boats in the wrong places. The company and battalion assembly areas were in some cases so far back … that the men could not help attracting attention as they laboriously carried their heavy equipment and boats through open fields and sparsely wooded forests.[16]

Walker was devastated, seeing his division's losses as being Clark's fault, but Clark later wrote that

> to suggest that the brave and able soldiers of the 36th made their sacrifice in vain would be to overlook the fundamental strategy of our drive towards Rome. The landing at Anzio was the key to that drive, and – as will be fully demonstrated – it was our assault along the Rapido [sic], co-ordinated with the other thrusts by the Fifth Army along the Gustav Line, that made it possible for General Lucas to avoid a bloody battle and to secure the beaches at Anzio with only 326 casualties, including 56 dead, among the 3rd Division in the first three days.[17]

Clark's assessment is not supported by the facts. True, Lucas landed at Anzio with complete surprise but 'not one single German soldier was withdrawn from the Rome area to the Cassino front as a result of 36th Division's attack'.[18] Böhmler goes on to state that 15th Division, supported by XIV Panzerkorps' artillery, smashed the American attack, supporting von Senger's comment that no reserves were drawn into the immediate battle. Moreover, Böhmler noted that the 'credit for drawing the German tactical reserve to the Cassino front belongs to the British X Corps', adding that the absence of 29th Panzergrenadier and 90th Grenadier Divisions from the Anzio front made no real difference because Lucas, failing to seize the advantage he had gained, made no move inland. In the most recent study of the Anzio campaign, Lloyd Clark notes that the arrival of the two reserve divisions on 19/20 January stopped X Corps' advance but their deployment had occurred *before* II Corps began Fifth Army's main effort.[19]

***

The second element of II Corps' plan was 34th Division's attack. Ryder's command, the most experienced US infantry division, had begun its attack on the 21st. On the same day Juin's corps had renewed its attack into the mountains, aiming for Monte Santa Croce, whence it would attack towards Atina. Part of 34th Division's attack would also be made onto high ground, but first the Red Bulls had to cross the Rapido north of Cassino before turning south, pushing one force towards Cassino to take the town and another, on the right flank, to capture high ground overlooking the town, including Monte Castellone and Colle Sant'Angelo, seizing Albaneta Farm and advancing towards Piedimonte. On the left flank X Corps was to continue its advance towards San Giorgio.[20]

34: The offensive along the Gustav Line was intended to draw German reinforcements from the Anzio area where VI US Corps was landing in Operation SHINGLE. US Army DUKWs come ashore in this image of an LST discharging at Anzio. (NARA)

While 34th Division crossed the Rapido north of Cassino, the third regiment of 36th, which had so far not been involved on the Gari, was to be ready to force another crossing north of Sant'Angelo; the Texas Division's other regiments, while deploying defensively, would feint a further crossing where they had come to grief. Clark's orders to Keyes were for 34th to cross the Rapido, defended in that area by the Vienna Division, before sending a column 'down the road into Cassino while other forces went through the mountains about Monte Castellone to take the high ground dominating the town and debouch to the enemy's rear near Piedimonte'.[21]

35: In the early stages of SHINGLE the lack of a landing ground meant that US and British AOP aircraft could not operate from the bridgehead. An AOP carrier was improvised by the US Navy, allowing aircraft to fly in support of the artillery. (NARA)

36: Also in II Corps, 34th Division fought its way across the Rapido north of Cassino and then into the town as well as into the mountains. These soldiers are moving forward in difficult conditions. (NARA)

Juin was also ordered to turn his corps south-west towards Terelle and Piedimonte to threaten Tenth Army's communications and supply lines.[22]

Major General Charles 'Doc' Ryder had an excellent reputation from the First World War, having earned the Distinguished Service Cross twice as well as a Silver Star and a Purple Heart. Thus far in the Second World War he had demonstrated 'tactical acumen and [a] level disposition',[23] qualities he would need in the task ahead. Facing his division were the 131st, 132nd and 134th Grenadier Regiments of the *Hoch-und-Deutschmeister* Division, with their supporting artillery, whose line ran from Cáira village, in the north, to the Liri valley via Cassino. Behind them in reserve were elements of the Hermann Göring and 29th Panzergrenadier Divisions.

> The enemy was ready. Before the troops lay the deep, icy cold, swift-flowing waters of the Rapido, with all strategic crossings heavily laid with mines. High up the river the enemy had blown a dam, diverting the stream so as to render the valley an area of quagmire. Incessant rains fell, often turning to sleet. Beyond loomed the great wall of mountains into which the Germans … had dug in to entrenched positions. Before those hills lay endless fields of mines, trip wires, booby traps and merciless enfiladed fire. Again, as with the 36th, surprise was impossible.[24]

The initial attack was made by Colonel Carley L. Marshall's 133rd Regiment, its objectives being Points 156* and 213, the former Carabinieri training barracks at Monte Villa, about two miles north of Cassino, and the southbound road from the barracks. Although the single-storey buildings had been damaged severely by artillery fire, the defenders had fortified them and debris camouflaged concrete pillboxes housing machine guns covering the river as well as the northern and eastern approaches to Cassino. Ryder believed 'possession of the barracks an essential preliminary for his attack, particularly the thrust to the strongly fortified town of Cassino'.[25] Colonel Mark Boatner's 168th Regiment would then pass through 133rd to take Monte Castellone, Colle Sant'Angelo and Albaneta Farm while 135th Regiment, under Colonel Ward, would attack the town from the north. From the barracks to the town, advancing troops would have some shelter from hostile artillery, since there is only a 'narrow shelf, no more than 300 to 400 yards wide, overshadowed by the steep-walled Cassino massif'.[26]

Following a heavy thirty-minute bombardment by five artillery battalions, 133rd Regiment began its advance at 10.00pm on 24 January, although enemy fire delayed 100th Battalion for thirty minutes. Both 1st and 3rd Battalions moved off on schedule but were then delayed by minefields. The supporting tanks of 756th Battalion tried crossing the river to clear lanes through the minefields but could not ford the stream. Little progress was made that first night: 3rd Battalion, in the centre, got some men right up to the riverbank but they were unable to cross due to sustained heavy fire from the barracks; 1st Battalion encountered a minefield only 200 yards from the start line and had to stop while 100th Battalion, on the left,

---

* Referred to incorrectly as Point, or Hill, 56 in most accounts.

reached the bank. At 4.30am on the 25th Ryder ordered 133rd Regiment to extend to the right where there seemed to be firmer ground. As a result 3rd Battalion redeployed to 1st's right flank while 100th sidestepped even farther north. With the regiment deployed in an assault line an artillery bombardment at 9.00am supported some men of 100th Battalion across the Rapido, only to meet another obstacle, a barbed-wire entanglement covered by machine-gun fire. Having cleared a lane through a minefield, several platoons of 1st Battalion were across early in the afternoon and, by early evening, 3rd Battalion had also formed a small bridgehead.

Once night had fallen all three battalions were reinforced so that, by midnight, 133rd Regiment had consolidated a bridgehead which Ryder ordered it to expand before dawn broke. He aimed to get tanks across into an enlarged bridgehead and deploy 168th Regiment on its advance to Cassino. However, 133rd's efforts to expand the lodgement failed; the soldiers within were forced to defend what they held. When night came on the 26th they had not advanced and 168th was still on the other side of the Rapido.

The most effective enemy fire was coming from the high ground, particularly Point 213, north-west of the barracks, and so Ryder ordered 135th Regiment to cross the river on the bridgehead's left flank and attack up the massif from the south towards Point 213 to 'eliminate enemy fire on the assault troops on the valley floor and open the way for an advance westward to Monte Castellone and beyond to the Liri valley'.[27] That night a company of 1st/135th crossed but struggled to overcome the many obstacles. Armoured support was impossible since tanks bogged in the marsh created by the flooding and six were stuck on the best approach. No further progress could be made with armour until engineers had improved the crossing site.

Keyes was pressing Ryder for progress so that more troops could cross, expand the two small bridgeheads and move into the hills above. Still hoping to launch armour into the Liri valley, Keyes urged on Ryder who ordered 168th Regiment to pass through 133rd on the morning of the 27th. Doing so, and deploying 168th north of the barracks, marked a change of operational emphasis and an

> increasing awareness of several vital factors in the situation: the need for better ground for river crossing operations; the strength of the German defences in Cassino; the necessity for depriving the Germans of the high ground; the urgency of reaching the flank of the Liri valley; and the course of developments taking place still farther north in the French zone.[28]

Ryder issued detailed orders to 168th Regiment for its revised task. Two battalions, each preceded by a tank platoon, would attack in line abreast under cover of an hour-long artillery bombardment which would become a rolling bombardment once the Rapido had been crossed. The tanks were to overcome the many obstacles employed by the Germans. Ryder considered this plan had a good chance of working, provided the tanks could reach the river by way of the narrow and muddy tracks across the flat land and then cross the Rapido.

The attack was launched before daybreak on the 27th. As the guns opened fire the tanks set off, followed by the infantry. However, only four tanks made it to the far bank of the Rapido, some sliding off the narrow tracks. So much did the leading tanks churn up the ground that those following were mired down, preventing further movement. As engineers deployed to construct corduroy tracks with logs, infantry followed the tanks and, in spite of heavy German fire, two companies of each assault battalion crossed. Although the four tanks that crossed were out of action by 1.00pm the infantrymen fought their way across the low ground on the far bank so that, as darkness fell, they were at the base of Point 213. Losses had been heavy but Company C crossed the Rapido after dark to ascend Point 213 with some troops reaching the top undetected by the defenders. However, this achievement proved illusory.

37: Both 34th and 36th Divisions suffered many casualties. In this image wounded men are being stretchered back to safety for treatment. (NARA)

38: Among the difficulties faced by Major General Ryder's 34th Division was ground flooded deliberately by the enemy, as seen here close to Pasquale Road in the shadow of Monte Cassino. (NARA)

Aware that his position would come under attack when day broke, and believing that his company could not hold it against sustained attack, the company commander decided to withdraw. He gave the order for withdrawal but the soldiers then broke and ran, possibly as a result of enemy fire.[29] Two other companies on the west bank also panicked and followed the fleeing men. The 'uncontrollable rout' was not stopped until the troops had reached the near bank, by which time all three companies were disorganized. Since the two companies remaining on the far bank would be too exposed and vulnerable to enemy attack, they were also withdrawn before being redeployed northward for 100 yards to another crossing site. Having negotiated the German minefields, aided by a French guide, both recrossed the Rapido and advanced about a mile towards Cáira village where, midway between river and village, two platoons dug in while the others created defensive positions for the route forward from the crossing point. Neither Ryder nor Keyes had lost sight of the plan for the Red Bulls to complete their crossing of the Rapido. That crossing depended on the engineers constructing a route forward for the tanks. Once that task was complete the division could accomplish its mission.[30]

***

At this stage it became clear that Fifth Army's envelopment of the Liri valley entrance would be 'deeper than originally intended, but the strength of the German defences required it'.[31] As it seemed more likely that Juin's CEF could produce 'more conclusive results', Clark ordered Juin to move his axis of advance leftward and take the heights looming over the head of the Rapido valley. These are the Colle Belvedere ridge, Colle Abate and the village of Terelle, an area dominating the valleys leading to Atina and to Roccasecca, from either of which the Liri valley might be reached; von Senger had his headquarters in Roccasecca. Taking this high ground would also secure 34th Division's flank in the envelopment of Cassino. Juin had renewed his attack on the 21st, aiming to strike through the most difficult terrain within the CEF's boundaries to reach Atina. He had no doubt of his men's ability to overcome the obstacles presented by the country which he believed was so bad that the defences would be much weaker than elsewhere. In this latter belief he was right; Kesselring later commented.

> Ability to cross country is especially notable among the French and Moroccan troops. They have quickly surmounted terrain considered to be impassable, using pack-animals to transport their heavy weapons, and have on many occasions tried to turn our own positions (sometimes in wide encircling movements) in order to break them open from the rear.[32]

Clark issued his revised orders to Juin on the 23rd and the French commander, having shifted his main effort towards his left flank, moved 3rd Algerian Division into place – Monsabert pivoting his command at a right angle to face west – and launched an attack towards the 2,530-foot (771 metres) Colle Belvedere on the morning of the 25th. The redeployment was difficult, Colonel Radiguet de la Bastaïe, the divisional artillery commander, describing the move as madness. His gunners had to move their weapons along narrow, twisting mountain roads in the darkness, uncoupling guns from tractors to manhandle them around the sharpest bends. However, at 4.00am 'the tone was different when he transmitted to Monsabert: "Artillery in position in the Cerreto bowl, according to your orders, at 6.00am".'[33] Bastaïe's 67th Artillery Regiment's (67 RAA) batteries, reinforced by those of 63rd and 64th Artillery Regiments, would prove invaluable to the infantry, as would the weapons of the American 13 Field Artillery Brigade.[34] The tank-destroyers of 7th African Chasseur Regiment (*7e Régiment de Chasseurs d'Afrique*, 7 RCA) would also deploy. At 5.40am Bastaïe's guns began a twenty-minute bombardment of enemy positions on Point 470 before switching to l'Olivella and other targets. Four squadrons of USAAF Martin B-26 Marauder medium bombers also targeted the objectives to keep German heads down.[35]

Once Belvedere was taken, Juin intended to push on towards Colle Abate, which was higher, more rugged and about a mile west of Belvedere. In ordering this change in Juin's axis of advance, however, Clark was forcing the CEF to extend an already over-extended front. Rather than reinforcing Juin's front as he ordered the change of direction, Clark waited until 26 January to tell Keyes to assist the French. In turn, Keyes ordered 142nd Regiment of 36th Division, under Brigadier General Frederick B. Butler, assistant divisional commander, to execute that task.[36]

Colonel Jacques Roux, commanding 4th Tunisian Rifle Regiment (*4e Régiment de Tirailleurs Tunisiens*) of 3rd Algerian Division, had briefed his officers on the 24th but had only some far-from-ideal aerial photographs to demonstrate the nature of the ground. (Colonel Roux was to die with many of his riflemen on the slopes of Belvedere on 27 January.) He had assigned his 2nd Battalion, under Commandant Berne, and 3rd Battalion, under Commandant Paul Gandoët, to take Belvedere; Commandant Bacqué's 1st Battalion supported the operation. The hurried nature of this change of axis of advance and the new tasks for 3rd Algerian Division meant that Roux's men had a lengthy march of almost a day to reach their start line. They had to descend from their previous positions and cross the freezing waist-high Secco before climbing Belvedere.[37]

For two days 4th Tunisian Rifle Regiment fought for Belvedere.[38] They spearheaded the CEF attack, their first objective being Monte Cifalco, held by *Gebirgsjäger*. Since Monte Cifalco dominated the Sant'Elia area and the valley of the Secco, a tributary of the Rapido, it was 'of primary importance' to the defenders.[39] The Tunisians crossed the Rapido with relative ease and threaded their way through the minefields to assault Point 470, on which were sited the German forward positions, but could not dislodge the *Gebirgsjäger* from the mountain itself. Point 470, a German flank position, fell to 9 Company of Gandoët's battalion, beginning a series of attacks and counter-attacks that saw the position neutralized, but back in German hands by dark. Monte Cifalco 'remained in German hands and was a thorn in the flesh of the French, for from its slopes the German artillery observation officers had a clear view both of the flanks and rear of the attacking French and of the Americans advancing southwards.'[40]

Meanwhile, Roux's 2nd and 3rd Battalions, having taken or by-passed German positions on the lower slopes, were making steady progress; armoured cars of 3rd Algerian Spahis (*3e Régiment de Spahis Algérien de Reconnaissance*, 3 RSAR) supported them, their drivers threading gingerly through the nerve-racking hairpin bends of the Terelle road. With Berne's 2nd Battalion advancing on a two-company front on Points 700 and 771, Gandoët's 11 Company began an advance worthy of a Holywood epic. By dusk both Points 700 and 771 were in Tunisian hands and vicious counter-attacks were repelled; during one fight Commandant Berne received serious wounds. Notin commented that 9 Company at Point 470 distracted some of the enemy's attention from the advance of 2nd and 3rd Battalions.[41]

Gondoët's men, meanwhile, were executing a spectacular advance that must stand as one of the most difficult of the war. Commandant Gandoët had identified a way up the mountain. On the steep face of Belvedere he had spotted a fissure, quickly dubbed 'ravin Gandoët', that would provide cover from enemy view, especially that of the gunners on Cifalco, although it was a very steep climb of about 2,000 feet. Lieutenant Jordy's 11 Company was given the task of ascending the fissure to Point 681 (2,234 feet). Jordy, with Lieutenants Tumelaire and Chol's platoons, worked their way up towards 681. As with all the division's soldiers, they carried a minimum of food and water (a single K-ration per man) to allow the maximum load of ammunition and weaponry. Their progress was slow, not aided by the need to be as quiet as possible, or the freezing conditions as cold wind and sleet assailed them. Nonetheless, Tumelaire's men were halfway to the top after four hours and took a German post by surprise; the occupants had never considered an attack from that direction while mist helped hide the Tunisians and mask sound. By nightfall 11 Company had reached its objective, emerging as if from nowhere to overwhelm the defenders and secure 681. Although surprised, the Germans fought tenaciously, each strongpoint having to be taken in close-quarter fighting by small groups of Tunisians.[42]

The Tunisians' success proved costly: artillery observers on Cifalco continued directing fire onto them. Even with their vision obscured by smoke or mist, the German gunners maintained their fire, inflicting casualties as the infantry ascended. Commandant Bacqué's 1st Battalion suffered heavily as it climbed the slopes with his company commanders killed or wounded. In spite of their losses, the attackers had taken Belvedere's summit on the afternoon of the 25th but were driven off by German counter-attacks to positions on the upper slopes. Roux's riflemen had made short work of 131st Regiment of 44th Division. Advancing with their left flank protected by 7th Algerian Rifle Regiment, they had inflicted severe hurt on the Austrian grenadiers to establish a firm lodgement on Belvedere; Roux perished two days later.[43] The commander of 131st Regiment was among the dead, killed during the first day of battle.[44]

The CEF were not finished as Tunisians and Algerians pressed on with their advance, the Tunisian 2nd Battalion taking Colle Abate and Point 862 north of it while pressure was maintained on the mountain village of Terelle. Although Juin's men continued to enjoy success, their tactical situation was becoming dangerous. German artillery harassed them constantly, causing many casualties, and their advance had gone so far that reinforcements were unable to reach them, nor were re-supply parties with ammunition and food, both of which were running short. All this was due to Clark's sudden decision to switch the direction of the CEF's advance. Juin wrote to Clark a few days later that 3rd Algerian Division 'At the cost of unbelievable efforts and great losses … had accomplished the mission which you gave them', but pointed out that their situation would be 'extremely precarious' until Monte Castellone and its neighbouring heights, south-west of Monte Cáiro, were in 34th Division's hands. As we have seen, on the 26th Clark had ordered Keyes to insert 36th Division's 142nd Regiment between 34th and the Algerian Divisions to advance towards Monte Castellone. Keyes, realizing that the CEF's progress held more promise than another attempt to cross the Gari near Sant'Angelo, happily re-assigned 142nd Regiment to Ryder's command. Perhaps a determined attack across the mountains could unlock the German defences, allowing Allied troops to penetrate the Liri valley from the flank.[45]

As this re-organization was underway the Germans were reacting to the French success by preparing a major counter-attack. On the 27th that counter-attack was made against Roux's Tunisians. Eighty guns poured some 5,000 rounds down on the Tunisian soldiers and 200th Regiment, commanded by Colonel Behr, struck at Colle Abate and Point 862. Although French artillery responded fiercely, both heights fell to Behr's men who, however, could make no further progress against the doughty defenders. Another prong of the German counter-attack struck elements of 4th Tunisian Rifle Regiment which had advanced into the Secco valley, on 44th Division's left flank, and regained some positions.[46]

As well as the counter-attacks, the German commanders acted to close a dangerous gap that had opened south of Colle Belvedere where an Allied stroke from the north threatened to roll up 44th Division. To insure against any such attack, von Senger ordered 191st Grenadier Regiment of 71st Division to fill the gap between Colle Abate and Monte Castellone. Senger had intended to use 71st Division to reinforce Rodt's 15th Panzergrenadier Division but Juin's push into the Terelle area forced a change of plan, von Senger initially considering using 71st Division for a counter-attack. Although part of the division was deployed in a counter-attack in the Belmonte valley this gained no ground, but sealed off the area. As 3rd Algerian Division pushed forward, XIV Panzerkorps' counter-attack plan was overtaken by events and 71st was used for 'fire-brigade' actions to close gaps in the forward defences. The defences of Cassino town, then lightly manned, were reinforced by 211th Infantry Regiment. Major General Wilhelm Raapke, commanding 71st Division, was temporarily redundant as his regiments deployed under command of 44th Division.[47] However, von Senger decided to pull 44th Division out: having suffered greatly at the hands of Juin's men, it 'was no longer able to defend the position'. He replaced it with 90th Grenadier Division, moved from the southern front.

***

Ryder was continuing his offensive while 142nd Regiment was en route by lorry or on foot from Monte Trócchio to the Colle Belvedere area. All three battalions of 168th Regiment were to cross the Rapido and advance across the low ground to attack Points 213 and 156, possession of which would facilitate an American attack on Monte Castellone, while 133rd Regiment might finally take the old Carabinieri barracks in readiness for an advance towards Cassino. Since Keyes had placed all available corps engineers at Ryder's disposal to keep the approaches to and exits from the Rapido crossing sites, plus the sites themselves, in condition suitable for use by armour, the engineers deployed to support 168th Regiment: 235th Engineer Battalion of 1108th Engineer Group performed sterling work creating routes useable by tanks, laying corduroy tracks using logs and steel mesh to allow tank tracks to grip. Ryder also placed 760th Tank Battalion and 175th Artillery Battalion under command of 168th Regiment, creating a strong combat team.[48]

On the morning of the 29th that combat team was committed to action. Led by tanks from 760th Battalion, and under a heavy curtain of artillery fire, both 1st and 2nd Battalions of 168th Regiment, the latter leading, crossed the Rapido against Points 156 and 213. Although German resistance was strong, seven tanks were on the far side by 7.00am.

> The Engineers, working as always under the most adverse conditions created by the rushing stream and constant fire from the enemy, had laid out three additional crossings. Tanks and troops moved over, encountering resistance which immobilized five of the seven vitally needed armoured monsters which had gained the other shore.[49]

Tank support proved invaluable, allowing all three battalions to cross the river and begin advancing steadily towards their objectives. During the afternoon Ryder committed 756th Tank Battalion. The appearance of twenty-three of the battalion's tanks at 4.00pm provided a major boost to the infantry. With tanks firing on German machine-gun positions, the infantry could move faster. Over 1,000 rounds were expended at close range by the advancing Shermans. By 6.45pm all three battalions had reached the foot of the hills. Tank shells tearing through the barbed-wire barricades allowed the infantry to climb the slopes. By dawn next day Points 156 and 213 were in American hands, although skirmishing and mopping up continued until noon.[50]

Success seemed to breed success, although the men of 168th Regiment on those hills had to fight off two counter-attacks on the 30th and another next day while plagued by inadequate radio communications with their supporting artillery and tanks. With the infantry on the hills the tanks could no longer give close fire support due to the gradient of the high ground. Surviving tanks sought cover from artillery and mortar rounds falling on the flat ground while the Stuart light tanks crossing the river to replenish fuel and ammunition were sought out by *Panzerjäger*. When two Stuarts brewed up, smoke was laid to screen the crossing site.[51]

Elsewhere, on the night of the 29th, an attack launched by 142nd Regiment would last two days. The independent task force, under Brigadier General Butler, began 'to reach the French in the nick of time' that morning. Operating close to the boundary between II Corps and the CEF, in the difficult ground between Monte Castellone and Colle Belvedere, Butler's attack protected Juin's right flank and helped improve the Algerian positions. The Tunisians had seized La Propoia ridge before advancing to cross the Secco to the foot of Belvedere while the Moroccans had taken Monte Marrone. Colle Abate had also been retaken by 3rd Algerian Division. Moreover, 142nd Regiment's southward advance led to the capture of Manna Farm and further progress towards Monte Castellone. When one of the 168th Regiment platoons blocking the Cassino-Cáira road probed north with a platoon of tanks on the 30th the little battle-group captured Cáira village, thereby helping CEF units consolidate their positions around Colle Belvedere.[52]

Success for 34th Division had been gained after five days of brutal battle, mostly in grim weather conditions with snow and cold rain falling, but the Gustav Line had not been broken nor had the expected drive into the Liri valley begun. On 34th Division's front the Germans still held the barracks north of Cassino where the division had yet to overcome the defenders to launch the assault on Cassino town; the barracks area was vital to the attack. However, Clark was aware that his men were tired, noting in his diary that defenders and attackers were 'like two boxers in the ring, both about to collapse. I have committed my last reserve and I am sure the Boche has done the same'.[53]

Clark's chief of staff, Gruenther, was of like mind but felt that Cassino would be taken by 6 February, although he noted that Keyes would not speculate on when the town would fall. Fifth Army was engaged on two fronts with Clark also having to pay attention to events at Anzio where VI Corps was in action against Fourteenth Army. Clark was at Anzio on 31 January when Gruenther sent a signal expressing his hope of taking Cassino within a week.[54] Lucas' first offensive moves had not begun until the 25th when 1st British and 3rd US Divisions deployed to take Aprilia and Cisterna respectively. Those operations met stout resistance while German aircraft also attacked the bridgehead and the shipping that was VI Corps' lifeline to Naples. Kesselring was gathering a strong bomber force in Italy by transferring aircraft from Greece, France and Germany. By 3 February he had some 140 bombers while Luftwaffe anti-shipping units in southern France received a boost of another sixty machines.[55] Attacks on shipping and the port included conventional bombs, torpedoes and radio-guided glider bombs, already used against Allied vessels at Salerno. As Clark visited the bridgehead on 31 January, a renewed VI Corps attack was underway but, against determined resistance, was called off with heavy losses, one British battalion suffering 653 casualties.[56]

With all three corps in action on the Garigliano-Gari-Rapido front – X Corps had renewed its action against a reinforced German front on 27 January – and VI Corps at Anzio, Clark still hoped for a breakthrough along the Gustav Line. His real goal, however, 'was to capture the strong defensive bastion, consisting of the Monastery Hill, Hangman's Hill,* and other nearby peaks which furnished all-round observation for the conduct of the defensive battle'.[57]

Although these words were written much later they reflect the contemporary situation. Clark had become fixated on Monte Cassino, or Monastery Hill, and other Allied commanders would share his obsession. However, the Cassino massif was the critical point of von Vietinghoff's defence plan and, on 31 January, he informed Kesselring that he was prepared to weaken LXXVI Panzerkorps by transferring troops from the Adriatic sector to reinforce von Senger's XIV Panzerkorps. Kesselring gave his 'full agreement'. While Clark, and Alexander, pondered on ways to break out at Anzio and break through the Gustav Line, the German intention was to smash the Allied bridgehead at the former and hold the latter. Since any advance out of the Allied lodgement at Anzio threatened German southbound lines of communication from Rome, such an advance would force Kesselring to abandon the Gustav Line, thereby giving up southern Italy. However, Allied pressure on the Gustav Line not only made it impossible to withdraw formations from the line to reinforce Fourteenth Army at Anzio, but made it imperative that the Gustav Line be reinforced to a manpower level hitherto not committed against Fifth Army. Kesselring would have to transfer troops from Anzio to maintain the Gustav Line defences early in February.

> If the Gustav Line could be held until enough units were gathered at Anzio to eliminate the beachhead, the situation in southern Italy would remain the same as it was before the amphibious operation. The Allied forces would have suffered a crushing defeat and would still be a considerable distance from Rome.[58]

Already the strength of XIV Panzerkorps along the Gustav Line had been increased from the four divisions at the beginning of January to the equivalent of six at the end of the month with more reinforcements appearing regularly despite Fourteenth Army's demands. Facing X Corps on the Garigliano, Steinmetz's 94th Division

---

* It had yet to be given the name Hangman's Hill. Its true name is Monte Venere.

continued holding the coastal sector with its eastern flank reinforced by part of 29th Panzergrenadier Division. II Corps faced a much-weakened 44th Division plus elements from 15th Panzergrenadier, 71st Infantry and 3rd Panzergrenadier Divisions, each of which was also represented in Fourteenth Army. On the eastern sector the CEF was opposed by 5th *Gebirgs* and part of 3rd Panzergrenadier Divisions. Other than 29th Panzergrenadier and 71st Divisions, every formation under von Senger's command had seen at least a month of continuous operational service; some had endured more. Most were very much understrength: von Senger noted that 44th Division's battalions had been reduced to 'no more than 100 men' with their young commanders leading them 'as if they were mixed assault companies'.[59] Blumenson wrote that 71st Division was 'seriously depleted' with insufficient replacements arriving; 44th Division received only about 1,000 replacements in January but lost the same number taken prisoner.[60]

***

As the battle moved into its next phase the opposing commanders contemplated their relative positions, strengths and possible courses of action. All were focusing on the area around Cassino and Monte Cassino and both Allied and German commanders made plans to re-deploy or reinforce formations. The defenders had already suffered heavily around Cassino with 44th and 71st hit hard; units of 3rd Panzergrenadier Division deployed there had also sustained serious loss. In line with the policy agreed with Kesselring on 31 January, von Vietinghoff ordered 90th Grenadier Division, the *Afrika* Division, from the Adriatic sector to von Senger's command, followed by the transfer of 1st *Fallschirmjäger* Division; elements of the latter already deployed to Anzio would move to join their comrades in the Cassino sector. With these two formations moving in, von Vietinghoff moved another out: 29th Panzergrenadier Division was sent to Anzio. The paratroopers deployed into the hills around Cassino and would prove to be very tough opponents for the Allied troops over the next three months. The first elements of 90th Division arrived in the Cassino sector on 7 February and the first *Fallschirmjäger* followed days later.[61]

General Alexander had also decided to transfer formations from the Adriatic front, held by Eighth Army, to the Fifth Army front. Fifth Division had been the first, joining X Corps to take part in operations along the Garigliano. Alexander had already offered Clark 2nd New Zealand Division, Eighth Army's most experienced, but Clark had declined the offer. The New Zealanders were now transferred from Eighth Army command to the Cassino area, to form the core of an army group reserve for Fifth Army. Leese, Eighth Army's commander, brought forward I Canadian Corps and 4th Indian Division from his reserve, only to have

39: Although German casualties were lower than Allied in the first battle, four of the six men buried in these graves perished in January 1944. (Author's photo)

Alexander call for the Indians to be transferred across the Apennines to join the New Zealanders. Leese had lost four divisions from his command (1st Division had been sent to Anzio), a loss that, combined with poor weather conditions and difficult terrain, compelled him to abandon any plans for major operations until spring.[62]

With 2nd New Zealand and 4th Indian Divisions as his army group reserve, Alexander considered how they might be used as a corps to support operations on Fifth Army's front. With their experience thus far in the war – they had fought in Greece, Crete, the Western Desert and Tunisia – the New Zealanders had a reputation for exploitative operations while 4th Indian Division, with experience in East Africa, Syria, the Western Desert and Tunisia, had demonstrated excellent mountain-fighting skills. Alexander's ruminations would lead to New Zealanders and Indians taking a prominent role in the battles for Cassino.

In the meantime, however, Alexander watched the efforts of 34th Division as Ryder's men tried to break through the Gustav Line.

Chapter Five

Juin's corps and 34th US Division had made significant progress in the January battles but no breakthrough had happened. According to Hougen, 'the eyes of the entire world were focused on the scene at Cassino'.[1] Although 34th Division's historian was guilty of hyperbole, there is no doubt that many eyes were focused on the battle. One reason for that was the threat to the Benedictine Abbey of Monte Cassino. US artillery men had been ordered not to fire at the building.

> Though the enemy was suspected of using the Abbey as an observation post, as a storage place for supplies and ammunition, and as a setting for probable gun positions, the Allies strove to avoid the destruction of this famous shrine, realizing the impact such an unfortunate result would have upon the Christian World.[2]

As yet Monte Cassino was not an objective: 34th Division's sights were fixed firmly on the barracks which was 133rd Regiment's objective on 1 February. At the same time 135th Regiment passed through their comrades of 168th on Point 213 to begin an advance towards Monte Castellone, the highest point of which is at 2,530 feet (771 metres). Tank support, from 753rd, 756th and 760th Battalions, was provided, but the tankmen were limited in the help they could give infantry climbing into the mountains.[3]

We have already noted (page 76) the actions of 142nd Regiment out on the right in taking Manna Farm, midway between Castellone and Belvedere. That action, as with those of the French troops, was aided by heavy mountain fog, which also helped 135th Regiment as it advanced from Cáira since troops could move without fear of observation. Monte Castellone fell to 3rd/135th Regiment who, when the fog cleared, could look across a valley and down on the Abbey. The regiment's 2nd Battalion, which had suffered some artillery fire from the defenders, took Colle Maiola to the left and continued towards Colle Sant'Angelo and the spur leading down to Monastery Hill. Next day both battalions moved forward again, 2nd/135th on the east flank where it winkled out defenders on Point 324 but suffered many casualties. Fighting continued on the 3rd with 3rd/168th inserted to the right of 135th Regiment's battalions following determined counter-attacks on 2nd/135th which, on the 2nd, had pushed halfway to Point 593. Counter-attacks on the 2nd Battalion were part of von Senger's counter-stroke against the Franco-American advance and occurred all along the front from Manna Farm to Point 706 at the south end of Castellone. German prisoners told their captors that Point 593 was garrisoned by men of III/3rd *Fallschirmjäger* Regiment, the first evidence of the move of 1st *Fallschirmjäger* Division from the Adriatic. Those counter-attacks limited any progress on 3 February, at the end of which 135th Regiment's soldiers were only a mile and a half from Highway 6. They had secured the line of Monte Castellone, which would remain in Allied hands, although Ryder had hoped that deploying 3rd/168th would allow a drive towards Highway 6. It was not to be: von Senger had sent in reserves to blunt the dangerous American advance.[4]

40: The ground on Monte Castellone still bears much evidence of its having been a battlefield in 1944, as this unexploded projectile suggests. (Author's photo)

Down in the low land, 133rd Regiment had assaulted the barracks on 31 January, securing the buildings that had so long defied attackers, clearing the start line for an attack southward to Cassino, with 3rd/133rd Regiment supported by two tank platoons from Company B 756th Tank Battalion on 2 February. One tank platoon used the road to Cassino while the second travelled down the river bed. The latter was stopped about 600 yards north of the town but the other made some more progress until engaged by anti-tank guns, firing under cover of smoke, forcing retirement to a quarry west of the road behind Point 156.[5]

The advance was resumed at 5.25pm with tanks and infantry protected by smoke. Within fifteen minutes the attackers were in Cassino's northern outskirts. Before long German infantrymen were attacking the tanks which, as darkness fell, became ineffective; trapped in a square, three were captured and two were damaged. A withdrawal of about 1,000 yards was carried out but, at 6.00am next day, the attack resumed with a company, supported by tanks, advancing on the north-east corner of the town. However, once again the attackers were repelled, but plans were made for two battalions, 1st and 3rd, to attack that afternoon. The 3rd Battalion seized its first objective, Point 175, considered the key enemy strongpoint north-west of Cassino. An estimated fifty Germans, supported by machine guns emplaced in three pillboxes and mortar fire from behind the hill, pinned down the attackers,

41: With a 50 pence coin for comparison, a piece of metal, possibly from a shell casing, collected by the author on Castellone. (Author's photo)

who sustained eight casualties.[6] With the company advance stalled, one soldier, Private First Class Leo J. Powers, a rifleman in an assault platoon, spotted one pillbox and, on his own initiative and disregarding terrific fire, crawled forward to assault it. Armed with hand grenades and knowing that, should he be seen, he faced almost certain death, Pfc Powers crawled to within fifteen yards of the pillbox before standing up in full view to lob a grenade into the small opening in the roof. The grenade entered the pillbox, killing two of the occupants; three or four more fled. The centre of the line resumed the advance. However, another machine gun opened fire from a second pillbox on the left. Powers, who had also located this pillbox, crawled forward with no cover from enemy fire before raising himself in full view some fifteen feet from the pillbox to throw in his grenade. The gun fell silent, one German was killed and others fled. Still acting on his own initiative, Powers crawled towards the third enemy pillbox in spite of heavy machine-pistol and machine-gun fire, making use of the scant cover. Crawling to within ten yards of the pillbox, he stood up and tossed two grenades into the small opening in the roof of the pillbox, killing two of the enemy. Four wounded men surrendered to Powers, who was now unarmed. He had worked 'his way over the entire company

42: Pfc Leo J. Powers of 133rd Regiment 34th Division was awarded the Medal of Honor after his initiative and courage 'broke the backbone' of the defences north of Cassino. (Courtesy John Griffith, California)

front, and against tremendous odds had singlehandedly broken the backbone of this heavily defended and strategic enemy position, and enabled his regiment to advance into the city of Cassino'. Leo Powers received the Medal of Honor.[7]

A second Medal of Honor was awarded posthumously to Second Lieutenant Paul F. Riordan who commanded an assault platoon in the advance. Attacking Point 175, his platoon was pinned down by machine-gun fire from the hill and a pillbox some forty-five yards to the right. In spite of intense fire, Riordan moved out in full view of enemy gunners to reach a position where he could throw a hand grenade into the pillbox. Getting to his knees, he hurled the grenade about forty-five yards, scoring a direct hit that killed one, wounded two other Germans, and silenced the gun. After this, as we have seen, Pfc Powers cleaned out the pillboxes on the hill itself, and the company took its objective. Riordan survived but, five days later, was to carry out another singlehanded attack in which he was killed.[8]

Having taken Point 175 the attackers came under fire from Castle Hill to the south. Castle Hill's almost sheer north face hid machine-gun posts and small strongpoints in caves which maintained a rate of fire that pinned down the attackers. However, with support from Company C 760th Tank Battalion, the infantry resumed their advance, although fire from Castle Hill persisted. A

43: One of the German defensive positions that took a toll of 34th Division was the castle above the town on Point 193. Castle Hill was fought over extensively in the following weeks. (NARA)

platoon of tanks and elements of Company I of 3rd/133rd Regiment reached a courtyard on the north-west corner of Cassino, consolidating there with walls and corners of buildings as cover. Their position remained precarious while the enemy held Castle Hill. In the meantime, 1st/133rd pushed into the north-east corner of the town and dug in.[9] The defenders, from 211th Grenadier Regiment, had pushed the Americans back by 1,000 yards on the 2nd and repelled every attack next day.[10]

In spite of the losses there was a belief that 34th Division, aided by artillery and tanks, would crack the Gustav Line. Already, in the first three days of February, Ryder's Red Bulls had achieved much: about a third of the critical area north-east of Cassino was in their hands while infantry and armour had forced a small lodgement in Cassino. American troops were engaging the Germans' strongest defences blocking the way into the Liri valley. In spite of the heavy losses already suffered, there remained a belief that II Corps' superiority in artillery and armour would enable the infantry to break through to Highway 6.[11]

It was not to be, but the realization that the operation had failed to achieve a breakthrough was not reached until several days later. Thus Fifth Army persisted in its attacks, Starr noting that three main drives were made over the following nine days. In both attacks on the town and into the mountains, heavy reliance was placed on artillery with Fifth Army's gunners providing 'virtually unceasing assistance'. In the first fourteen days of February 8-inch howitzers fired over 12,000 rounds in direct support of the infantry while 240mm (9-inch) howitzers hurled almost 900 rounds and 105mm howitzers expended nearly 100,000 rounds: guns of all calibres discharged nearly 200,000 rounds, 135th Regiment's cannon company alone firing 22,000 shells.[12] Böhmler commented that 'Cassino town was proving to be a tough nut, and not even the heaviest sledge-hammer in Alexander's well-equipped workshop proved powerful enough to crack it'.[13]

Bitter fighting occurred on 4 February in both Cassino town and the mountains above. With the support of 151st Field Artillery Battalion, whose 105s unleashed 4,568 rounds, 133rd Regiment tried entering the town from the north-eastern corner. However, the concrete and steel bunkers constructed by the Germans within the stone buildings proved impervious to howitzer rounds, and when half a dozen German tanks added their firepower to the defence the infantry had to withdraw. The 8-inch howitzers would be needed to deal with the armoured strongpoints.[14]

In the mountains 3rd/135th Regiment reached Colle Sant'Angelo, only to be forced back to Point 706 by a violent counter-attack while, in the centre, 2nd/135th came to within 500 yards of Point 593 and, on the right, 1st/135th gained a tenuous foothold on Point 445. Confused fighting lasted all day with opposing troops close enough to be throwing hand grenades over stone walls. At times opponents

44: Although artillery support was provided for the attacking formations, weather conditions and the fog of battle often made it difficult to direct accurately the fire of weapons such as this US Army 240mm howitzer. (NARA)

were but yards apart and, in such a situation, control of the battle was generally difficult and, at times, impossible. On the 5th the division regrouped, although 2nd/135th was more often engaged in fighting off counter-attacks. One platoon, reduced to squad strength, battled its way close to the Abbey, coming back with fourteen prisoners from a cave on Monastery Hill.[15] Böhmler commented on this achievement, noting that the Americans had advanced to beneath the Abbey walls, pressed on to Point 435 and 'in broad daylight drove a German observation post out of its position'.[16] It was the closest the Americans would get to the Abbey since reinforcements were arriving for von Senger, including 361st Regiment from Major General Ernst-Günther Baade's 90th Grenadier Division and the first of Lieutenant General Richard Heidrich's *Fallschirmjäger*.

Yet another platoon, under Captain Jack Sheehy of 168th Regiment, 'reached the walls of the Abbey but was forced to withdraw'.[17] It is unclear whether all these actions occurred on the 5th or 6th but Hougen was certain that they occurred on the latter day when Company L 168th Regiment led the attack. He added that the storming of the hill was bloody, 'troops advancing partway up the narrow defile only to be stopped in their ascent'. There they clung on.

In his history of 34th Division, Hougen commented that 135th Regiment fought desperately on 4 and 5 February to reach and cross Highway 6, only to be repelled.

> Never were fresh troops more greatly needed. None came. Indeed, thus far in the Italian campaign, reserves were an almost unknown quantity. One fresh battalion at this juncture might well have cut Highway 6 and forced a general withdrawal of the enemy. Men wondered then and wonder now, how planners of the campaign failed to have sufficient reserves on hand at all times to meet such situations which would obviously arise.[18]

Desperate attempts were made to advance on 6 February, all of which came to naught. In addition to Company L's attack against Monastery Hill, Company K was in action and, with Company L, was pinned down all day before retiring to Point 445 where both relieved 1st/135th which moved into reserve. Moving off at 6.30am, 2nd/135th had a little more success, gaining some advantage on both Points 593 and 569 before being forced off by counter-attack but recovering the north slopes of 593. Counter-attacked viciously all through the 7th, the much-weakened battalion held on.[19]

On the outskirts of Cassino 1st/133rd had withdrawn in the face of German tanks on the 4th, occupying Point 175 and permitting Company L to move to support the remainder of the 3rd Battalion on the edge of town. Next day 1st Battalion deployed from Point 175 to Castle Hill. Fighting its way through the difficult intervening terrain the battalion reached the hill but, after dark, was forced to return to Point 175. Meanwhile, on the edge of town, 3rd/133rd fought off yet another counter-attack, against its left flank, and secured another block of buildings.[20]

By 6 February the Red Bulls were pressing on the final German blocking points separating Fifth Army from Highway 6. The divisional advance was lapping up against the edge of the town, against Point 593, against Monastery Hill and against Castle Hill. However, 34th Division was exhausted, lacking the strength to make further efforts to reach Highway 6. But Alexander had ordered 2nd New Zealand and 4th Indian Divisions to form an army group reserve for exploitation through the Liri valley and, on 3 February, both were placed under command of a newly-designated New Zealand Corps in Fifth Army, to be joined later by the British 78th Division. The US Combat Command B was also to join in the exploitation phase (one of 2nd New Zealand Division's three brigades was armoured).[21]

With the new corps under his control, Clark ordered 2nd New Zealand Division to relieve 36th Division south of Highway 6. The relief was complete by the morning of the 6th, allowing Clark to provide the additional strength needed for the II Corps advance. Before the relief was complete, the Texas Division had been ordered to move to 34th Division's right to attack Piedimonte from the north-east while Ryder's division took Cassino and opened the way for armour to push into the Liri valley. The New Zealand Corps was then to pass through to continue the advance. II Corps' and New Zealand Corps' plans were integrated with a further plan for X Corps to attack south of the Liri. During the night of the 7th/8th X Corps was to attack towards Monte Faito before, next day, capturing the mountains behind Castelforte, attacks intended to force a German withdrawal and open the Liri valley.[22]

McCreery had already decided to take Monte Faito as a step towards attacking Castelforte from the rear. However, he had had to send a brigade to Anzio on 30 January with 168 Brigade of 56th Division the formation chosen. Although X Corps received 2 Special Service Brigade from Anzio, it was still losing manpower, especially as the remainder of 56th Division was to follow 168 Brigade to Anzio. Operations were launched to open the way to taking Monte Faito but the initial 9th Commando attack on Point 711 and Monte Ornito was beaten off and fresh plans had to be made. On the night of 7/8 February 138 Brigade attacked but without success, although 6th Lincolns twice reached Monte Faito before being pushed off by speedy counter-attacks. The Germans followed with a series of 'fruitless attacks' on Monte Ornito and Cerasola before both sides settled down to defensive warfare in rain, sleet and snow.[23] Starr suggests, inaccurately, that X Corps' attack 'was not mounted in strength and did not reach its objectives'.[24]

***

With 36th Division firm in the Monte Castellone–Manna Farm area on 7 February, II Corps was set up for a new drive to cut Highway 6. Ryder's plan was for 34th Division to attack at 10.00pm on the 7th, with 135th Regiment seizing Albaneta Farm to cover 168th's right flank in its attack on Monastery Hill, due to begin at 4.00am on the 8th. Since 135th Regiment was still fighting off counter-attacks it had no role in the attack, but 133rd would continue its battle for Cassino town.

As planned, 1st and 3rd Battalions of 168th Regiment left their start lines at 4.00am on 8 February in a concentric attack on Monastery Hill. Neither enjoyed success as heavy rain became a fierce blizzard that made life even more difficult for already exhausted soldiers. On the right the advance reached the base of Point 444, north-west of the Abbey, to be caught in enfilading fire. On Point 445's slopes attackers were also pinned down. Although both battalions attacked again at 3.30pm, following an hour-long artillery bombardment, no further success was gained and 1st/168th was stopped at the base of Point 444. At Point 593 a German counter-attack gained ground before being repelled. Such was the picture during the next two days.[25]

On the night of 7/8 February 100th Battalion joined the attack on Cassino town, allowing 133rd Regiment to launch all three battalions into action at 6.45am on the 8th. Tanks provided support, and smoke covered the attackers' approach. Clark's overall plan envisaged X Corps, II Corps and the CEF making simultaneous attacks but, as we have seen, X Corps made no significant gains. Juin agreed with Clark's plan but felt that his divisions 'were too exhausted to participate'.[26] II Corps was alone.

The fresh attack into Cassino by 133rd Regiment involved more force than hitherto, with all three battalions deployed and 8-inch howitzers in direct support as well as the tank battalion. Infantry used a new tactic for fighting in the built-up area, firing bazookas through walls but Cassino's walls were so strong and thick that up to nine rounds were needed to create a three-foot-diameter hole. (Fewer rounds were necessary to penetrate German concrete pillboxes.) A wide range of artillery was deployed, from 8-inch howitzers down to 37mm anti-tank weapons; armour-piercing rounds proved particularly effective.[28]

Even with all this firepower the infantry found progress difficult, advancing no more than 200 yards. Ruined buildings, rubble-strewn streets and enemy fire stopped the advance. During this attempt to push into the town Second Lieutenant Riordan's platoon was ordered to take the town jail, one of several strongpoints. Once again Riordan led and penetrated the ring of enemy fire covering the approaches to reach the jail. However, his soldiers, unable to follow, were cut off. Aware that he was alone, Riordan went on to attack the jail. One man against a well-placed, numerically superior enemy force was too much and, having killed at least two defenders, Riordan fell to small-arms fire. Added to his earlier actions at Point 175, his final act earned him a posthumous Medal of Honor, the citation noting that his 'bravery and extraordinary heroism in the face of almost certain death were an inspiration to his men and exemplify the highest traditions of the US Armed Forces'.[28]

***

Although 133rd Regiment's soldiers continued battling in the northern outskirts of Cassino for another six days in their efforts to evict the Germans it became clear that they could not pass through the defences. Above them both 135th and 168th Regiments had failed in their stubborn attempt to pinch out Monte Cassino while Walker's 36th Division, on Colle Maiola, found every attempt to advance the mile and a half from Albaneta to the Liri valley frustrated. Not only did the Germans fight them, the weather was also against them, as was the terrain. Lashing rain, heavy snow and bitter cold in the rugged ground of the Cassino massif assailed friend and foe alike and, although the Americans created ad hoc units from clerks, drivers and others to provide reserves for the companies in the mountains, the hope of a breakthrough was dying, even at army group headquarters. Although the offensive continued 'the infantry units were too exhausted, too numb from the cold, too battered by the German fire to do more than await relief'.[29]

Lemnitzer, Alexander's deputy, visited the front and reported 'that the troops were so disheartened as to be almost mutinous'. Little more could be asked of them and they were in sore need of rest. Alexander and Clark agreed that II Corps could not be expected to continue beyond 12 February; both divisions were so reduced as to be ineffective. On 13 February it was estimated that 36th Division's infantry regiments were at less than 25 per cent of their effective combat strength; 1st and 3rd Battalions of 141st Regiment totalled only twenty-two officers and 160 men. The situation in 34th Division was equally bad with 274 dead, wounded and missing in 3rd/133rd Regiment: Company I had only thirty men, Company K seventy and Company L forty. The other regiments were little better: 135th Regiment averaged only thirty men per company; 168th Regiment had only 793 men in all.[30]

In spite of all their efforts and courage, the men of II Corps had failed to make the breakthrough by covering that final mile to Highway 6. Fourth Indian Division's historian commented:

> After gallantry beyond all praise the American assault petered out on the bare hillsides. The survivors of 34th US Division clung grimly to their hard-won ground, buffeted day and night by the elements and by the foe. They had done all that men could do.[31]

***

45: Two GIs study the high ground they had been ordered to take, knowing that German observers on the snow-covered Monte Cáiro can see almost all that happens below. (NARA)

VI Corps' situation at Anzio was still difficult. An Allied advance at the end of January created a salient in a period of bitter fighting in which the Germans tried to overwhelm the Allied troops in that salient. The area known as the 'Factory' and Carroceto were held by elements of the British 1st Division and Colonel General Eberhard von Mackensen, commanding Fourteenth Army, sent two forces, *Kampfgruppe* Pfeiffer and *Kampfgruppe* Gräser to push out the British troops on the night of 7/8 February.[32]

Attacking along the Buonriposa ridge, and from the east side of the Factory, the Germans encountered tough opposition. Pfeiffer ran up against 5th Grenadier Guards of 24 Guards Brigade, an encounter that resulted in a Victoria Cross being

46: The exhaustion of battle is clear in the features of this GI who typifies the endurance of infantrymen in the first battle. Some of 34th Division's soldiers, unable to walk away from their sangars, had to be carried out as their limbs were frozen and cramped. (NARA)

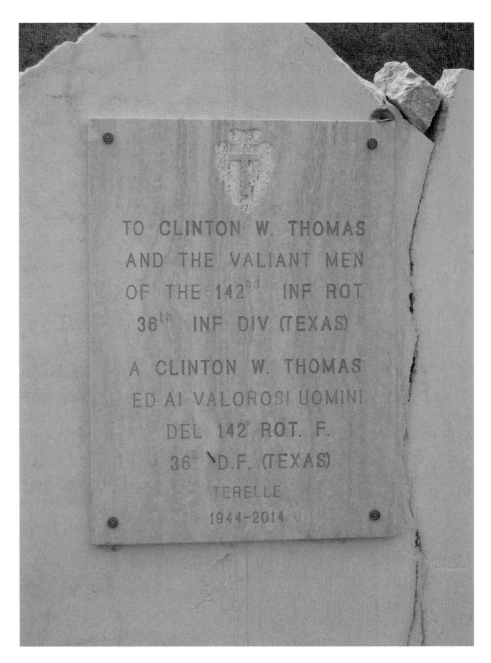

47: One regiment of 36th Division (142nd) was deployed into the mountains to support 34th. Above the village of Terelle a monument bearing this plaque commemorates Pte Clinton W. Thomas, a holder of the Bronze Star and Purple Heart, whose identity discs were discovered nearby in 2010 by Damiano Parravano of the Associazione Linea Gustav. (Author's photo)

awarded to a Grenadier officer, Major Philip Sidney, commanding 5th Grenadiers' support company. Sidney's company headquarters was to the left of the battalion headquarters in a gully south-west of Carroceto bridge. German infantry had by-passed the forward rifle company north-west of Carroceto, attacked the area of Sidney's headquarters and pushed into the gully. However, Major Sidney 'collected the crew of a 3-inch mortar firing nearby and personally led an attack with Tommy guns and hand grenades, driving the enemy out of the gully,' after which he sent the mortarmen back to their mortars. With a handful of guardsmen, Sidney positioned himself to again beat off the enemy who had renewed their attack in strength. They kept the majority of the Germans out, although some reached a threatening position some twenty yards away. Knowing that they could outflank him, Sidney dashed forward to engage the Germans with his Tommy gun, forcing them to withdraw, leaving a number of dead.

Back at his former position, Sidney sent all but two of his guardsmen to fetch more ammunition and grenades. At this stage the Germans attacked again. Major Sidney was hit in the face by a grenade that bounced off and exploded, wounding him and one guardsman and killing the other. Nonetheless, he singlehandedly kept the enemy at bay until the ammunition party returned. Once more the Germans were repelled. Believing that further attacks were not imminent he went to a nearby cave to have his wound dressed. Before that could be done the enemy attacked again and Sidney returned immediately to his post, engaging the attackers for another hour. By then the left of the battalion position was consolidated and the Germans were finally beaten off. At last Major Sidney allowed his wound to be attended to; by then he was weak from loss of blood and barely able to walk.

With the enemy in close contact all the next day Sidney could not be evacuated. However, 'although extremely weak, he [was] ... a tonic and inspiration to all with whom he came in contact.' He had shown 'efficiency, coolness, gallantry and complete disregard for his personal safety of a most exceptional order'. His action, taken in the face of great odds, ensured that his battalion's position was re-established 'with vitally far reaching consequences on the battle as a whole'.[33]

The action in which Sidney distinguished himself was typical of the many small actions of the battle being waged in those February days. Such was the pressure on the bridgehead that it was critical that Fifth Army should maintain the offensive at Cassino and prevent the diversion of German troops to Anzio.

***

On 9 February 1944 it was planned to commit the New Zealand Corps if II Corps had not gained its objectives by dark on the 12th; Freyberg warned 4th Indian

48: At Anzio a German counter-attack was launched on the Allied bridgehead on 7/8 February during which Major William Philip Sidney, commanding a company of 5th Grenadier Guards, earned the Victoria Cross for his courage and leadership although badly wounded. Sidney later succeeded to the title Lord de L'Isle and is seen here as Governor General of Australia. His father-in-law, Lord Gort of Limerick, also held the VC. (Taylor Library)

to be ready to attack immediately after that deadline. As a result of that order, 7 Indian Brigade, under Brigadier Oscar de Turville Lovett, moved forward on the 10th, concentrating near Cáira on the lower slopes of Castellone on the night of the 11th/12th, ready to relieve the US troops the following night and attack the night after.[34]

On the 12th the two corps HQs agreed the final details of the handover: 36th US Division would hold its positions on Monte Castellone whilst the Indians advanced southwards from Points 593, 450 and 445, the high-water marks of the American advance. Since 36th Division had no more than 700 men on Castellone, Walker might have to seek support from Freyberg's corps while Keyes was concerned about how long the Texas Division could hold out should 4th Indian's attack not be launched quickly. However, 7 Indian Brigade was expecting an orderly, normal relief rather than a handover on an active battlefield.

As the Indians assembled near Cáira two assault groups of 200th Grenadier Regiment attacked the Americans on Castellone 'under an unusually heavy barrage'.[35] The Germans regained the heights and 36th Division's defences were disorganized. In a speedy reaction, every possible soldier, including cooks and clerks, was sent into the fray and II Corps artillery unleashed such a storm of fire that the Germans could not hold what they had just taken. Both Germans and Americans were exhausted and sustained heavy casualties. The Indians had not been immune; 7 Brigade suffered about twenty casualties an hour as the battalions waited to move. With Germans infiltrating from around Terelle that afternoon, 7 Brigade deployed two battalions to support the Americans at Terelle and the planned relief could not be carried out that night. Thus the Indians' attack was postponed again by twenty-four hours.[36]

As darkness fell on 13 February the men of 7 Brigade started the difficult move into the mountains, a trek of almost four miles from Cáira by a rough mountain track under fire from enemy mortars and artillery. Supplies had to be brought up along the same route under cover of darkness, for which mules and pack-carrying soldiers were used. The task of bringing up supplies began immediately as American ammunition and stores could not be used; a new logistical chain was being created from 4th Indian Division's HQ north of Highway 6 to the forward locations, 7 Brigade being at the forefront, while 5 Brigade concentrated at Portella in the relative safety of the Rapido valley; 11 Brigade was based around San Michele, about three miles east of Cassino.[37]

Although the relief of the Americans in the mountains began on the 13th it did not end until 6.30am on the 15th when 7 Indian Brigade took over from the American infantry, some of whom were so exhausted that they could not move due to the cold and overwhelming tiredness; they had to be lifted from their sangars and carried to safety on stretchers. The British official history records

49: When the New Zealand Corps relieved II US Corps, soldiers of 4th Indian Division took over from 34th Division in the mountains. Indian soldiers are seen dragging supplies up an extremely steep rock face. (Author's collection)

50: Mules were critical for re-supplying troops in the mountains and for casualty evacuation, some even describing them as more important than tanks in such terrain. The average mule could carry about 160lb. (Author's collection)

51: Soldiers were also used to carry supplies into the mountains, several units of 4th Indian Division being dedicated to that role. (Author's collection)

that some 200 American soldiers in the area taken over by 1st Royal Sussex 'had suffered so extremely from exhaustion and exposure that while they could man positions they were unable to walk'. Carrying them out could be done only after dark on the 14th, prompting a further delay in the planned 7 Brigade attack; Point 593 would be attacked on the night of 15/16 February and the Abbey the following night.[38]

The move onto the heights gave 7 Brigade an idea of what would be involved in launching an offensive in such terrain. Senior officers of 4th Indian Division knew that their forthcoming attack would require striking a balance between operational demands and sustaining the assaulting troops. Two factors constrained planning: the number of men the division could support in its forward areas; and the number who could be deployed on the available jumping-off positions.[39]

It was decided that the maximum feasible force that could be launched into and sustained in action was a brigade group. II US Corps had deployed the equivalent of six British brigades, four on the Cassino massif, a fifth on Castellone and the sixth in the attack into the northern outskirts of Cassino. Since those formations had lost 80 per cent of their fighting strength 'in a series of fruitless encounters' in which it had never been possible to bring to bear the maximum assault strength, 4th Division's planners opted for 'a comparatively modest test of strength against the dominant feature of Point 593, followed by an all-out bid by 7 Brigade to reach the Monastery in a single bound'.[40]

Lovett was given two additional battalions – 1st/9th Gurkha Rifles and 4th/6th Rajputana Rifles – to reinforce 7 Brigade. To these were added 12 Field Company Royal Indian Engineers, B and C Companies 4th/6th Rajputana Rifles (a machine-gun battalion), a troop of 57th Light Anti-Aircraft Regiment and two companies of 2nd/7th Gurkha Rifles. The last named were to be deployed on portering duties, such were the difficulties of re-supply and the shortage of mules and human porters.[41]

However, at corps level, the problems of fighting in the mountains and seizing Monastery Hill had focused attention on the Abbey. That was to have both an immediate and an enduring effect on the struggle to break the Gustav Line. Before going on to study the Second Battle of Monte Cassino it is appropriate to look at what seemed to be concentrating the minds of commanders at corps, army and army group levels. (It is also appropriate to note that the Germans did not recognize the distinction applied by the Allies to the next phase of the struggle. Since, in their view, the New Zealand Corps performed a relief in place of II US Corps and continued attacking on the same axes of advance, the 'second' battle did not begin until 15 March, recognized by the Allies, as the opening of the Third Battle.)

Chapter Six

The baton was being passed to the New Zealand Corps. By 6 February 4th Indian Division had completed its move to the Cassino area where Freyberg had established his HQ. However, Major General Francis Tuker, known as 'Gertie', had fallen ill and command of the division devolved temporarily on Brigadier Harry Kenneth (Ken) Dimoline, the divisional CRA. Tuker referred to Dimoline as having 'officiating command of the division' while he remained as a presence in the background. With Lieutenant General Freyberg appointed to command New Zealand Corps, neither division would fight under its previous commander. In 2nd New Zealand Division, Brigadier Howard Kippenberger, commander of 5 Brigade, became temporary GOC. Organizing the corps required

52: Commanding 2nd New Zealand Division was Major General Howard Kippenberger, already a veteran of considerable active service. Unfortunately, Kippenberger was injured badly by a land mine on Monte Trócchio, losing both feet. (Author's collection)

some improvisation: the heads of services in 2nd New Zealand Division assumed double roles by taking on the corps-level job as well as that at divisional level, although Colonel R.C. Queree was promoted to brigadier as Freyberg's BGS.[1] Such an arrangement did not augur well for effective command and control at corps level. On 4 February Freyberg held the first of a series of conferences on the corps' role, which was attended by Dimoline as GOC 4th Indian Division. Although making firm plans depended on progress by II US Corps, it was agreed that their great experience in mountain warfare fitted 4th Indian Division to fight through the hills north of Highway 6 while the New Zealanders fought on the lowland should entry be made into the Liri valley.[2]

***

Lieutenant General Sir Bernard Freyberg, a giant of a man but inevitably known as 'Tiny', had served in the First World War, earning the Victoria Cross on the Somme in 1916 while commanding the Royal Naval Division's Hood Battalion, as well as being wounded four times. Although born in England, his parents had emigrated to New Zealand when he was a child. Blumenson described him as

53: Lieutenant General Bernard Freyberg VC commanded the New Zealand Corps but was not a good corps commander. It was Freyberg who demanded that the Abbey be bombed, thereby turning a neutral building that had been respected by both sides into defensive positions for the Germans. (IWM NA10630)

'an imposing figure with the reputation and prestige' of a war hero of the First World War who had, more recently, 'commanded troops in Crete and … fought magnificently in the desert campaign', noting that Clark was impressed by his strongmindedness, energy, aggressiveness, and optimism.[3] One veteran of the campaign wrote of him:

> In command of the [New Zealand] division, and of an expeditionary force whose tentacles stretched as far as Cairo, was the great father-figure, courtly in manner and resembling a giant teddy-bear of … Freyberg, on whose body Winston Churchill had counted twenty-seven battle scars – before more were added in the Desert. He had ended the Great War as a brigade commander, aged 29, with VC and three DSOs, had served with the Grenadier Guards in peacetime, and had returned to New Zealand on retirement as a major general, whence he was summoned to war again in command of the Expeditionary Force.[4]

Freyberg's Kiwis, experienced soldiers with 'a vast fund of battle wisdom', were 'self-reliant, adventurous and independent' volunteers who knew that their division had earned a high reputation and the support of their people at home. Blaxland likened them to a 'touring test team'.[5] Freyberg had commanded his division in Greece and Crete as well as in Eighth Army's battles in Libya and Egypt, culminating in the final battle of El Alamein before the pursuit into Tunisia and the left-hook operation to turn the Mareth Line. For that last operation, in March 1943, Freyberg was elevated to corps command: General Leclerc's Free French forces, 8 Armoured Brigade and additional artillery were added to 2nd New Zealand Division to create the New Zealand Corps.[6]

Although Freyberg's corps advanced rapidly to the Tebaga Gap, it was then faced by strong German resistance and had little success in its first attacks. As the attack by Leese's XXX Corps had come unstuck at Wadi Zigzaou on the main Mareth Line, Tuker's 4th Indian Division was deployed on a flanking move through the mountains while 1st Armoured Division was ordered to join Freyberg. However, X Corps HQ, commanded by Lieutenant General Brian Horrocks, moved with 1st Armoured Division, Montgomery having ordered Horrocks to take overall command. Montgomery's decision did not sit well with Freyberg who was six years older than Horrocks and much more experienced[7] (Horrocks had been a PoW for much of the First World War). Nonetheless, the re-organized corps went into action again in Operation SUPERCHARGE II on 26 March, gaining a tactical victory against doughty opposition from the remnants of 21st Panzer and 90th Light Divisions; the Desert Air Force provided close air support and 1st Armoured Division executed a novel night advance that caught the Germans off balance.[8] Following this the New Zealand Corps was disbanded. It appeared that Montgomery had doubted Freyberg's ability as a corps commander. Thus in Italy in February 1944 the New Zealand commander was being given another opportunity to prove himself at corps level. (His command on Crete in 1941, Creforce, might also be considered as corps level, and he had been acting commander of XIII Corps in the desert between the death of Strafer Gott and Horrocks' arrival in August 1942.)

In North Africa Freyberg had been very critical of British armour in the battles along the El Alamein line in July 1942 and had gained permission to convert one of his brigades to armour. Thus 2nd New Zealand Division had an integral armoured brigade but only two infantry brigades, which was a disadvantage when operating in circumstances with little opportunity to deploy tanks, as had happened recently at Orsogna and would happen again at Cassino.

The other major element of the New Zealand Corps, 4th Indian Division, included 'the only troops who could rival the fame of the New Zealanders'. Recent arrivals in Italy, 4th Indian, were the

> wearers of the Red Eagle badge and heroes of the earliest victories in the Desert, of the storming of the heights of Keren in Eritrea, of many other grim battles in the Desert, and of the night attack on the pinnacles above Wadi Akarit. There was an air of quiet confidence about the lithe and hardy men of the assorted battalions.[9]

As already noted, Tuker, GOC of 4th Indian Division was *hors de combat*. Suffering from rheumatoid arthritis, he was forced to take to his bed in his caravan, which allowed him to continue exerting influence on the division through Dimoline. Later he was removed to hospital, ending his vicarious influence. One of the tragedies of the Cassino battles is that this very able commander could not play a full part in planning operations involving his soldiers. Major General Francis Tuker, a very experienced commander, had a great intellect and an intelligent approach to operations and, after the war, wrote two excellent books on warfare, *Approach to Battle* (in which he noted the obsession with challenging the enemy's strength instead of exploiting his weaknesses) and *The Pattern of War*.

Commissioned from Sandhurst into the Royal Sussex Regiment in 1914, Tuker was transferred to 1st/2nd Gurkha Rifles and, during the First World War, served in India and Mesopotamia. By January 1918 he had been promoted to captain, took part in the Kuki Expedition and served in North West Persia in 1920 and 1921. By 1932 he was a major. Promoted to lieutenant colonel in early 1937, he was appointed commanding officer of 2nd Gurkha Rifles, took part in operations in Waziristan, was appointed OBE and Mentioned in Despatches.

In late October 1939 Tuker was promoted to colonel and shortly afterwards became Director of Military Training, India, as a temporary brigadier. On 1 October 1941 he was given command of the newly-formed 34th Indian Infantry Division, but then took command of 4th Indian Division on 30 December.[10]

Tuker commanded 4th Indian Division during the North African campaign but his formation was 'side-lined' by Montgomery in Operation LIGHTFOOT, the final battle at El Alamein in October 1942, probably because of Montgomery's prejudice against the Indian Army, for which he had been rejected at Sandhurst. Tuker went on to prove the skills and military worth of his soldiers in the mountains of Tunisia where they operated on terrain considered impassable by Europeans.[11] Thus it seemed that the Red Eagles were ideal for operations in the Cassino massif.

Although not fully active, Tuker was applying his mind to the problems facing Freyberg's corps. He presented a memorandum to Freyberg on 12 February recommending an outflanking manoeuvre around Monastery Hill, using the American gains on Monte Castellone, to cut Highway 6. He insisted that, if the Abbey had to be attacked, it should be regarded as a fortress since the Germans would be holding it 'as a keep'. The Abbey would have to be neutralized, which could only be done by aerial bombing, using 'blockbuster' bombs. Freyberg may have already known Tuker's views for, on the afternoon of the 12th, and probably before receiving Tuker's notes, he was visited by Alexander from whom he received permission to bomb the Abbey. However, Freyberg's and Tuker's concepts of 'bombing' were very different. Moreover, as Blaxland commented, Freyberg 'put great faith in the effect of the bombing' but did not give equally serious consideration to Tuker's recommendation for an outflanking manoeuvre.[12]

Freyberg believed that a strike by fighter-bombers, using 500lb bombs, would suffice whereas Tuker had said that such would be insufficient: heavy bombers dropping blockbusters were required to reduce the Abbey to dust. Since the Allies had hitherto refrained from firing at the Abbey, why did it become a target for heavy bombers?

***

It had been Allied policy to respect buildings, such as the Abbey, with religious and cultural importance, not only to Italy but to Christians across the world. President Roosevelt had written to Pope Pius XII in July 1943, undertaking that churches and religious buildings would 'to the extent it is within our power' be preserved from the devastation of war.[13] The British and US governments had assured the Vatican 'that the Abbey's safety would be provided for' while the German government had given

54: Freyberg believed that 36 Kitty-bombers could destroy this building. However, his request for such an attack developed into an opportunity for the airmen to make the first use of strategic bombers in support of ground troops but with unfortunate consequences. (Author's collection)

55: Much of the treasure of the Abbey, a repository for national archives as well as artwork, was removed by the Germans to Rome. Although credit for this is usually attributed to an Austrian officer, Julius Schlegel, it was Dr Maximilian Becker, a medical officer, who initiated the process. (NARA)

an assurance that their troops would not occupy it.[14] The decision to bomb was not taken lightly, as the controversy that still continues demonstrates. Since both sides had assured the Vatican that they would respect the Abbey, why was it bombed?

There is no evidence that the Germans used the Abbey for military purposes before the bombing, but Allied soldiers below Monte Cassino thought otherwise. Majdalany wrote:

> When you have been fighting a long time you develop an instinct for enemy observation-posts. You spot quickly where they must be, and you seem to know intuitively the exact moment you start being watched. And it is like suddenly being stripped of your clothes. We were being watched now, and we knew it. We were being watched by eyes in the Monastery every inch of the way up the rough little road through the olive groves.[15]

However, Majdalany was commenting about a time when the Abbey, or rather its ruins, *were* occupied by the Germans since his formation, 78th (Battleaxe) Division, did not arrive in the area, as the third division of New Zealand Corps, until after the bombing. Nonetheless, his comment chimes with those of many who had been there before the bombing – Americans, British, Indians and New Zealanders. Another Cassino veteran, Brian Harpur, who served in 1st Kensingtons of 78th Division, recorded a post-war conversation with Majdalany about the Abbey; as with Majdalany, Harpur was not at Cassino before the Abbey was bombed.

> That brooding monastery ate into our souls. You were there and I was there and there was never any doubt in our minds, nor in the minds of anyone else that it had to be bombed. No way could we or anyone else conceive that it was not occupied by those mad German paratroopers and crammed with enemy observation posts.[16]

The author has spoken to many veterans of the Cassino battles but never to one who believed the bombing was *not* justified. In 1944 the late Lieutenant Colonel Brian Clark MC GM was the adjutant of 1st Royal Irish Fusiliers (the Faughs) in 38 (Irish) Brigade. Brian Clark presented the author with some of his contemporary maps and other material on Cassino, including his notes for a lecture on the final battle to the Military History Society of Ireland in the 1980s. In that lecture the former Faughs' adjutant used a quotation from Alistair Horne's book *The Price of Glory*, about Verdun in the First World War, to illustrate how the ordinary soldier felt about the Abbey: 'You could not escape it. Like a small rodent under the unblinking eye of a hawk, it made you feel quite naked and unprotected. At the same time it beckoned with an irresistible magnetism.'[17]

At no time during the American assaults had bombing the Abbey been suggested, although many American soldiers would have agreed with such action. Harold L. Bond wrote that 'All of us were convinced that the abbey was a German strong point, and it was being used by them for the excellent observation it gave of all our positions'.[18]

Fifth Army had 'scrupulously tried to avoid firing into the Abbey until the second week in February when shells fell on the slope before the Abbey and some damaged the top floor.'[19] However, a diary maintained by one monk recorded 'the first Anglo-American shell' striking the entrance cloister on 11 January.[20] Bombing seems to have entered the equation with 4th Indian Division's request on 11 February for intense bombing of 'all buildings and suspected enemy posts on or near the objectives, including the Monastery'.[21] No American commander had felt such action necessary and it is significant that, when Freyberg made his request that Monastery Hill be 'softened up' before 4th Indian Division's attack, the American commanders did not agree. Freyberg telephoned Al Gruenther, Fifth Army's chief of staff, to request that 'thirty-six aircraft carrying heavy [sic] bombs should be used' against the Abbey. Since Clark was at Anzio, Gruenther contacted John Harding, Alexander's chief of staff, to tell him of Freyberg's request and

56: This modern image, taken from near the railway station, shows the Abbey and Hangman's Hill, indicating how Allied soldiers believed that they were being watched by Germans in the Abbey. (Author's photo)

inform him that he knew Clark 'believed there was no military necessity' to destroy the Abbey. On returning to his headquarters, Clark confirmed what Gruenther had said, telling the latter to repeat it to Harding. In further discussion with Harding, Gruenther reiterated Clark's view but was told that Alexander 'had decided the matter'. Later, when Clark spoke to Alexander and made clear his view, 'Alexander did not alter his decision, and General Wilson later concurred in it'.[22] At one point Gruenther offered Freyberg a squadron of A-36s* carrying 500lb bombs for his preferred target, which Freyberg stated to be 'the convent' [sic]; until then it had not been on his list of targets.

When his division was assigned the task of taking Monastery Hill, Tuker, finding that Fifth Army Intelligence Branch had little information on the Abbey, undertook what Majdalany described as 'one of the stranger acts of generalship of the war'. He had his driver take him to visit the bookshops of Naples in search of any printed material with details of the building. In a book dated 1879 he found the required information and included it in his memorandum to Freyberg. He

---

* The North American A-36 Apache was a dive-bomber variant of the P-51 Mustang fighter with strengthened wings fitted with slatted airbrakes.

emphasized that the building had been converted into a fortress in the nineteenth century (in fact that work was centuries older) with walls about 150-feet (46m) high, 'of solid masonry', and 'at least 10 feet (3m) thick at the base'. Noting that the walls were battlemented and pierced with loopholes, making the building 'a modern fortress', such a structure would be impervious to the work of field engineers and could 'only be directly dealt with by applying blockbuster bombs from the air, hoping thereby to render the garrison incapable of resistance'. He added that 1,000lb bombs would be 'next to useless'.[23]

Clearly Tuker was well informed on developments in aerial bombing. The 'blockbuster' to which he referred was a relatively recent development, such high-capacity munitions having first been used in a raid on the Renault factory at Billancourt, near Paris, on 3 March 1942.[24] With a very light cylindrical casing, some three-quarters of the weight was high explosive; traditional bombs were about 50 per cent explosive by weight. The designer of the 'blockbuster', known as a 'cookie' in the RAF, was subsequently appointed MBE for his efforts; Albert Cecil Brookes was also known as 'Mr Blockbuster'.[25] Blockbusters were designed to cause widespread blast damage and must have seemed ideal to Tuker. The basic blockbuster had been developed into a heavier weapon by combining two to create an 8,000lb bomb; this version had been introduced in December 1943. A 12,000lb version followed.

Freyberg was not as *au fait* as Tuker with the world of aerial bombs since he seems to have believed that fighter-bombers carrying 1,000lb bombs would achieve Tuker's desired result. His request to Fifth Army was for 'three missions of 12 planes each; the planes to be Kitty Bombers carrying 1,000 pound bombs'. (He was referring to the Curtiss P-40 fighter-bombers being used by the Desert Air Force, as Tomahawks or Kittyhawks, depending on variant, and the USAAF, as Warhawks. The P-40 could carry a maximum bombload of 2,000lb, with one 1,000lb bomb under the fuselage and a 500lb bomb under each wing.) The maximum load of thirty-six P-40s, eighteen tons, would have had little effect. It may be noted that Freyberg was told by Gruenther of Clark's objections to bombing, including the fact that destroying the Abbey might not reduce its military value as an obstacle.[28]

However, the proposal to bomb the Abbey soon had a life of its own. Christopher Buckley, British war correspondent and *Daily Telegraph* journalist (later killed by a mine in the Korean War), outlined the press debate with daily publicity accorded to the rights or wrongs of such a proposal. Noting that there was much 'to be said on either side of the case,' he commented that 'publicists in Britain and America saw to it that nothing was left unsaid'.[28] In addition to that debate, another aspect to the proposal was that only heavy bombers could drop the munitions Tuker demanded, placing the execution of the proposal with the staff of Mediterranean

Allied Air Forces (MAAF). MAAF, established on 10 December 1943 to succeed the previous Mediterranean Air Command (MAC), was initially commanded by Air Chief Marshal Sir Arthur Tedder. Transferred to the UK in January 1944 to become Eisenhower's deputy for the Normandy landings and subsequent liberation of Europe, Tedder was succeeded by the American Lieutenant General Ira C. Eaker, with the RAF's Air Marshal Sir John Slessor as his deputy (and Commander RAF in the theatre). MAAF, as with MAC before it, co-ordinated all American, British and other Allied aircraft in the Mediterranean. Within MAAF, the US Army Air Forces' Fifteenth Air Force, plus No.205 Group RAF and the US XV Air Force Service Command, formed the Mediterranean Allied Strategic Air Force (MASAF), from which would come the heavy bombers to strike at Monte Cassino. In addition, MAAF included the tactical air forces, the RAF's Desert Air Force and the USAAF's Twelfth Air Force, commanded by Major General John K. Cannon, operating medium bombers, fighter-bombers, fighters, reconnaissance machines and transport aircraft. Cannon even suggested to Alexander that his bombers be used against the Abbey which they would 'whip out like a dead tooth'.[29]

Freyberg may have thought that thirty-six P-40s were capable of demolishing the Abbey but the airmen did not agree. They had their own ideas, based on their strong belief in the power of bombing, for the first-ever opportunity to use heavy bombers to support ground troops and were determined to show how effective this could be. Eaker carried out a reconnaissance over the Abbey before agreeing to the mission. With General Devers, Deputy Supreme Allied Commander Mediterranean, he flew in a Stinson L-5 over Monte Cassino, probably on 13 February, at about 200 feet (some sources suggest more than 1,000 feet, which is where his fighter escort was) above the building and 'believed they saw at least one military radio aerial inside the monastery and enemy soldiers walking in and out of the building'.[30] German uniforms hanging on a clothesline in the Abbey courtyard and machine-gun emplacements only fifty yards from the walls were also reported.[31] In contrast General Keyes flew over several times with one of his senior staff, Colonel Robert Porter, and saw no Germans. Of the rumours that the Abbey was being used by the Germans and that they had been seen, Keyes commented 'They've been looking so long they're seeing things'.[32] Keyes, a devout Roman Catholic who attended the celebration of Mass each day, was unlikely to have allowed his faith to blind him to the presence of Germans. The Germans did not fire at light aircraft so as not to disclose their positions and attract attention from fighter-bombers.

Once the decision to bomb was taken, however, MAAF HQ, although recognizing that the mission was being flown at the request of a ground commander, chose not to co-ordinate it with New Zealand Corps HQ. For them, the factors deciding the

57: The Deputy Supreme Allied Commander, Mediterranean, General Devers, was one of those convinced that the Germans were using the Abbey for military purposes. He flew over the Abbey with Eaker, the air commander, and both persuaded themselves that there were Germans in the Abbey with uniforms hanging out to dry and wireless antennae. Devers is the centre figure in this photograph between Lieutenant Generals Sir Oliver Leese (L) and Richard McCreery. (IWM NA 13787)

mission's timing included the weather and the needs of the Anzio bridgehead, but not those of the soldiers they were 'supporting', who were waiting to learn when the bombers would strike so that their assault could be launched to take maximum advantage of the aerial onslaught. This was especially true for the soldiers of 1st Royal Sussex, of Lovett's 7 Indian Brigade, who were making their way onto the high ground and their start line.

Caddick-Adams comments, 'For the first-ever mission of an Allied strategic bombing force supporting a tactical mission on land, Eaker, for his own reasons, laid on a raid of epic scale, by way of demonstration.'[33] That 'epic scale' amounted to a heavy bomber force of 142 B-17s of Fifteenth Air Force, plus eighty-seven B-25 Mitchells and B-26 Marauders of Twelfth Air Force. (There are variations in the number of B-17s: Hapgood and Richardson give a figure of 144 while Blaxland states 135; Majdalany increases the mediums to 112 aircraft but agrees

58: Lieutenant General Geoffrey Keyes, commanding II Corps, a devout Roman Catholic, opposed the bombing but was over-ruled. Keyes is on the left with Lieutenant General A.L. Collier and General Juin. (NARA)

on 142 B-17s.) The US official history comments on the 'great difference' between Freyberg's original request for three Kitty-bomber squadrons and the strike that was delivered, although Freyberg did subsequently ask for the Abbey 'to be flattened'. Neither official records nor the personal papers of the main participants indicate why the attack was scaled up to such an extent.

> What seems likely is that air force planners seized upon the opportunity to demonstrate the power of the bomber, which had never before been used in concentrated mass directly in support of ground troops taking a tactical objective. If Freyberg wanted the building flattened, the building would be flattened. Probably General Eaker, and perhaps General Devers, persuaded General Wilson to let the air forces try the experiment.[34]

The B-17 Flying Fortresses were drawn from the 2nd, 97th, 99th and 301st Bombardment Groups, all from 5th Bombardment Wing, based around Naples and Foggia, where the Allies had established airfields.[35] Major Bradford E. Evans was the leader of the thirty-seven B-17s of 2nd Bombardment Group[36] and, as with the other 100-plus heavy bombers, his machines each carried a dozen 500lb bombs, making the overall weight dropped by the heavies 380 tons. However, no blockbusters were included for the simple reason that a B-17 could not carry a blockbuster due to the design of its bomb-bay which, situated between front and rear wing spars, was laid out vertically rather than lengthwise, as with British bombers.* Thus Tuker's request was not met and the damage to the Abbey was not as severe as it might have been had British bombers been deployed, but this would have involved aircraft flying from Britain. Not only was Sir Arthur Harris of Bomber Command unlikely to have approved such a mission, but it was clearly within the remit of the Mediterranean air forces.

In the early afternoon of 14 February US 105mm howitzers fired leaflets into the area around the Abbey. They bore a message in Italian and English, headed ATTENZIONE! and addressed 'Italian Friends':

> We have until now been especially careful to avoid shelling the Monte Cassino monastery. The Germans have known how to benefit from this. But now the fighting has swept closer and closer to its sacred precincts. The time has come when we must train our guns on the monastery itself.
>
> We give you warning so that you may save yourselves. We warn you urgently: Leave the monastery. Leave it at once. Respect this warning. It is for your benefit.[37]

The warning was intended for the many civilians taking shelter in the Abbey and for those monks and brothers who had not already left, including Abbot Gregorio Diamare, leader of the Monte Cassino community.

Meanwhile Freyberg's HQ expected the bombing to be carried out late on the 16th and had issued orders to 4th Indian Division for its soldiers to fall back to safe positions. However, Allied intelligence, through Ultra decrypts, had learned that a major German counter-offensive was to be launched on the Anzio bridgehead that day. Therefore, Fifth Army HQ informed Freyberg that the bombers would be assigned to Anzio. With clear skies forecast around Cassino on the morning of the 15th the bombing would take place then, leaving about twelve hours in

---

* The other American heavy bomber, the B-24 Liberator, also carried its bombs in a vertical arrangement, although it had twin bomb bays, each the size of the B-17's single bay. In both the B-17 and B-24 bomb-bay design was further restrained by a central longitudinal beam in the lower fuselage.

which to prepare. Dimoline was asked if he could bring forward his attack. In spite of his best efforts Dimoline could not persuade Freyberg that such a change would reduce considerably the chances of success. Kippenberger, GOC of 2nd New Zealand Division, felt that Freyberg was not really listening to Dimoline. Frustrated, the latter asked Kippenberger 'to make an appointment for us both with General Freyberg, as he thought his task was impossible and his difficulties not fully realized. The General refused to see us together: he told me he was not going to have any soviet of divisional commanders.'[38]

While Tuker might have been able to change Freyberg's mind, Dimoline was unable to do so. He was told by Freyberg that the bombing was at 4th Indian Division's request and that cancelling it meant that the division would not get air support again. Not only that, but the day-to-day delays were making New Zealand Corps look ridiculous, averred the corps commander. Told to inform Freyberg within thirty minutes if he could withdraw his forward troops to the 1,000-yard safety line and bring forward his attack on Monte Cassino, Dimoline answered that he could do neither.

Therein lay the basic problem with Freyberg's plan: with no control over the bombers he lost any advantage the bombing might have given him. The plan had been for the bombers to strike late in the day with the infantry attacking as the aircraft flew away, their last bombs having exploded, thus ensuring that the defenders would have been dazed and slow to re-organize. Moreover, it would by then have been night. The change of plan meant that the bombers would strike in the morning, making any immediate infantry follow-up suicidal. Thus the air strike would not be followed by an infantry attack. In such circumstances, Freyberg could and should have asked for the bombing to be postponed until the Indians were ready to mount an assault. He failed to do so.

***

US Army Air Forces' doctrine was for heavy bombers to fly to the target and attack in formation, a doctrine originating in part from the belief that heavy defensive armament would protect the bombers from enemy fighters. That belief had proved to be wishful thinking in northern European skies but with the Luftwaffe in Italy much diminished the danger was reduced. Nonetheless, the normal pattern of assembling the force before flying towards the target was followed. Major Evans took off at 6.55am on 15 February at the head of the thirty-seven B-17s of his group, the first of four such groups, in the largest bombing force yet sent against a small target. It took ninety minutes to assemble the bombers over southern Italy. Then, with Vesuvius, the Bay of Naples and the offshore islands visible from 20,000 feet, they set off towards their IP, the 'initial point' for the bombing run. However,

Evans, noting that they should have been a thousand feet higher, led his group in a spiral climb to reach the required altitude above the IP, a road intersection 'just north of a distinctive bend in the Volturno'.[39] By that time, streams of condensation trailed the B-17s as hot engine exhausts met colder air and water droplets from exhausts froze to form icy white contrails marking their passage through the skies. Those on the ground could see a 'perfect formation with that arrogant dignity [of] ... bomber aircraft as they set out upon a sortie'.[40]

Evans' B-17 released its bombs at 9.28am. For this 'most advertised single bombing in history',[41] a crowd of spectators had gathered.

> A holiday atmosphere prevailed ... . For almost all the men of Fifth Army, this Tuesday was a very rare day off from the war. Soldiers ... scrambled for positions from which they could watch .... Some stood on stone walls, others climbed trees for a better view. Observers – soldiers, generals, reporters – were scattered over the slopes of Monte Trócchio ... across the valley. A group of doctors and nurses had driven up in jeeps from the hospital in Naples. They settled themselves ... with a picnic of K rations and prepared to watch the show.[42]

Major Evans' bombs were probably the first to strike and seem to have landed about the entrance to the Abbey. Among those watching on the ground, Harold Bond recorded that the only sound was the drone of the aero engines since the 'land armies had stopped everything and were watching the show'. Nor did German anti-aircraft guns open fire. Bombs began falling 'like little black stones, and ... the ground all around us shook with gigantic shocks as they exploded'. Soon the Abbey had disappeared under 'a huge cloud of smoke and dust which concealed the entire hilltop'.[43] However, some watchers realized that not every bomb was falling on the intended target. Some fell among Indian soldiers waiting to assault the Abbey, causing twenty-four casualties, none of them fatal; the Indian positions were about 1,500 yards away.[44] The MAAF commander, Ira Eaker, had taken his friend Jacob Devers to watch the bombing. Both were lying on a rooftop some three miles away. Eaker's faith in 'precision bombing' must have been shaken when bombs landed close to the pair, amongst the vehicles that had carried them and their entourage.[45] Had the bombs fallen any closer, they could have preceded Leslie McNair as the highest-ranking US Army officers to die in Europe, killed by US bombers. (McNair was killed near St Lô in France in July 1944.) Clark was also fortunate to escape death by US bombs when a stick from one B-17 landed close to his command post at Presenzano, seventeen miles from Monte Cassino.[46]

The historian of 4th Indian Division recorded Brigadier Lovett's memory of a conversation with Colonel Mark Boatner of 168th Regiment, 34th Division, in the latter's command post. Told by Lovett that 7 Brigade was going to take the Abbey, Boatner opined that this might be possible if enough soldiers were thrown at it. When Lovett replied that, first of all, American bombers 'were going to destroy the monastery', Boatner pushed his cap back, bit on his cigar, placed his hands on his knees and looked at his allies sympathetically before commenting that 'Waal, if it is incumbent arn you to depend on our barmers, and I wuz in your shoes, I'd hie me back to dear old Pittsburgh.'[47] His remarks do not suggest any great faith in bombers. The author has heard similar caustic comments from two veterans of the Tunisian campaign, one from 2nd London Irish Rifles and the other from 5th *Fallschirmjäger* Regiment, albeit twenty years apart: 'When the RAF comes over,

59: A USAAF Boeing B-17 Flying Fortress over the Abbey on which bombs have already fallen. The clear day was ideal for the bombers but the timing was not suitable for an infantry assault to follow through after the bombing. (NARA)

the Germans take cover. When the Luftwaffe comes over, the Allies take cover. When the Americans come over, everybody takes cover.'[48]

The B-17s were followed by medium bombers flying from Sardinia. In the early afternoon, B-25 Mitchells and B-26 Marauders, also unopposed by anti-aircraft fire, added their contribution to the destruction. Almost 600 tons of bombs fell during the day; some eyewitnesses commented that the mediums 'were much more accurate'.[49] As well as high-explosive bombs the aircraft dropped 100lb incendiary bombs which did little physical damage but set fire to grass and growth on the mountain, in some places exposing German positions while clearing the defenders' field of fire. Allied artillery also fired on the mountain with an especially large concentration at 10.30am from II Corps artillery in a 'time-on-target' bombardment of 266 rounds from 240mm and 8-inch howitzers and 4.5-inch and 144mm guns.[50] This is described in more detail in Starr's history of Fifth Army as 'a special serenade … consisting of 5 rounds each from ten 240mm howitzers and twenty-four 8-inch howitzers and 4 rounds each from twelve 4.5-inch guns and twenty-four 155mm guns'. Starr claims that the Germans were occupying the Abbey and that while it was destroyed 'as a monument' its 'usefulness to the enemy was only impaired'.[51]

Many onlookers were convinced that they saw German soldiers fleeing from the Abbey[52] but others, including General Fred Walker, were emphatic that no Germans had been in the buildings.[53] However, the destruction caused by the bombs meant the Germans could occupy the ruins, using them as defensive positions, which they began doing two days later. Immediately after the bombing, 'German troops emerged from their shelters and occupied the ground abandoned by the Indian units when they sought safety before the bombardment'.[54]

Over the followings days, the Abbey and surrounding area was subjected to further bombing attacks, mostly fighter-bomber missions supporting ground troops. The bombardment had failed to break the Gustav Line or dislodge German troops from 'well-nigh perfect defensive positions'.[55] Rather than assisting the ground forces, the bombers made their task more difficult and their situation worse. Freyberg, who wanted an infantry attack launched as soon as darkness fell, did not know that Point 593 was still in German hands; he believed that 34th Division had taken it but, while the Red Bulls had assaulted the point they had been forced off and the small German garrison was positioned to disrupt any attack on Monte Cassino. Lovett made clear to Dimoline that he would not attack the Abbey until Point 593, 'the outer bailey, as it were, of the castle that had the monastery for its keep',[56] was in 4th Division's hands. Dimoline agreed and 7 Brigade's main attack was postponed for twenty-four hours to allow 1st Royal Sussex to secure 593, dubbed 'Monte Calvario' by its German defenders.

The decision to postpone the attack was 'a cruel one for the New Zealand Division', exacerbated by the knowledge that the delay allowed the Germans time

60: The heavy bombers were followed by medium bombers, such as this Martin B-26 Marauder. In both the attack on the Abbey and the later one on the town, the mediums proved to be much more accurate. (NARA)

to prepare for the attack. In the meantime, Lieutenant Colonel Glennie, CO of the Royal Sussex, was faced with an extremely difficult predicament. With movement by day impossible, he had to wait until nightfall to launch his assault but the terrain precluded using large numbers. Glennie chose to attack with C Company – three officers and sixty-three men – over unknown ground: the New Zealand official history notes that C Company 'was handicapped by ignorance of the ground, since daylight reconnaissance was impossible with the enemy at such close quarters'.[57] Clark criticized Glennie's tactics.

61: When the bombers flew away, this was the condition of the Abbey. However, some of the oldest parts of the building survived, including St Benedict's original chapel, on the bottom right. (NARA)

The attack was slow in getting under way and of a piecemeal character, so that the enemy was able to chop up the first thrusts and turn back the advance piece by piece. That night, for instance, the first advance was made by a single company against a commanding hill overlooking the monastery. By the time the company reached the hill the Germans had been able to rally some forces and offer opposition. The company reached the hill, but was not followed up by forces strong enough to hold it, and by early morning a counter-attack drove it off.[58]

It would have been all but impossible to deploy more than a company against Point 593. Clark, not familiar with the ground, failed to appreciate how failure to co-ordinate the bombing with the ground forces complicated the New Zealand Corps' problems.[59] Glennie's battalion was astride Snakeshead Ridge and, although 1,000 yards from the Abbey, only seventy yards separated his leading soldiers from the Germans; Point 593's peak was but another hundred yards away. Lovett's other battalions were nearby, 4th/16th Punjabis echeloned to the

A-36A 86th FG Apr 1944 (USAF via NARA)

62: Much more accuracy was obtained through the limited use of dive-bombers, North American A-36 Apaches, a version of the P-51 Mustang. A-36s would prove their worth in re-supplying the defenders of Hangman's Hill. (NARA)

left down the slope and 1st/2nd Goorkhas* held in reserve, only a few hundred yards to the rear.

C Company advanced two platoons abreast, the third following in reserve. Movement was very slow.

> On this ground there was a danger at every step of a stone being dislodged and rattling against another: and in those high places sounds of this kind were audible a long way off. On this ground, too, it was fatally easy to turn an ankle, or stumble. It was especially easy for a man laden with something heavy, such as a Bren gun. With every single step there was a danger of breaking the silence that was essential to their approach, with an alert enemy a bare seventy yards away.[60]

---

* The Regiment preferred to use this nineteenth-century spelling of Gurkha, although the latter version appeared in the *Army List*.

Hobnailed boots were certain to create noise on the rock-strewn ground and the defenders were alert for any sounds.

> The [Sussex] groped forward but when only 50 yards from their start line an impassable palisade of boulders was encountered. Intense fire at close range lashed the advance mercilessly. After several unsuccessful attempts to outflank and by-pass this obstacle the Royal Sussex withdrew.[61]

Thirty-four officers and men had become casualties to machine-gun fire and grenades. The latter were essential in such close fighting but the Sussex had insufficient. Nor had they artillery support, being too close to the enemy for the gunners to bombard the defenders.[62]

It was clear that more than a single company was needed to wrest Point 593 from the Germans and hold it against counter-attack. It was also clear that no attack could be made in daylight and that attackers required plenty of grenades while strong reserves would be necessary to defend Point 593. Nonetheless, a further attack was planned, this time with the full battalion. At least that was what Lovett called for but he failed to appreciate the terrain. Glennie deployed B Company, reinforced by a platoon from A; the remainder of A Company was to feint on the right and provide covering fire; D Company was to take over once 593 had been secured. The survivors of C Company were held in reserve.[63]

The attack was to be launched the following night, 16/17 February. Glennie would have preferred more time for reconnaissance, building up his supply of ammunition and obtaining oblique aerial photographs of his objective. However, he accepted that the pressures on Anzio meant that he had to attack that night, but insisted on a delay for the mule train to deliver a supply of hand grenades. The mules were late and the start time was twice delayed by thirty minutes. Only half the grenades requested arrived. With those doled out, the three companies moved off at 11.20pm.

Once again the Sussex suffered. Even forming up on their start line, C Company was hit by artillery fire, but Allied fire: aimed at the German artillery, some rounds failed to clear the ridgeline, exploding amongst the waiting infantry. Only D Company escaped without casualties. Following re-organization B Company advanced but met heavy machine-gun fire. Attacking with extreme courage some Sussex fought their way into the German positions but could not evict the occupants. Hand-to-hand combat ensued with some attackers falling down a small precipice and being captured. The diversionary group had also found one of these precipices but had stopped just in time. Although another group reached the rear of the peak, it encountered a larger enemy group approaching to reinforce the defenders. Eventually the struggle developed into a grenade battle in which the Germans had the advantage of a greater supply.

In the early hours the right company had suffered every officer killed or wounded and the left company was running out of ammunition. D Company was deployed, as were the survivors of C. However, D Company was not only stopped by the precipice that had halted the right company but also came under fire from both flanks. The attack having failed, the survivors withdrew to the start line. The toll was ten officers and 130 men killed, wounded or captured; twelve officers and 250 men had deployed. Over two nights 1st Royal Sussex had lost twelve of fifteen officers and 162 of 313 men in the struggle for 593: 'In two nights a fine battalion that had fought since the earliest days of the war and to which success had become a matter of routine had been cut to pieces'.[63]

Although Glennie re-organized his battalion into three smaller companies, it was clear that the Royal Sussex, having been knocked back twice, could not be asked to undertake another assault. However, the imperative to continue remained as von Mackensen's Fourteenth Army continued its push into the Anzio beachhead, penetrating a mile and a half. Thus 7 Brigade would make another attempt to take Point 593, this third effort to be made by three battalions. However, Freyberg was losing patience with Dimoline and Lovett and had already 'questioned whether the capture of Point 593 was the *sine qua non* that Lovett claimed it to be'.[64]

For the third attack 7 Brigade was reinforced by 4th/6th Rajputana Rifles and 1st/9th Gurkha Rifles, 'on loan' from 5 Brigade. Those battalions would join Lovett's 1st/2nd Goorkhas to attack on a broader front. The fresh plan was that at midnight on the 17th/18th the Rajputanas would pass through the Royal Sussex to seize Point 593, at which stage 1st Royal Sussex would follow, attacking along Snakeshead Ridge to take Point 444 at the further end of the feature, which bends like a boomerang with Point 593 at the bend. At 2.15am, under a rising moon, both Gurkha battalions would attack across the slopes towards the Abbey, their start line to the left of the Sussex. It is doubtful if any British commander would have asked any other battalion to carry out such an approach, so difficult was it with steep, boulder-strewn slopes and ravines to traverse; but the Gurkhas, 'born and bred in the foothills of the Himalayas, were the most expert mountain fighters in the Commonwealth armies. If anyone could negotiate the impossible mountain terrain, the Gurkhas could'.[65] To ensure adequate ammunition, food and water, two battalions (2nd Cameron Highlanders and 2nd/7th Gurkha Rifles) were organized as 'portering' units.

However, this was not simply a renewed 7 Brigade attack but an integral part of the planned corps attack, which Freyberg had urged upon Dimoline after the first rebuff of the Sussex.[66] As Lovett's battalions attacked, 2nd New Zealand Division would 'force the lower Rapido' and drive for the entrance of the Liri valley while 1/4th Essex and 1st/6th Rajputana Rifles of 5 Brigade would attack on the north of Cassino town to pin the German defenders 'between two fires'.[67] Elements of 34th Division were still in Cassino's northern sector.

The New Zealand Division's plan was to attack from Monte Trócchio into the town, an operation that fell to 28th (Maori) Battalion. Since the ground was inundated due to the German flooding of low-lying ground, the only suitable approach was along the railway embankment. Tanks were also to be deployed along the embankment but repairs would be necessary to demolitions carried out by the Germans, a task assigned to an engineer company following the infantry. The sappers would also clear mines and bridge the canal and the Rapido with Bailey bridges – both watercourses lay between the start line and the railway station. However, they would have to finish their work before dawn to allow tanks and anti-tank guns to reach the Maoris at the station by daylight. The New Zealand armour and the remainder of the division, under Kippenberger, waited behind Trócchio for the order to advance and exploit the Maoris' success.

> The Maoris had a special place in the New Zealand Division. They were cheerful ebullient men, with a keen sense of humour and a natural fighting spirit: great soldiers in the assault and pursuit. Temperamentally, they were the 'wild Irish' of the New Zealand Division.[68]

The corps' plan was that the two battalions of 5 Indian Brigade attacking north of the town would join with the New Zealanders while 7 Indian Brigade took Point 593 and the ruins of the Abbey and secured the heights. It was not to be.

Although the full Rajputana battalion was committed to attacking 593, they faced the same difficulties as 1st Royal Sussex. Edging along Snakeshead Ridge the Rajputs were pinned down by machine-gun and rifle fire at the base of the rock and on its lower slopes.

> They tried everything they knew to work their way round the boulders and ledges, and more than one small party succeeded in reaching the summit, but they were invariably killed or wounded. It developed into the same story as on the two preceding nights: successive small individual efforts that made no progress but always cost a few more lives. By two in the morning one company commander had been killed, two of the other three wounded.[69]

As the Rajputs fought for possession of 593 the soldiers of 1st/9th Gurkhas, who had struck out from about 300 yards to the left, were making for Point 444, their initial objective, at the end of the 'boomerang'. However, they came under crossfire from 593 and other German locations to their left. In trying to deal with the latter they came up on the left of the Rajputs but both battalions were pinned down by fire from 593 and neighbouring strongpoints above them. That left 1st/2nd Goorkhas who were approaching the Abbey via Point 450. Their final approach was via the northern slope of Monastery Hill, but first they had to descend a steep ravine. Doing so they closed on what looked like a belt of scrub. Spotted on aerial photographs, on which it appeared as a long shadowed area, this seemed out of place in a landscape where shellfire had destroyed so much vegetation. The 'belt of scrub' turned out to be part of a well-planned ambush for, as the leading riflemen approached, they were showered with grenades by Germans above and behind. As the scrub appeared to offer some cover from observation, the Goorkhas dashed for it.[70]

> the leading companies found themselves in a death trap because the scrub proved to be thorn thicket, sewn [sic] with mines and booby traps, ingeniously threaded together with trip wires. Men were blown up, killed and maimed as they floundered around in the thicket so that within fifteen minutes most of B and C Companies had been struck down. A few men broke through but had to fall back and dig in on the near side of the scrub belt.[71]

Lieutenant Colonel Showers, commanding the battalion, led his remaining two companies over the crest. Their assault met a torrent of fire and Showers, shot in the stomach, was one of many casualties. Although the survivors pressed on, taking one or two German positions, machine-gun fire from Monastery Hill stopped the Goorkhas. Those who survived until dawn consolidated close to what had been their start line under two hours earlier.[72]

Seven Brigade's attack had failed, the Rajputs suffering 196 casualties; only two of the battalion's British officers were unscathed. Losses in 1st/2nd Goorkhas were almost as heavy with 158 casualties, including twelve British and Goorkha officers. With ninety-four casualties, 1st/9th Gurkhas had the lowest casualty toll. For 448 casualties, 7 Brigade had nothing to show, the little ground gained by 9th Gurkhas being abandoned before sunrise.[73]

After the battle a story circulated that some Gurkhas had reached the Abbey walls, where they fought to the death in close-quarter combat. 'Birdie' Smith, a Gurkha officer and veteran of the Cassino battles, wrote that no evidence to support this story was ever found, but that if any Gurkhas had reached the Abbey they might have been from a platoon of C Company 1st/9th Gurkhas, commanded by Captain Arthur Bond, which had disappeared in the darkness. A wounded signaller later crawled back to state that Bond and some of his men had reached the Abbey. Since no Gurkha bodies were found there, Smith concluded that Bond's party perished on Point 593 rather than under the Abbey ruins, although Stevens suggests that they were killed on the approach to Point 569.[74]

None can gainsay the courage of those who fought on those adamantine slopes, a courage exemplified by Naik Birbahadur Thapa, 1st/2nd Goorkhas, who, although wounded severely, 'managed to burst through the copse [the booby-trapped thicket] and to seize a position in the midst of the stormtroopers' and Stretcher-bearer Sherbahadur Thapa who made sixteen trips across the deadly ground before being killed, or Lieutenant Ralph Loftus-Tottenham,* killed 'in a fearless rush' on a machine-gun post.[75]

The two battalions of 5 Brigade that were to strike towards Cassino town and link with 2nd New Zealand Division were not sent forward since the New Zealanders' attack had also come to naught. We have already seen that 28th (Maori) Battalion was to attack along the railway embankment into the south of the town, following which engineers would repair breaches in the embankment to allow tanks and artillery to follow and support them. As with the attacks in the mountains, the van of 5 New Zealand Brigade's advance was limited to two Maori companies since there was insufficient room for a larger force until the station had been secured. A possible second prong, a simultaneous crossing farther south in the vicinity of Sant'Angelo in Theodice, was considered but 'the hazards were deemed too great'.[76] An attack on a narrow front had to be accepted, contrary to divisional practice; 'the Division usually preferred to hit the enemy on a front of at least three battalions'.[77]

The success of this element of Operation AVENGER hinged on the engineers' ability to repair the remaining breaches before daylight. Reconnoitring the embankment had identified twelve breaches with engineers working to repair some of those from the 13th. Four were complete by the 16th, the engineers protected by infantry patrols and 'noise' from the artillery. There remained the major disadvantage of the narrow front but Kippenberger

> had in mind … the tactics that had won Badajos in the Peninsular War and similar fortresses. While the defence was distracted by feint attacks, a breach was made (or more than one breach) and reserves were poured into the hole. The example was that of existing divisions which had attacked successfully with single battalions and of the Germans' predilection for the stab rather than the broad blow.[78]

A broad attack was to be simulated by bringing forward supporting weapons to keep the German garrison 'passive and impressed'. Heavy and medium guns

---

* The young Irish officer was the son of Major General Freddie Loftus-Tottenham, later GOC 81st (West African) Division in Burma, who also lost a second son, John, in action in Burma with 6th Gurkha Rifles.

63: Cassino railway station in the 1930s. This attractive building was completely destroyed.
(Author's collection)

would shell the objectives first, followed by all available field guns firing until ten minutes after the infantry's H Hour. Thereafter counter-battery and harassing fire would continue for two hours; special targets were designated for machine guns and mortars. To the south the Divisional Cavalry and 24th Battalion would fire across the river as the Maoris attacked; after dawn they would lay smoke to screen the attackers.

Once the leading Maoris, B and A Companies, had taken their objectives, the tanks of 19th Armoured Regiment would follow through, a squadron to be in the station by daylight, to provide defence, with the other squadrons pushing into the south of the town and ready to climb the road to Monte Cassino to assist the Indians. This was to be followed by the division exploiting across the Gari into and up the Liri valley towards Rome.

A and B Companies left their assembly areas as the artillery opened fire at 8.45pm on the 17th. Crossing the start line after 9.30pm they made for the railway station. On an unpleasant evening they 'had to plod through the mud of the causeway and flounder across waterlogged fields and through an exasperating system of drains' and were further impeded by mines while machine guns and mortars ranged on them. Stretcher-bearers were soon busy. B Company had suffered badly in the minefields and took an hour to reach the station; A Company was also slow in reaching it. However, the Maoris pressed on. Before long the station building and the Round House had been cleared of the defenders from III/361st Panzergrenadiers. Machine guns firing from the outskirts of the town were making progress difficult and so artillery fire was called for, allowing the advance to continue. Lieutenant Colonel Young, commanding 28th Battalion, came forward at about 3.00am to check the situation and directed B Company towards its second objective. However, that objective, a group of houses on Viale Dante, was held strongly and the attacking platoon went to ground until A Company could seize the Hummocks and draw level with B on the left.

Unfortunately, A Company had been stopped at the foot of the Hummocks by a major natural obstacle, a swollen stream about twenty-feet wide, covered by wire and mines. Although this had been seen on aerial photographs its true nature had not been appreciated. A flanking route was sought, but to no avail. By 6.00am the sky was lightening and, coupled with moonlight, the attackers were exposed to enemy fire. Kippenberger ordered the Maoris to remain in position with smoke laid to conceal them.

The engineers who had gone to work behind the infantry had almost completed bridging both Rapido and canal and repairing the breaches in the embankment. However, they had suffered delays from the beginning and never caught up. In bright moonlight after 3.00am they were under enemy observation, providing good targets for marksmen. At 5.45am the entire embankment was hit by mortar and Nebelwerfer fire, killing three sappers and driving the others to cover. In spite of their strenuous efforts under fire, it was 5.00am before the bridge was complete but no vehicles could be sent across because 'work beyond the river was not far enough advanced to allow them to be usefully employed'.[79]

As day broke German mortar fire ensured that the engineers stayed under cover. Work ceased. Both companies of 28th Battalion, depleted by casualties, would have to hold out for almost eleven hours until dark with only the weapons they carried. Artillery fire could be called down but attackers and defenders were very close. Counter-attacks were launched and tanks appeared. One platoon was overrun in the station yard and by 4.00pm the survivors began withdrawing. The companies had suffered about 130 casualties while the engineers had sustained a further thirty; of a force of 200 men only sixty-six remained. All seemed to be in vain. That impression was heightened by the thought that, with the Germans still holding Monastery Hill, the opportunity for exploitation into the Liri valley was gone. Once 7 Brigade's attacks in the mountains failed the New Zealanders' efforts were also doomed. Although the Maoris had added to their reputation in the attack on the station, it had been 'a gesture which gained one small bridgehead over the Rapido but had no real significance in the overall battle for Monte Cassino'.[80]

What the New Zealanders did not then appreciate was how close they had come to success. Although the Maoris occupying a salient based on the railway station were outnumbered and overlooked by enemy defenders in the town, on the lower slopes of the mountain and on the Hummocks, the Germans were worried about the New Zealanders throwing in reserves and the possible convergence of both Allied attacks. Vietinghoff and Kesselring were prepared for the worst but the surrounding area was defended by soldiers of Baade's 90th Division and Baade had no doubt that he could carry the day. He did so by releasing 'the last possible reserves' from other sectors for the counter-attacks that forced the Maori withdrawal.[81] In a conversation after the New Zealand withdrawal von Vietinghoff told Kesselring that he had not thought 'we would do it', to which Kesselring replied, 'Neither did I.'[82]

***

Thus ended the Second Battle of Cassino. Majdalany wrote that it had demonstrated how, in history's most mechanized war, ground and weather could neutralize the machinery of modern warfare, leaving the infantryman to carry on 'with rifle, machine gun and grenade'. In spite of overwhelming superiority in tanks, artillery and airpower, and with tens of thousands of vehicles, Fifth Army had to rely on

64: Among the most capable German divisional commanders was Ernst-Günter Baade, commanding 90th Division. Baade's leadership and insight ensured that the Germans held the railway station against Allied attacks. (NARA)

the 'humble pack-mule': 'In the mountains above Cassino in February a mule was worth a dozen tanks.'[83]

Perhaps the most obvious lesson from the battle was that ground and air forces needed to work more closely together so that plans could be better co-ordinated.

This lesson was learned: the tactical use of heavy bombers in Normandy that summer showed better planning and co-ordination.

***

Freyberg was quick to call off the battle, which ended on 18 February, the day the German onslaught on the Anzio bridgehead climaxed. Mackensen's Fourteenth Army had launched Operation FISCHFANG on the axis of the Via Anziate, 'a very narrow front', on Hitler's orders.[84] Fourteenth Army had been reinforced by the arrival of 114th *Jäger* Division from Yugoslavia and 362nd Division from northern Italy, plus three independent regiments and two heavy tank battalions.[85] Supported by armour, including Tiger tanks, and aircraft, the Germans overran a brigade of the newly-arrived 56th (London) Division, transferred from X Corps, and pressed the Allied forces hard. However, the US 179th Regiment and British 1st Loyals, supported by artillery, tanks and mortars, although forced back to the final beachhead line, stopped the German advance in spite of severe losses. In turn VI Corps counter-attacked, deploying the US 1st Armored and 3rd Infantry Divisions, the latter commanded by Lucian Truscott who was soon to assume corps command, and by the 20th the offensive had been broken, at a cost of some 5,000 casualties; the Allies had suffered similar losses, including 400 killed. The narrow front demanded by Hitler had created a salient that became a deathtrap for von Mackensen's men.[86] Stalemate at Anzio thus allowed Alexander and Clark to focus more closely on Cassino.[87]

***

At Cassino 'the fortunes of the day rested with the dour and unyielding defenders'.[88] It seemed that no renewed offensive with existing manpower would succeed. Senger was very critical of the Allied planning for the second battle, summing up his criticism by writing that 'The plan was so similar to the first one (which was a combined attack by the US 36 Div. across the Rapido at S. Angelo, followed immediately by the US 34 Div. north of Cassino)'.[89]

The battle had been identified as siege warfare with the defensive ring of strongpoints at Points 593, 569 and 575 providing the German outer wall while the ruins of the Abbey formed the keep of their castle. The Maoris had launched a classic forlorn hope operation while the bombing was an echo of the use of sappers and miners in an earlier age.

Fourth Indian Division commander represented to the Corps Commander that before renewing the offensive he must re-organize with two brigades forward. General Freyberg agreed with this decision. 7 Brigade's front was defined as from Point 593 to Point 450, a distance of 800 yards fronting the main enemy defences. 5 Brigade would take over on the left of Point 450 and would carry the line along the Maiola ridge system above the valley of the Rapido.[90]

Thus the battalions of 4th Indian Division took over their new positions after a night's rest: 1st/2nd Goorkhas relieved 4th/6th Rajputana Rifles in their forward positions while 1st/9th Gurkhas set up a chain of posts between Points 450 and 445. Meanwhile 2nd Cameron Highlanders and 149th Anti-Tank Regiment accepted the role of portering and stretcher-bearing for 5 Brigade with 2nd/7th Gurkhas and 57th Light Anti-Aircraft Regiment doing likewise for 7 Brigade as divisional engineers began constructing a jeep track along the Maiola ridge into the forward area.[91]

As all this was happening, Freyberg was planning his corps' next moves.

Chapter Seven

As soon as the battle had been called off, Freyberg began planning a new offensive. His corps was being strengthened by the arrival of the British 78th Division, known as the Battleaxe Division from its divisional flash of a golden battleaxe on a black ground. Although Alexander believed that the New Zealand Corps could make one more attempt to break through, he was not overly optimistic and felt that failure would mean stopping offensive operations. In an Allied Central Mediterranean Force (ACMF) appreciation of 22 February, he noted that 'after the New Zealand Corps has shot its bolt, a certain pause in land operations will be essential to enable troops to be re-organized and prepared to continue the battle'.[1]

On the 18th, with the Anzio situation still critical, there was insufficient time to plan and execute anything other than a 'modified (and simplified)' version of recent operations. Notified that morning by Fifth Army HQ of the events at Anzio, Freyberg remarked that 'we must do our damnedest to make a diversion here'. That afternoon he told Dimoline that there was no time to reconsider the plan but the 4th Division GOC objected strongly to another attack on the Abbey and reminded Freyberg of

> the problem inherent in the siting of the defences in the Cassino promontory. A series of mutually supporting posts extended in a horseshoe eastwards from Point 575 to the monastery, and to attack without first subduing the westernmost strongpoints was simply to enter a pocket where fire poured in from all sides.[2]

This was the point at which Freyberg agreed to 4th Indian Division re-organizing on a two-brigade front, as noted on page 132. On the 19th Wilson and Alexander visited the front to see the ground for themselves. That visit led to Alexander writing an appreciation of the situation in Italy and of his plans for the conduct of the campaign. Addressed to Wilson as supreme commander, this stated that Alexander's object was 'to force the enemy to commit the maximum number of divisions to operations in Italy at the time OVERLORD is launched'.[3] Brooke wrote that day that 'the Italian attack is going well, and it should play its part in holding formations in Italy and keeping them away from the Channel'.[4]

Renewing the offensive created a dilemma for Alexander and his generals.

> I felt confident now that the bridgehead could be held, for, unless they could find fresh formations, a renewed German attack would have to be made in much reduced strength. I could concentrate therefore on Cassino and try to find some new method of taking this fortress which had twice defied our best efforts. I still had one division uncommitted, the 78th, but the weather was very bad and the Liri valley a sea of mud; it was no good putting my last fresh troops into a repetition of our former attacks unless I could produce some new tactics to give us a better chance of success.[5]

The answer was 'a really heavy air bombardment', this time on Cassino town. Major General Cannon 'was anxious to make the experiment too' and thought that, given good weather and the full bombing force in Italy, he could succeed. Although Alexander wrote that they both regarded this as an experiment 'without any certainty as to how it would work', it is likely that Cannon was more enthusiastic than Alexander.[6] Alexander discussed the plan with Clark and Freyberg and, on 20 February, decided that 2nd New Zealand Division would attempt to take Cassino following an aerial bombardment. Having gained the town, the New Zealanders would advance along Highway 6 past the southern face of Monte Cassino to link up with 4th Indian Division and close the ring around the enemy position, thus giving the Allies a strong bridgehead over the Rapido and opening the way into the Liri valley.

Other than the 'really heavy air bombardment', this was almost taking up from where Operation AVENGER had come to a halt, the main difference being that Kippenberger's New Zealanders would make the main effort on the ground and there would be no direct assault on the Abbey. Freyberg believed that 4th Indian Division's attacks had failed because the infantry had been unable to attack on a broad front whereas the Germans could quickly reinforce threatened points and concentrate defensive fire.[7] However, the bombing was to be the trump of the new assault, being of such ferocity 'as had never before been attempted in support of ground forces'.[8] Bombers would obliterate Cassino, from which the residents had long been evacuated. A fortified redoubt for the Germans, the half-mile square town was to be pounded into rubble before infantry and tanks attacked. It was hoped that no enemy soldier would survive Cassino's total destruction.[9]

With 78th Division under his command Freyberg was able to concentrate 2nd New Zealand Division on a narrow front for the advance into Cassino from the east. Meanwhile, 4th Indian Division would attack into the town from the north and once Cassino was secured those formations would advance to take Monte Cassino while 78th Division and the tanks of Combat Command B (CCB) of 1st

65: An Allied aerial photograph of Cassino, taken in November 1943, with Castle Hill in the right background. (NARA)

US Armored Division would enter the Liri valley to strike towards Valmontone. However, Clark did not agree with Freyberg's plan, commenting that he believed it to be 'absolutely impossible to mass for an attack down the Liri valley without first securing the commanding elevation on one flank or the other'.[10] Clark believed that Freyberg had 'weakened from day to day in his [belief in his] ability to take the monastery' but that the securing of the Cassino spur was essential before Allied troops could be despatched into the valley. Wilson agreed with Clark's assessment; otherwise entering the valley would be 'sticking one's head' into a trap. After discussion with Clark, Freyberg amended his plan to include an attack on Monte Cassino as the New Zealanders attacked the town.[11]

On 21 February Freyberg outlined the four phases of his revised plan: 4th Indian Division would seize Point 445, about 500 yards north of the Abbey, from where it would cover with fire Castle Hill, the western edge of the town and the eastern slope of Monte Cassino; bombers would then attack the town; 2nd New Zealand Division, supported by CCB, would capture Cassino and seize a bridgehead over the Gari at Highway 6 while the Indians took Monte Cassino and cut Highway 6 some miles west of the Gari; 4 New Zealand Armoured Brigade, under 78th Division control, would pass through the Gari bridgehead to seize Sant'Angelo from the north, after which CCB would exploit to the west along Highway 6 in the Liri valley and 78th Division would cross the river near Sant'Angelo while 36th Division kept a regiment in readiness to support the exploitation.[12]

Kippenberger, who would command the New Zealand attack into the town wrote, 'It was not a bad plan: the subsequent army report said it was the best that could have been produced in the circumstances'. However, he did note that his division, this time led by 6 Brigade, could still only attack on a narrow front 'down a single road, the ground on either side being flooded and mined, with sections in single file on either side of the road, that is on a front of two men'. Thus the battalions would have to be fed in singly rather than striking a united blow. Likewise the Indians could only advance onto Monte Cassino through the narrow entry of Castle Hill, once the New Zealanders had secured it. The craters and rubble created by the bombing would be obstacles as severe as intact buildings. Kippenberger also believed that the 610 guns available to the corps 'could have produced enough fire without waiting for the air'.[13]

Due to their importance to the operation, the air forces were to set D Day and H Hour any time after 24 February. As a prerequisite to the operation, Freyberg required a three-day period without rain, so that the ground would have dried out sufficiently to bear the weight of armoured vehicles and visibility would be adequate for the bombers and tactical support aircraft that would follow. Unlike the bombing of the Abbey, both ground and air commanders agreed a timetable of operations: the bombing would be in the morning with H Hour for the ground forces at midday. D Day would not be agreed until the meteorologists could promise weather conditions suitable for both air and ground forces to operate.[14]

What few realized was just how long it would be until optimum weather conditions occurred. Freyberg held a conference at his HQ on 21 February to discuss his plan, especially the role of the airmen. He had not learned from the bombing of the Abbey since he was convinced that 'at least 750 tons of bombs' would level the town, clearing the way for his infantry and armour 'to walk through'. The senior air officer present, Colonel Stephen B. Mack, commanding XII Air Support Command, agreed that bombers could drop that quantity of bombs and destroy the town but added two caveats: the air groups would need three hours to complete their missions since it was essential for smoke and dust to clear before each wave attacked; and the infantry would only be able to 'advance with difficulty' while armour would not be able to pass through for two days due to streets being blocked by debris. Freyberg refused to accept Mack's second caveat, insisting that he expected the tanks to pass through in no more than twelve hours. Freyberg's appreciation of bombing had not advanced since his request for three squadrons of Kitty-bombers.[15]

Freyberg's optimism regarding airpower was matched by that of one other man. General Henry H. 'Hap' Arnold, commander of the US Army Air Forces, suggested to Eaker that 'a massive air attack be launched'. Arnold recommended using all available aircraft in the theatre, including

> the Coastal Air Force, all the heavy bombers, medium bombers, and fighters of the strategic and tactical air forces – including crews in rest camps, those not yet quite ready for battle, and those in Africa – [pooled] to establish a force 'which, for one day, could really make air history'.[16]

Eaker was not so enthusiastic, responding by advising Arnold not to set his heart 'on a great victory as a result of this operation'. However, he was enthused by another plan: a bombing campaign against German coastal shipping and the road and rail networks south of the Pisa-Rimini line. This was Operation STRANGLE, to which we shall return; Eaker was confident that it would help Allied ground forces break the Gustav Line, advance on and liberate Rome and force the Germans back into northern Italy.

Nonetheless, Eaker was compelled to bomb Cassino. Determined to make the operation a success, and aware of deficiencies in the performance of his heavy bombers, he told Major General Nathan E. Twining, commanding the Mediterranean Allied Strategic Air Force (MASAF), that accuracy, formation flying and leadership had to be improved.[17]

Planning for the air and ground operations continued. The bombers would strike over a four-hour period and a heavy artillery bombardment would also occur. Some 360 heavy and 200 medium bombers would destroy Cassino and fighter-bombers would provide close support in the ground operation. As H Hour for the ground assault approached, bombing was to increase in intensity, reaching its maximum at H Hour. Freyberg also produced operational instructions for his ground forces. Concerned lest his tanks become embroiled in street fighting, he 'directed maximum use of fire and movement', an instruction that also applied to self-propelled artillery. So that Allied tanks might be more easily identified, those moving from the direction of German positions were to elevate their guns to the maximum. Such instructions applied to 4 New Zealand Armoured Brigade and the US armour of CCB, the latter deployed as two task forces. CCB had planned for exploitation, with control posts linked by radio, had chosen lines of advance and had recovery vehicles ready, but General Allen, its commander, was not optimistic, writing to Harmon, his divisional commander, who was at Anzio with the bulk of 1st Armored Division, that weather and ground conditions meant that operations would be restricted to the roads, 'only a few of which exist in [the Liri] valley'.[18]

Allen need not have worried. The weather was not co-operating with Freyberg's plans. When it was clear and dry at Cassino, airfields at Foggia might be shrouded in fog and those in Naples rained in, while the more distant airfields, in Sardinia, Corsica and North Africa, might be under thick cloud. As well as Freyberg's three consecutive dry days around Cassino for the ground forces, the overall plan required suitable weather conditions for aircraft over a much larger area; unless the ground dried out, for example, it would be impossible for heavy bombers to take off.[19]

Instead of dry weather arriving, conditions worsened. The weather broke completely: heavy rain fell on low-lying ground, increasing the boggy conditions, and making life miserable for those waiting for the news that D Day was impending. On a daily basis the attack was postponed. Bad as life was on the low ground, it became worse higher up as rain turned to sleet, then to snow at higher altitudes where strong winds created blizzards. This daily postponement meant that inter-brigade reliefs were not possible in 4th Indian Division, whose soldiers on the heights were suffering greatly.

> For three weeks while winter gales, driving snow and freezing rain pelted the exposed infantry, Fourth Division dourly waited, enduring an average daily toll of 40 to 50 casualties. No hour passed in which the crump of mortars, the whine of shells or the crack of a sniper's rifle did not herald the call for stretcher-bearers.[20]

Stevens described the outstanding courage of one Indian soldier during this period. On 24 February Subedar (Lieutenant) Subramanyan, 11 Field Park Company, Queen Victoria's Own Madras Sappers and Miners, led the 'search for an officer who was thought to have walked into a minefield' near the railhead at Mignano.

With five sappers, Subedar Subramanyan checked the ground with a mine detector, a sapper following to mark the cleared path with white tape. Suddenly there was a small explosion and Subedar Subramanyan realized that the man behind had trodden on an anti-personnel mine. Knowing that within four seconds the mine would detonate, Subramanyan 'sprang towards the man behind him and deliberately flung himself on top of the mine, at the same time endeavouring to push the other man aside'. Subramanyan's body 'largely neutralized' the force of the explosion but he suffered such severe injuries that he died minutes later. He was awarded the George Cross posthumously, becoming the first Indian recipient of the award, instituted by King George VI in September 1940.[21] * His actions were described as being 'of unsurpassed bravery, performed in an instant and without the excitement of battle'.[22]

Meanwhile 7 Brigade's soldiers in their positions on ridge crests and hillsides endured the unceasing battering of the winter elements.

> When darkness fell the men emerged from the freezing cramp of their foxholes to prepare for the next miserable day. The enemy likewise came to life, searching the trails and assembly areas with mortars and artillery fire in the hope of intercepting supply columns. Paratroopers crept forward to strike down unwary sentries, with abysmal ignorance of British psychology they tried propaganda – shouting the names of prisoners taken and promising creature comforts to all who would surrender. They likewise dropped leaflets. Often the Urdu leaflets reached the Royal Sussex and the English leaflets 4/16 Punjabis; or else they reached 1/2 Gurkhas who could read neither. In spite of their aggressiveness the Germans were feeling the strain. An officer of 31st Field Regiment picked up six prisoners on Point 593 who were only too willing to be brought in while 4/16 Punjabis every now and then found outpost sentries in a mood to surrender.[23]

There was even wry humour. A battery commander of 11th Field Regiment, who had spent 'a long and exhausting tour' in an observation post under regular machine-gun fire only a few hundred yards from the Abbey's rear walls, returned to his battery to find that his mother had written to him telling him that he should visit the famous Benedictine Abbey 'should he ever be in the neighbourhood'.[24]

***

---

* His name is given as Subramanian in the *London Gazette* and is amended from Subramanyan in the citation for his award.

For Kippenberger's New Zealanders there was 'a period of preparatory reliefs and explorations' with 6 Brigade and elements of 5 Brigade taking over positions north of Highway 6 from US troops of 133rd Regiment. These included a wedge-shaped sector, with the 'blade' forming the front, of some 500 yards, among the buildings in the north of the town. The right, or western, boundary abutted the hillside, 'resting on the positions being dug by the Indians', while the left boundary lay along Pasquale Road, running north-east from the town. The road was so named because it passed through San Pasquale village and through the barracks of painful memory for the soldiers of Ryder's 34th Division. This handover was completed, although not without difficulty, on the night of 21/22 February.[25]

The Carabinieri barracks was the rendezvous for 24th and 25th Battalions of 6 Brigade with their American guides who led them to their new positions. Their forward area was about 500 to 600 yards square with its extremities at Point 175 and at the town's eastern edge, 100 yards south of the junction of Pasquale and Parallel roads. All 6 Brigade's forward positions were overlooked by German positions on Castle Hill (Point 193). The New Zealanders used surviving walls and remnants of roofs to provide cover from surveillance while 3- and 4.2-inch mortars, 6-pounder anti-tank guns and mined road-blocks north of the town were employed as active defences. On the left of 6 Brigade an improvised force, including anti-tank gunners and machine gunners deployed as infantry under command of 27th Battalion, provided 5 Brigade's right wing, relieving 91st Reconnaissance Squadron. The force held an outpost ring some 300 to 400 yards from the Rapido which had overflowed to create a marsh, 'that most irksome of military obstacles'.[26]

Other reliefs had been carried out to the south with 24th Battalion relieving 28th (Maori) Battalion on the Rapido sector facing the railway station before, in turn, being relieved by 23rd Battalion.

> The enterprise of enemy patrols kept the New Zealand infantry on edge and tempted sentries to fire at shadows. One night, in what the Germans justifiably called 'a bold and skilful assault', a patrol from *I Battalion 129 Panzer Grenadier Regiment* ambushed Second Lieutenant Esson and a sergeant of C Company 23 Battalion on their rounds and spirited them away with such silent efficiency that the mystery of their disappearance was only unveiled after the war.[27]

At this stage 78th Division, under Major General Charles Keightley, first introduced soldiers to the Cassino front. The division had left its previous positions, and Eighth Army, in the Apennines to join the New Zealand Corps and Fifth Army in early February. Relieved by 3rd Carpathian Division of the Polish II Corps, the Battleaxe Division moved to Capua where it was complete, save for 56th

Reconnaissance Regiment, by the 19th. The divisional historian noted that this was where 'a Carthaginian army had once frittered away its victories in idleness and luxury' but this would not be the case for 78th Division in 1944.[28]

Although Freyberg intended to keep the Battleaxe Division solely for the pursuit, if possible, and therefore had prescribed no active role for it in the planned assault, it was to be ready with bridging equipment to cross the Rapido should it be required to support exploitation by 2nd New Zealand Division. In the interim, 11 Brigade relieved the New Zealand Divisional Cavalry and B Company of 23rd Battalion along the Rapido on the night of the 23rd/24th. One battalion, 1st East Surreys, moved into forward positions while the other two, 2nd Lancashire Fusiliers and 5th Northamptons, were in reserve.[29]

The Battleaxe Division expected to be advancing towards Rome as soon as the town and Monte Cassino had been taken and CCB had set off into the Liri valley.

> But the weather remained unfavourable, and day after day the attack had to be postponed. The Division trained and exercised in a dreary landscape of pools and semi-liquid quagmires until it went into the line brigade by brigade. Eleven Brigade, which was intended to lead the river-crossing in assault-boats, learnt its new trade on the stretches of grey rainwater, while patrols were already active in covering the groups of RE who were working against utterly depressing and frustrating conditions in trying to prepare reasonably solid tracks down to the river. The Germans were patrolling strongly too, and clashed time and again with patrols of the East Surreys, manning the forward positions. With a gradual inevitability the Division got sucked into the battle before the great assault was even launched. Eleven Brigade took over a sector of the river on 23 February, and 36 Brigade moved up three days later.[30]

On the other side reliefs had also been taking place. Baade's 90th Division had been handing over its positions in Cassino to Heidrich's 1st *Fallschirmjäger* Division which also relieved 90th Division on Monte Cassino and Castle Hill, as well as Colle Sant'Angelo, Point 593 and Monte Cáiro. The paratroopers were about 6,000 strong (the division's full war establishment was 16,891 men), 'well fed, well clothed and in high fettle'. Its heavy weaponry on 14 March included thirteen Italian assault guns, twenty-eight medium anti-tank guns, including eight self-propelled examples, a battery of 100mm parachute guns and one of 75mm mountain guns. Supporting artillery included two batteries of medium guns and three light batteries; 71st *Werfer* Regiment, with its multi-barrelled equipments, was also available – the regiment totalled eighty-eight barrels.

Baade's 211th Grenadier Regiment, having performed sterling service in defending the town, was relieved by II/3rd *Fallschirmjäger* Regiment, a unit that would put up a doughty defence against the New Zealanders. Third *Fallschirmjäger* Regiment's first battalion had been the first German unit to enter the Abbey after its destruction, a detachment of eighty setting up a strongpoint in the ruins on 23 February.[31]

***

In the meantime plans for the New Zealand Corps assault, codenamed Operation DICKENS, were refined. The foul weather showed no signs of abating, although it had appeared earlier as if Freyberg might get his three dry days when both the 21st and 22nd 'were fine, bracing days'. It was not to be: the 23rd broke dull and overcast with heavy rain beginning after noon and snow falling on high ground. The first of many twenty-four-hour postponements was announced. February ended with no sign of improved conditions. On 7 March a period of several dry days began but the armoured commanders now insisted that, since the ground was so saturated, four dry days would be needed for the tanks, with another two fine days for them to exploit. Clark became impatient and Freyberg considered a less ambitious operation to ease the pressure on Anzio but, by the 9th, tracks had hardened to the extent that it seemed that DICKENS might be launched on the 10th. However, the bombers were unable to fly from a waterlogged Foggia. The story was the same on the 13th, but the wait finally ended next day. The bombers would fly on the 15th. At 6.00pm on the 14th Mediterranean Allied Air Force HQ announced that D Day would be the following day: Cassino was to be obliterated on the Ides of March.[32] The code-word 'Bradman' was signalled throughout the New Zealand Corps. For weeks the signal 'Bradman won't bat today' had been received by 'all units with monotonous regularity'.[33] The action was about to begin.

***

The signal 'Bradman' cued a withdrawal of about 1,500 yards by forward elements of 2nd New Zealand and 4th Indian Divisions to the bombing 'safety line'. Once again there was a gathering of spectators with Clark and Gruenther driving to Cervaro to witness the bombing with Alexander, Devers, Eaker, Freyberg and others from an observation post 'set up in an old stone house overlooking Cassino'.[34]

As 8.30am approached the distant sound of aircraft was heard: a 'locust-like drone' in the distance, rising to an 'uncertain murmur [that] swelled gradually; a steady, pulsing throb' and then 'the specks began to appear, high and small against the sky'.[35] The medium bombers, seventy-two B-25 Mitchells and 105

B-26 Marauders, arrived first, fighter escorts wheeling high above them, their contrails criss-crossing the sky. Approaching the targets the bombers, in waves of about a dozen machines each, seemed to fly past before banking left, opening their bomb bays and dropping their bombs before banking again onto their homebound course. It was believed that about 80 per cent of the bombs from the first wave of aircraft 'fell into the heart of Cassino'. Some missed their target, landing on the Allied side of the Rapido.

Fifteen minutes later the heavy bombers, 114 B-17 Flying Fortresses and 164 B-24 Liberators, approached, as did A-36 Apache dive-bombers, and unleashed their cargoes.* The pounding lasted until noon, during which 992 tons of high explosives, a total of 2,223 thousand-pounder bombs, were dropped.

> The bomb plot confirmed that 47% of the bombs fell within one mile of the centre of the town and 53% near the town and on Monastery Hill. Some other aircraft went astray and four Fortresses and thirty-nine Liberators bombed Venafro, Pozzilli, Montaquila, and other places, all situated, as was Cassino, on the western side of a river. The similarity may have misled the pilots. Ninety-six Allied soldiers and one hundred and forty civilians were killed in these mistaken attacks. So much for the cold figures. On this morning in roaring explosions and invisible blast, under clouds of black smoke and yellowish dust the town of Cassino was blown asunder and beaten into heaps of rubble studded with the tottering remains of houses.[36]

The New Zealand official history noted casualties 'rising to as many as twenty in a single regiment … in British, American and New Zealand artillery areas' while fifty men were hit in 4th Indian Division's B Echelon in the upper Rapido valley.[37] One young subaltern of 4th Indian Division, taking cover near Point 593, felt the bombing 'was a terrifying exhibition of sound and fury'. His location should have been safe but that was not the case.

> After a few minutes I felt like shouting that's enough; but it went on and on until our ear drums were bursting and our senses were befuddled.

---

* As with the bombing of the Abbey, there are discrepancies between sources in the numbers of bombers involved, the US official history agreeing with the UK official history only on the number of B-25s; the former states 101 B-26s and 262 B-17s and B-24s. The British total of 455 is twenty greater than its American equivalent. Starr does not quantify the mediums but gives an overall figure of 503 bombers, including 120 B-17s and 140 B-24s.

Several bombs fell on my company and I found myself shouting curses at the planes. The chance of being killed or maimed by one's own side is somehow more terrifying even if the end result is the same. 'Dear God, take pity on those poor devils in the town.'[38]

'Birdie' Smith also noted that bombs had fallen in the Allied gun lines, in 4th Indian's B Echelon – where fifty men and 100 mules became casualties – as well as on a Moroccan hospital and the town of Venafro, ten miles south of Cassino, which lay at the foot of a hill resembling Monte Cassino.[39] Such errors were described by Clark as an appalling tragedy which he attributed to 'poor training and inadequate briefing of crews'.[40] The Venafro incident, involving a number of aircraft, killed seventeen soldiers and forty civilians and injured seventy-nine soldiers as well as a hundred civilians. Venafro was also the site of Eighth Army's tactical headquarters, which had moved there from Vasto on 11 March. The move had been completed on the 13th, in time for the HQ to be bombed two days later; there was immense desolation and one officer expressed his bitterness 'against the American Liberators, especially when they tried to do it again about ½ hour later'. Eighth Army's commander, Leese, was away from his HQ at the time, watching the bombing.[41]

The US official history is critical of the heavy bombers:

The medium bomber attacks were generally punctual, their bombing concentrated and accurate. The heavy bombers were often at fault on all three counts. Thus, the target received less than the full weight of the bombs dropped. Only about 300 tons fell into the town … . The remainder landed on the slopes of Monte Cassino and elsewhere. … In addition, there were frequent and long pauses between the attacking waves.[42]

Nonetheless, the bombing had razed the town. More was to come: a massive artillery bombardment with over 800 guns and howitzers ready to support the infantry and armour as they attacked into the ruins and support from fighter-bombers of the Desert Air Force and XII Air Support Command. Cloud cover in the afternoon prevented further heavy bomber strikes at targets to the rear of the town but the fighter-bombers were able to attack. Between 1.00 and 3.00pm forty-nine machines dropped eighteen tons of bombs on the railway station while, between 1.45 and 4.30pm, no fewer than ninety-six A-36 Apaches, P-40 Warhawks and P-47 Thunderbolts struck the Colosseum area south of the town with forty-four tons, and thirty-two A-36s and P-47s bombed Monastery Hill's forward slopes. Other targets received thirty tons from sixty-six A-20 Havocs and P-40s.

66: A formation of Consolidated B-24 Liberators of the US 15th Air Force. As well as taking part in the bombing of Cassino in March, Liberators played a major role in Operation STRANGLE, the bombing attacks on German lines of communication. (NARA)

The artillery opened fire at noon, firing concentrations on a range of targets, including enemy artillery, and following that with a rolling bombardment by the New Zealand Corps 25-pounders, 144 guns in all; this commenced at 12.40pm and the guns 'crept' their fire from one end of the town to the other ahead of the advancing troops. In the eight-hour period beginning at midday almost 196,000 rounds were fired by New Zealand and X Corps artillery, supported by US II Corps and the CEF.[43] Freyberg was confident that the bombing and artillery bombardment would neutralize the Cassino garrison; those not killed by the bombs and shells would be too shocked and dazed to offer cohesive resistance. In this he was mistaken.

> The bombing was an erroneous concept inasmuch as it failed to destroy all life in Cassino. The bombing of the Abbey had already shown that the many arched cellars provided secure shelters because aircraft bombs are not designed to penetrate deep into the ground.
>
> At Cassino the bombing was not directed against frightened refugees but against the Wehrmacht's toughest fighting men. The 1 Parachute

67: Bombs fall on Cassino, reducing the town to rubble, as a prelude to Operation DICKENS. Once again heavy bombers preceded the mediums, the latter being more accurate. Dive-bombers and fighter-bombers also deployed. (NARA)

Rifle Division had slowly relieved 90 Pz. Gren. Div., thus allowing the new troops gradually to familiarize themselves with the terrain. Their commander, General Heidrich, had taken over on 26 February.[44]

Many of Colonel Heilmann's II/3rd *Fallschirmjäger* Regiment's soldiers had been killed, caught in the open by bombing or shelling. Both Heidrich and Heilmann were convinced that nothing could survive the aerial and artillery onslaughts.[45] Stevens noted that it was believed that a battalion of Heilmann's regiment 'died to a man in the ruins of Cassino'. Many, however, had survived and, although dazed, recovered quickly. Sheltered in basements or bunkers, they waited for the bombing to end before crawling out. Böhmler summarized the battalion's losses: of 300 men and five guns it had mustered the previous day, some 160 men and four assault guns had been buried under the rubble. No.7 Company had suffered the heaviest losses with only 'a mere handful' surviving the bombing and shelling; survivors were cut off but some fought their way back to their own lines. No.6 Company had no losses but the other companies were each reduced to fifteen or twenty men. No.6 Company's survival, fortuitous for them, proved disastrous for the New Zealanders. When the bombers had

68: Artillery fire followed the bombing with heavy artillery that included fire from weapons such as this Royal Artillery 7.2-inch howitzer firing 202lb (92kg) shells. (9th HAA Regiment Archive)

first appeared the company had been in reserve with the battalion's battle HQ in the cellars of a substantial building, the Excelsior Hotel. When the first wave of bombers had departed, Major Foltin, commanding the battalion, had transferred his HQ staff and No.6 Company 'to a rock cavern at the foot of the monastery hill'.[46] However, regimental HQ had no idea of the fate of the battalion since wireless contact had been lost, telephone lines destroyed and runners could not get through.

Regimental HQ had also lost touch with von Senger's HQ. Heidrich, knowing that he could not give his men any support other than artillery fire during daylight

69: The bombing of March 1944 is commemorated by this stone in Cassino. (Author's photo)

hours, decided that this was his most important task. He believed that he would have a clearer idea of the situation in the town by evening, which would allow him to deploy his reserves. First, however, he committed the bulk of his artillery to firing on Cassino and engaging New Zealand concentrations in the northern sector of the town and outside it. His artillery included 71st *Werfer* Regiment, commanded by Lieutenant Colonel Andrae, which proved exceptionally effective with its 'shrieking salvoes and plunging fire [having] the same effect as carpet bombing'. This brought the attackers to a standstill, while fire from heavy anti-aircraft guns at Aquino airfield added to Andrae's rockets.[47] Senger was at Aquino and left there on foot to join Heidrich and Heilmann at the latter's command post, about a mile and a half south of Monte Cassino. He had a difficult journey on which his 'only accompaniment [was] the jarring explosion of shells, the whistling of splinters, the smell of freshly thrown-up earth and the well-known mixture of smells from glowing iron and burnt powder'.[48] From time to time he was aware of hidden batteries, their gunners dashing from cover to man their weapons for sudden bombardments. He was reminded of the Somme in 1916 and commented that Hitler was right in describing Cassino as the only battlefield 'of this war that resembled those of the first'.[49]

The intensity of the German fire, combined with the tenacity of the surviving paratroopers, stopped the New Zealanders. As evening fell it was clear that the defenders had won the day, as an OKW communiqué reported:

> On the southern front, after an exceptionally heavy air attack, the enemy, strongly supported by tanks and artillery, attacked Cassino. The attack failed in the face of the heroic resistance of the 3 Parachute Regiment under Colonel Heilmann and the effective support afforded to him by 71 Mortar Regiment under Colonel Andrae.[50]

In spite of this note of triumph in OKW's report, most of Cassino was in Allied hands by the end of the day. The Germans held only the town centre and railway station but those were critical to the New Zealanders' plans. To pass through Cassino along Highway 6, the Allies had to fight their way through the centre of the town and secure the railway station.

***

After noon, and the bombers' departure, the New Zealand infantry and armour attacked, led by 25th Battalion, of 6 Brigade, and the tanks of B Squadron, 19th Armoured Regiment. Lieutenant Colonel MacDuff's infantry moved southwards down Caruso Road 'at a brisk walking pace' with A and B Companies in the van, moving in single file with A on the left; this was the axis of advance used previously by 34th Division. The remainder of 25th Battalion took position in an old quarry north of the town while both leading companies and their supporting tanks moved towards Cassino under cover of the bombardment and a smokescreen. Although they regained their old positions unopposed 'a challenge awaited them' beyond the line of the jail as German defenders opened fire with rifles and machine guns from Castle Hill and from the debris of the town. The old axiom that no plan survives first contact proved itself true once again: at 1.00pm the wireless link with battalion HQ was lost, and remained so all afternoon. Runners could not get through and infantry and tanks lost contact with each other. However, all knew to keep moving southward, with the mountain to their right.[51]

As 2nd New Zealand Division went into action in the renewed assault on the town, it did so with a new commander. On 2 March Howard Kippenberger had attended a corps conference in the early afternoon, after which he and his ADC, Frank Massey, went up Monte Trócchio. Returning down the mountain Kippenberger trod on a mine which exploded, blowing off one foot, injuring the other and tearing a thumb. Massey was injured slightly. Kippenberger lost both feet as the injured one had to be amputated, with the lower parts of both legs. He was succeeded as GOC by Brigadier Parkinson while Lieutenant Colonel Bonifant assumed command of 6 Brigade. The loss of Kippenberger was 'seriously felt' in the division 'to the great distress of all New Zealanders in the field'.[52]

There was to be no simple progress into and through Cassino as Freyberg had intended. Phillips wrote that any contested advance in an urban setting is at best 'a staccato sequence of pauses under cover and dashes for fresh cover'. In Cassino most remaining cover was held by Heilmann's soldiers.

> The way forward to the next breathing space lay over ground that slowed down infantry and exposed them to short-range fire. They had to plunge down cavernous craters up to sixty feet across, scramble over piles of debris or find a way round, get on through churned mud and keep direction under the pall of smoke whose protection alone made advance possible.[53]

The determined survivors of Heilmann's battalion showed remarkable ardour and ingenuity. With most of their heavy weapons destroyed, they relied on their personal weapons and artillery support. One NCO, however, ensured that at least one heavy weapon would oppose the Allied advance. Oberfeldwebel Neuhoff had a StuG III reverse into the reception area of the ruined Continental Hotel; this faced down Highway 6 as the road approached the base of Monte Cassino. With machine guns and mortars sited to cover every approach, Neuhoff created an impassable roadblock. Described by Böhmler as 'an outstanding platoon commander' who was not prepared to give an inch to the attackers, Neuhoff's defence was critical in preventing 26th Battalion crossing Highway 6 inside the town and advancing southwards; the battalion was stopped at the hotel while 24th Battalion, moving to support it, 'also failed to make any impression'.[54] This operation was ordered by Bonifant, commanding 6 Brigade, with the intention of pressing on towards the railway station and the 'Hummocks'. As well as Neuhoff's post in the Continental Hotel, other factors militated against 26th Battalion. It was already dark, craters had been filled by rain and progress was very difficult. The leading company took three hours to advance 650 yards. Eventually the entire battalion assembled along Highway 6 ready for an attack at daybreak.[55]

Lieutenant Colonel McGaffin's 19th Armoured Regiment had deployed B Squadron to support 25th Battalion onto the first objective, codenamed *Quisling*, after which A Squadron was to work with 26th Battalion's advance to *Jockey*, the second objective. Also under command of McGaffin's HQ were the guns of 392 Self-Propelled Battery, 98th Field Regiment, to provide close support. Although the armour advanced initially on both Caruso and Parallel roads, when the leading troop on the latter found the road cratered so badly that it was impossible to carry on all tanks had to use Caruso Road. Although obstructed by a bomb crater, a diversion was found and the tanks advanced towards Cassino, albeit thirty minutes behind the infantry. However, the leading troop, finding an insurmountable wall of rubble at the edge of the town, had to stop beneath Castle Hill.[56]

70: Little recognizable was left of Cassino as this image of the castle ruins overlooking the devastation of the town shows. (NARA)

Finding some progress possible on the left flank 8 Troop wound its way through a maze of 'ragged skeletons of buildings, then nose down into pits and nose up over heaps of rubble, like a flotilla headed into a stormy sea'. With commanders reconnoitring and guiding on foot, and covered by a smokescreen laid by C Squadron from Pasquale Road, the troop reached the boundary road east of the Convent (actually the Chiesa del Carmine, or Carmelite church) by 2 o'clock and was ordered to move south-west. Although Major Leeks led on foot and called for sapper assistance to make a path, the sappers were unable to enter the town due to continuous fire from Castle Hill. Crews dismounted to clear a path.[57]

***

Böhmler commented on the New Zealand advance, noting how the infantry 'advanced gaily and for the most part in close formation' while tank commanders stood upright in their turrets as if they were on parade, although the latter practice was common for British tank commanders. However, such a practice ensured that commanders were the first targets for German riflemen and those who survived the fire hastily dropped into their turrets, slamming hatches over their heads. Once the Allied bombardment had passed, *Fallschirmjäger* left their shelters and, from whatever cover was available, engaged the infantry.[58]

The supporting creeping bombardment was extended for almost ninety minutes on its final line but ceased at 3.30pm. It was too far ahead of the leading infantry to provide effective cover. The plan had been for the infantry to advance at a rate of a hundred yards every ten minutes but they found that it took an hour to cover a hundred yards, so determined was the opposition and so difficult the ground. Soldiers had to negotiate bomb craters, crawl round or over mounds of rubble and squelch through mud.[59] Rather than aiding the armour/infantry ground attack the bombing had given the Germans excellent defensive positions and the best anti-tank obstacle they could have asked for. Meanwhile German artillery added its weight to the punishment being meted out to the New Zealanders. Fighting was bitter and close quarter with grenades being used by both sides.

The tanks' advance had become a separate battle. Not only did commanders have to take cover from German riflemen but they also had to fight through masses of rubble. That meant that officers had to guide tanks through the rubble

> with crews at times dismounted to ply pick and shovel, with tanks in the last resort charging like bulls against obstacles, [but] little progress was made. When darkness fell three troops … were entangled in the ruins … and the rest of the regiment was banked up along the two roads which entered the town from the north.[60]

In spite of all their difficulties the New Zealanders made some progress. By nightfall the infantry had advanced some 200 yards into the ruins and all but reached Highway 6. However, the plan had been that they should have been in the town centre by 2.00pm. There was one high point when D Company 25th Battalion captured Castle Hill (Point 193) in what Phillips describes as 'a brisk, resourceful action', Molony as 'a brilliant escalade' and Böhmler as 'a hard fight' that overwhelmed the garrison. Molony noted that, in spite of the action being so hard, 25th Battalion's losses were light with only forty-one casualties sustained. Twenty-two prisoners were taken in the Castle.[61]

The tanks had also made some progress. Eight Troop had advanced a short distance and 'for the first time' provided direct support to the infantry by shelling German positions around the Convent. However, another crater barred the route ahead and the following 5 Troop moved out to 8 Troop's left to advance south along the eastern boundary road, only to be foiled by further cratering. At that stage Major Leeks was wounded by rifle fire; Major McInnes came forward to relieve him with orders from the commanding officer to 'keep cracking'.[62]

The squadron was dispersed with troops in different locations, largely ignorant of where the forward infantry positions were. Tanks also made good targets for enemy artillery. In addition they suffered from bombs dropped by American fighter-bombers falling close to the leading tanks or blocking the road behind them. McInnes had reconnoitred towards Highway 6 and reached the conclusion that 'further armoured advance was at present impossible'. On a further recce mission, McInnes was wounded and Lieutenant Carey took command of the squadron.[63]

As darkness fell it was clear that Freyberg's plan had not worked out as he had intended. Although there were infantry in the town, Castle Hill was in New Zealand hands, and some tanks were also in the town, another setback befell the plan when rain began to fall. The forecast had been wrong: torrential rain fell on Cassino. Every bomb crater became a pool. Fighting died away slowly and 26th Battalion's advance came to a standstill. It seemed as if the weather was on the side of the Germans.

> If General Heidrich had had the power and the ability to call for rain at any stage in the Third battle then it is doubtful if he would have changed the date and time that Fate selected on his behalf. The heavy rain lashed down, turning craters into ponds, ponds into small lakes, and making the engineers' task of clearing one narrow approach route through the rubble doubly difficult. No glimmer of moonlight appeared so that confusion, always likely in any night operation, was increased.[64]

71: Another image shows the wreckage of a Panzer IV in the area of the present-day Via San Giacomo; it was knocked out by US tanks close to the jail on 3 February. (NARA)

Meanwhile, 4th Indian Division's 5 Brigade was going into action as darkness fell. Each of Brigadier Bateman's three battalions was assigned a task, 1/4th Essex, under Lieutenant Colonel Noble, deploying to relieve the New Zealanders on Castle Hill before seizing Point 165, some 300 yards above the hill, at one of the hairpin bends on the road up to the Abbey. The sector had been held by 2 Company 3rd *Fallschirmjäger* Regiment which had been wiped out, only one survivor reaching the Abbey bearing the news of the fate of his comrades. Then 1st/6th Rajputana Rifles, commanded by Lieutenant Colonel West, were to pass through the Essex to take Point 236, another hairpin above 165 and some 300 yards distant. Finally 1st/9th Gurkhas were to pass through the Rajputs, advance another 600 yards and seize Point 435, Hangman's Hill.[65]

    The timing of 5 Indian Brigade's operation was unfortunate with pitch darkness and heavy rain adding to an already difficult task. Moving off at 6.15pm on the 15th,

72: An oblique aerial photograph of Cassino and the castle marked to show the areas of operations of units of 2nd New Zealand Division; the bombing made nonsense of all the careful planning. (NARA)

the Essex had to negotiate a steep ascent and overcome small groups of Germans en route. (As Birdie Smith points out, 'steep' really meant a climb of 500 yards for every 1,000 horizontal yards.[66]) Not until midnight did one company relieve the New Zealanders on Castle Hill. C Company, under Major D.A. Beckett, held the Castle while A secured the approach from the edge of town and D Company secured Point 175, across the ravine behind and to the north of the ancient structure; B Company was in reserve to the north. At 3.00am C Company was sent forward to the south-west to attack Point 165, which it seized. Thus 5 Brigade held the route 4th Indian Division would use to enter the battle.[67]

A and B Companies of the Rajputanas had passed through 'the turmoil around and on Castle Hill' at 11.50pm on the 15th. They had already been caught in heavy enemy fire on the outskirts of the town with C and D Companies being scattered by the fire; neither reached the battalion's destination and were dispersed in little groups along the town's northern approaches. A Company left the Castle at 2.45am to cross the hillside and attack Point 236, the second hairpin, a position that would be vital to the divisional operation as 'Its possession opened the slopes for a drive upwards towards Hangman's Hill and ended intimate enemy surveillance of the Castle area'. By 4.30am on the 16th the Rajputs were nearing their objective but, with under 150 yards to cover, they were spotted. Heavy rifle and machine-gun fire swept the hillside. When defensive artillery fire was added, A Company was forced to withdraw to the Castle.[68]

That left 1st/9th Gurkhas, whose commanding officer, Lieutenant Colonel Nangle, had been ordered to support the Rajputs and then continue the attack towards Hangman's Hill. When he learned that only two Rajput companies had reached Castle Hill, Nangle deployed his C and D Companies with the former skirting the edges of Cassino onto the hillside, thereafter being lost to sight. D Company was sighted by an enemy machine-gun team which opened fire, causing fifteen casualties among the Gurkhas in less than a minute. Before the company commander could re-organize D Company to resume its advance, dawn had broken, making forward movement impossible.[69]

C Company of 1st/9th Gurkhas was out of touch and out of sight with no one knowing its fate. Not until the following morning was it known that the Gurkhas had reached Hangman's Hill. Their presence was discovered when Corps HQ asked if it would be safe to fire on the hill. The gunners chose not to fire without clearer information about the missing Gurkha company. During the afternoon came reports that figures could be seen 'below the gibbet platform' and then a faint wireless signal brought the news that 20-year-old Captain Michael Drinkall and his Gurkhas had found their way across the hillside, evading enemy defences, to seize the prominence which lies not far from the Abbey. Later it was learned that Drinkall's men, in two groups, had climbed towards Hangman's Hill and met only a single German outpost, which was eliminated by a volley of grenades that brought no retaliation from other posts. By dawn C Company held Hangman's Hill, less than 300 yards from the Abbey, and settled down to defend it.[70]

During the night there was another daring but small operation when Lieutenant Angus Murray of 4 Field Company and Sergeant Alan Morris of 20th New Zealand Armoured Regiment set out to reconnoitre 4th Indian Division's battlefield to ascertain if tanks could traverse the hillside. Evading enemy strongpoints at the hairpin bends, they examined the winding road to Hangman's Hill before descending into Cassino to find themselves in the midst of enemy soldiers.

In a dugout in a ruined building Sergeant Morris captured a prisoner. While exploring an underground passage he fell riddled with bullets. A Wild West pistol duel followed in which Lieut Murray killed three Germans. In a running fight in the early dawn he outfooted his pursuers and returned safely to the Castle.[71]

Murray and Morris's reconnaissance had taken them deeper behind German lines at Cassino than any other Allied soldiers to that time. However, Murray's report on his return was that Monte Cassino was impassable for tanks except by the road.[72]

Thus 5 Brigade had marked out the ground from which 4th Indian Division would do battle, with 1/4th Essex, two companies of 1st/6th Rajputana Rifles and two companies of 1st/9th Gurkhas in the forward positions. The Essex held the Castle and Point 165, with the Rajputs also at the Castle, Drinkall's Gurkha company on Hangman's Hill and the remainder of the Gurkha battalion forming a rough perimeter close to the Rajputs' HQ and behind the Castle area. Both scattered Rajput companies would be withdrawn to the upper Rapido valley for re-organization.[73]

Chapter Eight

The battle continued on the 16th. Heidrich, with an excellent bird's eye view of the battlefield, 'could follow every move below him as intimately as a player above a chess board'. He concentrated his force in the critical area around Castle Hill, moving troops from the Monte Castellone area and preparing to strengthen his line at any threatened point. The sectors his *Fallschirmjäger* held could be reinforced with relative ease; troops could be moved to Monastery Hill via the ravine north of Castle Hill and by streambeds, while additional troops could filter into the town along Highway 6. German artillery and mortars were directed on the town's northern approaches while the *Fallschirmjäger* 'were told that they were to stand firm man by man until death closed on them'.[1]

Allied artillery tried to spoil Heidrich's overview by laying a smokescreen below Point 236. Thus covered, 1st/6th Rajputana Rifles made another attempt to take the strongpoint, but met a firm rebuff. Almost as soon as the Rajputs left cover they were lashed with heavy fire from many directions. Simultaneously battalion HQ was struck by a mortar round, wounding five officers, including Lieutenant Colonel West and the adjutant. Major P.R. Inwood immediately took command. During the day the scattered C and D Companies were extricated by Major Marshall for re-organization in the upper Rapido valley.[2]

Fourth Indian Division's units consolidated positions to meet counter-attacks while preparing for further advances. The corps artillery maintained a counter-battery programme whilst also hitting at the German defences. The US official history notes that 71st *Werfer* Regiment suffered heavily on the 16th with almost all its equipments knocked out. In part this can be attributed to the high visibility of the rocket launchers which created great clouds of dust and smoke on discharge, making them easier for observers to pinpoint. Blumenson also quoted a German source as saying that the Allies appeared to be using 'the tactics of El Alamein; namely concentrated fire from planes and guns, and infantry attacks on a narrow front'.[3]

Allied tactical aircraft were also punishing the defenders. The weather was good on the 16th, allowing 133 medium bombers and 167 fighter-bombers from US Twelfth Air Force and the British Desert Air Force to strike at gun positions. Fighters ensured that German aircraft were unable to attack the Allied troops, a task they had performed for the bombers over Cassino on the 15th. Targets for the day included artillery positions at Belmonte, Aquino, Pontecorvo and

73: An American soldier examines a captured Nebelwerfer. The rocket-launchers were crude but effective. (NARA)

Pignataro in the Liri valley and some points south-west of Monte Cassino, as well as Atina. However, opposing forces were so close that air support from the fighter-bombers was not possible.[4] In addition, the air forces were involved in Operation STRANGLE, interdicting the enemy's logistical train.

Once the presence of Drinkall's Gurkha company on Hangman's Hill was confirmed, a new task presented itself to 4th Indian Division: reinforcing and maintaining those men. Two companies, A and B, of Rajputs were to make another attempt to take Point 236 while the remainder of 1st/9th Gurkhas would follow C Company and infiltrate to Hangman's Hill.

74: Pilots of 332nd Fighter Group discuss a mission. The group's African–American airmen, the first black personnel to serve as pilots, gained fame as the Tuskegee airmen. (NARA)

> It would be an exaggeration to suggest that the toehold near the Abbey was a great gain but equally it was an opportunity to try to force open a way to the Abbey, and this might be achieved by sending the rest of the battalion to Hangman's Hill – as originally planned. On hearing this, Major Evans of the Ninth wrote: 'We thought what a bloody relief it was to get out of the town where we were losing men and achieving nothing'.[5]

At the same time the New Zealanders were to keep the Germans in the Continental Hotel occupied. Corps artillery provided cover for all these operations, and concentrations of fire on the mountainside at 7.00pm.

At 9.00pm the Rajputs' A and B Companies began climbing from Point 165 and an hour later, after hard fighting, 'stormed the upper hairpin bend'. However, insufficient ammunition and casualties meant they could not exploit up the slopes beyond Point 236 where the defenders were rallying. A counter-attack could be expected. As the Rajputana companies fought their way to and onto Point 236, the Gurkhas began their trek towards Hangman's Hill. It was difficult: the companies had to move up through the Castle and along the mountainside in single file on a clear moonlit night,

75: MAAF bombers strike at Siena's railway marshalling yards in Operation STRANGLE. (NARA)

a slow and frustrating business. When the leading soldiers left the outskirts of the town they found that the track leading up to Castle Hill was being fired on by German snipers so that an alternative way into the Castle had to be found. The original curtain walls ran from the fort down the side of the hill and were obstacles until a hole was found through which, one by one, the Gurkhas passed and thence made their way up to the Castle itself. It was nearly 0400 hours on the 17th March before the whole force had reached the Castle and was ready to cover the last part of the journey up to join C Company on Hangman's Hill.[6]

A and B Companies of the Rajputana Rifles had suffered several counter-attacks and, running low on ammunition, withdrew to 'a none too securely held Point 165'.

However, C and D Companies seized Point 202, holding it tenaciously throughout the daylight hours of 17 March. The Rajputs' battles were instrumental in the Gurkhas crossing the mountainside below the Indians and above the Continental Hotel to Hangman's Hill with little interference from the Germans. On their journey the Gurkha companies adopted a 'sort of open formation' but were shelled intermittently from below by one Allied tank crew who, presumably, believed that the slopes above Castle Hill were all German-held.[7]

The leading elements of 1st/9th Gurkhas reached Hangman's Hill just before dawn where the battalion deployed with C and D Companies on the platform of the knoll. A Company covered the road bend to the left and B the feature's northern slopes. Hardly had the reinforcements arrived than the Germans counter-attacked from the Abbey. However, the *Fallschirmjäger* hit the centre of the Gurkha positions, where there was strength in depth, and were rebuffed. With the Rajputanas losing Point 236 the slopes were under German control but a substantial Allied force still held Hangman's Hill. The Germans were determined to knock the Gurkhas off Hangman's and the Essex out of the Castle.

The Gurkhas on Hangman's Hill were in a precarious position, especially C Company who had been forty-eight hours in action with only a day's rations and water. Thus it was necessary to establish a battalion re-supply chain. As night fell on the 17th a pioneer company deployed as porters, as did a Bengal Sappers and Miners company, to re-supply the Essex at the Castle. Escorted by A and D Companies of 4th/6th Rajputana Rifles, they set out to take supplies to 1st/9th Gurkhas. The column moved down the Rapido valley but came under fire, suffering nineteen casualties. At 10.10pm they finally reached the Castle and ninety minutes later the pioneers began moving out from there along the mountainside. Once again the Germans intervened, launching a heavy raid on the lower hairpin bend at Point 165. Although this raid suffered repulse, enemy mortar and shellfire continued striking along the slopes and the pioneer porters refused to leave the Castle. This refusal was reported by Lieutenant J.R.M. French MC at 1.45am on 18 March whereupon the escorting companies of 4th/6th Rajputana Rifles were ordered to fight their way across to the Gurkhas on Hangman's Hill. A party of gunners from 11th Field Regiment volunteered to help with portering duties. Under Sergeant Parfitt they reached the Gurkhas and when they returned next night Parfitt brought a wounded Gurkha officer with him.[8]

Although the New Zealanders were pressing hard against the town's defenders, German snipers and machine-gun teams were slipping into the ruins on the northern edge of Cassino and from there sweeping the slopes above them with fire. With their targets including the Castle gateway, such was the persistence of their fire that it was possible only to leave the Castle in single file and at the double. Thus the Rajput companies faced this threat as well as mortar bombs and shells along the mountainside as they left the Castle to take succour to the Gurkhas.

> The infantry shouldered as much of the porters' loads as could be carried and moved off to run the gauntlet. Three hours later a welcome message reported that with the loss of eight men the supply party had got through. It was too late to return before dawn so the Rajputanas spread out among the Gurkhas and spent the day on Hangman's Hill.[9]

In addition to the loads carried by the Rajputs an airdrop was made on the afternoon of 18 March when forty-eight aircraft dropped containers on Hangman's Hill. Although the drop zone was very small, the airmen performed well and, guided by coloured smoke, most of the containers were on target. Although many then bounced down the hillside out of reach of the defenders, enough were retrieved to improve the garrison's situation. The aircraft involved were USAAF A-36 Apache dive-bombers which, between 18 and 24 March, flew 191 supply-dropping sorties. Each dropped two containers, suspended on parachutes.[10]

**

The fighting in Cassino was intense from the 16th to the 18th as the New Zealanders tried to winkle out the defenders. While Freyberg and Parkinson

76: A USAAF ground-crew member checks a drop-tank on an A-36 Apache being prepared to drop supplies to the garrison of Hangman's Hill. (NARA)

77: Soldiers on Hangman's Hill scramble to retrieve supplies dropped by Apaches before they tumble over the edge. (NARA)

anticipated a southward thrust by 6 Brigade, to clear the town and the area south of it, including objectives such as the Colosseum, the Baron's Palace, the railway station and nearby Hummocks, and an attack by 5 Indian Brigade to seize the hairpin bends on the road up to the Abbey plus Points 236 and 202, from which line an assault on the Abbey's ruins could be launched, this was not be be. Rather than developing operations at corps and divisional levels, the fighting became a tactical affair controlled by company, platoon and section commanders. Why? In the town's ruins radio-telephone and landline communications had all but broken down while runners could not make fast progress through the obstacle course of devastated streets. Similar communications difficulties beset 5 Indian Brigade on the high ground.[11]

In Cassino the fighting began with a two-company-strength advance co-ordinated by 24th and 25th Battalions. Both companies advanced across Highway 6 at 6.15am to clear the area below Castle Hill and the nearby Botanical Gardens where Highway 6 turned sharply to the south. Bitter, slow fighting, supported by tanks from 19th Armoured Regiment, led to the capture of some houses and the Convent just to the south of Highway 6. The tanks had entered Cassino from the east, having crossed the Rapido over a bridge constructed by 48th US Engineer Battalion during the night of the 15th/16th. Engineer tanks, carrying folding bridges, had seen the Shermans across some lesser obstacles. But no great progress was made; engineers were unable to clear tracks through the rubble for tanks since the area was swept

78: The hairpin bends on the road to the Abbey and the high ground overlooking them also played their part in the battles. This is the fourth hairpin after Castle Hill. (Author's photo)

by enemy fire at close range. Another problem was that *Fallschirmjäger* still had a firm grip on the railway station and the Hummocks.[12]

Meanwhile Brigadier Bateman had proposed the plan that saw the Rajputana Rifles attack Point 236 and 1st/9th Gurkhas reach C Company on Hangman's Hill. This had been accepted by Sandy Galloway, acting GOC of 4th Indian Division, who had relieved Dimoline on 9 March, and by Freyberg who then ordered 6 Brigade to continue its advance on the 17th. When it was suggested that more infantry should be committed in the town, Freyberg rejected the idea, believing that enough foot soldiers were already fighting in a confined space.[13]

Senger considered this a tactical mistake by Freyberg, writing that such mistakes 'made our task less difficult'.[14]

> The slow tempo of the first infantry attack was in line with the reluctance to throw in reserves at the very places where the attack needed backing. During the first two days the enemy had no battalion staff in the town. This went against our principles. With us, if the situation demanded it, the battalion commander would normally be seen in the front line, sometimes even rushing out of his bunker armed with a hand grenade,

like any patrol leader. Thus he could be expected to send back tactically relevant situation reports and to make his own decisions.[15]

The senior German commanders had little information from Cassino in the first two days, von Senger noting that Heilmann's men were not in the habit of 'reporting the smaller losses of ground, because they hoped soon to recover it'. However, reports from XIV Panzerkorps' artillery supporting the *Fallschirmjäger* were more accurate.[16] Vietinghoff and Westphal, Kesselring's chief of staff, were impressed with the exemplary courage with which the airborne soldiers were defending the town, although von Vietinghoff believed it was too soon to judge whether it could be held. Senger felt that another heavy bombing attack might render Cassino 'indefensible because troops and weapons were useless if buried under a mountain of rubble'. To strengthen the defence, von Vietinghoff assigned additional man-portable anti-tank weapons, the German equivalents of bazookas and grenade launchers, to Heidrich's division while von Senger placed III/115th Panzergrenadier Regiment, from 15th Panzergrenadier Division, under Heidrich's command. (By this stage of the battle all Heidrich's division had been committed to the Cassino sector.) While German higher commanders were philosophical about the outcome of the battle, 'they wished that the Luftwaffe would come to the help of the ground troops, or that – better still – heavy rain would continue'.[17]

***

On the 17th, the third day of battle, Freyberg issued verbal orders to Parkinson stressing that it was essential that the New Zealanders 'push through to the Gurkhas [on Hangman's Hill] tonight', adding that wherever he could push in tanks he was to do so. Thus, at 6.45am on the 17th, 25th Battalion, with a company from 24th and a Sherman troop, advanced towards the Botanical Gardens and Continental Hotel, pushing forward steadily to within 200 yards of the hotel. Their advance allowed 26th Battalion to attack southward from the short east-west stretch of Highway 6 within the town.[18]

The attack by 26th Battalion had an inauspicious start 'that would have thrown less seasoned troops into hopeless disorder'. This advance, 'a rough and ragged affair', was to be supported by two troops from 19th Armoured Regiment. At 11.00am the Shermans moved off from the Convent to cover the 700 yards to the railway station but poor communications meant that not all the infantry knew the advance was underway. Companies were ordered to a rendezvous point whence they were directed to the start line. Unfortunately the start line was under fire from the west but from it groups of infantry were sent to follow the tanks which were 'ploughing their way through heaps of rubble and scattered mines, engaging any enemy posts which they could spot with their [main] guns and machine guns'. By noon two tanks had reached the station. A further pair soon joined them. The Shermans prompted a speedy German withdrawal, allowing the infantry to pass through and secure the Hummocks. However, 26th Battalion, having sustained ninety-one casualties, was exhausted and too disorganized to continue the advance southward.[19]

Nonetheless, this had been a success which encouraged Bonifant to order 24th Battalion to move from the northern outskirts of Cassino, pass through the town and clear Highway 6 between the Continental Hotel and Colosseum. His order was not easy to execute: the battalion discovered that the town was a 'confusing and dangerous shambles' in which 25th Battalion was still engaged in a dozen disparate vicious actions, either against determined defenders who were proving hard to move or to repel others who had been evicted from their positions but were trying to infiltrate again into those positions. Not surprisingly, 24th Battalion did not make the progress Bonifant had hoped for. When darkness fell, only two companies had reached positions just south of the Convent. Moreover, they were off their intended axis of advance.[20]

***

During that day a German assault had been launched against the Gurkhas on Hangman's Hill who had attempted to attack the Abbey ruins but had been driven back by heavy fire. At dawn on the 17th Hauptfeldwebel Steinmuller led an assault platoon of I/3rd *Fallschirmjäger* Regiment in a determined attack. The Germans took the crest, pushing the Gurkhas back but an immediate counter-attack prised them off the crest, sending them back to the Abbey. The *Fallschirmjäger* did not have sufficient reserves to organize a fresh attack strong enough to destroy the Gurkhas.[21]

The Gurkhas' presence on Hangman's Hill and their determination not to be beaten off caused concern at XIV Panzerkorps HQ and at Tenth Army since the Abbey was being surrounded from south and west. Both von Vietinghoff and von Senger urged an immediate restoration of the situation, but Heidrich preferred to drive the Gurkhas off by fire rather than risk the heavy casualties inherent in an assault. Not only did the harassing fire lead Freyberg to re-supply the defenders by air but it also caused many casualties. (Böhmler noted that a German patrol on 29 March, by which time Hangman's Hill had been evacuated by the Gurkhas, found 165 dead Gurkhas as well as four wireless sets, twenty machine guns, thirty-six tommy guns and 103 rifles in the positions that 1st/9th Gurkhas had held.)[22]

In addition to the ground operations on 17 March the air forces had dropped 171 tons of bombs on enemy positions. As well as 185 single-engine fighter-bombers, including A-36 Apaches, P-40 Warhawks and P-47 Thunderbolts, two dozen A-20 Havocs and four dozen B-25 Mitchells had flown in the operations in which Heidrich's HQ at Castrocielo was targeted; forty-two tons of bombs were dropped on the HQ area.[23]

***

At the end of that Saint Patrick's Day the New Zealand Corps had made some progress but was still well short of objectives that, in the planning stage, had been considered the work of a few hours. The town had proved a mixture of a battlefield and no man's land with Freyberg's men dominating neither. Second New Zealand Division's casualties had been 'surprisingly low' at 130 officers and men with only twelve tanks damaged or destroyed. The toll, however, does not reflect the ferocity of the fighting, nor the difficulties facing the attackers. On the mountain, 5 Indian Brigade 'had scored a notable success in capturing Hangman's Hill' but it remained to be seen if it could be held. Freyberg considered committing more infantry in the town, either 5 New Zealand

79: The Abbey from Hangman's Hill today. (Author's photo)

Brigade* or a brigade of 78th Division. Once again he decided not to, believing that 6 Brigade had sufficient strength and drive to clear Cassino without adding a further brigade, which would be needed for exploitation should the battle end as Freyberg hoped. Both Parkinson and Bonifant agreed with him, but Galloway of 4th Indian Division was unsettled by his decision; he was concerned for 5 Indian Brigade.[24]

***

On the positive side Freyberg could see a slightly brighter picture. The New Zealanders' seizure of the railway station left only a small part of the town in German hands while 5 Indian Brigade had secured a jumping-off location for an assault on the Abbey. However, the Germans in the Continental Hotel, the Hotel des Roses (about 200 yards south of the Continental) and the surrounding area could engage any troops moving across Monastery Hill towards Hangman's with enfilading fire and also, from behind, anyone moving up the mountainside from Castle Hill towards the Abbey. If 5 Brigade was to attack the Abbey it was essential that the Gurkhas on Hangman's Hill be well provided for with food, ammunition and water while, in the town, tank paths had to be cleared to allow the armour to play its full part in attacks on the Continental Hotel and Hotel des Roses.

Engineers had been involved heavily from the beginning but had been thwarted in efforts to clear paths for tanks through the town. Both US and New Zealand companies continued to work through the night of 17/18 March, the US 48 Engineer Company building an additional bridge across the Rapido, where Highway 6 crossed east of the town. A ford on the Rapido was completed, and some 200 yards of Highway 6 cleared; craters and shell holes were filled in, while New Zealand engineers turned the bombed and mined railway embankment into a track for jeeps and tanks, useable as far as the station by such vehicles; other vehicles could travel almost to the station.[25] However, progress in Cassino was limited; New Zealand engineers using mechanical equipment 'could clear a route only as far as the Botanical Gardens'. That left 300 yards of 'impenetrable wreckage' between any tank and its most desirable target, the Continental Hotel.[26]

Another positive for Freyberg was that Allied air forces still dominated the skies with over 400 sorties flown on the 17th. There was little sign of the Luftwaffe and

---

*   2nd New Zealand Division had two infantry brigades since its re-organization to include an integral armoured brigade in 1942.

80: Among victims of Operation DICKENS was 34-year-old Gunner F.C. White of the New Zealand Artillery who had earlier earned the Military Medal. (Author's photo)

81: The deepest point of 2nd New Zealand Division's advance into the railway station was marked after the war by this memorial. (Author's photo)

82: In May 2014 the 70th anniversary of the battle was marked by the addition of a second plaque to the memorial. (Author's photo)

German artillery and Nebelwerfer positions suffered heavily from US and British tactical aircraft, as did their supply routes from Villa Santa Lucia.[27]

Allied artillery continued expending vast amounts of ammunition while smoke shells or smoke generators screened Allied positions. Expenditure of smoke shells was very heavy, with 21,700 rounds used on 18 March alone. The guns continued in action on the 18th as the battle entered yet another day. For the infantry there were more skirmishes while C Company of 24th New Zealand Battalion set out from Point 165 to seize Point 202 which had been held by the Rajputana Rifles the previous day; 202 overlooked one of the western hairpin bends on the road to the Abbey. It was intended that the company should link up with the Rajputs and send a platoon to keep touch with the Gurkhas on Hangman's Hill while the other platoons would attack the Continental Hotel and Hotel des Roses from the rear. The attack failed, in spite of support from tanks in the town, but C Company remained in place above Cassino. Second Lieutenant Charles Klaus MM, commanding 13 Platoon, had led his men to Highway 6 but was killed outside the Hotel des Roses.[28]

In the town the strongest German counter-attack yet experienced on the flat was launched on the station's defenders. As dawn broke, some sixty *Fallschirmjäger*,

83: The smokescreen known as Cigarette concealed the approaches to the forward Allied positions from the view of German observers on the heights. (NARA)

from the motorcyle company of the Machine Gun Battalion, supported by some badly-aimed artillery and Nebelwerfer concentrations, attacked, trying to pass themselves off as Indian as they approached the station, passing between the Hummocks and the Round House. Some entered the Round House but the attack was beaten off by 26th Battalion, the Germans suffering at least ten casualties.[29] However, 26th Battalion made little progress that day while 25th spent the day taking an enemy strongpoint close to the Continental Hotel.[30] German artillery, mortars and riflemen continued targeting the New Zealanders while the Luftwaffe made a rare appearance, although the bombs dropped in the 'hit-and-run' attack fell in flooded fields in front of 26th Battalion, showering soldiers in their dug-outs.[31]

Stalemate seemed to be settling over the battlefield on the 18th and Freyberg issued orders that afternoon for efforts to break it next day. Twenty-eighth (Maori) Battalion, of 5 NZ Brigade, was to come under command of 6 Brigade for a renewed attack on the Continental Hotel and Hotel des Roses at 3.00am. Meanwhile 4th Indian Division was to assault the Abbey. Both battalions of Rajputana Rifles, much reduced in strength, were to combine as a composite unit under 5 Brigade and relieve the Essex on Castle Hill and Point 165, allowing that battalion to join the Gurkhas on Hangman's Hill, whence both battalions would attack the Abbey. At the same time 7 Indian Brigade was to launch an extemporized armoured force along Cavendish Road to capture Albaneta Farm before moving south-eastwards along the ridge to the Abbey. Meanwhile, 2nd New Zealand Division's troops on the flat also had a role: 24th Battalion was to cross the lower slopes to attack strongpoints at the Continental Hotel and on Point 202. Thus the Abbey was to be the target of a pincer move, with infantry forming one part of the pincer and armour the second. Molony described this as

> a complicated plan for 4th Indian Division because time was short, the preparatory moves would have to be made in darkness and almost certainly under fire, while detailed reconnaissance was as impossible as it had been throughout the battles of Cassino, even if time for it were possible.[32]

It was truly a complicated plan without sufficient attention given to detail, as was typical of Freyberg's temporary corps HQ. However, one aspect had received considerable attention; that was Cavendish Road, the work of the Sappers and Miners of 4th Indian Division, intended as a jeep track into the mountains for re-supply and casualty evacuation of units on the heights. Porters and mule trains brought supplies forward on a nightly basis and casualties were carried out by stretcher-bearers or mules before being handed over to jeep ambulances on lower ground. The availability of a route for wheeled vehicles improved the lot of those serving on the heights. On 16 February the Indian sappers began work on the track that was to become Cavendish Road, named for a former CRE of 4th Indian Division.

By the 25th the field companies had created a jeep road from an old track, little more than a narrow goat track, but useable by men on foot, leading into the mountains from a narrow road out of Cáira. Ascending to the top of a slope on the north side of Colle Maiola, it rose 800 feet in one and a half miles, ending with a one-in-four gradient. Stevens described it as traversing 'the Monte Cassino ridge system by way of Massa Albaneta, between the razor-backed summit crowned by Point 593 and the next ground to the west, Point 575', while Majdalany commented that it allowed 'access to a usable defile and track sweeping round to the rear of the Monastery'.[33] Studying the jeep track on a map, Freyberg believed that it could assist his operations and ordered its upgrading to allow tanks to use it. 'It was hoped that the appearance of tanks from this direction would cause something like the consternation that greeted Hannibal's elephants after their Alpine crossing'.[34]

That work began on 1 March with a section of 6 Field Company New Zealand Engineers reinforcing the Indians. From then until the 11th sappers worked tirelessly at widening and strengthening the track. Pickaxes, shovels, explosives, bulldozers and compressors were all used to widen Cavendish Road to twelve feet from about eight with a solid well-drained surface to bear the weight of tanks. Those stretches exposed to view from above were screened off with camouflage nets. It seems the Germans never realized the significance of the work underway almost under their noses, although the track could be observed from three angles 'and the enemy obviously knew that work was in progress ... and that the track was open to mule traffic'. Side and overhead cover was provided where observation was mainly from on top or on the flank, or of the movement of jeeps; eighteen-foot-long timber poles at six-foot intervals supported camouflage screens over a total distance of 320 yards.[35]

To launch an attack along Cavendish Road, Freyberg established a small armoured force of 7 Indian Brigade Reconnaissance Squadron, C Squadron 20th NZ Armoured Regiment and Company D 760th US Tank Battalion, plus three M7 Priests of Combat Command B. The New Zealanders deployed sixteen Shermans and the Americans sixteen Stuart light tanks, five of which also equipped 7 Brigade Reconnaissance Squadron, in addition to three Shermans. (Interestingly, it seems that the Germans believed these AFVs 'had been specially modified to enable them to operate in mountain country'. Böhmler, who made that comment, also described the Shermans as Grants and the Stuarts as 'Commandos'.) The Sherman, weighing about thirty tons, was under ten feet wide, the Stuart was about half the Sherman's bulk and seven-and-a-half feet wide while the M7, built on a Grant hull, was the same width as the Sherman and weighed about twenty-two tons. Negotiating Cavendish Road would be difficult for all three types, especially the Sherman, with drivers and commanders having to work closely to ensure their vehicles stayed on the track since there were steep drops to one side for much of the route. The plan had the advantage of surprise: the Germans would not expect tanks in such country, especially as they had failed to realize what the sappers were doing on Cavendish Road.[36]

Stevens wrote that the plan, codenamed Operation REVENGE, called for 'timing and speed of movement [that] asked a great deal of the participants'. The Essex in the Castle were to complete a complicated handover before crossing the mountainside under fire to join the Gurkhas on Hangman's Hill in time to attack the Abbey in Operation HECTOR. However, the Germans on the upper slopes were making it very difficult for anyone to leave the Castle. Nonetheless, the composite Rajput battalion reached the Castle to relieve the Essex and two Essex companies began their journey across the slopes to join 1st/9th Gurkhas. All seemed to be going well and the other two Essex companies were completing their

84: Cavendish Road, the result of the work of the engineers of 4th Indian Division whose Red Eagle emblem is displayed on the marker board. Creating the road out of a simple track eased the supply problems and allowed the planning of an attack involving tanks. (Public domain)

handover to the Rajputs in the Castle before moving out to follow their comrades. It was then, at about 5.30am, that 'a fierce hail of machine-gun fire swept the [Castle] walls'.[37]

The defenders of the Abbey, I/4th *Fallschirmjäger* Regiment, had chosen that time to sortie forth and attack the Castle. A short but sharp artillery and mortar bombardment preceded the attack, which Smith reckoned to include between 200

85: Part of Cavendish Road today. (Author's photo)

and 300 men, although Stevens described it as 'heavy attack' without estimating figures; but he wrote that the Essex and Rajput platoons 'at the lower hairpin bend disappeared in a smother of enemies'. The attackers swept on towards the Castle, coming 'down hill like a rolling stone'.[38]

As the Germans attacked, the Castle garrison included two Essex companies, less a platoon, a company of 4th/6th Rajputanas, two platoons of 1st/6th Rajputs, some Sappers and Miners and an artillery observation group, under Major Ronald Oswald, 1st Field Regiment, a total of 150 men commanded by Major Frank Ketteley MC of the Essex. Major Oswald was unable to call down defensive fire since it was not known whether the defenders of the lower hairpin bend were still in position or had been overrun.[39]

With riflemen on the slopes firing at anyone who appeared on the battlements, the *Fallschirmjäger* reached the walls over which grenades were hurled into the courtyard. The garrison fought back vigourously, and Bren gunners fired through arrow slits. It seemed as if a medieval siege was being re-enacted with modern weaponry. Corporal Edwin Parker of the Essex, stationed at the north-west corner, broke up two attacks with his Bren and grenades before being killed.[40]

The first onslaught led to twenty minutes of sharp fighting, after which the attackers were pinned down. They were recalled by a flare signal to re-organize and renew the assault, under cover of smoke, at 7.00am. During this phase Major Ketteley was wounded fatally and was succeeded by Major D.A. Beckett, who was already wounded and whom Ketteley was treating when he was shot. Such was the attackers' determination that they tried scaling the walls but, once again, co-ordinated defensive fire wrote *finis* to their endeavours. In spite of this second rebuff the *Fallschirmjäger* launched a third assault which was held off by mortar and shellfire, the artillery having established fire lines. While spotting for the mortars, Beckett was wounded a second time. When the fighting died down briefly he deployed some Rajputana riflemen outside the gate with orders to establish themselves under cover on the mountainside and counter German riflemen who were firing from higher ground.[41]

However, the picture at the Castle had become perilous, the garrison being reduced to three officers and sixty men who were still on their feet. Ammunition supplies were being exhausted; more than 8,000 rounds had been fired by the machine gunners while the mortars had shot over 1,500 bombs. So many rounds had the Essex mortars fired that barrels had become red hot, and some had even bent out of shape due to the heat. The RSM of 1/4th Essex, WOI Rose DCM, had shuttled back and forth to the mortar pits with loads of bombs while an eight-man party had brought bags of ammunition, risking the crossing of the ravine in so doing.[42]

86: A memorial to the soldiers of 1/4th Essex who defended Castle Hill stands at the castle. (Author's photo)

At 9.00am German troops from the town began threatening the Castle from below, pouring machine-gun fire at the gateway. Reaction came from both Essex and Rajput machine guns and mortars from across the ravine, which protected the western wall, while New Zealand Shermans fired in the path of the attackers ascending from the town. The defensive fire had the desired effect, stopping the Germans. Then a German stretcher-bearer appeared under a white flag to seek a ceasefire during which wounded could be collected. Galloway permitted a thirty-minute armistice and both sides began collecting wounded. Several Essex casualties were dug out from under a collapsed part of the Castle wall. Some reinforcements, A Company 2nd/7th Gurkhas, under Major Denis Drayton, reached the Castle at noon, thus strengthening the garrison.[43]

The *Fallschirmjäger* had not given up. Another attack was made in the afternoon when a small party laid a demolition charge under a buttress on the northern battlements; the resultant explosion brought down part of the wall, entombing two officers and twenty men of the Essex A Company. However, those Germans who tried entering the Castle through the breach were shot down as they did so. One wounded soldier crept into the Castle to surrender, telling his captors that of the 200 who had taken part in the first assault that morning only forty remained alive and uninjured. Beckett was wounded for a third time as he defended the breach in the wall. He was fortunate not to have been killed and owed his life to a German soldier. There were several *Fallschirmjäger* prisoners in the Castle, all of whom, except a sergeant major, volunteered as stretcher-bearers;

87: The ruined castle standing above the town in 1944 on Point 193. (NARA)

88: The Castle restored to its erstwhile splendour. From Castle Hill the visitor can appreciate how the building dominates the town and its importance to those who fought there. (Author's photo)

89: The visitor can also appreciate how the Abbey and Castle formed part of an integrated defence. This image shows the proximity of the buildings. (© Damiano Parravano, Chairman, Associazione Linea Gustav)

one saw a sniper aim at Major Beckett and threw the officer out of the line of fire. In the fighting two German prisoners were killed while rescuing British wounded. The sergeant major, who had disdained cover, walking openly 'with the air of a supervisor of events', subsequently commended Beckett on a soldierly performance, presenting him with his fur-lined airborne gauntlets as a memento of their shared experience.[44]

With that attack the defenders' ordeal ended. One more assault was beaten off by curtains of defensive fire before it reached the walls. Some defenders had been men of B and D Companies of the Essex who had just begun their journey to Hangman's Hill when the first attack struck. A number of men of the rear company went back to aid their comrades in the Castle but only a few made it before the attackers threatened to overrun them. Those who avoided being captured or killed rejoined their comrades en route to Hangman's. As a result, when day broke, they were wending their way across the mountainside in plain view and not until 10.15am did they reach the Gurkhas' positions. Of those who had set out, only seventy-five completed the trek and then had to watch as attack after attack was made on their fellow Essex in and around the Castle.

The gallant handful of Essex, in spite of their mauling, were in no mood to stand by and see their comrades assailed. They asked permission to strike down the slopes … onto the rear of the paratroopers. Permission was refused, for the assault upon the Monastery had been set for 1400 hours. By noon, however, it was apparent that it would be folly to commit the Hangman's Hill force, thin on the ground and with scanty replenishment, to a major assault while a critical battle raged on its line of communication. The culminating attack therefore was abandoned and the Essex were ordered as soon as night fell to return to the Castle. That evening they once more crossed the fire-swept slopes and took a pummelling from enemy outposts. Shortly after 2200 hours, some reached the Castle; others, finding the way blocked, returned to Hangman's Hill.[45]

That afternoon the Essex had suffered another casualty when the commanding officer, Lieutenant Colonel Arthur Noble, was wounded whilst touring the battlefield with Major General Galloway. Major L.W.A. Chapell MC succeeded him.

***

Since the joint Gurkhas/Essex assault on the Abbey had to be cancelled as a result of the attacks on Castle Hill, commonsense would suggest that the ad hoc armoured force's attack along Cavendish Road, Operation REVENGE, should also have been cancelled. However, the armour went ahead in spite of there no longer being a second arm to the pincer, leaving the tanks to operate alone. Stevens commented that 'Research historians doubtless will be puzzled by the fact that 7 Brigade's diversionary filibuster in the rear of the Monastery was allowed to proceed' and it is difficult to understand why, although Phillips noted that at 'this time the outcome of the contretemps round Castle hill was still obscure' while Galloway 'did not despair of the infantry assault on the monastery'. In fact, Galloway ordered the Gurkhas to attack as soon as they were ready but accepted that the sequence of the operation would be reversed, with the armoured attack 'preceding instead of following the onset of the infantry'.[46]

The difficulties facing the tanks were clear to Major Patrick Barton, OC of C Squadron 20th Armoured Regiment, who undertook a reconnaissance on 18 March. He realized that not only did he have a difficult task liaising with Juin's troops around Monte Cáiro but his squadron was a small detail in a mixed force directed on to a somewhat vague objective under command of a British artillery colonel without tank experience; and he was so concerned at the total lack of infantry support that he made representations to Corps, but fruitlessly since the Indian brigade, steadily drained of men by weeks of fighting and exposure in the hills, could spare no infantry for the operation.[47]

His concerns were valid, nonetheless. The armour, and M7s, having ascended Cavendish Road from Cáira, was laagered in an open bowl-shaped area, codenamed Madras Circus, in the Indians' forward defensive localities ready for H Hour on the 19th. However, a German aircraft spotted some tanks parked on Cavendish Road on the 18th and made a strafing attack, an incident the officer commanding the US tanks, Lieutenant Herbert Crowder, believed might have influenced the decision to send the armour into action next day. Until then the force commander, Major Malcolm Cruickshank, had understood that the tanks would not be deployed until the infantry had taken the Abbey and the New Zealanders cut Highway 6 south of Cassino. Moreover, when told early in the afternoon of the 18th that the attack would take place next day he was also informed that the overall commander would be Lieutenant Colonel John Adye, acting CRA of 4th Indian Division.[48]

Whatever the reason for the change of plan, the tank force moved off from Madras Circus at 6.00am on 19 March, driving west of Colle Maiola along the jeep track to Massa Albaneta, encircling Points 479 and 593 and firing on German outposts on the western slopes of those features. Tank commanders found the going to be the main worry since, although the track was passable, elsewhere the ground was soft in places which led to some tanks bogging; others lost tracks to rough terrain. About a quarter of a mile from Albaneta Farm opposition began strengthening. This completely unexpected attack was a major shock to the Germans who, having considered the terrain completely unsuitable for armour, had not taken notice of the sappers' preparations along Cavendish Road. 'Agitated wireless messages were overheard' and men of III/4th *Fallschirmjäger* Regiment, with no anti-tank guns, used mortars and called down artillery fire, as well as their personal weapons 'with such accuracy and persistence from the cover of scrub and boulders that it was death for tank commanders to show their heads for more than a moment above the turrets of their tanks'. Having to advance with hatches closed, the commanders were almost blind and several tanks 'trundled into difficulties' while turrets filled with fumes from guns and engines. However, they broke through the lightly-defended line before wheeling and advancing by a narrow defile between Albaneta Farm and Point 593 towards the rear of the Abbey, targeting local defences with their main guns. 'Had [the attack] been integrated with infantry attacks it seems possible that the Cassino defences might have collapsed.' But no infantry supported the armour and the planned attack from Hangman's had been delayed.[49]

While some of C Squadron's Shermans engaged German infantry, Lieutenant Harold Renall led his troop, and some American Stuarts, past the southern shoulder of Point 593. The Abbey ruins lay before them, the way to it open 'over a good cobbled road'. On the right they could see the Liri valley. The absence of infantry doomed their efforts. 'One by one they came to grief, hit or stuck in the mud.' The Stuarts were the focus of intense fire although two of the light tanks effected the rescue of some of the crew of a crippled Sherman. While high-explosive and solid shot hammered Albaneta Farm to raise dust, the Stuarts dashed in under the cover of the dust cloud to rescue the Sherman crew. However, Harold Renall had been killed.[50]

The limit of what the armour could do had been reached. No infantry were coming to support them, although, at 10.20am, Freyberg had decided that, should the armour reach a position from which it could fire effectively on the Abbey ruins, the force on Hangman's Hill would attack. But at midday the battle described above was underway and the route to the Abbey was blocked. Fighting continued into the afternoon as tanks tried battling their way forward to the Abbey's rear walls. Had they done so, it was unlikely that their guns, or those of the M7s, would have wrought much damage. By 5.30pm a dozen tanks had been knocked out. Barton and the commander of the reconnaissance squadron agreed that the operation should be called off.[51]

Nothing else could be achieved by the armour without infantry support and, as darkness fell, the German infantry would take the upper hand; in the meantime the *Fallschirmjäger* were secure in sangars or dug-outs on the hillsides. Signs of preparations for a counter-attack from Phantom Ridge were noted which could have provided a serious problem for a withdrawal. Galloway had realized that the force had reached its limit earlier in the afternoon as the track forward needed sappers to work on it and so there was no rationale in continuing. The column limped back to Madras Circus, some *Panzerfaust* rounds speeding it on its way.[52]

Three Shermans and three Stuarts had been destroyed with nine Shermans and seven Stuarts damaged, although eleven damaged tanks were subsequently recovered. Galloway described the attack as having been 'as successful as he could have expected'. Majdalany suggested that it had been a gamble worth taking while Phillips wrote of it as victory psychologically if not materially 'even though it may have prevented the Germans from thinning out in that area to find reserves for the main battle'. Heidrich was concerned enough to create a reserve, relieving III/4th *Fallschirmjäger* Regiment on Point 593 with 15th Panzergrenadier Division's reconnaissance unit. This gave him three battalions, albeit understrength: I/ and

90: Another significant building in 1944 was Albaneta Farm, once a convent on the Abbey's estate. (Author's photo)

II/1st *Fallschirmjäger* Regiment and III/4th. Senger considered the town the weakest point since it formed a lightly-held narrow sector against which the Allies could deploy strong forces.[53]

On the 19th, as battle raged against Castle Hill and the armoured force made its sortie behind the Abbey, the town's defenders continued demonstrating their tenacity. Freyberg had deployed 28th (Maori) Battalion to join the infantry in Cassino but only two companies entered the fray. Alongside 25th Battalion they had been rebuffed by the defenders of the Continental Hotel and Hotel des Roses while their supporting tanks tried to fight their way through mounds of rubble and the craters left by bombing. Fifty men from 5 Field Park Company had tried clearing Highway 6 behind the Maoris but such work was impossible in the thick of battle; even the reconnaissance patrol had led to two officers being wounded. On the outskirts of the town engineering work had improved communications with two good lateral routes into town, one being the railway embankment, and US engineers were about to complete the alternative bridge over the main road.[54]

Fighting in the town continued to be close and brutal with the New Zealanders finding that buildings that had been cleared 'were apt to be re-occupied by the enemy a few hours later'. Colonel Hanson, the New Zealand Division's CRE, believed that a system of tunnels under Cassino was being used by the Germans but it seemed more likely that they were infiltrating back via the southern stretch of Highway 6 or the steep gully between Points 445 and 193. In some cases opposing troops occupied adjoining rooms in the same building and fighting became deeply personal.[55]

Böhmler described the 'desperate struggle … for the possession of the Via Casalina' [Highway 6] as the Maoris entered the fight and advanced into the corner where Highway 6 made its sharp southward turn. They could get no further than the Continental Hotel while 25th Battalion 'had been equally unsuccessful in its attacks' on the slopes of Castle Hill where

> Lieutenant Jamrowski was the soul of the defence. With a handful of haggard, exhausted men he had not only repulsed every attack delivered against him, but had also launched a number of counter-attacks and dealt the New Zealanders some shrewd blows.[56]

He continued by describing the fighting on both sides as 'exceptionally grim'.

> Hidden from view amongst the chaotic masses of rubble, man fought man in single combat, until one or the other could fight no more. Quarter was neither asked nor given, and though the fighting was perhaps the

bitterest yet seen in the Italian campaign and every yard was contested to the end, both sides observed the decencies of war.[57]

Of those decencies the most noteworthy was the chivalrous treatment accorded the wounded by both sides. Majdalany wrote that the special circumstances of Cassino, where for weeks it was impossible to move or bury the dead and where evacuation of wounded was so difficult, led to a situation in which 'medical orderlies of both sides fell into the habit of wandering, almost at will, in a mute kinship that in its spontaneous charity was perhaps the most ironic witness of all to the folly that made it necessary'.[58] Reflecting on this practice in his own memoirs, von Senger quoted those words of Fred Majadalany, adding that 'I associate myself with these sentiments

91: German troops of 1st *Fallschirmjäger* Division march into captivity, having been taken prisoner by New Zealand soldiers. (NARA)

of my young friend, and I bow to those New Zealanders, Indians and Germans who in the midst of a hellish, death-dealing battle saved others at the risk of their own lives'.[59]

***

Concerned about the pressure on his units in the heights, Galloway was becoming more frustrated with the unfolding of Freyberg's plan. When he learned of the assault on Castle Hill he reported this to Freyberg, telling him that 'the two battalions in the town were two battalions too few' and that 4th Indian Division could not achieve much more until Cassino was cleared. Since it was evident that some of those attacking the Castle had come up from the town, and that the area near Castle Hill was a route for Germans filtering into the town, Freyberg agreed that the Germans were stronger in the town than had been believed and that it should be garrisoned against such interlopers, whether from the south or north-west. That done, Cassino would be cleared north of a line from the station to Hangman's Hill.[60]

This led to redeployments within the corps, the most significant being the introduction of a battalion from 78th Division into the battle. Fourth Indian Division was to be reinforced by 6th Royal West Kents of 11 Brigade and was to establish itself firmly on Point 193 (Castle Hill) and recapture Point 165. Second New Zealand Division was to reduce its frontage to increase its strength in the town, 5 Brigade coming into line in the northern sector, assuming command of 25th as well as its own 23rd and 28th Battalions, plus 19th Armoured Regiment, less C Squadron. Seventy-eighth Division was to close up on the left, assuming some of 2nd New Zealand Division's tasks in the south. During the night of 19/20 March the re-organization took place, in spite of 'lively enemy gunfire'. Once established, 5 Brigade was 'to comb out the rest of the town and open up [Highway] 6 to the south, so that the posts on Points 435 and 202 should be no longer isolated'. The defenders of Points 435 (Hangman's Hill) and 202, Gurkhas and New Zealanders respectively, were in precarious situations and being re-supplied by airdrops. They could not hold out indefinitely.[61]

***

It was clear that the Germans had scored another defensive victory, even if Freyberg did not want to believe that. Paradoxically, von Senger was worried about the situation, especially in Cassino, noting that the Germans' real weakness lay in their inability to carry out proper reconnaissance. While the intelligence service that worked through the general staff organization was still operating, formations and units on the ground could not 'use the normal means of reconnaissance'.

The Luftwaffe, a shadow of what it had been in Italy when the Allies landed, 'could barely venture into the air for routine reconnaissance' while few prisoners were being taken. Although it was possible for agents to pass behind the lines by sea, von Senger was aware that not only would they know nothing of preparations for attacks but they 'probably worked for and got paid for both sides'. Thus every Allied major attack 'came as a complete surprise'.[62] Allied air supremacy meant that light aircraft could spot for artillery with airborne observers allowing Allied guns to be directed onto any part of the German lines. That advantage often proved ineffective since so many Allied attacks moved slowly, allowing XIV Panzerkorps to move reserves during the night, but von Senger did not allow that to blind him 'to the fact that our successes were … temporary … '. Once the Allies could initiate a war of movement it would no longer be possible for the Germans to move reserves by night. 'Only if there were parity in the air could restrictions be imposed on the day movements of the enemy, and this would also re-establish parity in the conduct of operations'.[63]

92: From the area of the former Pasquale Road north of Cassino three major features of the battles dominate the view: Castle Hill, left, below Hangman's Hill, centre, and the Abbey atop Monte Cassino. (Author's photo)

Böhmler was unimpressed with Freyberg's progress, describing it as 'not very convincing'. What had been achieved – the advance to Highway 6 in the town, pushing the defenders back to the Rapido in the eastern sector, taking the station and Hangman's Hill – did not amount to a great deal when '[m]easured against the immense amount of material expended and the severe losses suffered', especially as German troops still held the heart of the town and the Abbey when, according to the Allied plan, the armour should have passed through Cassino into the Liri valley and along the road to Rome.[64]

***

Freyberg, although not yet prepared to admit defeat, realized that success had to come within forty-eight hours since the men on Hangman's Hill and Point 202 could not be expected to hold out any longer. Clark was also keen to see progress, if only because he knew that Alexander was already planning to sidestep Eighth Army across Italy to engage on the Cassino front. For his part, Alexander allowed Freyberg one further opportunity for his corps to break into the Liri valley.

The re-organization Freyberg had ordered allowed him to prepare for continuing operations, including sending 6th Royal West Kents, who had relieved the survivors of 1/4th Essex in the Castle, against Point 165, the lower hairpin bend, and a company of 2nd/7th Gurkhas to take Point 445, on the northern edge of the ravine below the Abbey and Castle Hill, to prevent the Germans reinforcing the town by that route. Similarly, Point 165, another 'leak' point, was to be seized by a company of West Kents from the Castle. Neither attack succeeded. The single company of Gurkhas, moving downhill, 'kept up their attack for two hours but were unable to cover the last few yards to their objective; a continued blaze of defensive fire caused some twenty casualties and the attempt had to be abandoned'.[65] Had 11 Brigade been able to spare more than one company there might have been a different outcome.

The West Kent company was also rebuffed but without making quite as much progress as the Gurkhas. Leaving the Castle to move down to the lower hairpin the leading men encountered a recently sown minefield, setting off mines that caused injuries and alerted the Germans. All hope of surprise evaporated. Although the company returned to their start line and re-organized for a second attempt, that also came to naught on more mines near a small mound en route to Point 165. The explosions caused further casualties and brought down intense enemy fire, forcing the West Kents to abandon the attack.[66]

While these two unsuccessful attacks were underway the Germans were attempting to surround and capture Castle Hill. As dawn broke on the 21st the 'extreme confusion of the night's fighting resolved itself ... into a determined attack' on Castle Hill which was beaten off by the defenders, supported by a strong defensive shoot by the artillery on the approaches to the Castle which were accurately registered for just such tasks. Such was the intensity of that fire that groups of *Fallschirmjäger* 'doubled forward to gain the shelter of the Castle walls and thereafter to surrender'. Some forty prisoners were taken.[67]

Fourth Indian Division had done all that it could. Previously both Castle Hill and Point 175 had been considered jumping-off platforms for further attacks. Thereafter they were turned into defensive strongpoints and 5 Brigade set about the task of converting them to the defensive role.[68]

***

In the town battle continued on the 20th with little progress. That day's plan had been to commit 21st Battalion, reinforced by two companies of 24th, to seize and hold a line between Point 202 and the Continental Hotel as a prelude to effecting a junction with the Hangman's Hill garrison. At 11.00pm on the 20th the attack was launched but faded out next day. Little was achieved. The next day 23rd and 25th Battalions also 'struggled fiercely and unavailingly' in the mess of ruined buildings east of a line between the Hotel des Roses and the base of Castle Hill. The New Zealanders' front was to be narrowed further by 5th Buffs and 56th Reconnaissance Regiment of 78th Division relieving 26th Battalion and the Divisional Cavalry. The Battleaxe Division took over the area around the station and extended to the right as far as the crossroads north of there.[69]

For the New Zealanders the stress of combat was taking its toll. Phillips noted that the infantry in Cassino were in as much disarray as their opponents with newly-arrived soldiers mixing with the 'muddy, stubble-chinned veterans of several days' standing' while many others, such as gunners and signallers, stretcher-bearers and sappers, and dismounted tankmen, were mingled together in the heat of battle, often with enemy soldiers intermingled with them. All six New Zealand infantry battalions were in the line, four of them (from the right, 25th, 23rd, 28th and 21st) deployed north of Highway 6 and 24th and 26th south of the road. In practice, however, the picture was not as tidy as on paper.

Several battalion HQs located in the convent formed a control centre of sorts that helped co-ordinate ration parties and casualty evacuation parties, for which the convent also provided a basic shelter, as well as a rallying point for lost soldiers. Communications could be troublesome, making it difficult to accurately track unit and sub-unit locations while the ruined town 'was a place of unexpected encounters'.

One company … was awakened to the presence of Germans in the next room by bazooka fire through the dividing wall. There was one period of three days when more than forty Maoris shared a house with the enemy and only took their departure because their ammunition was spent.[70]

The attacks by the New Zealand Corps on the 21st were seen by the Germans as a desperate effort to bring the battle to a conclusion. Freyberg still believed that 21st Battalion could link up with the men on the hill but the day's efforts resulted in no more progress than 'a matter of odd buildings'. Before leaving for a conference with Clark and Alexander that afternoon Freyberg asked 21st Battalion's commanding officer if his unit could achieve its objective by a night assault, but the answer, although long, was negative. Nonetheless, the conference decided to continue with the offensive. Churchill had signalled Alexander expressing the hope that the operation would not be halted, commenting that 'Surely the enemy is very hard pressed too'.[71]

The enemy was indeed hard pressed, retaining only a very small portion of the town, but enough to prevent Fifth Army breaking into the Liri valley. No night operation proved possible but hard fightng resumed with first light on the 22nd. That day the New Zealanders 'battled with a vehemence born of the knowledge that the sands were running low'. Their efforts were in vain, Heidrich's soldiers holding their ground with equal determination. No gains were made. Indeed the Germans even attacked the Castle from below, with engineers hurling charges over the walls into the courtyard. They were beaten off by the West Kents who took over thirty prisoners and inflicted perhaps as many casualties. Stevens commented that the attack with assault engineers arose from Heidrich realizing that his opponents were preparing the Castle as a fortress 'from which mobile forces might sally to take up a battle of manoeuvre on the slopes' and tying it in defensively with the upper Rapido valley by means of a minefield and wire entanglements. Hence that assault on the morning of 22 March.[72]

There was to be no breakthrough for the New Zealand Corps as *Fallschimjäger* held firm wherever and whenever New Zealanders attacked. At the end of that day Parkinson confirmed that his day's objectives were still in enemy hands. Heidrich believed that 'the Allies had lost their dash' and his confidence was buoyed by the fact that he had two battalions in reserve. In the air the Luftwaffe had also flown more sorties than the Allies, although the latter numbered only twenty-seven, mostly supply-dropping, missions.[73] Weather conditions had deteriorated since the first bombing mission on 15 March, restricting the support air forces could give ground troops. Between the 21st and 26th, except for the 24th, conditions 'could hardly have been worse for flying'. However, the re-supply of the garrison of Hangman's Hill was maintained, the last drop being made on the 24th, just before the withdrawal. In spite of the weather conditions Allied aircraft of all kinds had dropped 1,859 tons of bombs in support of the third battle with another 205 tons on targets along the approaches to the Cassino front. This was in addition to providing direct and indirect air support to VI Corps at Anzio.[74]

There was another obstacle to flying during the third battle, also provided by nature but from a source the planners had not considered. Vesuvius, Monte Vesuvio, the volcano that had destroyed Pompeii and Herculaneum in AD 79 began to grumble on the 18th. At 6.30pm it was seen 'to be more active than normal and, from RHQ at Torre [Annunziata] several streams of lava were visible on south slopes of hill'. The lava continued flowing during the night and by next morning had reached the tree line and was flowing in the direction of Torre del Greco but did not appear to present a danger to Torre Annunziata. Ash and dust erupted into the air above, a heightfinder of 25 HAA Battery recording the cloud as reaching 20,000 feet. Eruptions continued for over a week, not easing until the 28th; dust continued falling after that date. AA sites in the area had to go out of action while many USAAF aircraft on the airfields they were protecting were destroyed or damaged by falling ash and dust. Radio communications were also disrupted while roads became impassable and service personnel were deployed to assist civilians evacuate their homes. At San Giuseppe cinders fell to a depth of six inches. One veteran told the author that he was never more frightened during the war than in the days that Vesuvius erupted. Needless to say the loss of aircraft had an immediate effect on the air support that could be given over Cassino.[75]

On the 22nd Luftwaffe aircraft strafed and bombed the New Zealand positions on Highway 6, attacking the anti-aircraft emplacements, although seven German aircraft were brought down. The strain was growing, not only on the infantry but also on the gunners who maintained fire support throughout the battle. On 22 March 4th Field Regiment, which had supplied much of the smoke cover, had to borrow thirty anti-aircraft gunners to keep their 25-pounders in action, so exhausting was an arduous week of firing. That day saw the regiment fire 7,456 smoke rounds and 570 HE rounds, an average exceeding 330 rounds per gun, a typical daily expenditure at Cassino.[76]

***

There was skirmishing on the 23rd, a windy day with flurries of snow, on which Freyberg convened a council of war with Lieutenant General Sidney Kirkman, XIII Corps commander, the divisional commanders of New Zealand

93: Vesuvius erupts in March 1944. Ash from the eruption blocked roads, damaged and destroyed aircraft on airfields in the Naples area and disrupted operations. Troops in the vicinity were deployed to assist civilians whose homes were threatened. (NARA)

Corps – Parkinson, Galloway and Keightley – and his Corps Commander Royal Artilley and Chief Engineer. The two-hour conference debated Fifth Army's problems at Cassino. It was accepted that both 2nd New Zealand and 4th Indian Divisions were no longer fit to prolong the offensive but the comparatively fresh 78th Division might be capable of assaulting the Abbey from the area of Point 593. Other possibilities were considered but, recognizing the inherent difficulties, it was agreed that there should be a pause in operations.[77]

The Third Battle of Cassino had all but ended. Although the Gurkhas remained on Hangman's Hill, they would be recalled. Other ground taken would be held and fortified since defending such areas would keep the enemy's resources extended and maintain the Allied wedge in the German line until it could be hammered in completely by a fresh and stronger force. No one, however, was keen to hold a line that was the high-tide mark of a blocked attack rather than being chosen for its defensive attributes. Galloway argued that Castle Hill would be difficult to hold, requiring major engineering to make it defensible, as well as securing Point 175 'beyond all risk' and the area around Cassino jail. Even with such effort he believed the Castle would attract much enemy fire with resultant casualties.[78]

Regrouping in Cassino and on the heights meant that the garrisons of Hangman's Hill and Point 202 had to be evacuated since their positions formed a salient that would be extremely difficult to hold and re-supply. However, the north-west sector of the town, abutting Castle Hill, the Botanical Gardens and the railway station would be held; the Allied front line was to run from the eastern slopes of Point 593 to Point 175 and then by way of the north-western sector of Cassino to the Botanical Gardens, to the railway station and the Hummocks and, finally, to the confluence of the Gari and Rapido rivers. 'All posts were to be mined and wired and well dug-in where the ground permitted. Offensive action would be restricted to vigorous patrolling and local counter-attacks when necessary.'[79]

To recall the Gurkhas and their Essex and Rajput comrades from Hangman's Hill, and the New Zealanders from Point 202, orders were sent to both locations by word of mouth, three officers volunteering to take them, one each from three of the battalions concerned. They set out on the night of 23/24 March, each with a carrier pigeon to bring back the acknowledgements that the orders had been received. The pigeons were named Saint George, Saint Andrew and Saint David, representing the nationalities of the officer volunteers: Mallinson of the Essex, Normand of the Gurkhas and Jennings of the Rajputanas. Although Jennings was forced to return to Castle Hill by German patrols, the others reached their destinations and Saint George and Saint Andrew took the news back. On the night of the 24th/25th, feint attacks in Cassino and from the Castle, plus an artillery bombardment on the Abbey, covered the evacuations of both garrisons without loss, although the Germans later claimed to have recaptured a stubbornly-defended Hangman's Hill on the 27th.[80] From Hangman's Hill, no fewer than 263 officers and men returned (six gunners, 185 Gurkhas, thirty-two Essex and forty Rajputs) while forty-five New Zealanders returned from Point 202.[81]

Over the previous week C Company 24th New Zealand Battalion on Point 202 had provided a collecting post for stragglers, especially wounded, from other units but the company commander, realizing that he might have to fight a rearguard withdrawal, told the wounded that he would have to leave them behind. However, he left a keg of rum and a Red Cross flag made from parachute fabric – there had been a generous supply drop that day, all of which had to be abandoned – with a promise to collect them next morning. Although he was not permitted to return in person, a volunteer party, under a New Zealand medical officer, set out next morning to fulfill that promise. Failing to find the men where they had been left, they began a search that ended with the discovery of the party who had decided to 'struggle down under their own steam', perhaps given strength by the rum and the desire not to be captured. At much the same time as the rescue party came on the wounded so did a German soldier who told them that they could go no further without permission from the local commander.

'A delegation duly presented itself and the German officer then handed them a written note addressed to "The English Commander".' The note informed the 'English Commander' that this would be the last party allowed to pass through. A German orderly then escorted the party along 'a devious route' to prevent them noting the layout of German positions and took his leave of them when they had cleared those positions, finally wishing them luck and shaking hands with them. It was a perfect example of the gentlemanly behaviour shown by both sides to the wounded.[82]

Those who had been evacuated felt disappointed, the Gurkhas even asking who was relieving them. While 2nd New Zealand Division took up its new positions on the Cassino front, 4th Indian Division was relieved by 78th Division before moving into reserve and later transferring to V Corps on the Adriatic front. The Indians had suffered heavily and rest was needed. Tuker would not return to his Red Eagles and, on 25 March, Major General A.W.W. Holworthy DSO MC took over as GOC. That day 11 Brigade of 78th Division began relieving both 5 and 7 Indian Brigades: 2nd Lancashire Fusiliers took over Point 175 and the hillsides overlooking the Rapido; 5th Northamptonshire Regiment relieved three battalions, 1st Royal Sussex, 1st/2nd Gurkhas and 4th/6th Punjabis, along the hillside betwixt Point 593 and the ravine, and 8th Argyll and Sutherland Highlanders became the new custodians of Castle Hill. During the third battle the Indian 11 Brigade had been used to reinforce the other two brigades and had seen little action as a discrete formation. The divisional machine-gun battalion, 4th/6th Rajputana Rifles, 'had fought its last battle with the Red Eagles on its shoulders' and was to return to India.[83] The former 4th Battalion (Outram's) of 6th Rajputana Rifles would become an airlanding battalion of 44th Indian Airborne Division.[84]

Reliefs by units of 78th Division were executed in a blizzard with some unable to complete their task that night. According to the diarist of 4th/16th Punjabis:

> The quickening dawn saw many of us still in the Rapido valley. Men who had spent long days in foxholes and whose knee joints and muscles had weakened through lack of normal exercise had to move carefully. The blizzard was still just thick enough to hide us from view. As we neared the transport that was to carry us away, the smokescreen cleared and the edge of the now shattered Monastery loomed out dressed in a mantle of snow as if to hide from us her scars of battle. It was a fitting farewell.[85]

Fourth Indian Division had finished with Cassino. So, too, had the New Zealand Corps, which was disbanded on 26 March with Kirkman's XIII Corps taking over its responsibilities. Second New Zealand Division would transfer to V Corps and play no part in the fourth and final battle of Cassino. The New Zealanders had suffered 1,316 casualties in the third battle and the Indians about 3,000.[86] Neither was fit to continue.

As XIII Corps settled in on its new front, plans were already in place for a further offensive at Cassino. The Germans were certain that another attack would come, but not when, or where, it would be launched.

Chapter Nine

Three attempts to break through the Gustav Line into the Liri valley had failed at the cost of many lives on both sides. Alexander faced increasing pressure from Churchill who appreciated neither the difficulties of the terrain nor the strength and resolution of the defence. Two days before the end of the third battle, the premier had demanded to know why Alexander persisted on attacking on such a narrow front.

> I wish you would explain to me why this passage by Cassino, Monastery Hill, etc., all on a front of two or three miles, is the only place which you must keep butting at. About five or six divisions have been worn out going into those jaws. Of course I do not know the ground or the battle conditions, but, looking at it from afar, it is puzzling why, if the enemy can be held and dominated at this point, no attacks can be made on the flanks. It seems very hard to understand why this most strongly defended point is the only passage forward, or why, when it is saturated (in a military sense), ground cannot be gained on one side or the other. I have the greatest confidence in you and will back you up through thick and thin, but do try to explain to me why no flanking movements can be made.[1]

Majdalany commented, apropos the third battle, that 'the Fifth Army front was between 20 and 25 miles but for a week they would fight the Germans on a front of less than 1,000 yards'.[2] This was what puzzled Churchill and also frustrated him to the point that he became more critical of his Army commanders. Brooke noted that the Cabinet meeting on Monday 20 March was one 'of the worst with Winston in one of his worst moods! Nothing that the Army does can be right and he did nothing but belittle its efforts … .'[3] A week later Brooke recorded 'Alexander stuck at Cassino'.[4] The following day he was concerned about the prime minister's health, describing Churchill as being 'in a desperately tired mood. I am afraid that he is losing ground rapidly … [and] seems incapable of concentrating for a few minutes on end'.[5] Brooke attributed this to the pneumonia attack Churchill had suffered earlier that year, later writing that, at the time in 1944, he had felt that the burden Churchill had been carrying was 'gradually crushing him'.[6]

Thus Churchill's physical condition may have contributed to his frustration at the lack of progress in Italy. However, he seems to have been mollified by Alexander's response, outlining plans being drawn up by his chief of staff, John Harding. These involved both Fifth and Eighth Armies attacking on a much broader front than had the New Zealand Corps and with larger forces than before. Churchill responded:

> Thank you very much for your full explanation. I hope you will not have to 'call it off' when you have gone so far. Surely the enemy is very hard-pressed too. Every good wish. The war weighs very heavy on us all just now.[7]

After the second battle Alexander had decided to 'carry out a thorough regrouping of forces and re-organization of command, the main lines of which were reported by General Harding, my Chief of Staff, to Allied Force Headquarters [AFHQ] in an appreciation dated 22 February'.[8] This regrouping meant bringing Eighth Army HQ west of the Apennines to assume command of all British troops, save for a corps in the Adriatic sector and the two divisions at Anzio, and using that army to take Cassino and break into the Liri valley. Meanwhile Fifth Army would advance on a parallel axis south of Eighth through the Aurunci mountains; VI Corps would break out of Anzio, advance towards Valmontone and cut Highway 6 behind Tenth Army. Apart from the timing of the VI Corps breakout from Anzio this was the plan implemented in May.[9]

The regrouping was intended to ease the logistics and command problems of having formations and units from two nations under a common command; Alexander preferred to have corps that were either completely American or completely British. (The French were organized along American lines, with Commonwealth formations and the Poles on British lines.) Although the first three attacks had failed to achieve the breakthrough, they had left the army group 'with solid advantages'. Those included holding most of Cassino, with a bridgehead over the Rapido in which 'we could concentrate the proper force for a renewed offensive', as well as a significant salient into the German right, or southern, flank, gained by McCreery's X Corps in January, which proved its value to Fifth Army in May. The once-threatened VI Corps at Anzio was positioned to 'cut all the enemy's communications when they should break out, or to threaten directly the possession of Rome on which the Germans set such value'.[10] As a result of the re-organization Fifth Army moved all its supply dumps from the axis of Highway 6 to that of Highway 7, the Via Appia, while Eighth Army's field maintenance centres were established along Highway 6. All this was happening while the New Zealand Corps was carrying out its March operations and required considerable co-ordination. Matters were not helped by the weather and it was the late March before the necessary reliefs and transfers were complete. McCreery's X Corps quit Fifth Army on 31 March, being relieved in the Garigliano sector by Keyes' II Corps and Juin's CEF.[11]

***

General Wilson, supreme commander in the Mediterranean theatre, was concerned about Alexander's planned pause in operations and its possible effects. On the other hand, he was optimistic about the effects of air power, his general plan being 'to use the air to deprive the enemy of the ability either to maintain his existing positions or to withdraw his divisions out of Italy in time for OVERLORD'. Alexander was not so much in thrall to the arguments for air power and felt that AFHQ's optimism

> was based largely on an over-estimate of the disorganization caused by bombing attacks on marshalling yards; but even the more effective policy of creating blocks at defiles, especially by the destruction of bridges, which was subsequently adopted with the support, and, in part, on the advice of my staff, never in fact achieved this desirable result though it did seriously reduce the enemy's margin of maintenance.[12]

Alexander was referring to Operation STRANGLE, the air offensive 'to destroy German rail, road, and sea communications south of the line Pisa-Rimini' thereby reducing the ability to supply their forces south of Rome. Operation STRANGLE began with a directive issued by Major General John K. Cannon, commander of MATAF, on 19 March which classified the importance of targets: railway marshalling yards and repair facilities were of 'first importance' with bridges, tunnels, viaducts and some stretches of track of 'secondary importance'. Although not an integral part of STRANGLE, operations by MASAF, when the heavy bombers and the Wellingtons were not required to participate in the Combined Bomber Offensive against Germany, would also be conducted against targets beyond the range of lighter bombers, such as marshalling yards in northern Italy.[13]

***

On 21 March Alexander held a conference with his army commanders, Clark of Fifth Army, with whom we are already familiar, and Lieutenant General Sir Oliver Leese Bt of Eighth Army. Leese had succeeded Montgomery at the beginning of January when the latter left to take command of 21 Army Group in the UK. Although he had been commanding XXX Corps in England, preparing for the landings in France in 1944, Leese was no stranger to Eighth Army. He had commanded XXX Corps for the final battle of El Alamein, having been brought out from England by Montgomery following his accession to command, in the subsequent pursuit into Libya and the campaign in Tunisia. Thereafter he helped plan the landings in Sicily, Operation HUSKY.

Leese was commissioned in the Coldstream Guards early in the First World War and soon became a casualty, being wounded on 20 October 1914. Less than

94: Lieutenant General Sir Oliver Leese Bt, who succeeded General Sir Bernard Montgomery as commander Eighth Army. In preparation for the final battle, Eighth Army was sidestepped across Italy. (IWM TR1759)

two years later, as Sniping and Intelligence Officer of his battalion, he earned the DSO at Flers Courcelette, the first battle in which tanks were deployed, on 15 September 1916. He was also wounded in the stomach, the bullet passing through a whiskey flask, a twenty-first-birthday present from his mother, and being deflected from his heart. To return to his battalion in time for the battle Leese had illicitly commandeered a vehicle in Paris. His commanding officer, receiving a signal to send him back there to face an enquiry, replied that Lieutenant Leese had been killed; no further action was taken. This was the third occasion on which he had been wounded.

As well as the DSO, Leese was twice Mentioned in Despatches. Remaining in the Army after the war, by 1939 he had been promoted to colonel and had commanded 1st Coldstream. An instructor at the Indian Army Staff College, Quetta (now in Pakistan),* when war broke out, he was ordered home to command a brigade but, because of the German invasion of France, was posted to HQ British Expeditionary Force as Deputy Chief of Staff. Leese was evacuated from Dunkirk with Field Marshal Lord Gort VC.

Thereafter he commanded the newly-formed 29 Infantry Brigade Group which he was to train. In December 1940 he was appointed GOC of West Sussex County Division before being appointed to command 15th (Scottish) Division. Then, in June 1941, he was given the task of forming and training Guards Armoured Division, remaining as its GOC until Montgomery asked for his transfer to Eighth Army and command of XXX Corps. He had proved an extremely capable divisional commander and made a great success of converting guardsmen from infantry to armoured soldiers.[14]

Leese was a complete contrast to Montgomery, shunning the limelight, but he shared his predecessor's belief in maintaining morale by visiting units on the ground. When he became Eighth Army commander the advance east of the Apennines had come to a halt. With the front temporarily inactive, save for some Canadian operations in mid-January 1944, Leese had an opportunity to become familiar with his new command and assess its problems and capabilities. He was not to know then that Eighth Army would be transferred west of the Apennines to bring the full weight of Allied Armies Italy to bear on the Gustav Line.

***

---

* Today the Pakistan Army Command and Staff College. During the war a Middle East Staff College was established in Haifa; Galloway, later GOC 4th Indian Division, was an instructor there.

Alexander continued to see his role as being 'to force the enemy to commit the maximum number of divisions in Italy at the time of OVERLORD'. Although unaware of the exact date of OVERLORD, he knew that the target date was early May and thus intended his army group to launch its offensive about fifteen to twenty-one days beforehand. He considered that the most effective way to attain his object was 'not merely to push back the enemy's line but to destroy enemy formations in Italy to such an extent that they must be replaced from elsewhere to avoid a rout'. He quoted Nelson's axiom that 'only numbers can annihilate', adding that he needed to achieve a local superiority of three-to-one in infantry, emphasizing that this was a local, not an overall, superiority.[15]

Since the Germans still had eighteen or nineteen divisions south of Rome and probably five, including three still being formed, elsewhere in Italy, it would be essential to reinforce the Allied strength of twenty-one divisions to the equivalent of about twenty-eight and a half by mid-April. However, four would be armoured divisions, 'of less value than infantry for fighting in Italy'. (Alexander had been critical of the deployment of 5th Canadian Armoured Division to Italy since he believed he had sufficient armour for the conditions in which his command was fighting.)[16] Eventually, he would be able to field a force equal to fourteen divisions in Fifth Army, of which six, plus the Special Service Force, were at Anzio, and the remainder, including Juin's CEF, reinforced to over four-division strength, were on the main front from the Tyrrhenian coast to the junction with Eighth Army. For its part, Eighth Army had twelve divisions and the equivalent of a further two, nine on the main front, in addition to three armoured brigades.

Fifth Army had II Corps in the main line with 85th and 88th Infantry Divisions, plus a group from 1st Armored Division, the bulk of which was with VI Corps in the Anzio bridgehead. The two infantry divisions were relatively raw, especially when compared to 34th, 36th and 45th Divisions: 85th Division, the Custer Division, had been re-activated in Camp Shelby, Mississippi, in May 1942, under Major General Wade H. Haislip. Before its training was complete, Haislip, promoted to command a corps, was succeeded by Major General John B. Coulter who took the Custermen to war and Italy; 339th Infantry Regiment disembarked in Naples in March 1944. Within days it was in the line, to be followed by other elements of the division with its HQ 'in an olive grove about ten miles behind the front' on 3 April. Five days later the Custermen took over part of Fifth Army's line, although 339th Infantry already held Fifth Army's extreme left sector, anchored on the Tyrrhenian sea near Minturno. On 10 April the division took over the coastal sector of II Corps' line and 'was committed to action as a [formation] for the first time in its history'. Although there were no major actions, casualties were suffered from enemy artillery, mortars, Nebelwerfer rounds and riflemen.[17]

The Custer Division's sister formation, 88th Division, also known as the 'Blue Devils' or the 'Cloverleaf Division', was re-activated at Camp Gruber, Oklahoma, in July 1942 under Major General John E. Sloan, a veteran with thirty-one years' service. Basic training was followed by participation in the Louisiana manoeuvres before the division left for North Africa in December, arriving in Italy at the end of the month. Some personnel entered the line with Fifth Army in early-January and Sergeant William A. Streuli, of Paterson, New Jersey, became the Blue Devils' first fatal casualty in a Luftwaffe bombing raid west of Venafro on the 3rd. On 27 February the division was first committed to front-line combat when 2nd Battalion 351st Regiment relieved 141st Infantry on Point 706 near Cervaro.[18] Thus elements of both divisions covered II Corps' front from the sea to the left boundary of the French-held Monte Fuga bridgehead, north of the Garigliano.[19]

These two infantry divisions formed the backbone of II Corps as it prepared for the fourth assault on the Gustav Line. In the Anzio bridgehead VI Corps included 3rd Division, now commanded by Major General John W. 'Iron Mike' O'Daniel, Ryder's 34th Division, 45th Division, commanded by Major General William W. Eagles, 1st Armored Division, 1st Special Service Force, and the British 1st and 5th Divisions. The British formations were commanded by Major Generals Ronald Penney and Philip Gregson-Ellis respectively, Penney being the first officer commissioned into the Royal Corps of Signals to achieve divisional command. One other US formation, 36th Division, was held in army reserve but would later move to the Anzio bridgehead. Fifth Army also held 509th Parachute Infantry Regiment in reserve, plus an Italian brigade group.

Juin's *Corps expéditionnaire français* included four divisions, three groups of *tabors* and an armoured group. General Brosset's *1ère Division de Marche d'Infanterie*, formed of the *1ère*, *2ème* and *4ème Brigades d'Infanterie*, arrived in Italy in April; it was also known as the Free French Division or 1st Motorized Infantry Division. General Dody continued to command *2ème Division d'Infanterie Marocaine* with *4ème*, *5ème* and *8ème Régiments de Tirailleurs Marocaines* while Monsabert's *3ème Division d'Infanterie Algérienne* included two Algerian regiments (*3ème* and *7ème Régiments de Tirailleurs*) and *4ème Régiment de Tirailleurs Tunisiens*. General Sevez's *4ème Division Marocaine de Montagne* had arrived in February, after the corps' last action, and included the *1er*, *2ème* and *6ème Régiments de Tirailleurs Marocains*. General Augustin Guillaume commanded the *Groupement de Tabors Marocains*, consisting of the *1er*, *3ème* and *4ème Groupes*; each *groupe* included three *tabors*, each of three *goums*, the last-named equating to an infantry company.[20]

Each French division included field and anti-aircraft artillery as well as engineers; Brosset also had a regiment of naval fusiliers, while Dody, Monsabert and Sevez each had regiments of *spahis*, light cavalry units recruited in French North Africa. Attached to Brosset's division was a unit of *chasseurs d'Afrique*, also light cavalry, and 757th US Light Tank Battalion. Monsabert had a *chasseurs d'Afrique* regiment and 755th US Light Tank Battalion.[21]

***

Eighth Army's order of battle included four corps with an armoured reserve of 6th (South African) Armoured Division, formerly 1st Infantry Division, veterans of the Desert campaign, commanded by Major General Evered Poole. Kirkman's XIII Corps was composed of the British 6th Armoured (Major General Vyvyan Evelegh), 4th Infantry (Major General Dudley Ward in the final battle) and 78th Infantry Divisions, and 8th Indian Division (Major General Dudley 'Pasha' Russell); it also included 1 Guards Brigade and 1 Canadian Armoured Brigade (Brigadier W.C. Murphy). McCreery's X Corps included only one full division, the recovering 2nd New Zealand, as well as three brigades, 24 Guards, also recovering after their experiences at Anzio, 2 Parachute, and 12 South African Motorized with General Umberto Utili's Italian *1° Raggruppamento Motorizzato* (1st Motorized Group). The other two corps were I Canadian, under Lieutenant General E.L.M. 'Tommy' Burns, including Major General Christopher Vokes's 1st Infantry Division and Major General B.M. 'Bert' Hoffmeister's 5th Armoured Division, as well as the British 25 Tank Brigade, under Brigadier J.N. Tetley, of the famous Yorkshire brewing family. Lieutenant General Władysław Anders commanded the Polish II Corps, which disposed two infantry divisions and an armoured brigade. Rather than the normal three-brigade order of battle, Anders' divisions, 3rd Carpathian and 5th Kresowa, had but two brigades each and were commanded by Bronisław Duch and Nikodem Sulik-Sarnowski respectively. The division also included 2 (Warsaw) Armoured Brigade, under Brigadier General Bronisław Rakowski. Anders' command relieved 78th Division in the Cassino sector on 27 April.[22]

***

At Alexander's conference on 21 March Freyberg reported on his corps' situation. Alexander's two immediate options were discussed: reinforce New Zealand Corps with the hope that it might secure the Abbey within days, or abandon the operation. With the latter the agreed choice, it was decided to plan a fresh offensive with Eighth Army making the main effort. Planning was already underway for Eighth Army's move, its headquarters having begun moving from Vasto to Venafro on 11 March. Complete at Venafro by the 13th, Leese's HQ was in place for the bombing of Cassino two days later with the consequences already noted. As the army followed, leaving Lieutenant General Charles Allfrey's V Corps under Allied Armies in Italy command on the Adriatic sector, Alexander faced a problem. Planning for the landings in France included a landing in southern France, Operation ANVIL, for which his command was to supply major formations, including Juin's corps. However, he obtained an agreement to delay the transfer with ANVIL delayed until August, and renamed DRAGOON. Assured that the French would remain with Fifth Army, Alexander was confident that he would enjoy the manpower superiority needed to crack the Gustav Line and break into the Liri valley.[23]

Two other problems faced Alexander's staff, about which he had limited influence. He had none over the first, a shortage of ammunition for 25-pounders and medium artillery. This was because industry was unable to keep pace with the demand for such munitions, expenditure of which had been especially high in Italy. During the final battle of El Alamein, from 23 October to 4 November 1942, Eighth Army's artillery had fired 1,027,000 25-pounder rounds and 200,000 medium rounds; the daily rate of fire for 25-pounders was 102 rounds per gun; with only forty-eight medium guns the daily rate per gun was over 300. From October 1942 until May 1943 British armies in North Africa had used 10,000 tons of ammunition each month. In the final three months of 1943 in Italy the monthly rate had more than doubled to 22,000 tons.[24] To deal with the crisis, Alexander introduced a rationing system on 21 March. Thereafter, 25-pounder ammunition was not to exceed fifteen rounds per gun per day, with the quota for mediums ten per gun per day. Exceptions were permitted to repel attacks, or support operations ordered, or approved, by Alexander.[25] Neither the gunners nor the infantry were ever aware of the true extent of the ammunition famine. It was known only to Alexander, his higher commanders and staff officers, thus averting a morale crisis. On the ground the problem would not have been obvious: sufficient ammunition was usually available for most purposes whilst the rationale of stockpiling was appreciated at all levels.

Although the other problem facing Alexander was one of demographics, he could do something about it. Such was the strain of war that the United Kingdom was reaching the limits of its available manpower, not only for the armed forces but also for industries essential to the nation's war effort, and very survival, such as agriculture, coal-mining and manufacturing.* The level of casualties in Italy had also been much higher than expected due to the nature of the fighting in the mountainous terrain. Earlier in the year Alexander had been informed that 13,250 infantry reinforcements were being sent to the Mediterranean but that he could

---

* The wartime British aviation industry built a very limited number of transport aircraft, depending on supplies from the USA, thus saving on manpower that could instead build fighters and bombers, but giving the UK a disadvantage in the commercial market in the post-war years.

expect no more until September, thus compelling him to make arrangements within the theatre for battle casualty replacements.[26]

The Mediterranean Allied Air Forces continued playing their part in the build-up to the new offensive, codenamed Operation DIADEM. Some two thirds of air operations were carried out in preparation for DIADEM, the other third being on targets outside Italy. Excluding anti-shipping missions and raids on ports, 60,345 sorties were flown between 1 April and 12 May, an average of 1,472 per day, an increase of about 20 per cent on the rate in March, when the weather had been less favourable and the Vesuvius eruption had also affected flying.[27] These included attacks as part of Operation STRANGLE in which MATAF aircraft flew 15,329 sorties, the majority, 9,263, by fighter-bombers against 'small marshalling-yards, moving trains, stretches of track in open country, and motor transport'. The fighter-bombers' targets were usually at a hundred miles from the fighting front so that rail traffic would be stopped far enough away to put almost impossible strain on German motor transport by increasing the distances road vehicles would have to travel to supply front-line troops. Almost all daytime road movement was stopped as a result. Medium bombers were MATAF's most powerful weapons, capable of carrying much larger bomb loads than fighter-bombers, with their efforts concentrated against bridges. Improved bombing techniques, combined with experience, increased considerably the accuracy of their attacks. However, the fighter-bombers were more flexible: they flew at low levels and could operate in most weather conditions whereas the mediums needed to fly higher to bomb effectively and thus were more constrained by weather.[28]

By the time Operation DIADEM began on the night of 11/12 May, the Allies had achieved complete control of the air. STRANGLE had had a major effect on the German ground forces. In its first phase, from 19 to 31 March, 1,136 tons of bombs fell on railway marshalling yards, 1,692 tons on 'Interdiction' targets, including road and rail bridges, and 200 tons on roads and transport. Fighters also flew sorties to strafe German road vehicles. Those first dozen days may not have brought German road and rail transport to a standstill but had impeded both considerably. Kesselring noted, on 4 April, that Tenth and Fourteenth Armies were receiving a daily supply of only 1,357 tons against the necessary 2,261. As the bombing continued more serious impediments were inflicted on Kesselring's forces with roads blocked, bridges destroyed and railway lines damaged. At the same time MASAF heavy bombers, plus RAF Wellingtons, flew no fewer than 2,815 sorties during STRANGLE, mostly against targets north of the Pisa-Rimini line. These included RAF B-24 Liberators bombing the Vicenza marshalling yard on the night of 2/3 April while, on the 7th, B-17 Fortresses and B-24 Liberators hit marshalling yards at Treviso, Mestre (Venice), Ferrara and Bologna, with 397 tons, 219 tons, 59 tons and 214 tons of bombs respectively. Treviso's station buildings were destroyed and tracks damaged badly; through traffic was halted at Mestre which also suffered severe track damage and demolished buildings, while rail traffic near Bologna was disrupted completely for two weeks.[29]

Such was the effect of the STRANGLE attacks that, on 11 April, Kesselring appointed a Luftwaffe officer, General Wenninger, as 'General with special responsibility for the maintenance of rail communications in Italy', under whom railway construction battalions planned and carried out repairs, using army engineers for skilled work and local units, the Todt Organization and conscripted civilians as labourers. Wenninger's organization displayed considerable skill and ingenuity in devising ways around blockages, moving supplies from train to train or to road vehicles, building diversions for road traffic and often employing small vessels to move goods along the coast between small harbours or suitable beaches.[30]

***

It had not escaped the notice of soldiers on the ground that something big was being prepared, although their war continued in its usual, sometimes brutal, often boring, fashion. While some were in positions well separated from their foes, others were uncomfortably close to them. Alexander described the intimate closeness of many front-line adversaries: 'The Germans were at most 150 yards away; at least in the next-door room.'[31] On 26 March the British 4th Division, veterans of the Tunisian campaign with First Army, transferred from Fifth Army to Eighth. Under Fifth Army command the division had already sampled that form of static warfare that was the lot of the soldier facing the Gustav Line. The division had been relieved from that routine for rest and maintenance before relieving Monsabert's Algerians north of Cassino in the mountains. Major General John Hayman-Joyce, the GOC, reconnoitred the sector on 26 March during which his CRA, Brigadier Ivan Smith, was killed by shellfire.[32]

Fourth Division's new sector was an eight-mile front 'across the wild and mountainous country of the Upper Rapido' with positions overlooked by Germans; frequent shelling and mortaring caused many casualties. The division's soldiers found the enemy more aggressive than their previous opponents along the Garigliano, 'possibly because here it was their turn to hold the dominating positions'. Hayman-Joyce deployed 10 and 12 Brigades in the line, with Prestonforce (4th Reconnaissance Regiment, 2nd Somerset LI, and a detachment of No.2 Support Group) on the right of the line, commanded by Lieutenant Colonel Preston of 4 Recce. Prestonforce was positioned north and north-west of Vallerotonda covering the mountain village of Valvori and the Ancina valley. In the centre 12 Brigade, north and north-west of Sant'Elia, blocked the Secco valley and the road from Belmonte, while 10 Brigade, on the left, guarded the heights covering Monte Belvedere and the

95: While reconnoitring the positions in which the British 4th Division was to relieve Algerian troops north of Cassino, Brigadier Ivan Smith, commanding the divisional artillery, was killed by German shellfire. (Author's photo)

southern portion of the road wending upward through a series of corkscrew bends from Cáira to Terelle. The terrain was very difficult with wooded and scrub-covered ground interlaced with deep gullies, all providing cover for enemy patrols at night-time. Such patrols frequently passed without a shot being fired from either side, the Germans having no desire to provoke a battle and the British because they had failed to observe their foes. Although the infantry had orders to fire only at Germans within twenty-five yards, ambushes were organized for unwary enemy patrols.

Often the Germans would shout a few words in English, to gain time in a surprise encounter. Sometimes they would carry out a full-scale raid: during the day they would bring down prolonged harassing fire on a company position, perhaps make some sort of demonstration, and then after dark put in the raiding party, covered by a box barrage, on one of the more isolated platoons.[33]

The German ability to see all that happened on the lower ground made re-supplying and relieving front-line units difficult. However, the problems were overcome in a logistical programme that was typical for maintaining formations in such positions. All necessities were brought forward under cover of darkness to forward positions where mule trains waited to carry the loads uphill where they were needed. Each nightly re-supply of a battalion required some fifty mules.

A mule could carry 160lb, thus making it necessary to sort out the food carefully to avoid overloading. It was essential to put the more valuable items, such as rum, tea, sugar and milk on separate mules in case one did not complete the journey. Mail was put in metal boxes to keep it dry. Water was carried in cans. Loads were tied together with metal rings on them in order that they could easily be fixed to the saddle, and were placed side by side with a space in between. Thus when all the tying up was completed there would be a double row of loads. At 1800 hours … the mules would be led up the centre of these two rows and the loads hooked on to each side of them.[34]

Of course there had been an earlier, and also hazardous, journey before the mules were loaded for the uphill trek. All re-supply materials, whether rations, ammunition or equipment, were transported by lorry from field maintenance centres (FMCs), or supply dumps, well to the rear to assembly areas that were well hidden from German artillery observers. There the vehicles waited until nightfall.

when it was dark enough, a military policeman would give the order to 'move' and everybody rushed off. 'Rushed' was the appropriate term. There was one section of road along which everyone drove like people possessed in spite of the state of its surface; it very quickly received the soubriquet of 'The Mad Mile'. Along the route were posted notices such as 'Shell Trap – No Halting' just in case there were any unwary drivers. The journey forward was anything up to eight miles … accomplished by wheeled transport and then by mules, which made the trek up to the units whose locations were otherwise inaccessible. Many mules were killed by mortar fire, or fell to their deaths from the difficult mountain tracks.[35]

The other infantry divisions of XIII Corps were 8th Indian and 78th, the former having been part of V Corps on the Adriatic sector and the latter of New Zealand Corps. XIII Corps held the seven miles between Cassino and the Liri Appendix, an apex of land bounded by the confluence of the Gari and Liri rivers. We have already noted that 4th Division was in the line north of the town where, on 21 April, 8th Indian Division's 21 Brigade relieved 2 Independent Parachute Brigade while, ten days later, 17 and 19 Indian Brigades moved to a training area along the Volturno to begin training in river crossings, use of assault craft, bridging, and working in battle with 1 Canadian Armoured Brigade, with 11th (Ontario) Armoured Regiment assigned to 17 Brigade and 14th (Calgary) Armoured Regiment to 19 Brigade; 21 Brigade, on its relief in Cassino, went into divisional reserve. Alongside 4th Division, Dudley 'Pasha' Russell's 8th Indian Division was to assault across the Gari when Eighth Army opened its attack on D Day.[36]

Seventy-eighth Division, as part of Freyberg's corps, had been partially sucked into the third battle with 6th Royal West Kents having relieved the Essex at the Castle, a position that remained probably the most vulnerable of those for which 78th Division was responsible. Those Germans on Monastery Hill could look down into the courtyard of the ruined fortification which was also menaced by the paratroopers still in the town. (At that time all that remained of the medieval building was the central courtyard, part of a stone tower and the remains of a curtain wall about ten feet high and up to five feet thick. The Castle has since been restored.) The West Kents had to climb almost vertical rocks to reach it.

> At first it was held by two complete companies, but this was later considered … unnecessary. It was more economical to hold the vulnerable spot with just two platoons, each of which was relieved after forty-eight hours. It was further decided to rotate this onerous task so that the two platoons were taken from each company, and each battalion in [36 Brigade] in turn. Everyone was to have the 'honour' of holding the castle.[38]

The Castle also hosted an OP party from 138th Field Regiment. Defence depended greatly on the infantry being able to call down gun and mortar fire, since they could not be reinforced quickly; artillery and mortars had repelled earlier German attacks. One enemy bombardment cost the lives of nine men of 8th Argyll and Sutherland Highlanders while the entire gunner OP party was injured in another.[39]

Thirty-six Brigade was also responsible for the station, where, in the following weeks, 5th Buffs were shelled and mortared heavily, losing sixty casualties, including a company commander killed. Their supporting artillery, 358 Battery of 138th Field, engaged enemy gun and mortar positions regularly. The station was

96: Little was left of the town after the bombing. (NARA)

on one flank of the divisional line, which extended to the slopes of Monte Cáiro, with stretches where only yards separated British and German troops.[40]

Fred Majdalany commanded a company of 2nd Lancashire Fusiliers in 11 Brigade in the mountains. With the enemy less than fifty yards away at some points, any daylight movement invited a mortar bombardment.

> The men lived behind stone sangars, crouching under cover, during the hours of daylight in cramped immobility. One company, relieved after six days in the forward area, could hardly march out for stiffness. In the forward sangars the only hot nourishment available was tea boiled over tommy cookers; rats abounded and, as the weather grew warmer, the air was heavy with the stench of corruption, and alive with flies.[41]

Death was all around and the stench of putrefying corpses, human and animal, was something veterans never forgot. Majdalany wrote with feeling about one sight witnessed by them.

> One of the most touching sights on these corpse-littered mountains was a Gurkha cemetery. The graves seemed too short for a man, and the boots at the end of each one, too small. (There was always a steel helmet at one end of the grave, boots at the other.) The rows of little boots always gave the impression that this was a burial ground of children.[42]

The third brigade of 78th Division, 38 (Irish) Brigade,* was also deployed in the mountains. Brigade HQ and the three battalions were clustered around Cáira and Monte Castellone with 1st Royal Irish Fusiliers in the valley from Cáira up towards Monte Cáiro and both 6th Royal Inniskilling Fusiliers and 2nd London Irish Rifles on Castellone. It was believed in 78th Division that Cáira was the most shelled spot in the line, if not in Italy.[43]

The 'most extraordinary position' held by the Irish Brigade was that of 6th Inniskillings, whose right company overlooked the Abbey and one of the few tracks leading into the German positions. That track was a supply route leading from Villa Santa Lucia, one of three to the front-line positions. German troops were very active in their efforts to keep the track open and had inflicted many casualties on the Algerians who had previously held the positions. In part that had been due to the Algerians not patrolling actively; in fact, they seemed not to

---

* Formed at the suggestion of Churchill, the Irish Brigade included battalions of the three surviving Irish line infantry regiments.

97: The Gurkhas whose original graves were described by Major Fred Majdalany now lie in Cassino War Cemetery. (Author's photo)

believe in patrolling. The unit relieved by the Inniskillings had been 4th Tunisians, part of 3rd Algerian Division. During the handover, the Tunisian CO explained to Bala Bredin that his men had done little patrolling as most were young recent reinforcements who were not long with the unit.[44] Lieutenant Colonel H.E.N. 'Bala' Bredin, commanding the 'Skins', had very different views and believed that his battalion should dominate no man's land. An Ulster Rifleman with an MC and Bar from Palestine, where he had commanded Wingate's Special Night Squads in Wingate's absence, Bredin had also fought in France in 1940. Posted to Tunisia as brigade major of an airborne brigade he had found life so dull after the campaign, that he transferred himself to the Irish Brigade, assuming the position of second-in-command of the Irish Fusiliers, the 'Faughs', as they embarked for Termoli; he told the author that he donned a Faughs' side-cap on the quayside and threw his maroon beret in the harbour. Subsequently Bredin was appointed to command the Inniskillings.[45]

British doctrine called for domination of no man's land as a matter of principle, which fitted Bredin's belief in aggressive soldiering. His battalion contested the in-between ground and before long owned it. Each night patrols from both sides moved into no man's land and sought cover from which to launch ambushes. More than forty years later Bredin recalled that 'The Skins always won and we

98: When 38 (Irish) Brigade deployed onto Monte Castellone, 6th Royal Inniskilling Fusiliers took up positions overlooking the Abbey. This image illustrates how close the 'Skins' were to the German defenders. (Author's photo)

99: Irish Brigade HQ was established in a farmhouse overlooking Cáira village. A modern building now occupies the site. (Author's collection)

soon established our superiority over the Germans'.[46] They also closed one of the German supply routes from Villa Santa Lucia.

John Horsfall, second-in-command of the Irish Rifles, oversaw the move of the battalion onto Monte Castellone and its re-supply. Commenting that the 'month on Castellone was the most static of any period that I ever knew while actually in the line' he noted that the nightly 1,800-foot climb to battalion HQ 'was hardly more than similar ones in … our Scottish Highlands, though Castellone had too much of the Glencoe about it for my liking'. He emphasized the difficulties of providing cover since digging in was impossible in the rocky ground.

> our pickets and observation posts had to lie up behind rough sangars built out of loose boulders. Most of these were pushed together during the night in the vain hope of protecting our men from small arms fire. Certainly they provided for nothing else and new ones had to be built most nights, if only to mislead the enemy as to which ones were occupied.

100: 'Too much of the Glencoe about it' was Major John Horsfall's comment on 2nd London Irish Rifles' Castellone positions. This is the area held by the Irish Rifles today with the Abbey to the left. (Author's photo)

The Germans had no problems on the opposite crags, having had months to prepare their positions with explosives.[47]

Another officer of the Irish Brigade provided a vivid account of life on Castellone.

Sangar life engulfed us now. No digging down into the sandy soil of Capua – laborious piling of rock with a pathetic little roof took place on these adamantine slopes. ... These were no Pathans or Afridis facing us here. This enemy dealt not in the single brain-splashing shot of the rifle, but in generalized and wholesale death. No need to view Dead Mule Corner for proof. By day and night the stench was eloquent testimony to their efficiency. ... We were many times better off than the [Inniskillings] directly facing the Monastery, where throwing the contents of his lavatory tin out the back of his sangar earned for many a man a hail of mortar bombs. Just try sharing a rock hole about the size of two coffins with

101: A contemporary image shows just how close the Inniskillings were to the Abbey. The ground between was patrolled and dominated by them during the hours of darkness, depriving the Germans of one of their re-supply routes from Villa Santa Lucia. (Author's collection)

102: The nature of the ground on Castellone is clear from this image, showing why sangars had to be built from the rock lying about. (Author's photo)

three others, then, in a prone position, lower your costume and fill a small tin held in the hand. The stink of excrement competed with the death smell on every position. Bowels will not wait for nightfall.[48]

The terrain in the area has been described earlier, but a quick reminder will not go amiss. Limestone travertine rock is very hard, an excellent, hardwearing building material that splinters easily when struck by explosives, such as bombs, shells, mortar rounds or even bullets. Shells and bombs landing on normal ground will penetrate the earth, which absorbs much of the explosion's kinetic energy, but those bursting on a rocky surface will have their destructive power increased as the rock splinters, adding to the shower of metal from shells or bombs. Such splinters fly much farther than those from explosive devices bursting on normal ground and can kill or wound at more than a hundred yards. As a result, many more men needed treatment for head wounds than before; shells bursting overhead would cascade splinters into sangars in which overhead protection was either flimsy or non-existent. Eye wounds became more common, with many being blinded. Head and facial injuries, including eye wounds, were so numerous

103: Allied troops overlooking the Abbey were in turn overlooked by Germans on Monte Cáiro. This German observation post on Cáiro was at about 5,000 feet (1,500 metres) above sea level, almost twice as high as Castellone. (© Damiano Parravano, Chairman, Associazione Linea Gustav)

that 92nd General Hospital became largely an opthalmic establishment while 65th General Hospital treated head and facial wounds as well as neurological cases.[49]

***

Formations of XIII Corps were also training for the planned offensive. As noted earlier, 8th Indian Division trained with 1 Canadian Armoured Brigade along the Volturno. Fourth Division had preceded them in the training programme with battalions relieved to train with Canadian armoured units at Viticuso, as well as with 26 Armoured Brigade of 6th Armoured Division at Alife. River-crossing training was conducted at Barracone on the Volturno and near San Giorgio Dragoni under the eyes of a Canadian training team.[50] Set-piece attacks by infantry and armour were practised, as was assisting attacking infantry by engaging enemy strongpoints and providing close fire support on designated targets.[51]

    In mid-April 4th Division was relieved by 2nd New Zealand Division as X Corps assumed responsibility for the northern sector of the line. This allowed

104: A German mortar team in action. (NARA)

105: The remains of a German observation post. (© Damiano Parravano, Chairman, Associazione Linea Gustav)

the division's units to enjoy a spell of rest in the Volturno valley before another training phase. As with 8th Indian Division, the brigades trained with armour for their assault role: 17th/21st Lancers, commanded by Lieutenant Colonel Val ffrench-Blake, would support 10 and 28 Brigades while 2nd Lothians and Border Horse with 12 Brigade formed the divisional reserve. At much the same time there was a change of GOC, as Major General Hayman Joyce handed over to Major General Dudley Ward DSO. Commissioned in the King's Regiment, Ward had commanded a brigade of 5th Division at Anzio and would lead 4th Division in its role as one of XIII Corps' assault divisions.[52] Before that, however, there was another change of scenery as 12 Brigade relieved 1 Guards Brigade in Cassino from 2 April.[53] This task continued until the three battalions were relieved by the Guards on the nights of 4 and 5 May.[54]

> Cassino town was like another world. The conditions in which the garrison had to live were so bad that troops were allowed to stay there for only eight days, and the foremost positions … could be occupied for only half that time. The place could be reached only at night, and even then the approach had to be covered by a heavy smokescreen, known as Cigarette.[55]

Life was very difficult and very dangerous during those eleven days in Cassino. Some of 12 Brigade's positions were extremely close to enemy positions; all were subject to shelling or Nebelwerfer salvoes fired from behind Monastery Hill. A Squadron 4th Reconnaissance Regiment held the station area at the beginning of May. They could watch Allied aircraft bombing German positions in the mountains and see the bombs fall to earth and explode. 'We gloried then. Now, I don't want to see it again,' wrote Bob Pite of 2 Troop. The Recce squadrons suffered the constant haemorrhage of casualties common to every unit in Cassino: when the station was mortared on 4 May a soldier of A Squadron was killed and eight others wounded while C Squadron suffered five dead and fifteen wounded from German artillery fire, one of the wounded dying later.

> The outstanding [memory] was … a defensive position in Cassino Station, through one window the Baron's Castle, from the next – not window but [a] dug-out under the wall – the monastery with the road zigzagging right in front of us up to the top and the 'hill' to the right. At night, and we stayed three whole days living under the floor with just enough room to sit up, the fireflies. I'll never forget the sight of them, little red sparks glowing and hovering everywhere.
>   I got my closest shave … here. We were stretching our legs and moving about the passageway above ground one midday. Someone pushed his

camera through a hole in the wall and took a photograph of the Baron's Castle. A minute later there was a sharp ping behind me, and there was a bullet with the tracer just dying, resting amongst the tickets of the ticket board inches from my backside. ... Nobody took any more snaps, I can tell you.[56]

German shelling, mortaring and Nebelwerfer salvoes took a constant toll. Stretcher-bearers risked their lives collecting wounded. So too did one of 78th Division's chaplains, Father Dan Kelleher of the Irish Brigade, who was at 1st Royal Irish Fusiliers' Battalion HQ near Cáira when heavy shelling struck the village, causing many casualties in one platoon.

> The Rev. Kelleher immediately raced to the village, which was under very heavy shelling. He found the wounded men and assisted the stretcher-bearers in their work, carrying wounded in his arms, at great personal risk, to the shelter of a ruined building.
>
> He comforted the badly wounded ... and assisted the overworked stretcher-bearers in applying bandages to their wounds.[57]

***

Meanwhile plans for the new offensive carried on apace. An essential element of Allied Armies' Headquarters' plan was designed to give the assaulting force, especially XIII Corps in the centre, the necessary numerical superiority to defeat the defenders and break into the Liri valley. To achieve that, Alexander's chief of staff, Lieutenant General A.F. 'John' Harding, devised an elaborate deception plan, Operation NUNTON. Harding, a gifted fighting general and staff officer, intended to keep the Germans guessing exactly where the Allies would strike and in what strength.[58] The deception plan included three discrete but inter-related aims.

Knowing that the Germans, with no real experience of such operations, worried about the possibility of further Allied amphibious operations, NUNTON's first aim was to convince Kesselring and his commanders that landings were being planned. Thus 36th US Division was deployed to Naples and Salerno for amphibious exercises. Not only did the Americans give any German agents the impression that another landing was in the offing, but they also masqueraded as Canadians, thus, hopefully, misleading the enemy as to the location of I Canadian Corps. American vehicles, military traffic signs and buildings bore the Canadian maple leaf symbol but the Canadians, in unmarked transport, had returned to the front, assembling behind XIII Corps along the Gari; this was the second aim of NUNTON.

Further strengthening German fears of another amphibious landing, Allied photo-reconnaissance aircraft flew over the beaches near Civitavecchia, under forty miles north-west of Rome, while radar stations nearby were bombed and seaborne beach reconnaissances made. This was intended to make the Germans believe that the landings would be made on 15 May with the aim that the beginning of DIADEM, scheduled for 11 May, would be seen as a prelude to an amphibious operation in the Civitavecchia area; thus the third aim of NUNTON. A XIII Corps instruction to brigades ordered each headquarters to draw up and distribute a programme of reliefs and training until, and including, 21 May.[59]

Eighth Army had been reinforced by the Polish II Corps, which had moved into the Cassino sector to take part in the offensive. The Poles' move was masked by the simple expedient of British signallers taking the place of Polish signallers, thus ensuring that monitoring of Allied radio traffic would pick up only English signals, an effective and successful deception.[60] Generally, however, radio silence was enforced until it became necessary operationally with communications meantime being conducted by telephone, liaison officers and despatch riders.[61]

Allied deception measures were aided immeasurably by air superiority with the Luftwaffe unable to fly sufficient reconnaissance missions over the Allied rear areas to provide any accurate intelligence picture. Other than knowing that a build-up was occurring, and that much of Eighth Army had moved from the Adriatic sector, German intelligence analysts had little accurate up-to-date information. Alexander's intelligence staff, in contrast, had an accurate picture of their foes' dispositions and knew the location of almost every German artillery piece, mortar or Nebelwerfer.[62]

Kesselring suggested later that Harding's deception scheme did not fool him. The evidence suggests otherwise since reserves were deployed to meet a range of threats, including the possible seaborne landings at Civitavecchia to counter which two divisions, Hermann Göring and 92nd Infantry, were positioned while 26th Panzer and 29th Panzergrenadier Divisions made ready to engage further Allied landings at Anzio while 90th Panzergrenadier Division was deployed in the Liri valley against any Allied airborne landing near Frosinone. Such deployments meant that those divisions could not move immediately to meet the real threat. If NUNTON worked well it would be some days before the Germans appreciated that the only threats were those they already faced along the Gustav Line and the Anzio bridgehead.[63]

Meanwhile Allied air forces were continuing Operation STRANGLE missions against the German logistical chain while Allied forces were well supplied; troops in even the most difficult front-line locations enjoyed good arrangements for re-supply. The army group communications system was working well, co-operation with the tactical air forces was effective and 'comfortably large' stocks of petrol and diesel fuel were held; an average division needed a daily supply of 49,000 gallons (222,754 litres) of fuel, although the humble mule had come to play an important part in the logistics plan.[64] Although the shell famine persisted, an adequate stockpile of 25-pounder and medium-gun ammunition had been created; artillery would be an important element in Operation DIADEM.

***

The training programme for those involved continued. As mentioned, Eighth Army's two assault divisions, 4th British and 8th Indian, conducted combined-arms training with British and Canadian armoured units. Following behind those two formations to expand XIII Corps' bridgehead would be 78th Division which also underwent 'serious training' from 1 May, including 'river-crossing exercises, street-fighting, and co-operation with tanks' for a formation in which 'morale had been badly bruised by a series of hard and furious battles and heavy casualties'. Within the division 38 (Irish) Brigade trained with B Squadron 16th/5th Lancers of 26 Armoured Brigade (the Irish Brigade had earlier been the lorried infantry brigade of 6th Armoured Division, the parent of 26 Armoured Brigade, a role assumed in March by 1 Guards Brigade) in a brigade battle-group that also included 214 Field Company Royal Engineers and 152nd Field Ambulance.

The linking of 16th/5th Lancers and 38 Brigade was appropriate: 5th Lancers had once been the Royal Irish Lancers, to which history an Irish harp on their NCOs' chevrons attested. Commanding B Squadron was Major Robert Preston Gill from County Meath. Each battalion of the Irish Brigade had a squadron of Lancers' tanks affiliated and the intensive training led to an excellent rapport between infantry and armour that helped dissolve the distrust and suspicion that had long existed between the two arms.[65] Moreover, the inevitable socializing deepened the sense of mutual respect and trust, prompting John Horsfall to comment that 'The bigger the blind, the better the battle'.[66]

Soldiers were also granted six days' leave, for some the last they would ever enjoy, which could be spent at rest camps at Maiori, Ravello or Amalfi. Some took day trips to Capri, or to see the ruins at Pompeii, the 'squalid, cheerful, captivating squalor of Naples', or that city's San Carlo Opera House where many were enraptured by the beauty of music. However, Naples had another side to it.

> Many a stolid soldier … felt a pang of pity as he saw the hard face of
> hunger mirrored in the patient eyes of some ancient Italian crone, or

saw the need rather than the impudence in the unselfconscious pose of a begging child little bigger than a baby.[67]

US soldiers visiting Neapolitan cafés found Italian espresso coffee unpalatable. Enterprising café owners quickly resolved the problem by topping off espressos with hot water, dubbing the resultant concoction 'Americano' and giving the world a new drink.[68]

Some cheer may have been gained from a short spell of leave, a visit to a rest camp, or the San Carlo, but each passing day brought closer the inevitable encounter with the doughty defenders of the Gustav Line.

***

The soldiers of II US Corps were the subject of some speculation since 85th and 88th Divisions were composed largely of wartime draftees, thus marking, as General Marshall later commented, 'the great psychological turning-point in the building of a battleworthy army'. II Corps' part in the forthcoming battle would be the 'first real test of the US Army's wartime training and replacement system'.[69]

Both divisions showed themselves to be well trained in their time in the line before D Day, experiencing front-line warfare under the eyes of an enemy who usually could see into both forward and rear American areas. The Custermen held Tremensuoli, a little town in a salient in the front line; its main street was dubbed 'Purple Heart Alley' since it was estimated 'that a man could appear on the street for no longer than twenty seconds without drawing enemy fire'.

> Both sides maintained an active defence … sending out nightly patrols for security, information, and prisoners. During many phases of the Italian Campaign there were what probably appeared to be monotonous reports of 'patrols were active on the Italian Front', carried in the newspapers and over the radios in the United States and other countries. Perhaps the chief reason for this 'inactivity' was the treacherous, steep, mountainous terrain, with its poor network of roads. In heavy snow or in the deep, slick mud that followed heavy rains, it was literally impossible to move tanks, bulldozers, and heavy guns up precipitous mountainsides. The most sensible thing to do was to await favourable weather.[70]

Nevertheless, patrolling, 'a highly important and dangerous assignment', was carried out every night 'in all kinds of weather'.[71] Soldiers of both divisions distinguished themselves, gathering information, taking prisoners and fighting the enemy, with many earning gallantry awards.

Although 88th Division's soldiers had been told 'back home' that they were 'one of the best outfits', those in the ranks were not convinced. These were men who

> soon were to go into their first attack and start playing for keeps up where bullets, and not words, settled the arguments. This was their first attack coming up – defensive war was over and the time was rapidly approaching when they'd have to carry the fight to the enemy. Would they go through that line or would they be thrown back?
>
> It took time – and blood – to answer those questions.[72]

During early April Fifth Army's line was held by 88th Division and 4th Moroccan Mountain Division while 36th Division, 2nd Moroccan and 3rd Algerian trained for mountain warfare in the Avellino-Salerno area. Efforts were made for infantrymen, 'weary of rocky slopes and dark days', to rest and recuperate in a morale-building programme. Reinforcements were also absorbed, each US division being assigned an additional 750 men over normal establishment so that rifle company casualties might be replaced more speedily in the forthcoming offensive. All Fifth Army's artillery pieces were calibrated by 30 April while equipment across the army was repaired or replaced. As with XIII Corps' formations there were infantry-armour co-operation exercises in addition to the mountain training. 'Above all the sunny Italian spring restored the morale of Fifth Army to the point it had reached at Salerno.'[73]

***

II Corps had a competent and experienced commander in Major General Geoffrey Keyes, a cavalryman who had gained armour experience under Patton in Tunisia and had assumed command of the corps in Sicily. His was one of three corps in Fifth Army, the others being VI Corps under Major General Lucian Truscott Jr at Anzio and General Juin's *Corps expéditionnaire français* on II Corps' left on the Cassino front. In total, Fifth Army held a narrow front of only twelve miles, whereas Eighth Army's stretched over seventy-five miles from the southern end of the Liri valley across the mountains to its left boundary overlooking the eastern coastal plain held by V Corps.[74] In manpower terms, Fifth Army, at 350,276, was stronger than Eighth, with 265,371, a difference that 'would help account for the somewhat different approaches to tactical problems on the part of the two army commanders'.[75]

Both armies were multi-national, a factor that also created problems. Although Fifth Army included the French corps, Juin's formations were American-equipped and organized on lines close to those of the US Army, but his soldiers were largely North African and thus cultural and religious differences were added to ethnic ones. (The US Army's fighting element was almost entirely white, segregation still being a matter of course in the services, although efforts were being made to include black Americans in front-line units and there was a Nisei, or Japanese-American unit, 100th Battalion, in 34th Division.) VI Corps at Anzio included British formations which were equipped differently, thus presenting an additional problem for the logisticians. This was the exception to the earlier re-organization that had placed British and British-equipped formations under Eighth Army and US and US-equipped under Fifth.

Eighth Army not only included British formations but also those from the Commonwealth and Empire. The Canadian Corps, 2nd New Zealand Division and 8th Indian Division showed how Eighth Army drew its soldiers from across the globe. To those were added Polish II Corps, which had made a remarkable journey to join Eighth Army in the shadow of Monte Cassino.

The Poles arrived in Italy with a mission. 'Their motives were as clear as they were simple. They only wished to kill Germans', according to John Horsfall. When 38 (Irish) Brigade was relieved in the Cáira-Castellone area it was by units of 6 Lwów Brigade, one of 5th Kresowa Division's brigades, whose commander, Colonel Witold Nowina-Sawicki, made a considerable impression on Brigadier Pat Scott. By the time of the relief the Poles knew that they would have

> the unenviable task of capturing the monastery and breaking through behind it in the next battle. Pat said that their attitude was unusual by British standards, and there was some question as to which brigade would lead the assault. Pat went on, '… after their general had expounded the plot one of them got up and asserted that his men had fought at Tobruk, were seasoned warriors and would naturally do the attack. But the other brigadier at once rose and immediately said no – he was the senior and he would do it.' Apparently feelings became so strong that compromise was impossible, and General Anders, their corps commander, had to resort to Solomon's solution. '… the brigades were split in half and the brigadiers commanded parts of each.' Pat also observed that such zeal in our army might have been misinterpreted.[76]

The handovers on Castellone and at Cáira were businesslike, as Horsfall noted: 'they did not bother at all about the usual refinements when taking over our posts. They just walked in with their weapons and that was that. They were quite imperturbable.' Ion Goff, commanding 2nd Irish Rifles, did his best to brief his

Polish counterpart of 16th Lwowski Infantry Battalion as he handed over his sector but they had no common language, nor, it seems, did anyone in either battalion headquarters. For 1st Royal Irish Fusiliers that problem did not arise with the incoming 17th Lwowski Battalion since the adjutant of the Faughs, Captain Brian Clark, discovered that he and his Polish counterpart, although unable to communicate in English, Polish or French, could both speak German. Although the brigade war diary noted that the Irish Fusiliers' companies all handed over to the newcomers 'after a certain amount of difficulty', that comment did not apply to the handover between the respective battalion headquarters. As Clark commented to the author many years later there was an irony in the use of German for the handover.[77]

***

The Poles had arrived from the Middle East but their journey had begun much farther away. On 1 September 1939 their homeland had been invaded by German forces following the Gleiwitz (Gliwice in modern Poland) incident the previous day in which, according to the Germans, 'Polish' troops had attacked the German radio station at Gleiwitz in Upper Silesia. However, the 'Polish' aggressors had been SS personnel dressed as Polish soldiers in an incident staged to justify the invasion. That invasion began the Second World War since both the UK and French governments issued *ultimata* to Germany demanding withdrawal from Polish soil. When Hitler's regime failed to comply, both countries declared war.

The Germans used combined-arms operational tactics as they invaded Poland from several directions. Fast-moving armoured formations, with mobile infantry, were supported by aircraft operating in close support. The media in the UK and elsewhere dubbed this style of warfare *blitzkrieg* or 'lightning war', as if it were a new form of warfare. However, the Germans had simply adapted British operational techniques from 1918, using tanks, mobile infantry, and air support, to traditional German military doctrine to create a more modern variation of the theme. Intended to unbalance a foe, it succeeded in doing so to a large extent in Poland, but the greatest unbalancing of Polish forces occurred when the Red Army invaded from the east on 17 September. The Poles had not been aware that Germany and the USSR had signed a non-aggression pact, the Molotov-Ribbentrop Pact, a week before the German invasion.

In spite of great courage and sacrifice Poland was overrun by her neighbours and carved up between them. Repression began immediately with the Soviet secret police, the NKVD (*Narodnyi Komissariat Vnutrennikh Del*), eliminating most of Poland's cultural and military elite. Among NKVD measures was the mass murder of Polish officers, over 20,000 of whom were shot near Smolensk and buried in mass graves in the Katyñ forest. Tens of thousands were sent to Siberia to provide slave labour, many dying in the horrendous winter conditions of Russia's far east. Men were worked to death in freezing conditions with temperatures well below zero; those who fell whilst hauling timber or on other hard labour were left to die or were shot, as were any who offered succour.

Some Poles escaped to continue their war against Germany in France, from where about 35,000 Polish service personnel were evacuated to the UK, the army contingent forming the Polish I Corps, based in Scotland. Another Polish formation in exile was created in Syria, then under French control. This was the Carpathian Rifle Brigade which, when France capitulated in 1940, moved to Palestine to offer its services to the UK; its men had escaped via Romania. Having fought under British command in North Africa, the brigade would form the basis of the Carpathian Division which served at Cassino.

Some of Poland's military commanders were imprisoned in Russia, among them Lieutenant General Władysław Anders who had been captured by the Red Army in Jesionka Stasiowa (Yasenka Stets'ova), a southern Polish village. Anders had commanded the Nowogródska Cavalry Brigade, which fought with distinction, and had been wounded many times, including during the battle after which he was captured, putting him on a par with Freyberg. Poland's tortured history meant that he had been born to a Baltic-German father in Western Russia, a territory that had earlier been Poland, as it is today. During the First World War he had served as an officer in a Russian cavalry regiment. Following his capture and treatment for his wounds, he was invited to join a Polish government under Soviet suzerainty. His refusal led to his being taken before NKVD 'judges' accused of having 'betrayed the international proletariat by fighting the Bolsheviks in 1918-20', to which was added the crime of fighting Soviet troops in 1939, causing casualties in their ranks. He was also accused of being a spy for refusing to join the Polish 'government' and of organizing an underground army in Lwów.

Anders was eventually taken to the Lubianka prison in Moscow, a former hotel that also housed NKVD headquarters. There he was held in basic conditions, interrogated frequently, beaten from time to time, and misinformed about events in the outside world. His cellmates changed regularly. Then, one day, he heard explosions and the crack of anti-aircraft guns and realized that the Soviet Union had been attacked. Hitler had decided to invade the USSR and Operation BARBAROSSA had been launched in June 1941. Shortly afterwards Anders was released and given a flat in which to live. Later he learned that a Polish military mission, led by Major General Zigmunt Bohusz-Szyszko, who had commanded the Polish Highland Brigade in Norway in 1940, was in Moscow and he was able to contact him. Through Bohusz-Szyszko he met the head of the British military mission, Major General Noel Mason-MacFarlane, who handed him a letter from General Władysław Sikorski, prime minister of the Polish Government in Exile in London. Sikorski informed him that he was to be acting head of the Polish army in Russia, in lieu of General Haller, whose whereabouts were unknown. The Polish army in Russia was formalized in an agreement with Stalin's government on 14 August 1941. In practice Anders' command was to be the Polish II Corps.

Anders found that things were never simple with the Soviets. Obstructions were placed in his way, although prisoners were released from camps across the USSR to join the new army with its headquarters at Buzuluk. From them it was learned that large numbers of Polish prisoners, as many as 15,000 officers and NCOs, had disappeared. Even with the new army being formed, apparently to fight alongside the Red Army, Soviet assistance seemed to be given only reluctantly; winter clothing for men training in the Russian east was provided by the UK.

While Sikorski believed that Anders' army could help liberate Poland, Anders believed that he had to get his men out of the Soviet Union to a better climate where they could enjoy better rations and healthcare. The Poles were moved to Uzbekistan where Anders learned that the Soviet government would allow them to leave for Persia, a country that the UK and USSR had invaded in the late summer of 1941 to secure its oilfields. Anders had been trying to persuade Stalin and the NKVD to do just that and the Soviet decision led to the exodus of about 115,000 Poles from the USSR, including soldiers' families who would support their menfolk as the war progressed. From Persia the corps moved to Palestine where Anders learned that it would later move to Italy; Churchill had secured an agreement for this deployment at the QUADRANT conference in Quebec. In the meantime soldiers were issued with British battledress, although retaining Polish rank badges and other insignia; the corps received British weaponry, including artillery, tanks, armoured cars and mortars, and transport.

II Corps absorbed the Carpathian Rifle Brigade which had served in Eighth Army in the desert campaign and moved from Palestine to Egypt to continue training and fitting out. Eventually, in autumn 1943, the corps' performance in manoeuvres proved its readiness to fight. The British commander-in-chief in the Middle East, General Maitland Wilson, soon to be Allied Supreme Commander, Mediterranean, agreed: II Corps would join Eighth Army in Italy. The first element to move to Italy was 3rd Carpathian Rifle Division, built on the Carpathian Rifle Brigade, which travelled to the peninsula in mid-December 1943 on a Polish ship, the MS *Batory*, escorted by Polish destroyers and submarines.

II Corps included two infantry divisions, each of only two brigades, and an armoured brigade. Third Carpathian Division included 1 and 2 Carpathian Rifle

Brigades, each with three battalions, organized on British lines, plus a divisional reconnaissance regiment (12th Podolski Lancers), a machine-gun battalion, three field artillery regiments, an engineer company, a signals battalion and medical, provost, electrical and mechanical engineers, and ordnance services. Alongside 3rd Carpathian Division, the corps would deploy 5th Kresowa Division with 5 Wileńska and 6 Lwówska Brigades and similar support and service elements; 15th Poznanski Lancers, the Poznań Uhlans Regiment, served as the divisional reconnaissance regiment. Two Armoured Brigade disposed three regiments, 1st Krechowiecki, 4th Skorpion and 6th Children of Lwów Armoured Regiments, as well as 7th Reserve Tank Battalion.[78]

There were also the usual corps units, plus the Polish Women's Auxiliary Service, *Pomocnicza Służba Kobiet*, or *PSK*, driving ambulances and lorries and serving as nurses, mechanics, despatch riders, teachers of orphaned children, couriers, and in other roles. Other women and underage males formed the Labour Auxiliary Service. Polish women probably got closer to action than women in most Allied nations, other than the Soviets, and the personnel of the PSK, known as the *Pestki*, wore with pride a slouch hat on the Australian model.[79]

The Labour Auxiliary Service had a unique member. In addition to underage male and female personnel, it included Private Wojtek, who became a Polish hero. However, Wojtek was a bear and an unlikely hero. His story began when hunters killed his parents and the orphaned cub was given to a small boy to be looked after until the hunters could sell him to someone who would train him as a dancing bear, a common sight in the market places of the Middle East. Wojtek was saved from that fate when Polish soldiers, on their journey across Persia, came across the starving boy with a hessian bag around his neck. Lance Corporal Peter Prendys, a 46-year-old, was one of a group who bartered for the bear cub with a small selection of local currency and their own worldly goods, although it was the inclusion of a tin of bully beef that persuaded the boy to part with Wojtek, a name the Polish soldiers chose after some discussion: it means 'happy soldier' or 'happy warrior'.[80]

Wojtek eventually became not simply a mascot but an accepted member of II Polish Corps, with his own military identification and even a role with 22 Supply Company. Before long he had achieved legendary status, helping to carry boxes of ammunition from lorries to gun positions.

> Standing upright, he held out his front paws into which men loaded the heavy boxes of shells. Effortlessly, he carried the munitions to their storage areas …. It was the company's proud boast that he never dropped a single shell.[81]

106: Polish troops relieved 78th Division in the mountains. Included in their Labour Auxiliary Service, and a member of 22 Supply Company, was Private Wojtek, a bear earlier adopted by soldiers in Persia. (IWM HU16546)

Such was Wojtek's contribution and his popularity that II Corps HQ approved the adoption of an official symbol for 22 Supply Company – a bear holding an artillery round[82] – which was emblazoned on company vehicles and worn as a sleeve badge on uniforms.

As we have seen, Polish troops relieved 78th Division in their front-line positions in late April. Those included the positions held by the Irish Brigade in the area of Cáira village and on Monte Castellone.[83] Pat Scott, the Irish Brigade commander, had been asked by his friend Major General Charles Keightley, GOC of 78th Division, to devise a plan to capture the Abbey but 'as I did not altogether take to the idea I said that I thought the best plan was for someone else to capture it'.[84] The 'someone else' would be Anders' II Corps.

Chapter Ten

On 5 May Alexander's headquarters issued the operation order for DIADEM, noting that the Germans could be expected to:

(a) Fight stubbornly for [their] present positions and … further resistance is to be expected on the Piedimonte-Pontecorvo line [the Hitler Line], for the defence of which all reserves at the disposal of … Tenth Army are likely to be used. It is also expected that when driven from these positions the enemy will make every effort to stabilize his front south of Rome by organized resistance on the general line North of Avezzano-Valmontone-Velletri [Caesar Line]. For the defence of that line all reserves of … Fourteenth and Tenth Armies are likely to be deployed.

(b) Once the enemy has been driven North of Rome, it is probable that he will withdraw fighting to the Rimini-Pisa line [the Gothic, or Green, Line] imposing the maximum delay on our advance by strong mobile rearguards and demolitions.[1]

Alexander intended:

To destroy the right wing of the German Tenth Army: to drive what remains of it and the German Fourteenth Army North of Rome; and to pursue the enemy to the Pisa-Rimini line, inflicting the maximum losses on him in the process.'[2]

The intention was unambiguous: destruction of the enemy's field armies rather than geographical objectives.[3] This would be critical after VI Corps' breakout from the Anzio beachhead in Operation BUFFALO.

Alexander outlined the roles of his two armies, and that of V Corps in the Adriatic sector. Eighth Army was to:

(i) Break through the enemy's position into the Liri valley and advance on the general axis of Highway 6 to the area East of Rome.

(ii)   Pursue the enemy on the general axis Terni-Perugia.

(iii) Thereafter advance on Ancona and Florence, the main objective at that stage to be decided later.

Fifth Army was to:

(i)   Capture the Ausonia defile and advance on an axis generally parallel to that of Eighth Army but South of the Liri and Sacco rivers.

(ii)   Launch an attack from the Anzio Bridgehead on the general axis Cori-Valmontone to cut Highway 6 in the Valmontone area, and thereby prevent the supply and withdrawal of the troops of ... Tenth Army opposing the advance of Eighth and Fifth Armies.

(iii) Pursue the enemy North of Rome and capture the Viterbo airfields and the port of Civitavecchia.

(iv)   Thereafter advance on Leghorn (Livorno).

V Corps was to 'hold its present front with the minimum of troops; will harass the enemy; and will vigorously pursue him should he attempt to withdraw, inflicting the maximum losses on him in the process.'[4]

Three subsidiary operations were mentioned, including French troops under AFHQ taking Elba, Fifth Army mounting a seaborne operation against Civitavecchia and V Corps doing likewise against Ancona, although the latter pair became redundant. Based on experience in North Africa and Italy, Alexander anticipated that such a large-scale set-piece operation could last for two to three weeks before a decisive outcome. He believed he might have to fight two El Alamein-scale battles, about twelve days each, en route to Rome but hoped to advance at about four miles a day, an estimate that was reasonably accurate: his armies fought from the Rapido/Gari to the Eternal City at a speed of between three and just under four miles per day.[5]

The operations of both armies were to be co-ordinated closely, thus putting maximum pressure on the Germans, reducing their ability to reinforce threatened formations. In Eighth Army Leese did not issue a written order for Operation HONKER, but emphasized to his corps commanders his intention 'To break through the enemy's main front in the Liri valley and advance on Rome'.[6]

Leese's command methods differed from those of his predecessor, Montgomery. He chose to announce his plans and consider details in conference with his commanders before making decisions. Conferences, attended by everyone concerned, were convened when necessary, thus ensuring that 'simultaneous planning [could] go on, on the right lines, at every level'.[7] What he planned for Eighth Army was a two-pronged attack by XIII Corps and Polish II Corps.

On Eighth Army's right, Anders' corps would operate north of Cassino while Kirkman's corps struck into the Liri valley.

Each corps attack was in two phases. The Poles' first phase was to isolate the Monastery Hill-Cassino area from the north and north-west and dominate Highway 6 until linking up with XIII Corps and to attack and capture Monastery Hill, including the Abbey ruins. That was to be followed by an advance to the Hitler Line north of Highway 6, developing 'operations with a view to turning it from the North'. XIII Corps' first phase was to capture and secure a bridgehead over the Gari between Cassino and the Liri river, isolate Cassino from the west, cut Highway 6 and link up with the Polish Corps, then clear Cassino of enemy forces and open Highway 6. The second phase for Kirkman paralleled that for Anders: advance on the Hitler Line south of Highway 6 and 'develop operations against it with a view to a break through'.[8]

Leese's plan was dictated by the ground, which allowed him room to deploy four divisions along his front but he felt that Monastery Hill had to be secured before successful operations could develop in the Liri valley; thus the simultaneous attacks by both corps. Each would assist the other's efforts, Polish Corps' mountain warfare on the heights aiding Kirkman's opposed river crossing while the latter ensured that German forces could not redeploy from the river line to assist those on the mountains. Eighth Army did not have a mountain corps to fight through the mountains to Atina, whence it could advance via the Melfa valley to the Liri. Such an operation had been advocated by Juin and Tuker, both men with knowledge of mountain warfare, but Leese, having examined the possibilities, decided that it was a non-starter for him.[9]

XIII Corps was suited to break-in and breakthrough operations with three well-trained experienced infantry divisions and an armoured division, the units of which, as already noted, were creating battlegroups with infantry formations, with 1 Canadian Armoured Brigade also involved. Anders' corps, with its two two-brigade infantry divisions was probably as large a force as could operate in the mountains and, as Leese deduced, 'would positively welcome a task in which American, British and Commonwealth troops had failed, as an opportunity to show their fighting quality'.[10]

Molony noted that 'two kinds of warfare contrasted sharply with each other' on Fifth Army's front with the French corps

> demonstrating mountain warfare in all its simplicity and subtlety, by laying hold of the tactically important summits, by exploiting along the high ridges with lightly equipped infantry, and by thrusting its mixed columns of armour and lorry-borne infantry along the few bad roads. The two kinds of manoeuvre were beautifully harmonized and the result

was that the Germans found the country too big to defend with their available troops.[11]

And so it would be.

Lucian Truscott's VI Corps at Anzio was to break out of Anzio in Operation BUFFALO to advance on Valmontone. Alexander visited Truscott's HQ for a long discussion about the breakout and 'made it abundantly clear that Valmontone had to have priority over other mooted objectives'.[12] Truscott's attack was to cut Highway 6 'thereby preventing the supply and withdrawal of the German Tenth Army on the southern front'. Truscott was to hold VI Corps in readiness for this operation which would be launched on twenty-four hours' notice from Alexander's HQ at any time from D Day plus 4.[13]

***

The Germans had re-organized their defences, re-aligning the XIV Panzerkorps-LI Mountain Corps inter-corps boundary: von Senger's corps became responsible for the ground from the Liri to the Tyrrhenian coast while General Valentin Feurstein's corps held the line north of the river, including the heights around Monte Cassino. Heidrich's men still defended the German-held part of the town and thence to the mountains and Point 593, but as part of Feurstein's command. To the north 5th *Gebirgs* Division held the sector to Monte Cáiro with, to their left, the Vienna Division. Feurstein, an Austrian with service in the old Imperial Army, also had Major General Alexander Bourquin's 114th *Jäger* Division under his command. Bourquin's 721st and 724th Regiments were deployed farther north in the Abruzzi but his reconnaissance battalion was with 71st Division in XIV Panzerkorps.

Senger's command included 104th Panzergrenadier Regiment of Major General Rodt's 15th Panzergrenadier Division on Tenth Army's extreme right, covering the coastline from Terracina to Gaeta. Steinmetz's 94th Division deployed from Gaeta to Minturno, covering the Gulf of Gaeta and the Allied Garigliano bridgehead. On 94th Division's left Lieutenant General Wilhelm Raapke's 71st Division, reinforced by elements from other divisions (including 94th), continued the line from the Ausente river to Sant'Ambrogio.

Senger had expected Alexander's renewed offensive to strike against XIV Panzerkorps in the coastal area since the Allies had suffered so heavily around Cassino that they would not choose that area again for the main thrust, the *Schwerpunkt*. Because the first attack in January on the right flank of the corps combined with a 'simultaneous deep outflanking movement … from the sea' had come close to breaking Tenth Army's front, he believed such a move would feature

107: Lucian King Truscott Jr, wearing the three stars of a lieutenant general. Commander VI Corps in the Anzio beachhead and break-out, he was the second-youngest corps commander in the US Army. Truscott, later commander Fifth Army in the final campaign in Italy, was arguably the finest American field commander in the European theatre. (NARA)

highly in plans for a renewed assault as 'a logical exploitation of the Anzio success, where the mere holding of the bridgehead was in itself a victory for the Allies'. He made those points in an appreciation dated 13 April and, by the end of the month, the German command agreed that the Allies would attack XIV Panzerkorps' front at several points, and land seaborne forces in the Gulf of Gaeta or north of there.

108: Major General Hans Valentin Feurstein, commander LI Mountain Corps which opposed the main elements of Eighth Army's advance in Operation HONKER. (NARA)

As a result, von Vietinghoff ordered the re-organization outlined, considering that von Senger's HQ 'would have too much on its hands' in such a situation.[14]

The re-organization order was promulgated on 24 April, the task to be complete by 10 May which, unknown to the Germans, was but a day before D Day for DIADEM. Vietinghoff's final orders, on 7 May, placed 1st *Fallschirmjäger* Division under LI Mountain Corps and reduced XIV Panzerkorps' area of

109: A joint Army/RAF team controlling close air support aircraft. The Army officer, a major of the Queen's Royal Regiment, wears an Eighth Army flash on his sleeve while the RAF squadron leader wears pilot's wings and the ribbon of the Distinguished Flying Cross. (Public domain)

responsibility. However, even on 10 May Tenth Army's order of battle was not finalized; further inter-divisional and even inter-regimental boundary changes followed while elements of some divisions were deployed under command of others. As already noted, 114th *Jäger* Division's reconnaissance battalion was with Raapke's 71st Division, as were elements of other divisions; these included 94th Füsilier Battalion* of 94th Division, 131st Grenadier Regiment and 44th Reconnaissance Battalion from 44th Division, and II/115th Panzergrenadier Regiment of 15th Panzergrenadier Division; 115th Reconnaissance Battalion of 15th Panzergrenadier Division would also come under Raapke's command on 13 May.

Molony described the German arrangements as 'markedly untidy' with decisions and orders changing constantly, not as a result of caprice but because of the need to create local reserves for the two front-line corps and the effects of Allied air superiority disrupting and slowing movements of units and formations, making any timetable impossible.[15] It should suffice to note that, on 12 May, the Allies

---

* Füsilier Battalion was the title used by some divisions for the reconnaissance unit.

had 3,960 operational aircraft, excluding transport machines, in Italy, Sardinia and Corsica, against a Luftwaffe with but 565 aeroplanes available, of which the majority, 343 (including 103 bombers and dive-bombers and 200 fighters and fighter-bombers), were based in Italy; 222 were in southern France, including 125 bombers and sixty-one fighters or fighter-bombers.[16]

Perhaps the best example of that untidiness was the Bode Blocking Group in LI Mountain Corps. Named for Colonel Bode, commander of 576th Grenadier Regiment of 305th Infantry Division, the ad hoc group included Bode's regiment, his division's 305th Füsilier Battalion, and I/ and III/115th Panzergrenadier Regiment; all answered to HQ 44th Division. In part this had occurred because Kesselring had approved moving 44th Division from the Terelle-Belmonte area to cover between the Liri and Cassino. Only the HQ had moved by D Day and, less than twenty-four hours after H Hour for Eighth Army's Operation HONKER, the Bode Group was placed under Heidrich's command. Heidrich's division deployed 1st *Fallschirmjäger* Regiment at Colle San Magno and Roccasecca, the 4th in Cassino and on Monte Cassino, and the 3rd at Albaneta Farm (Point 468). (Each regiment had only two battalions, the third having been moved out of Italy as training cadres.) Also under command of 1st *Fallschirmjäger* Division were II/100th *Gebirgs* Regiment and 4th Alpine Battalion from 5th *Gebirgs* Division, plus 44th Division's 132nd Grenadier Regiment. Lieutenant General Hans-Günther Schrank's 5th *Gebirgs* Division deployed its own 100th, less II/100th, and 85th Regiments, 3rd Alpine Battalion and 134th Grenadier Regiment from the Vienna Division.* As already noted, Bourquin's 114th *Jäger* Division deployed only 721st and 741st Regiments.

Tenth Army also included Major General Friedrich-Wilhelm Hauck's *Korpsgruppe* Hauck, deployed in the Adriatic sector, facing Lieutenant General Charles Allfrey's V Corps. Hauck's corps included 305th and 334th Divisions, but one of the former's regiments and its recce battalion were, as already noted, in the Bode Blocking Group.[17] Whereas Allfrey had 23 Armoured Brigade under command, in addition to 4th and 10th Indian Divisions, Hauck had no significant armour support. Kesselring had deployed 26th Panzer Division into army group reserve, along with 29th and 90th Panzergrenadier Divisions, the first two to support Fourteenth Army but the third divided between both armies. In northern Italy Kesselring had *Armeegruppe* von Zangen, of four infantry divisions, plus the OKW reserve formation, the Hermann Göring Panzer Parachute Division, near Leghorn (Livorno).[18] Thus the most mobile German formations were badly placed to meet the Allied attack: the Hermann Göring and 92nd Divisions were to counter a

---

* Schrank had succeeded Ringel in command of the division in February.

seaborne operation in the Civitavecchia area, 26th Panzer and 29th Panzergrenadier Divisions awaited further landings at Anzio and 90th Panzergrenadiers stood ready to engage an airborne assault near Frosinone in the Liri valley.[19]

That Tenth Army's re-organization was still underway when the Allies launched their attack is proof of the success of Operation NUNTON. Kesselring later wrote that his staff had lost track of Juin's corps, the role of which and its 'composition and direction of possible thrust remained an important and dangerous unknown factor till the fourth day of the offensive'.[20] Likewise he had no idea that the Poles were in the Cassino sector, nor that I Canadian Corps was located behind XIII Corps.[21]

Perhaps the most successful aspect of the Allied deception was convincing the Germans that the timing would be later in May. Senger wrote that when the attack was launched 'it came as a complete surprise'. He proved this by noting that he and von Vietinghoff had been 'superfluously ordered to meet Hitler to receive our decorations' while Kesselring's chief of staff was ill.[22] Having met Hitler, both von Vietinghoff and von Senger went on leave. XIV Panzerkorps had been handed over to von Senger's deputy, General of Artillery Otto Hartmann, a 60-year-old formerly of Kesselring's staff but earlier described by Field Marshal von Kleist as unsuited for operational command due to poor health and family problems. Hartmann erred in also allowing XIV Panzerkorps' chief of staff to go on leave, depriving corps HQ of that worthy's 'experience to fall back on'. Senger described Hartmann as an 'excellent but not so young general' who was 'not up to his task in this major battle', a comment that confirms that the German command was taken completely by surprise when DIADEM was launched. In fact, Senger felt that the Allies would land in France before renewing their advance on Rome.[23] Brooke wrote that Alexander's attack was due to start at 11.00pm and prayed that it would be successful as 'A great deal depends on it'.[24]

***

Vietinghoff's Tenth Army disposed nine divisions of varying strength (Heidrich's *Fallschirmjäger* Division with 4,627 men was weakest; 5th *Gebirgs* was strongest at almost 10,000) with an overall army fighting strength of 81,932. Fourteenth Army had a fighting strength of 76,873.[25] (The US official history quotes a total assigned strength for all German units in Italy as approximately 412,000.)[26] German defences were very strong and included the Hitler Line, renamed Senger Line, some miles west of the Gustav, running southwards from Monte Cáiro to the coast at Terracina by way of Piedimonte, Aquino, Pontecorvo, Monte Faggeto and Fondi. The Hitler Line had two subsidiary systems, the Dora and Orange Lines: the former branched off near Sant'Oliva in the direction of Esperia and thence via the lower slopes of Monte Fammera to Gaeta; the latter departed from the Hitler Line near Sant'Apollinare and protected the entrance to the Ausonia valley by way of Vallemaio and Coreno to Monte la Civita. The Dora Line could serve as either a layback to the Gustav or an outwork of the Hitler. Yet another line would face Allied troops as they advanced towards Rome: the C, or Caesar, Line through Valmontone to Velletri was north of Avezzano.

Although German defences were well-constructed and provided strength in depth, Allied air superiority remained a potent threat, not only in terms of attacks from the air but also from the intelligence advantages that command of the air afforded the Allies. Brigadier Pat Scott wrote that, by D Day for DIADEM, Allied intelligence knew the location of almost every German artillery piece and mortar.[27] German artillery strength was believed to be 'no more than 400 guns and rocket launchers supporting the units manning the Gustav Line in the valley'.[28] Allied artillery outnumbered German artillery while Alexander's rationing of ammunition had allowed substantial stockpiles to be built up. In Eighth Army, with almost 2,000 guns, excluding anti-aircraft and anti-tank pieces, there were 200 shells for every heavy gun in XIII Corps, 350 rounds per medium gun and 650 per 25-pounder. II Polish Corps had no heavy weapons but each medium gun had 700 rounds and every 25-pounder had 1,090. In the Polish sector were 300 guns while XIII Corps had 700; Operation HONKER would open with a bombardment by 1,100 guns on Eighth Army's front.[29] Another 600 guns, plus naval gunfire, would join in on Fifth Army's front.[30]

***

XIII Corps' task was to deliver the *Schwerpunkt*. First, however, it had to cross the Gari. Alexander's planners had considered every possible problem attackers might face. Their deception plan had been so successful that the German command had been disrupted by the absence of senior commanders, their re-organization had not been completed and their logistical support system had suffered significant damage from Operation STRANGLE. Reinforcements and matériel had managed to reach the front, but not to the hoped-for extent.

Allied artillery also came into play in the final countdown to the attack. On the evening of 11 May, D Day for DIADEM, and Eighth Army's Operation HONKER, the guns laid the smokescreen as usual, so that a change of routine would not suggest the possibility of an attack. On that day the weather had been fine but cloudy 'with a little rain, but the night was clear'[31] and 'a vast canopy of stars shone down brightly from a clear sky'.[32] It was one of the quietest evenings along the front in a long time. Suddenly, at 11.00pm, the calm was shattered by a storm of gunfire. The earth shook as some 1,600 guns opened fire from the coast to the mountains in the north. A US Navy heavy cruiser added the power of its 8-inch guns to the bombardment on II Corps' front. The bombardment's initial phase, lasting forty minutes, was directed on known German artillery positions after which Allied guns switched to their infantry's first objectives.[33]

As the guns adjusted their fire to their second task, the infantry of XIII Corps prepared to attack. Their H Hour was 11.45pm while II Polish Corps' H Hour was 1.00am on the 12th. Alexander had anticipated the usual German determined defence and several days of hard fighting for every yard of ground. His assessment was accurate. In spite of the absence of von Vietinghoff and von Senger, German defence was tough and well organized.

XIII Corps' leading divisions were 4th British and 8th Indian. Their experiences were bloody and confused as they sought to cross the fast-flowing Gari in small assault boats under a moon that had risen at 11.31pm. A mist had settled over the river complicating their task and making it virtually impossible to cross by boat. German machine-gun teams fired on fixed lines at obvious bridging points while mortars and artillery engaged registered targets along the river. Some small groups of infantry crossed but were cut off and wiped out. Thus the sappers were unable to put bridges across, while anyone approaching the river on Eighth Army's side, especially at planned bridging points, was caught in the German fire.[34]

Fourth Division planned two crossings, 10 Brigade on the right and 28 on the left. The respective commanders, Brigadiers Shoosmith and Montagu-Douglas Scott, had each selected a pair of crossing points; 10 Brigade had forty-two assault boats while 28 had thirty. Crossing points were codenamed Rhine and Orinoco for 10 Brigade and X and Y for 28. Rhine was located where the Ascensione stream enters the Gari; Orinoco was some 600 yards downstream while X was another 550 yards beyond Orinoco with Y about 250 yards farther on. Between Rhine and Orinoco the sappers would build Amazon bridge; Blackwater and Congo bridges would be constructed south of both X and Y crossings. A squadron of 17th/21st Lancers reinforced each brigade.[35]

Major General Ward's intention was that both assaults would 'advance as quickly as possible to a depth of some three thousand yards beyond the river' where he planned to push his reserve brigade, 12, forward, preferably through Shoosmith's formation, to wheel right to seize that part of Cassino still in German hands. The divisional advance was designed as four 'bounds', each to successive reporting lines, Brown (1,000 yards beyond and parallel to the Gari), Blue (on high ground another 1,000 to 1,500 yards farther on), Red (a bulge about 2,000 yards in depth beyond Blue), and Green (approximately another 1,500 yards forward). Consolidation of the Brown Line was intended to protect the crossings from counter-attacks. Holding Blue Line, on the first high ground beyond the river, would hide the crossings from enemy observers in the Liri valley. The Green Line extended right in a deep salient towards the rear of Monte Cassino and the planned junction point for XIII and II Polish Corps.[36]

Leading 10 Brigade's attack were Lieutenant Colonel R.O.V. Thompson's 1/6th East Surreys, the formation's TA unit (there were three TA battalions in the division, one in each brigade). Once across the Gari, Thompson planned to advance on a two-company front, with D on the right and A on the left; C Company was to protect the crossings and battalion HQ while B formed the battalion's reserve. Lieutenant H.G. Harris led his platoon across the river to 'get a simple assault-boat ferry working at each crossing-place'[37] by swimming the Gari with a rope and establishing a ferry anchor point.[38] The operation was successful but not everything went as planned for the division.

The East Surreys were to land in a flat area of overgrown fields, crossed by drainage ditches, with the Piopetto stream to the left, and behind that an area dubbed Square Wood, only 100 yards from the Gari, in which were enemy positions. To the right was Point 36, a small defended feature riddled with caves. The area's western boundary was 'Queen Street', the road from Cassino to Sant'Angelo. In such flat ground the enemy had been unable to site many positions overlooking the river but the ground was liberally strewn with mines, and sharpshooters waited in trees thereabout.[39]

The battalion's advance was met by heavy machine-gun and mortar fire, in spite of which A and D Companies gained footholds within fifteen minutes. Two A Company boats had been sunk but D Company's beach-master, Captain W.G. Spencer, had launched his reserve boats while Harris' ferry also assisted A Company. With platoons mixed up, forming up on the far side was not simple, a situation made more confusing as the mist was thickened by the dust of battle, especially that raised by artillery and mortar fire. Such was the fog thus created that tracer rounds fired by Bofors guns to guide the leading companies were shrouded completely. Both companies blundered into a minefield, suffering many losses. 'Blinded and confused, their comrades falling around them and the battle going against them, officers and men rallied into groups and fought their way towards their objectives.'[40]

Pressing ahead, both A and D Companies fell behind the bombardment. B Company then crossed without loss and moved up 200 yards from the bank, followed by C. Heavy machine-gun fire from Point 36 brought A and D Companies to a stop; they were joined by C. Thompson's HQ had also crossed but remained close to the bank. Mortars and machine guns forced it to move three times during the night. Just before dawn B Company moved forward, joining elements of 2nd Bedfordshire and Hertfordshire Regiment, also of 10 Brigade. Point 36 fell to A and D Companies in a bayonet charge in which thirteen machine guns were captured, plus two dozen prisoners. However, an attack by B Company and some Bedfords on Point 63, the Surreys' second objective, was repelled.[41]

Thompson consolidated around Point 63, summoned his carrier platoon, on foot, to reinforce his position and distributed the surviving members of D Company, which had suffered most from the mines, amongst the other companies. All that day and night the Surreys held their position despite heavy and constant enemy fire. The Bedfords had all four companies across and had advanced, some linking up with the Surreys as we have seen. They had found their compasses to be erratic, probably the cause of two companies straying into the minefields. Nonetheless the Bedfords continued and by dawn, in spite of stout German resistance, were on

110: Commemorating 2nd Beds and Herts of 4th Division's 10 Brigade, this memorial stands on their line of advance from the Gari. (Author's photo)

Queen Street, where they received orders to dig in while 10 Brigade secured its bridgehead; for this they were joined by the remaining battalion of the brigade, 2nd Duke of Cornwall's LI, whose task was securing the left flank. Ward had decided that such a consolidation was necessary before advancing to Blue Line.[42]

The mist that had fallen the previous night did not clear in the early morning. It shrouded the valley well into the morning, fortuitously for 10 Brigade since the Germans could see neither crossings nor the consolidating troops; it was thickened with smoke-bombs from 2-inch mortars. When it cleared at last the ferry and bridging operations had to be stopped as German machine-gun fire was directed along the river line.[43]

Ward, concerned that the infantry might be attacked by tanks, thus threatening the precarious bridgehead, ordered 'only minor advances and consolidation until each Brigade had four [anti-tank] guns on the west bank'.[44] Difficult as 10 Brigade's situation was, 28 Brigade was in even worse position, having been pinned to the riverbank. Both assaulting battalions, 2nd King's (Liverpool) and 2nd Somerset LI, had suffered heavily. The Kingsmen had reached their crossing point thirty minutes late, losing the benefit of the counter-battery programme which was then coming to a close. Then, as they launched their boats, enemy fire fell on them, destroying many of the flimsy vessels. In spite of this, three companies crossed but, having lost so many men, were disorganized. Thus when B Company advanced the soldiers ran into a minefield. D Company had been reduced to an officer and ten men while C Company also lost heavily while crossing a minefield under heavy fire.[45]

Yet more confusion beset 28 Brigade as 2nd Somersets set off to follow 2nd King's. Such was the disorganization that one company even withdrew, mistakenly believing that an order to do so had been received. Thus the brigade's attack had failed and in a manner that raised questions about leadership in Brigade HQ and in the King's and Somersets, both regular battalions from whom more had been expected. The GOC, Ward, although commissioned in the Dorsets, had transferred to the King's in 1937 and cannot have been happy with the battalion's performance. The result was that 28 Brigade was withdrawn on 14 May for re-organization, not rejoining 4th Division until the 20th. However, its third battalion, 2/4th Hampshires, a TA unit, remained with the division, attached to 12 Brigade.[46] The commander of 28 Brigade, Brigadier C.A. Montagu-Douglas Scott, had taken over only on 12 April, at much the same time as Ward had become GOC. Scott remained in command until 28 July.[47]

*** *** ***

To the left of 4th Division, 8th Indian Division's assaulting brigades crossed in much the same locations as 36th Division in January, overlooked by the village of Sant'Angelo. However, lessons had been learned from American mistakes and 17 and 19 Indian Brigades were well prepared, even though German defences on the far bank had been strengthened since January. Indian engineers had strung wires or ropes across the river so that assault boats could be hauled across. In 17 Brigade's sector, on the divisional left and including Sant'Angelo, 1st Royal Fusiliers attacked on the left, north of the village, with 1st/12th Frontier Force Rifles on the right. Farther south, 19 Brigade's attack was led by 3rd/8th Punjab Regiment, on the left, and 1st Argyll and Sutherland Highlanders.

The bridging points along the divisional front were, north to south, Cardiff, London, Oxford, Plymouth, Quebec, Edenbridge, Tonbridge and Swindon, the last-named just before the Liri and Gari meet to form the Garigliano; the first seven were tank-bearing. Armoured support for 8th Indian Division was provided by 1 Canadian Armoured Brigade.

> As the shoot went down, the meadowland to the east of the Gari suddenly became alive with men. Leading companies moved forward to the riverbank. Among them staggered sappers under the weight of assault boats. Mules floundered over the dykes and drainage ditches, laden with machine guns and ammunition. At 2345 hours the first assault boats were launched, and both brigades struck for the opposite bank. The shoot on the enemy back areas abruptly switched on to a tight barrage advancing from the bank of the Liri at the rate of 100 yards in every six minutes.[48]

Brigadier Charles Boucher's 17 Brigade had little difficulty crossing, in spite of the fast-flowing waters. However, problems were encountered when the advance began. Once again, mist, a help in the crossing, proved a hindrance. The Royal Fusiliers found themselves in a pea-soup fog – German smoke shells, dust and cordite fumes had added to the mist – that their 'native London could not have bettered'.[49] Before long the fusiliers found themselves unable to maintain formation with deep drainage ditches also conspiring to make following the bombardment impossible. When the bombardment moved on, enemy machine guns and mortars began sweeping the area.

Nevertheless, the fusiliers persevered and, by 1.00am, had passed Sant'Angelo on the right but were flanked by the village's defences and 'Platform' knoll on the other side. Until those had been cleared, further advance was impossible; the battalion dug in some 500 yards forward of the Gari and re-organized as many had become detached in the fog.

> by 0400 the Commanding Officer signalled the leading companies to halt and later to re-organize on the river bank. ... The Commanding Officer

went boldly forward into the mist to locate the line of advance and, encountering wire, made the complete circuit of an enemy strongpoint. But no attack could be launched in such conditions [and the fusiliers] proceeded to dig in and wait for the mist to clear. It cleared all right the following morning and the sun came out at 0900 hours. But with it came … enemy fire … and the slightest movement brought down fire.[50]

On the brigade left 1st/12th Frontier Force Regiment had also had a relatively straightforward crossing. Hampered by fog and enemy fire while organizing for the advance, by 2.00am, however, the Frontiersmen were deployed for action. Their advance was more a case of stumbling forward, setting off trip-wires that released smoke canisters to thicken the fog and give the German machine gunners the lines on which to fire. A and D Companies approached 'Bank' position where they encountered wire, mines, grenades and machine-gun fire, prompting a change of direction. Moving to their right the companies fought into Bank from the flank while C Company fought through to the lateral road, Queen Street, knocking out enemy posts. Communication was difficult as wireless sets failed and flares were snuffed out by fog as they were fired. Modern techniques having failed, a Mussulman war cry – 'Maro nari haidriya Ali' – succeeded in giving the commanding officer locations for his positions. The Frontiersmen had taken their first objectives.[51]

German resistance had not been overcome completely. Some positions had not been seen and had been by-passed and, from those, German troops engaged the flank and rear of the Frontiersmen while machine-gun fire from Sant'Angelo also raked the Bank position. Among the casualties was Major Amar Singh, an outstanding company commander, who was killed. The reserve B Company was called forward and, making use of dead ground, eliminated a series of German positions en route.

Boucher's third battalion, 1st/5th Gurkhas, was called on to cross but encountered problems, beginning with twelve of their sixteen assault boats being destroyed by shell- or mortar-fire. It took five hours to cross, after which two companies deployed to the start-line for an attack on Sant'Angelo while the others awaited the order to advance. Two attacks on Sant'Angelo were repelled during the morning. However, all three battalions were across.

Brigadier Thomas Dobree's 19 Brigade also encountered many problems in the crossing and subsequent assault. While 3rd/8th Punjabis moved up to their launching area they came under heavy fire, suffering many casualties. A and B Companies embarked and made the crossing but on the return trip many boats were swept downstream and lost, with Major Wright, commanding B Company, among those carried away. Other boats were damaged badly or sunk by enemy fire, leaving one company front with a single boat and two improvised rafts with which to cross. In spite of this, the remainder of the battalion was ferried over before dawn. Such was the delay that the battalion, far behind the artillery programme, had to attack without either that support or the cover of darkness. What followed was a remarkable demonstration of the courage and professionalism of the Indian Army.

Captain Douglas Treman MC led A Company forward until a wire-and-mine barrier was encountered, exploding mines drawing machine-gun fire in which many *jawans* were injured. Treman was among those wounded but, in spite of grievous injuries and loss of blood, gathered fifteen survivors and advanced to the lateral road, although six of his men fell. At the road Treman ordered his remaining soldiers to dig in. They subsequently engaged a number of Germans who approached their position in fog but that afternoon, when the mist had lifted, only Treman and three men remained. With no contact with their battalion HQ and low on ammunition, they were forced to surrender.

The Punjabis' other forward company, Major Sujan Singh's D Company, had also been frustrated by the smoke but, having located their first objective, Point 63, the Sikhs charged in line abreast. Brought to a stop by barbed wire, four machine guns engaged them at close range. Major Singh, who had been at the head of his men, was killed and one platoon completely wiped out, its soldiers having charged into the German position. Their bodies were later found under the muzzles of the German machine guns.[52]

B and C Companies had also crossed and moved up to consolidate the gains of A and D. Subedar Sumera Ram took command of B Company in Major Wright's absence but Major Gardhari Singh took overall command of the attack which was quickly pinned down by intensive fire from the front and both flanks. Attempts to move brought fire and the promise of death 'until the shining heroism of young Kamal Ram saved the day'. The 19-year-old, in action for the first time, was crouched near his company commander when the machine guns forced the Punjabis to take cover. One gun on the right was especially dangerous and the company commander called for a volunteer to get to the rear of it and silence it.

> Volunteering at once and crawling forward through the wire to a flank, Sepoy Kamal Ram attacked the post singlehanded and shot the first machine gunner; a second German tried to seize his weapon but Sepoy Kamal Ram killed him with the bayonet, and then shot a German officer who, appearing from the trench with his pistol, was about to fire.

Still alone, Kamal Ram attacked a second machine-gun post which continued holding up the advance. After shooting one machine gunner, he threw a grenade into the post and the remaining enemy surrendered. Then, seeing a havildar reconnoitring for an attack on a third post, Kamal Ram joined him. Having first covered his companion, he went in and destroyed that post also. But he had not finished his work. When a platoon that had been pushed further forward to widen the position was fired on from a house, Kamal Ram dashed towards the house, where he shot one German in a slit trench and captured two more.

> By his courage, initiative and disregard for personal risk, Sepoy Kamal Ram enabled his company to charge and secure the ground vital to the establishment of the bridgehead and the completion of work on two bridges.
> … His sustained and outstanding bravery unquestionably saved a difficult situation at a critical period of the battle and enabled his battalion to attain the essential part of their objective.[53]

(Kamal Ram was the youngest man to earn the Victoria Cross in the Second World War. He received the VC ribbon from King George VI in Italy in July but his Cross was presented to him in India by the Viceroy, Lord Wavell.)

On the divisional left the terrain over which the attackers, the Argylls, approached the near bank was overlooked by German-held high ground in the Liri Appendix. As the Highlanders moved up for their crossing they came under heavy artillery fire. Their many casualties included the gunners who were to provide forward observation for the artillery. Not only did German artillery take the lives of Scotsmen, but mines laid by the Americans did likewise. The devices had been laid when the Americans withdrew in January after 36th Division's failed assault. US soldiers had sown mines on both river banks to counter any German attempts to follow up but it was believed that all had been lifted: 19 Brigade's third battalion, 6th/13th Frontier Force had spent several days in mine-clearing work. However, as the Argylls spread out along the riverbank, a number of men were blown up by mines. The unexpected threat in the launching area not only disorganized the crossings but disrupted the timetable and meant that 1st Argylls lost their artillery support.

(Some American artillery units which had served along that stretch of river in January were among the artillery supporting XIII Corps' attack and their knowledge of the front along the Gari prompted American gunners to offer ten-to-one odds against 8th Indian Division succeeding in crossing. British gunners serving with the division reputedly relieved their American counterparts of much cash.)

Only the equivalent of five platoons of Argylls crossed with those who did showing tremendous spirit by pushing forward through barbed-wire belts and machine-gun fire which cost the life of one officer and wounded another. A platoon

111: HM King George VI pins the ribbon of the Victoria Cross on Sepoy Kamal Ram of 3rd/8th Punjabis, the youngest VC laureate of the war, who was later invested with his VC by the Viceroy of India, Field Marshal Lord Wavell. (Author's collection)

of D Company reached the lateral road, crossed it and dug in for a tenuous grip 'on a narrow triangle of waterlogged ground within 200 yards of the main German position'. That platoon was Eighth Army's flank guard, all that stood between the Punjabis and any German attack.[54]

> Everywhere, except on the extreme left, the Indian infantry had made good its footing on the German side of the river. It now became a race to bring up support arms, to reinforce the firing line, and to strike the next blow. The enemy had no river to cross, no bridges to build, so that the race began with the attack carrying a handicap of several hours.[55]

Both assaulting divisions had fallen well behind schedule and the bridgehead remained shallow. The follow-up division, 78th, strengthened by armour from 6th Armoured, could not be brought forward until there was sufficient manoeuvre room. However, the sappers had excelled themselves along XIII Corps' front. On 8th Indian Division's front, in spite of machine-gun and mortar fire, work had begun on two bridges.

> On the night of the 11th of May 4 Division secured only a shallow bridgehead across the [Gari], and bridging was not possible. Two rafts were operating by 5.30am but their use could not be continued in daylight. On 8 Indian Division's front the advance made better progress. By 2.00am two rafts were operating at Oxford, and a class 30 bridge was opened there by 8.15, while by 10.30 a tank-launched Bailey was across at Plymouth.[56]

Plymouth was the first Bailey assault bridge to be built in the field. A 100-foot double-single* Bailey, it was carried by two telephone-linked Sherman tanks, one just forward of the mid-point, the second at the tail. Resting on rocking rollers on top of the lead Sherman, the bridge was launched by the second tank, the 'pusher', when the first reached the bridging point. This was done by the rear tank pushing. To complete the operation both had to move forward with the leader descending into the gap. When launching Plymouth the front tank was lost when it toppled into the Gari and submerged, the crew escaping as it slipped below the water. The concept behind Plymouth had been conceived in the HQ A Mess of 8th Indian Division by its GOC, Russell, his CRE, GSOI and the CO of a Canadian armoured regiment; concept was turned into reality by a Royal Canadian Electrical and Mechanical Engineers officer, Captain Tony Kingsmill. German prisoners expressed considerable interest in this British 'secret weapon'. 'A new type of bridge, a triumph of mechanical improvisation, was open for its first trial in action.'[57]

Shermans of 14th (Calgary) Armoured Regiment crossed Plymouth before its approaches were damaged and use restricted temporarily to light vehicles. (The problem may have been a combination of a near miss from a German shell and damage to the ramps due to the bridge 'rocking' on the carrier's rollers.)[58] Both Plymouth and Oxford were in use by 9.15am on 12 May, the latter remaining secure

---

* The term 'double-single' referred to (a) the number of trusses used and (b) the number of storeys; thus the 'double-single' had two trusses but was only one storey high whereas a 'double-double' had two trusses and was two storeys high.

and providing the route over which the Ontarios moved to support 8th Indian Division. Plymouth and Oxford were the work of the Royal Indian Engineers.

The arrival of armour was a major boost to the infantry, a certain sign that the attackers were reducing their handicap in the race to secure ground, and the end of the crisis on the Indian front. Until then 1st Royal Fusiliers had been pinned down north of Sant'Angelo and only an Argylls' platoon held the left flank; neither Punjabis nor Frontiersmen could advance without flank security. By dusk five Sherman squadrons had crossed into the bridgehead, allowing 8th Indian Division to advance, clear enemy troops from part of Sant'Angelo and make for Panaccioni. This was in spite of some difficult terrain, including marshy areas where it was unwise to venture, and little dead ground to hide Shermans from observation. That marshy ground hindered the renewed Gurkha attack on Sant'Angelo as tanks bogged before they could enter the fray; the completion of the liberation of Sant'Angelo had to be postponed until the following day.[59]

> Had Eighth Indian Division not completed its bridges, German armour, held in reserve at a focal point between the British and Polish thrusts, would have had twelve hours of daylight in which to destroy infantry west of the Gari. There is reason to believe that the enemy counted on this advantage, and that the gallantry, skill and speed of the bridge-builders upset his plans. Indian Sappers and Miners and Royal Canadian Engineers had collaborated to turn the tide of battle.[60]

Although three bridges were planned in 4th Division's sector, none was completed until the 13th when Amazon came into use. Ward had ordered its construction during the night of 12/13 May. Fourth Division's three sapper field companies (7, 59 and 225), supported by 578 Field Company from XIII Corps Troops, undertook the work, 225 leading while 8 Field Squadron of 6th Armoured Division cleared mines from the enemy bank; 586 Field Company of Eighth Army Troops also assisted. Amazon was complete by 5.30 on the morning of 13 May at a cost of eighty-three sapper casualties. With all the bull-dozers knocked out, the bridge was pushed into place by a 17th/21st Lancers' Sherman, the commander of which, Lieutenant Wayne, crossed the Gari to reconnoitre the exit.[61]

C Squadron 17th/21st Lancers crossed over Amazon as did 2nd Royal Fusiliers and 6th Black Watch of 12 Brigade. Then tanks of 2nd Lothians and Border Yeomanry followed, ready to support a 12 Brigade attack on Queen Street in which Brigadier A.G.W. Heber-Percy deployed his two battalions on a 600-yard front, Royal Fusiliers against Point 31 and Black Watch against Point 33. Both battalions and supporting tanks made good progress against determined opposition, the

112: Terence Cuneo's painting of Royal Engineers working under intense fire to build Amazon Bridge across the Gari. The work was finished during the night of 12/13 May at a cost of eighty-three casualties amongst the sappers. (Reproduced by kind permission of The Royal Engineers Museum)

Fusiliers reaching Point 41, about 1,500 yards west of the Gari, by noon; 6th Black Watch, 1,000 yards to the south-west, had reached Massa de Vivo (Point 69). In the advance the Lothians and supporting artillery had helped destroy several 115th Panzergrenadier Regiment strongpoints. That afternoon 10 Brigade's 2nd Duke of Cornwall's LI and 12 Brigade's 1st Royal West Kents, supported by Shermans of 17th/21st Lancers (the 'Death or Glory Boys', from their skull-and-crossbones cap badge, known in the regiment as 'the Motto'), took up the baton with the DCLI and their supporting tanks reaching Point 63 quickly to find that positions held by Heidrich's Machine Gun Battalion, sited to cover Cassino, were open to an approach from the rear. The Germans were taken completely by surprise by British armour and infantry assailing them from behind. Such was their shock and confusion that some hundred prisoners were taken while survivors fled. Success also greeted the Royal West Kents who advanced for about a mile along the Piopetto's north bank with a company crossing the stream to occupy Casa Petracone until darkness fell.[62]

The most successful of 12 Brigade's units was 2/4th Hampshires, on loan from 28 Brigade which was being re-organized. Supported by Lothians' tanks the battalion advanced along the Piopetto to Point 33 on Queen Street before wheeling south to roll up, one after another, enemy posts facing the Gari. During this advance Captain Richard Wakeford, commanding the leading company, armed only with a revolver and accompanied by his orderly, attacked an enemy post, killing several Germans and making twenty prisoners.

> On the final objective a German officer and five other ranks were holding a house. After being twice driven back by grenades Captain Wakeford, with a final dash, reached the window and hurled in his grenades. Those of the enemy who were not killed or wounded surrendered.[63]

These actions, combined with others the following day, led to Wakeford earning Eighth Army's second Victoria Cross of the battle.

Encouraged by the success already achieved, Lieutenant Colonel Fowler-Esson, commanding the Hampshires, led his men 'unswervingly onwards until he reached Points 50 and 46', which were half a mile north of Sant'Angelo and within 8th Indian Division's boundary.[64] It was clear that the time spent on training with armour before DIADEM had been a major factor in this success as infantry and tanks operated in harmony, demonstrating that the British Army's great problem earlier in the war, poor co-ordination between armour and infantry, was being eliminated. Tank and infantry units had come to know each other on a squadron/company basis culminating in that day on which five infantry battalions and two armoured regiments had crossed the Gari to enlarge the bridgehead to the depth of about a mile. In addition, all the infantry anti-tank guns were in the bridgehead, as were two troops of 14th Anti-Tank Regiment. The sappers were working on Blackwater and Congo bridges to allow even more men and machines into the bridgehead.[65]

On the 14th the attacking divisions maintained their momentum. Eighth Indian cleared the Liri Appendix while 4th Division advanced towards the Cassino–Pignataro road, both brigades making steady progress. Richard Wakeford distinguished himself once again when attacking a hill feature.

> a tank became bogged on the start line, surprise was lost and the leading infantry were caught in the enemy's fire, so that the resulting casualties endangered the whole operation. Captain Wakeford, keeping his company under perfect control, crossed the start line and although wounded in the face and in both arms, led his men up the hill. Halfway up the hill his company came under heavy spandau fire; in spite of his wounds, he organized and led a force to deal with this opposition so that his company could get on.[66]

Heavy mortar fire was falling and Wakeford was again wounded, in both legs. Continuing to lead his men, he reached his objective, organized and consolidated the survivors and reported to Fowler-Esson before seeking medical attention.

> During the seven-hour interval before stretcher-bearers could reach him his unwavering high spirits encouraged the wounded men around him. His selfless devotion to duty, leadership, determination, courage and disregard for his own serious injuries were beyond all praise.[67]

***

While 10 Brigade was advancing towards Highway 6, the Gurkhas, with Canadian tanks, were attacking the remaining Germans in Sant'Angelo. With the final defenders routed, the garrison of the nearby Platform Knoll strongpoint surrendered, perhaps intimidated by the reputation of the Nepalese riflemen; 1st Royal Fusiliers, who were preparing an assault on the position, were spared the effort. While there were some other incidents of less than dogged German resistance, the *Fallschirmjäger* who beat a hasty retreat near Cassino being another, most German soldiers still held out determinedly, including a group of mountain warfare students facing an attack by 6th/13th Frontier Force who

113: Captain Richard Wakeford of 2/4th Hampshires also earned the Victoria Cross during Operation HONKER and received his award from HM King George VI. (Public domain)

fought fanatically as the Pathans swarmed in amongst them. After the position had been overrun little groups which had fled in the face of the onslaught returned to dig in and to die in last stands. Prisoners emerged with their hands above their heads, holding grenades which they hurled as their captors went forward to secure them.[68]

Elsewhere an attack by 12 Brigade towards the Cassino-Pignataro road, led by 6th Black Watch supported by Lothians' tanks, saw the adoption of a battle drill from history. On ground shrouded by heavy mist, Lieutenant Colonel Madden, commanding the Black Watch, formed his battalion into a hollow square around the tanks before advancing. Thus infantry and armour could maintain contact and the battlegroup took a strongpoint defended by an anti-tank gun that had been unable to engage the mist-cloaked Shermans. As always, mist clears and when this bank burned away 6th Black Watch were ahead of their flanking battalions, thus offering the Germans a target for counter-attacks. Although the Germans accepted the offer, every one of a series of attacks was repelled, the Black Watch holding out until that evening when 1st West Kents, supported by tanks, relieved them.[69]

Although the armour was working closely with the infantry, tanks were encountering problems other than German guns and man-portable anti-tank weapons, mist, a feature of the early mornings, being one. Another was the fact that the ground, not yet fully dried out, was not as firm as it would be in later weeks, resulting in some tanks bogging, as already noted, reducing the momentum of the advance, or leaving infantry groups with reduced or no support. Although, from high ground, the terrain looks flat, this was not so: folds in the ground, sunken lanes and hedges or walls all allowed anti-tank gunners to conceal their weapons and engage tanks at very close range. Such weapons took heavy toll of Allied tanks as 17th/21st Lancers discovered in six days of action during which the regiment suffered fifty-seven killed or wounded. In their case this literally was a case of 'death or glory'.[70] The regiment's historian, their CO at Cassino, wrote that

> Cassino contained all the elements of warfare in Italy; difficult broken ground seamed with marshes, rivers and gullies, merciless artillery fire directed from mountain observation posts; brave and skilful defensive fighting by the Germans; beauty – here fireflies and nightingales – amid the desecration of war.[71]

114: A squadron of 17th/21st Lancers supported each brigade of 4th Division. The *Death or Glory Boys'* casualties included Cpl Norman Edward James Daley of Wimbledon, Tpr George Coulson Taylor of Glasgow and Tpr John Nugent of Liverpool. (Author's photo)

XIII Corps had succeeded in doing much of what had been asked of it. With the Gari bridgehead secure, it was time to isolate Cassino from the west, cut Highway 6 and link with II Polish Corps. To do so required bringing 78th Division into the bridgehead to pass through the first two formations and assist in cutting Highway 6.

Before considering the Battleaxe Division's role in the battle, however, we should consider progress elsewhere along the army group front, beginning with Eighth Army's other attacking corps, Anders' Poles.

Chapter Eleven

Eighth Army had codenamed its part in DIADEM Operation HONKER. That name, chosen almost at random, was seen as inspirational to the soldiers of the Polish II Corps. To them it alluded to the call of wild geese and they saw themselves as 'wild geese', exiled from their homeland, an imagery they shared with the Irish 'wild geese', who had served for generations in the French and Spanish armies. Whatever the intentions at Eighth Army headquarters, Anders appealed to that same Polish spirit in his special order of the day before HONKER, in which he noted that it was the time for battle and 'revenge and retribution' on Poland's traditional foe.

> Shoulder to shoulder with us will fight British, American, Canadian and New Zealand divisions, together with French, Italian and Indian troops. The task assigned to us will cover with glory the name of the Polish soldier all over the world. At this moment the thoughts and hearts of our whole nation will be with us. Trusting in the Justice of Divine Providence we go forward with the sacred slogan in our hearts: God, Honour, Country.[1]

For the Poles the coming battle was more than a clash in a war between nations. It was part of a crusade to free their land from German control. To the Polish soldier the invasion in 1939 evoked memories of centuries of injustice suffered by Poland at the hands of her major neighbours, Germany and Russia, and others.

Leese originally intended both corps to have the same H Hour but, reconsidering, delayed H Hour for the Poles until 1.00am on 12 May. At that time the infantry of 5 Wileńska Brigade (5th Kresowa Division) and 1 Carpathian Rifle Brigade (3rd Carpathian Division) attacked enemy positions on the massif between Colle Sant'Angelo and Points 593 (Monte Calvario) and 569. They faced 3rd *Fallschirmjäger* Regiment, whose 2nd Battalion was on Colle Sant'Angelo and near Albaneta Farm while the 1st Battalion held the areas around Points 593 and 569. Protecting the attackers' flanks were 6 Lwówska Brigade, covering the right, and 2 Carpathian Rifle Brigade, protecting the left from positions on Colle Maiola and part of d'Onofrio ridge.[2] Previous attacks, by American and Indian forces, had been executed on a single axis, along Snakeshead Ridge. Anders, however, realized

115: Lieutenant General Władysław Anders and members of his staff with the ruins of the Abbey behind them. In Operation HONKER, Anders' Polish II Corps was assigned the task of taking the Abbey and that mountain terrain in its vicinity not already in Allied hands. (NARA)

that he could deploy on two narrow axes, both reached from Cáira via Cavendish Road.

Having taken their objectives, 5th Division's soldiers would 'immediately organize strong defences' allowing good observation over the Liri valley while, from north and west, they would also cover 3rd Division's operations against the Abbey. The troops on Castellone would cover all the corps' operations.[3] The ultimate objective, defined by Leese as taking Monte Cassino and operating against Piedimonte, was to break through the Gustav Line and attack the Hitler Line, 'or to be exact the hinge connecting the two lines, i.e. Piedimonte'.[4]

Surprise was impossible since the artillery bombardment two hours earlier and XIII Corps' attack had alerted the Germans. Moreover, Heidrich had anticipated that the next large-scale Allied attack in his sector 'would be directed against Albaneta Farm and the knolls north-west of it'. Anders' staff, knowing they would lack the advantage of surprise, had hoped that their soldiers would have more moonlight to assist in crossing the difficult ground.[5] Anders believed that the double attack would prevent the Germans co-ordinating their fire and force them to disperse reserves.

The remaining strongholds, Monte Cassino monastery to the south, Passo Corno to the north, were to be kept under overwhelming fire and blinded by smoke, to prevent them as much as possible from bringing their fire to bear on the area of attack. It was necessary to use our full strength in the attack, for we had no men to spare for reserves.[6]

Leading 5 Brigade were 13th Wileńska Rifle Battalion, on the right, and 15th Wileńska, on the left, their respective objectives the northern area of Phantom Ridge followed by Colle Sant'Angelo, and the southern part of the ridge followed by Point 575. Following 15th Battalion, but with orders not to leave its forming-up positions until that battalion had begun moving to Point 575, was 18th Lwowski Battalion of 6 Lwów Brigade. The Kresowa Division's artillery, with additional guns allocated from the corps artillery (Army Group Polish Artillery, equivalent to a British AGRA) was to neutralize the German mortars before engaging the defensive posts on the various objectives as they were attacked. The additional artillery for the attack included Polish units (7th Horse Artillery Regiment and two medium batteries), 4th New Zealand Field

116: The Poles faced strong opposition in the face of German paratroopers in well-sited positions with good fields of fire. (NARA)

Regiment and the British 140th Medium Regiment (5th London TA), plus a battery of 102nd Medium Regiment (Pembroke Yeomanry). Added to Kresowa's three field regiments, this represented a very strong array of firepower. Their task was difficult but the Polish artillery would receive high praise for their work at Cassino.

> At the battle of Cassino the problems which faced the Polish Gunners were exceedingly formidable. Located on the extreme flank of the front of attack, they were required to apply their fire obliquely on to mountainous hillsides. The technical orders which they had to interpret from a foreign language were based on a foreign procedure, and yet the support they provided to British units on their flank was always superb. The capture of Monte Cáiro and the Monastery at Monte Cassino will stand out, among the triumphs of a great military nation, as evidence of the quality of Polish infantry and Polish artillery.[7]

Eighth Army HQ also provided II Polish Corps with seventy-two 4.2-inch mortars, or four-and-a-half mortar companies. With no Polish mortarmen trained on 4.2s, anti-tank gunners from the divisional anti-tank regiments hurriedly trained to use mortars. Since there was insufficient time to achieve a high proficiency level, the accuracy typical of British mortarmen could not be expected of the Poles but their officer commanding, Major Offenkowski, believed that they achieved much as they 'were excellent gunners, enthusiastic and eager to learn'. (Eventually, they fired 7,000 rounds in the first attack.) Nor was lack of familiarity with their weapons their sole problem. To protect their positions they had to fill sandbags but without sand and with very few spades. Sandbags were filled with soil with spoons used for the task.[8]

The Polish infantry's problems were almost insurmountable. Although they had artillery support, its effect was limited by the topography. Many German positions were immune from fire; soldiers in natural caves extended by explosives could sit out the bombardment to emerge and engage attacking infantry who had not only to contend with difficult terrain, but also German artillery and mortar fire, the latter from reverse-slope positions that the Polish artillery could not hit. Although the gunners had no direct sight of enemy artillery positions, they did have the assistance of No.651 Squadron with its Auster AOPs; of the squadron's five aircraft two were allocated to the corps artillery (AGPA), one each to the divisional artilleries and one for other tasks.

Anders' infantry had some armour support but this was also limited by terrain. Two squadrons of Shermans, 2 and 3 Squadrons, of 4th (Skorpion) Armoured Regiment, plus two regimental HQ tanks and two batteries of self-propelled anti-tank guns (American M10 tank destroyers, known as Wolverines) deployed from San Michele as the bombardment began. The regiment's 1 Squadron was held at San Michele with 17th Lwowski Battalion as a corps reserve. For the tanks their route forward was along a narrow mountain track, known as the Polish Sappers' Road, on which movement was difficult. When one tank crashed into the mountainside, blocking the route, it had to be pushed over the edge after attempts to move it failed as the armour strove to reach the infantry they were to support.[9]

Those infantrymen were from 1 Carpathian Brigade whose 2nd Battalion was to attack from about Point 596 towards Snakeshead Ridge to take the ridge and Point 569. On its right, 1st Battalion's objective was Albaneta Farm, its four companies advancing one behind the other through the gorge leading to the feature. A troop of tanks would protect the northern flank, using the track from Colle Maiola to Albaneta, that protection strengthened by two SPGs, a medium machine-gun company and 12th Podolksi Lancers, the divisional reconnaissance regiment, acting as infantry.[10]

The attacking battalions had mixed fortunes. On the left, 2nd Battalion achieved success on Snakeshead, overrunning the enemy positions and even

117: The defenders had the advantage of being able to overlook the Allied positions and most of their axes of advance. (NARA)

118: A German shelter under Point 593. On the reverse slope for Allied artillery it would have been immune from fire. (Author's photo)

the northern part of Point 569. But casualties had been severe and the Germans were recovering their equilibrium. The resultant storm of fire led to more losses, especially as many Polish soldiers showed recklessness by standing up to shout defiance. In the gorge 1st Battalion also met stout opposition, sustaining many losses. Attackers met both frontal and enfilade fire, pinning them down throughout the hours of darkness. With daybreak and further artillery support, the battalion, backed by tanks, advanced with difficulty. Some elements infiltrated the slopes up to Albaneta but encountered heavy artillery fire that drove them to cover. Meanwhile the tanks found that the gorge had not been cleared of mines and that they were being observed by the Germans on Monte Cáiro. In spite of courageous efforts to move forward, Lieutenant Białecki's reinforced 4 Platoon was stopped by mortar and artillery fire. Białecki's Sherman suffered a direct hit, exploding its ammunition, blowing off the turret and killing three of the crew. Białecki and one crewman escaped, their uniforms aflame, but the other man died in hospital. Left with no radio contact with either their own HQ or the infantry, the surviving Shermans could not advance under the hail of enemy fire. Some elements of 1st Battalion probing out of the gorge were driven back by fire from Albaneta and Point 575. Communications were also breaking down.[11]

Although the Carpathians had taken Point 593 and 5 Brigade had ascended Phantom Ridge to engage the Germans in bitter hand-to-hand fighting, the defenders had regained their poise and held the advantage.

> The battle went on hour after hour. Dawn found them still fighting and the struggle lasted until the afternoon. Small groups penetrated the slopes of the next objective, but the main mass fought on Phantom Ridge.[12]

It was clear to Anders that 'it was easier to capture some objectives than to hold them'. He concluded that the attackers could not sustain the action and that, since it was impossible immediately to insert fresh troops, the assaulting brigades should return to their start lines to be relieved later by others that would continue the attack.[13]

The battalions of both divisions withdrew on the evening of the 12th but remained in their positions until the following day. Anders already appreciated that the critical feature in the defence was Point 593 rather than the Abbey but, after the initial assault, he also appreciated that Polish artillery fire, in spite of its ferocity, 'was unable effectively to silence the enemy batteries or to destroy the enemy infantry in their battle stations'.[14]

***

119 & 120: Polish armour deployed to support the infantry assault but this Sherman of 4th Skorpion Regiment became a casualty. Commanded by Lieutenant Białecki, it received a direct hit and only Białecki survived. (NARA)

121 & 122: Białecki's Sherman remains where it was hit, a poignant memorial to the tank crews who fought for Monte Cassino. A cross fashioned from tank tracks stands atop the wreckage which is a place of pilgrimage for the many Polish visitors to Cassino. (© Damiano Parravano, Chairman, Associazione Linea Gustav)

123: Not only did the Poles have to overcome determined opponents, but they had to deal with very difficult terrain, such as this rock face. (Author's photo)

Leese visited II Polish Corps' HQ on the afternoon of 12 May. In spite of the setbacks his men had suffered and their losses, Anders was pleased that Leese considered that the Poles had contributed effectively on Eighth Army's front. By keeping the Germans on Monte Cassino tied down, and drawing upon themselves the fire of German artillery from other sectors, they had prevented Feurstein deploying reserves, especially in XIII Corps' area. In so doing, II Polish Corps had been 'of great assistance' to XIII Corps as its divisions crossed the Gari and established a bridgehead. Although Anders wanted to attack again as soon as he could relieve his attacking brigades, Leese suggested that he await XIII Corps' progress in the Liri valley, thus ensuring that II Corps did not have to fight a battle in isolation.[15]

With a renewed offensive delayed, the Poles began reconnoitring the enemy positions, on which they directed harassing fire, as well as mounting aggressive patrols and local attacks. As XIII Corps pushed deeper into the Liri valley on the 16th, Leese ordered Kirkman and Anders to co-ordinate operations to maintain as much pressure as possible on the enemy, preventing him from exercising 'free use of his reserves or his artillery'.[16] The new Polish offensive was to be launched on the 17th with 7.00am as its H Hour, by which time the operations of both corps were interlinked and 78th Division was nearing Highway 6.[17]

***

Before moving on to 78th Division's battle in the Liri valley, a brief study of the work of the sappers in bridging the Gari in the face of furious opposition and in constructing roads and paths for the advancing formations is appropriate. The launching of Plymouth Bridge, using two turretless Sherman tanks in an innovative operation by Indian sappers, has been described. However, the original site reconnoitred for the bridge could not be found in the confusion of the first night's battle and an alternative was chosen with a seventy-foot water gap and a hundred-foot bridging gap. The history of the engineers in the Italian campaign details the work on Plymouth.

0.15am	Bridging lorries arrived at the bridge assembly point, within [150] yards of the bridging site.
3.30am	A track to the bridging site was completed, involving filling of eight ditches and a sunken lane.
5.00am	Tanks arrived at the bridge assembly point, having had great difficulty in finding the place.

5.30am	Off-loading of bridging equipment was completed, and a start made on assembling the bridge.
7.30 to 9	A launching ramp was constructed by eight sappers using fifty pounds of ammonal. At this point the bank was only six inches above water level, and the ramp had to be constructed under water.
9.15am	The bridge assembled ready to move to the river. There was still a heavy mist.
9.23am	The mist cleared suddenly, just after the bridge had arrived at the river. The Germans immediately opened fire.
9.30am	Launching of the bridge was completed. Difficulty was encountered in unhitching the rear tank, but this had been foreseen, and a prepared two-pound guncotton charge severed the connection without damage to bridge or tank.
9.30 to 10.30	Efforts were made to unload the near side ramp, which was carried in a spare tank, but fire became so intense that the effort was abandoned. The tank officer and one of the crew were wounded, three sappers killed, and five wounded. An improvised ramp was made later with sleepers, and tanks crossed successfully.[18]

Plymouth was a Class 30 bridge while Oxford and Amazon were Class 40, the number referring to the maximum weight, in imperial tons, the structure could support. Amazon spanned eighty feet and its construction lasted almost twelve hours, during which the sappers were under constant fire; fifteen were killed and fifty-seven wounded.

The sappers also built tracks for tanks and other vehicles from the river into the Liri valley; these were Ace, Spade, Heart, Diamond and Club tracks. They also converted the railway line into a track by removing the rails and sleepers, as well as much of the ballast.[19]

*** *

Early on Sunday 14 May Major General Keightley's HQ received the order that 78th Division was to cross the Gari and the 'troop-carrying lorries that had brought [the division] from Cassino only two weeks before headed north again along Highway 6'. The Battleaxe Division, with an armoured brigade under command, was to pass through 4th Division 'and swing right to cut Highway 6 west of Cassino' with its entry into the final battle spearheaded by Pat Scott's Irish Brigade.[20] For HONKER, Brigadier Pat Scott's command had been strengthened by the addition of B Squadron 16th/5th Lancers, an appropriate 'marriage' as described on p.224.[21] In addition to their friends of 17th Field Regiment (who dubbed themselves Royal Hibernian Artillery) the brigade group also included 214 Field Company RE and 152nd Field Ambulance RAMC.

That afternoon the brigade, led by 6th Royal Inniskilling Fusiliers, entered the bridgehead. One young officer, Lieutenant Jim Trousdell, 1st Royal Irish Fusiliers, remembered his first sight of the German positions covering the Gari. 'They had been very well dug and camouflaged, all the spoil removed and until you were right up to them they were practically invisible – also safe from anything but a direct hit, they were so deep.'[22] Brigadier Scott was aware that his brigade was the vanguard of XIII Corps' operation to link up with II Polish Corps and that his battalions' performance was critical since the Poles, having been pushed back by the Germans,

> could only shoot one more bolt, that bolt must succeed or the whole operation be jeopardized. The final attack on the Monastery could not, therefore, be made by the Poles until the threat to the Germans in the Liri Valley was such that success would be almost certain.[23]

However, the German right flank was beginning to collapse under Fifth Army's pressure, Juin's corps having displayed great resourcefulness, courage and skill as they fought through the Aurunci mountains. By the morning of 15 May the French and II US Corps had dislodged 94th and 71st Divisions on their front and Juin's men were preparing to strike towards the Liri valley. Scott, Keightley and Kirkman were unaware of the full extent of the situation to their far left and so Eighth Army's imperative remained 78th Division's thrust to fulfil Leese's plan and bring Anders' corps into action again.

***

The bridgehead situation remained fluid with the locations of friendly troops less certain than those of XIV Panzerkorps. Therefore the Irish Brigade was to attack in daylight with 6th Inniskillings leading, followed by 2nd London Irish Rifles and then 1st Royal Irish Fusiliers. Before the Inniskillings (the 'Skins') attacked, the commanding officer, Lieutenant Colonel H.E.N. 'Bala' Bredin,* deployed nocturnal patrols to ascertain locations of friendly and hostile forces: it was known that 2/4th Hampshires were to the right with a West Kents' battalion 'somewhere in front of them' but Bredin wanted clarity. Bredin's plans were upset by orders that his first objective, the Cassino-Pignataro road, codenamed *Grafton*, the start-line for the main divisional attack, had to be secured by dawn. Although believed to be free of enemy troops, the Inniskillings found otherwise and had to fight for the line.

The Skins were to move off at 3.00am but without tank support because a tank had bogged at one end of the bridge across the Piopetto. A new bridge was under construction but would not be ready before dawn. Undaunted, Bredin revised his plans. By 4.00am his two leading companies had occupied Massa Vendittis without opposition with the other pair about to assault Massa Tamburrini when they came under heavy machine-gun fire. As day dawned, both leading companies were just seventy yards short of the German positions in standing corn that provided some cover. German tanks were unable to engage; their crews were blind as heavy mist had fallen and infantry and armour milled about.

A very difficult situation for the Inniskillings was averted when the sappers completed the new crossing and, at 8.00am, Robert Gill's B Squadron 16th/5th Lancers crossed to support the infantry, some of whom guided them forward through fog and across marshy ground. The fog cleared just before 9.00am and the Lancers reached the forward companies with whom they began the attack, following a bombardment of the German positions. With tanks and infantry advancing together, the objective was taken quickly, together with three 75mm anti-tank guns and several machine guns. No time was wasted in preparing the next phase, an attack on high ground at Point 86 to consolidate *Grafton*, earlier

---

* Commissioned in the Royal Ulster Rifles in 1938, he saw active service in Palestine during the Arab Rebellion where he had served in Wingate's Special Night Squads, earning the MC and Bar and commanding the SNS in Wingate's absence. He was also twice Mentioned in Despatches. Having served with 2nd Rifles in France in 1940 he undertook parachute training and was posted as brigade major to a parachute brigade from which he sought a transfer to the Irish Brigade since he considered life in the parachute brigade too quiet. He joined 1st Royal Irish Fusiliers (the Faughs) as their second in command as they embarked for the landings at Termoli in October 1943, borrowing a Faughs' coloured side-cap on the dock and throwing the maroon airborne beret into the harbour. He would earn a DSO at Cassino, a Bar to that in northern Italy and a second Bar in Operation MUSKETEER in 1956, commanding a parachute battalion in the last British large-scale airborne assault.

124: The first obstacle facing the Irish Brigade of 78th Division was the Piopetto stream. Although it did not delay the infantry it caused a problem for the armour as a tank bogged at one end of the bridge across it and 16th/5th Lancers had to wait until the sappers built a second bridge. (Author's photo)

125: Once across the Piopetto infantry and armour had to advance to the ridge in this image, taken from close to the Piopetto. (Author's photo)

the objective for an unsuccessful attack by 1st Royal West Kents, supported by New Zealand tanks.

Bredin asked for Point 86 to be bombarded before his attack. At 10.00am the divisional artillery fired a five-minute concentration on *Grafton*, their seventy-two 25-pounders supplemented by two regiments of self-propelled 105mm howitzers, firing airburst rounds over positions south-east of Point 86 while 16th/5th Lancers added their guns and machine guns to the chorus. B and C Companies advanced when the gunfire died down, supported by the Lancers' Shermans. The Skins established themselves in the ditches and dug-outs south-east of Point 86 while D Company moved up, passed through and consolidated north-east of Point 86. *Grafton* had been taken with very light losses and some tanks immobilized by mines. German losses had been about twenty dead and sixty taken prisoner; equipment losses included a Mark IV tank, two self-propelled guns, five anti-tank guns and many small arms.

As the Inniskillings consolidated and awaited the customary counter-attack, 2nd London Irish prepared to take up the baton. Their advance was to begin at 3.00pm and, in the meantime, Skins and Rifles suffered harassing fire worse than anything hitherto experienced in Tunisia, Sicily or Italy. Field artillery, mortars

126: German defenders in positions such as this faced the advancing Allied troops. (©
Damiano Parravano, Chairman, Associazione Linea Gustav)

and Nebelwerfers took heavy toll of the Irish infantry, threatening the Inniskillings'
thin salient.[24]

The Rifles were to attack onto *Pytchley*, the ridge between Casa Sinagoga and
Colle Monache. As the Germans bombarded their concentration area Major
Desmond Woods MC, commanding H Company, moved his platoons into a
streambed that afforded some protection but when the mist lifted they sustained
several casualties from sudden German fire. Worst of all, a shell landed in the
commanding officer's O Group, fatally injuring both Ion Goff, commanding the
Rifles, and John Loveday, commanding 16th/5th Lancers. Others were wounded
seriously, including Major Geoffrey Phillips, commanding G Company, and
Lieutenant Ken Lovatt, the signals officer, with most of his signals team. This
tragedy caused a four-hour delay in the Rifles' H Hour, to 7.30pm.[25]

Bredin, who had been ordered back to the Rifles' O Group, arrived into a scene
of destruction, having crawled along a ditch for over 400 yards, and radioed Irish
Brigade HQ on the only surviving wireless set. Meanwhile, Major John Horsfall
MC also arrived. He had been but a few hundred yards away and to him fell the
task of taking command and finalizing the attack. Pat Scott arrived soon afterwards,

by which time Horsfall had been briefed fully by Bredin and Major Paul Lunn-Rockcliffe of 17th Field Regiment. However, an order from divisional HQ put H Hour back to first light next day. Keightley had decided to widen his front and the additional time allowed 11 Brigade to deploy 2nd Lancashire Fusiliers. A further delay became necessary for the Lancashires to reconnoitre the ground and plan their attack.[26]

At this point a departure from the narrative is called for to emphasize that 38 (Irish) Brigade was delayed by a combination of factors: the shelling of the O Group, followed by Keightley's decision to expand the front and, finally, the Lancashire Fusiliers' need to reconnoitre for and plan their attack. In recent years it has been suggested that the Irish attack was delayed by the intervention of a platoon of *Fallschirmjäger* pioneers commanded by Leutnant Jupp Klein, sent from Cassino into the Liri valley. Klein's account of causing chaos appears in Holland's *Italy's Sorrow* with the author editorializing that

127: During an O Group the commanding officers of both 16th/5th Lancers and 2nd London Irish were wounded fatally by shellfire. Colonel Bredin of the Inniskillings was called back to meet the Irish Brigade commander, Brigadier Pat Scott, and the second-in-command of the Rifles, Major John Horsfall. With their artillery commander, Paul Lunn-Rockcliffe, they completed plans to continue the advance. Scott is in the centre of the trio at the jeep's bonnet with Bredin on the left, Horsfall on the right and Lunn-Rockcliffe on the radio. (Painting by David Rowlands; reproduced by kind permission of Regimental HQ Royal Irish Regiment)

'Once again, a tiny force of carefully concealed men had beaten off a concerted Allied assault by men from 78th Division's 38th (sic) Infantry Brigade'. The story also appears in much more detail in a recent history of the Cassino battles but, in this case, with the author's caveat that is 'difficult to place the encounter precisely ... but Jupp appears to have been between Lines Pytchley and Fernie, while his opponents were almost certainly 38 Brigade and the 16th/5th Lancers'.[27]

However, no such incident occurred on 38 Brigade's front. Klein probably confused an action in which his platoon *may* have taken part with resistance to the Irish Brigade at Casa Sinagoga, which involved much more than a platoon and which will be examined shortly.

John Horsfall held an O Group at first light in the comparative shelter of a former German gun emplacement. He intended 2nd Rifles to advance on a three-company front with Major Desmond Woods' H in the centre, E, under Major Mervyn Davies, on the left and G, under Peter Grannell, on the right; F was in reserve. The attack was supported by 400 field and medium guns and when they opened fire 'the landscape ahead just vanished under pitch-black thundercloud, pierced by the dancing orange lightning of the shell bursts'. The Rifles had to advance almost a mile. Horsfall had ordered them to keep close, or lean into, the bombardment, ignoring the risk from 'shorts' to give the enemy least possible time to recover.[28]

Early in the advance, Woods learned that one platoon was being hit by 'shorts' which turned out to be German fire, the intensity of which increased; one platoon commander was killed and the other wounded.

> I will never forget the noise. ... One tried to move from one shell-hole to the next and I remember diving into a shell-hole and a chap ... landing on top of me and I said, 'get up, we must go on'. There was no movement; he was dead – he had a bit of shrapnel through his neck. ... About halfway through the attack ... the barrage dwelt for ten minutes and we were able to get down to the ground. One wondered would anybody be able to live under this barrage as far as the Germans were concerned but by God they could.[29]

During those ten minutes Major Woods brought his reserve platoon forward. H Company had taken some prisoners who were held at company HQ and also suffered the shelling. Mortars, machine guns and Nebelwerfer rockets pounded them and the supporting tanks of 16th/5th Lancers. Woods noted that the German bombardment had begun as the Shermans moved forward. H Company's objective was Casa Sinagoga, a cluster of farm buildings, including the Sinagoga family home. As the riflemen closed on it the Shermans were engaged by anti-tank guns, knocking out the leading tanks.

One of Woods' NCOs, Corporal J.A. (Jimmy) Barnes, from County Monaghan, then seized the initiative. With his platoon commander seriously wounded and his sergeant also out of action, Barnes led his section in an attack on the gun that had been doing most damage.

> one by one the men were cut down by machine-gun fire on their left flank until Corporal Barnes remained alone. He went on by himself and then he fell dead, cut [down] by a machine gun, but by then the crew of the 88mm* had baled out and the tanks were able to get forward once again.[30]

Barnes had thrown a grenade at the gun, killing at least one gunner. Although recommended by Desmond Woods, supported by John Horsfall, for the Victoria Cross, no award was made, nor was he Mentioned in Despatches.[31]

Finally, H Company was on its objective. Woods had finished the assault with one sergeant, a few corporals and a handful of riflemen, about a dozen all told, 'smothered in brick dust, and their eyes the only bright thing about them'.[32] E Company had taken its objective, Sinagoga wood, and its commander, Major Mervyn Davies, also recorded the operation. He too was unaware of enemy artillery shelling the company 'until we saw the odd man fall' but his men were able to approach the wood under the protection of their own 'very accurate' artillery.

> I remember trying to communicate with the tank troop commander by using the telephone on the outside of his Sherman. Of course the thing would not work. But the tank commander obligingly opened his turret when I hammered on it with a rifle. I showed him where I supposed some German fire was coming from.[33]

E Company covered the last few hundred yards to the wood with about a dozen casualties and took some sixty prisoners from 90th Panzergrenadier Division. Davies walked through the wood to discover that Grannell's G Company had also reached the objective. Having comforted an elderly couple in their farmhouse, he returned to E Company 'as a dreadful Nebelwerfer Stonk arrived', killing two of the best soldiers in the company, Sergeant Eddie Mayo MM and Corporal Edward O'Reilly MM.[34]

---

* This was probably a 75mm and is described as such in the divisional history.

Horsfall prepared for a German counter-attack but with heavy mortars and Vickers machine guns from 1st Kensingtons* emplaced, together with a troop of Shermans and 17-pounder anti-tank guns from 64th Anti-Tank Regiment, the threat was countered quickly; a tank attack was beaten off by 16th/5th Lancers.

Although 2nd London Irish had twenty dead and eighty wounded, they had taken their objectives, captured 120 prisoners and nine tanks and, in the wake of battle, buried over a hundred dead Germans. Having treated both their own and German wounded, with the assistance of German medics, E and H Companies pushed on to secure Colle Monache. *Pytchley* had been taken. It is impossible to see how the claim that Klein's platoon delayed this attack can be sustained since there was no delay other than those caused by the shelling of the O Group and Keightley's order to delay H Hour for 2nd Lancashire Fusiliers to conform with the London Irish.[35]

***

Keightley's broadening of the front had brought 11 Brigade into the picture with 5th Northamptons leading. The battalion fought forward to their first objective without armoured support and succeeded in spite of strong opposition, taking 126 prisoners. En route, Lance Corporal Allkin and Private McGill had knocked out an SPG with a PIAT while Lieutenant Hillian earned the Military Cross by charging a German patrol that he spotted approaching a position overlooking his platoon. 'Firing a Bren gun from the hip as he ran, he drove off the patrol, killing and wounding five of its members.' However, C Company's commander, Major Reggie Cook, was killed. Having linked up with 38 Brigade the Northamptons were bombed by Kittyhawk fighter-bombers.[36]

The Lancashire Fusiliers relieved the Northamptons for the second phase with two companies attacking, supported by 17th/21st Lancer tanks. As with the London Irish, the Lancashires stayed close to their own artillery 'and rushed into the dust as soon as their shells lifted from one bound to the next' so that the Death or Glory Boys saw little of them but occasionally used their main guns or Besas to deal with stubborn strongpoints, whether 'in a concrete lair or in the rubble of a farm building'.[37]

By 4.00pm both battalions were on *Pytchley* but with the Lancashires' right flank exposed. An anti-tank ditch prevented the Lancers closing up in support and the

---

* The 1st Bn Princess Louise's Kensington Regiment was 78th Division's support battalion, providing medium machine guns and 4.2-inch mortars. Each brigade was supported by a Kensingtons' company, or support group.

128: Following the O Group tragedy, the Rifles went on to take their objectives, including Casa Sinagoga, pictured here. During the battle for the farmhouse, Cpl James Barnes of the Rifles was fatally wounded attacking an anti-tank gun that had delayed the advance of the supporting Shermans. (© Damiano Parravano, Chairman, Associazione Linea Gustav)

Lancashires had no anti-tank guns. This weak spot was exploited when a German counter-attack, with machine-gun and mortar support, struck C Company via a sunken lane. Two self-propelled guns (StuG IIIs), sometimes identified as Panzer Mark IVs, wiped out a section, killing a PIAT group.[38] There followed another remarkable instance of one man changing the face of a battle. As with Jimmy Barnes at Sinagoga, or Kamal Ram on the Gari, one soldier saved the day: Fusilier Francis Jefferson, a native of Ulverston.

As the StuGs advanced on C Company's partially-dug trenches, Jefferson, a company runner, seized a PIAT and ran forward under heavy fire to a position behind a hedge. Although untrained in the use of the PIAT, he proved effective. Unable to see properly from his first position, he moved into the open where,

> standing up under a hail of bullets, [he] fired at the leading tank which was now only twenty yards away. It burst into flames and all the crew were killed.
>
> Fusilier Jefferson then reloaded the PIAT and proceeded towards the second tank, which withdrew before he could get within range.

129: A Sherman of 16th/5th Lancers moves forward past dug-in riflemen while a 17-pounder anti-tank gun is emplaced for additional support. (Author's collection)

By this time our own tanks had arrived and the enemy counter-attack was smashed with heavy casualties.

Fusilier Jefferson's gallant act not merely saved the lives of his company and caused many casualties to the Germans, but also broke up the enemy counter-attack and had a decisive effect on the subsequent operation. His supreme gallantry and disregard of personal risk contributed very largely to the success of the action.[39]

The 78th Division advance had made good ground. The next phase, to *Fernie*, would threaten Highway 6. Early on 17 May, 1st Royal Irish Fusiliers, the

130: Soldiers of 6th Inniskillings move forward through the Rifles' positions to prepare for the next 'bound'. (Author's collection)

Faughs,* advanced, supported by a heavy artillery bombardment and tanks of B Squadron 16th/5th Lancers. Also advancing were the tanks of 2nd Lothians, striking out via the left front of 38 Brigade through and beyond Piumarola. The Faughs moved forward with C and D Companies leading, A and B remaining in reserve for the next phase.[40]

Opposition had been strengthened by some *Fallschirmjäger* (Klein's platoon?) and before long the two companies were assailed heavily with mortars, artillery and machine-gun fire. Although rounds fell with deadly accuracy back to the start line, there were few casualties and apparently relatively few foes. Jim Trousdell, commanding a platoon of C Company, recalled:

> It was still dark as we waited on the start line for the barrage to lift and our advance to begin. The noise was terrific. When we did move forward I found it difficult to keep up with the barrage due to various interruptions such as keeping in line with the troops on either side of us. The only Germans that I saw were two dead, killed by our shellfire

---

*   From their Irish Gaelic motto *Faugh a Ballagh!* (Clear the Way!)

on the objective. I recall coming up to a farmhouse and throwing a 36 grenade inside in case it was still occupied but the late inhabitants had left – in a hurry it appeared as a half-eaten breakfast was on the table.

There was a certain amount of enemy shell and mortar fire. The only [company] casualties as far as I can remember during this battle were the company commander and his runner both killed by a shell, both a great loss.[41]

Jim Trousdell's company commander, Major Laurie Franklyn-Vaile, had been killed within fifteen minutes of the attack beginning. Also killed early in the action was the squadron leader of B Squadron 16th/5th Lancers, Major Robert Gill, who had been caught in a mortar blast while climbing into his Sherman. Although at first reported wounded, he had been killed instantly.[42] Within two hours, C Company had taken its objective, as had D, commanded by Major Jimmy Clarke MC, and the supporting arms were in place. The adjutant, Captain Brian Clark, brought the battalion Tactical HQ forward and A and B Companies passed through to engage in battle throughout the afternoon, ending with the two companies securing their objectives, key points dominating Highway 6. At 3.00pm Captain Clark reported to Scott that *Fernie* had been taken. The Faughs were ordered to exploit and D Company moved up close to Highway 6 while, after dark, Lieutenant Jimmy Baker took out a patrol to disrupt traffic on Highway 6 which it achieved by calling down mortar fire on the road.[43]

There followed another task for the Inniskillings. Pat Scott had been unable to obtain accurate information on the Lothians, whose brigade commander was convinced that the regiment was well beyond Piumarola, their objective. If so, such success had to be consolidated and exploited by infantry and so Keightley ordered the Irish Brigade to seize the ground overlooking Piumarola, a task Scott entrusted to Bredin and his Skins. After reconnoitring the area, Bredin laid his plans, delivering them at an O Group that 'was a memorable affair, each paragraph of the orders being punctuated by the arrival of a salvo of Nebelwerfer bombs'. For thirty minutes the Inniskillings endured shelling and mortaring in their forming-up positions. Then, as they assembled on the start line, Bredin was wounded in both legs. However, refusing treatment, he advanced with his men, strapped to the bonnet of a jeep. Only when he passed out through loss of blood did he leave the battlefield, his place taken by Major John Kerr MC who, only twenty months earlier, had been a battalion signals warrant officer. Bala Bredin need not have worried: his men advanced farther than intended originally, capturing over a hundred prisoners, three StuGs, several anti-tank guns and many small arms. The *Fallschirmjäger* in Piumarola, preparing a blocking position partway between

131: As 1st Royal Irish Fusiliers made their attack, Major Robert Gill, squadron leader of B Squadron 16th/5th Lancers, was killed by a mortar blast as he climbed into his Sherman. (Author's photo)

the Gustav and Hitler lines, were bounced by 38 Brigade and did not finish their work.[44]

***

XIII Corps' progress had been such that Leese had given Anders permission to renew the Polish assault, which was begun on the evening of the 16th. By then 12 Brigade of 4th Division was closing on its final objectives and, sensing 'an easing of the opposition on this morning of 17 May [advanced] to the very foot of the hill, there to dig in on either side of Highway 6. Meanwhile 1 Guards Brigade in Cassino still held down the defenders. As light faded on the 17th there was a break in the artillery's incessant pounding and a voice over a loudspeaker called, in German, on Heidrich's men to surrender before dark. Reminding them that they had fought well, they were told that continuing was pointless; the Poles were at the Abbey gates. 'If you don't believe us, send out patrols. Cassino is lost to Germany.' No one surrendered.[45]

However, the Germans had already been preparing their exit from Cassino and the mountains. By late on 16 May von Vietinghoff and Kesselring had accepted that Eighth Army had punched a mile-wide gap through LI Mountain Corps' sector, splitting Heidrich's men from Baade's. On Tenth Army's right, Fifth Army's attacks, by Juin's CEF and Keyes' II Corps, had made good progress with the critical Formia-Itri-Pico road threatened. Moreover, Kesselring's intelligence staff had identified the presence of the Canadians while both von Vietinghoff and von Mackensen were concerned about possible outflanking Allied landings on either side of the Anzio bridgehead. Studying the operational situation, it was agreed that Tenth Army would withdraw to the Hitler Line, as proposed by von Vietinghoff, a move phased over three nights via three delaying lines.

> 'Then we shall have to give up Cassino?' asked Kesselring, and von Vietinghoff replied 'Yes'. In this fashion the fate of this famous position, soaked with the blood of so many soldiers, was settled. Cassino's fall from being a position of pre-eminent tactical value was sudden, but there is no doubt that the senior German commanders now believed that the most important object was to prevent the Allies from breaking through in the Liri valley.[46]

Heidrich's men in Cassino and on the heights were not prepared to surrender 'their' Monte Cassino, Kesselring recording that he 'had personally to order these last, recalcitrant as they were, to retire, an example of the drawback of having strong personalities as subordinate commanders'.[47] That recalcitrance also explains why Heidrich's reserves were not echeloned to the right behind 90th Panzergrenadier Division's exposed flank and why LI Mountain Corps' withdrawal was delayed.

In the town Kesselring's order was complied with around midnight when 3rd Grenadier Guards

> 'suddenly saw the Germans rise from the ruins and swarm over the shoulder of Monastery Hill, moving in groups and by quick dashes from rock to rock. The whole slope was heavily bombarded, but undoubtedly

the majority of the parachutists safely passed through the barrage.' Royal Fusiliers, Bedfords and West Kents, of 4th Division, were waiting for them along [Highway] 6. They killed about a score of them and netted seventy prisoners. This may have amounted to a quarter of the garrison of the town's edge and the hill.[48]

***

On XIII Corps' right Anders had launched II Polish Corps on its second assault at 6.00pm on the 16th. Both divisions sought the same objectives as on their first attacks, but with 5th Kresowa attacking first in a two-battalion operation against Phantom Ridge, from the right flank. Not until over twelve hours later did 3rd Carpathian Division launch its assault from the left. Both were successful but, to understand that success, it is necessary to go back to the aftermath of the first attacks on the 12th in which the Poles had to relinquish ground taken at a high cost.

In the interval between the first and second attacks we carried out reconnaissance of the enemy positions and kept the Germans in suspense by artillery fire, local attacks and patrol activity. At the same time [XIII Corps] made further progress in the Liri valley. On 16 May General Leese ordered that the operations of the British and the Poles should be so co-ordinated that the enemy would not be able to make free use of his reserves or his artillery, and he set 7.00am on 17 May as the hour for the second attack.[49]

The renewed attack was assigned to fresh battalions. However, 5th Kresowa Division's brigades had suffered very heavy casualties in the first assault and the GOC, Major General Sulik, organized four ad hoc infantry battalions to deploy as reserves and for mopping up in the wake of the main attack. Those battalions numbered about 250 men apiece, included only two three-platoon companies, and were commanded by majors or captains. Anders refers to two battalions but, since the Poles had a sub-unit known as a half-battalion, it would seem that sub-units formed two small battalions. This excellent example of improvisation involved combing units such as the divisional anti-aircraft and anti-tank regiments, the machine-gun battalion, transport companies and workshops. The Polish Commandos (6 Troop of No.10 Inter-Allied Commando) and the Poznan Lancers' assault squadron, transferred from a defensive sector, also reinforced the attackers.[50]

Anders' staff had produced an excellent picture of enemy positions through their reconnaissance work and that of the air forces' photo-reconnaissance aircraft. That layout was in the form of two linked rings, creating a figure of eight. The northern ring included Point 593, Phantom Ridge, Colle Sant'Angelo, Point 575, Point 505 and Albaneta Farm; the southern ring featured Colle d'Onofrio, Point 569 and Monastery Hill. Such was the effectiveness of the German layout that their strongpoints covered the perimeters and the ground within the rings, as well as providing mutual support. Thus capturing or knocking out a strongpoint or two would not suffice because remaining posts could still engage attackers, preventing further advance into the system, or spreading out from the area taken. In addition to the strongpoints the *Fallschirmjäger* also held reserves within the rings, ready for counter-attacks to prevent attackers consolidating and making further advance. For the attackers the conundrum was how to take a minimum of half a ring when the terrain meant that no attack could be made over a front that covered even half a ring.[51] However, Anders

> estimated that the enemy must be quite as exhausted as we were, or even more so, and that in the next day's fighting therefore, our attack, even if less powerful than our first effort, would achieve a definite success. That critical moment of a battle had, indeed, arrived when both sides face each other in a state of complete exhaustion, apparently incapable of making any further effort, and when the one with the stronger will, who is able to deliver the final blow, wins. German commanders' reports found after the war confirmed that my estimate was right.[52]

This absolute conviction permeated the Polish soldiers. In 5th Division, Sulik's deputy, Colonel Rudnicki, led a group created for the assault, including what was left of 13th and 15th Battalions of 5 Brigade, 16th, 17th and 18th Battalions of 6 Brigade, the Polish commandos, elements of the Poznan Lancers and 3 Squadron 4th Armoured Regiment. Seventh Anti-Tank Regiment deployed 8 Troop with 3rd Division and 9 Troop with 5th Division. Equipped with Wolverines, the anti-tank troops were to use their 3-inch (76.2mm) guns against strongpoints to support the infantry and 4th Skorpion Armoured Regiment.[53]

The plan was for an infantry attack following an hour-long artillery bombardment, H Hour being 6.00am on the 17th. However, during the previous night a company from 16th Lwowski Battalion, reconnoitring Phantom Ridge, attacked and seized posts held by 3rd *Fallschirmjäger* Regiment on the ridge's northern end. That success was exploited immediately and, an hour before midnight, the battalion was firm on the ridge, its first objective. Forward observation officers of 5th Light Artillery Regiment, positioned on the side of Point 706, some 100 yards from the Germans, directed artillery fire on German machine-gun posts and infantry emplacements. Those operations unbalanced the Germans and had a positive effect on the assaults that followed.[54]

Leading the advance in the morning, 17th Battalion passed Point 706 to reach Phantom Ridge, where the assaulting troops moved through 16th Battalion to storm Colle Sant'Angelo. So speedy was the advance that the forward infantry evaded defensive artillery fire, although the porters and others at the back of the battalion were hit. The north-eastern slopes of Colle Sant'Angelo were soon in Polish hands but the defenders of the western slopes fought back vigorously from pillboxes, counter-attacking the Poles, leading to ferocious close-quarter combat. Heavy fire was also put down by German troops on Passo Corno while mortars from Villa Santa Lucia added their contribution. The attackers became the attacked; 17th Battalion's forward soldiers exhausted their ammunition and were pinned down, the ammunition porters unable to reach them. A series of German counter-attacks culminated in their recapturing Colle Sant'Angelo.[55]

The original plan for 15th Battalion was to attack Point 575 but this was changed to a renewed assault on Colle Sant'Angelo in conjunction with 16th and 17th Battalions and the commandos. That attack began at 4.00pm after an hour-long artillery and mortar bombardment. The southern slopes were taken, but the attackers lacked the numbers, ammunition, and sufficient artillery support to take the northern slopes and Point 575. Attempts to do so came to naught in the face of doughty defence. With heavy casualties and ammunition running low, the attackers, now intermixed, remained in position throughout the night.[56]

> For ten hours the fighting had continued, and the Poles had again suffered heavily. General Anders had become desperate; his reserves had been exhausted, and he was still as far as ever from his objective. He threw in the last thing he had – a weak battalion made up of drivers, mechanics and clerical personnel; but that, too, failed to turn the scales.[57]

Also involved in attacking Phantom Ridge were tanks of 4th Armoured Regiment, whose 3 Squadron was to support the infantry attacks on Colle Sant'Angelo and Point 575 while 2 Squadron, advancing through the gorge, was to take Albaneta Farm to support 3rd Carpathian Division's attack.

The Carpathians had begun their operation at 7.30am on the 17th, deploying 'the untried' 2 Brigade, including 4th, 5th and 6th Battalions. Using ropes to scale the steep side of Snakeshead Ridge, the division began its assault on Point 593. This objective was assigned to Lieutenant Colonel Fanslau's 4th Battalion which made its first attack on 593 at 9.23am. As ever the defence was determined, heavy machine-gun fire stopping the first attacking company. The company commander tried again and again, suffering severe casualties each time. When he accepted that his company could make no inroads on the position, Fanslau deployed other companies against the defence. Although some progress was made, and there are Polish claims that 593 'changed hands repeatedly' during the morning, the Germans still held on at noon. Fanslau decided on a further attack, supported by all available artillery. Launched at 2.30pm, Fanslau led the first wave. The Poles went forward again, only to be mowed down like corn by machine-gun fire, Fanslau dying at the head of his men. The attack was broken on the southern slopes of Point 593, only fifty yards from the enemy machine-gun positions. It was impossible to continue; the soldiers were exhausted 'and on the verge of complete nervous and physical collapse'. Not even fire support from tanks of 2 Squadron, which had reached Massa Albaneta to fire onto Point 593, could unlock the position for the infantry. Sixty-five minutes after launching its final attack, the battalion, accepting the inevitable, assumed defensive positions to secure what had been captured.

132: In the mountains the Poles had suffered heavily with their first assaults rebuffed, but they regrouped for a further attack. This memorial on Point 575 commemorates the men of 5th Kresowa Division. (© Damiano Parravano, Chairman, Associazione Linea Gustav)

The tanks had almost reached Massa Albaneta, beyond which lay the ruins of the Abbey.[58]

While 4th Battalion was enduring its purgatory, two 17th Battalion companies worked their way along the ridge from Point 593 towards Massa Albaneta, as did sappers who, under heavy fire, were clearing mines and physical obstacles as well as destroying bunkers to allow the tanks to advance. Late on the 17th soldiers of 6th Battalion were no more than 150 yards from Albaneta Farm but taking the strongpoint meant passing through a minefield and, as dusk was approaching, it was impossible to clear the mines. Moreover, the infantry were so exhausted that they could not protect the tanks overnight, so that Colonel Glinski asked for volunteers from reserve tankmen and recovery personnel for that role. Volunteers were forthcoming and began arriving at 8.00pm. During the night the tanks were targeted by German artillery and mortars while, at the request of 2 Armoured Brigade's commander, eight tanks deployed from 1 Squadron to the gorge where they were to reinforce 2 Squadron.[59]

At 9.00pm Anders issued fresh orders. Both divisions were to consolidate and hold the ground they had gained, re-organize and send out patrols while, next morning, 5th Division was to take Point 575 as 3rd Division took Albaneta Farm. What Anders did not know was that Kesselring had already ordered the evacuation of the mountain positions, including the Abbey, and that part of the town still held by Heidrich's men. The advance of XIII Corps threatened to envelope the defenders. However, Kirkman's troops had been ordered not to cross Highway 6. Indeed they were not to go any further than a ridge overlooking the road, a little over a quarter mile away, to reduce the risk of an unintended clash with Polish troops. Since the road was within the boundary of the still embattled Polish corps, an escape route was thus left open for the Germans.[60]

A German despatch rider was sent to take the evacuation order to the *Fallschirmjäger*. That man, whose personal courage has to be admired, 'found only sorry remnants of their companies'. The defenders had suffered exceptional losses, especially in I/3rd Regiment. No.1 Company which had defended Monte Calvario, Point 593, for six days, had borne the brunt of battle. Only three men survived: one officer, one NCO and one private soldier. The despatch rider's order received, the *Fallschirmjäger* began withdrawing, slipping away silently from ground they had defended at great cost for many weeks, although some rearguards remained. Those defending the town, from II/4th Regiment, could retire only by climbing the slopes of Monte Cassino where Dead Man's Gully claimed its last German victims and British and Polish harassing fire sought them out on their way to Piedimonte and the Hitler Line.[61]

***

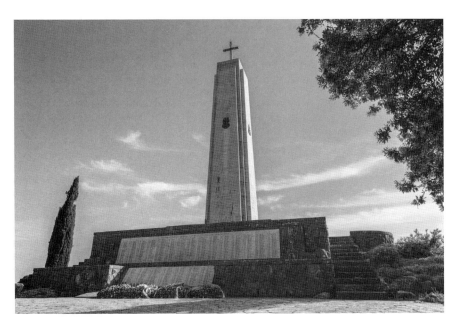

133: On Point 593 this obelisk commemorates the soldiers of 3rd Carpathian Division. (© Damiano Parravano, Chairman, Associazione Linea Gustav)

134: A patrol of 12th Podolski Lancers entered the Abbey on the morning of 18 May to find it abandoned save for wounded. To signal that the Abbey was in Polish hands, the patrol commander, Second Lieutenant Gurbiel, made a regimental pennant from a Red Cross flag and a blue handkerchief and flew it over the ruins. (NARA)

Unaware of the German evacuation, 3rd Carpathian and 5th Kresowa Divisions, supported by 4th Armoured Regiment, prepared for the renewed assault. Shermans of 1 and 2 Squadrons were first into action, advancing towards Massa Albaneta to support the Carpathians. Infantry patrols, from 6th Battalion, entered an empty Albaneta Farm while 4th Battalion assaulted Point 593, only to hit thin air, as the Germans had gone, except for the dead. The only fighting was at Point 569 which was overrun by 10 o'clock, after which troops moved towards the Abbey. In fact, a German wireless message ordering the garrison to withdraw had been intercepted, but so exhausted were the infantrymen that the Carpathians' reconnaissance regiment, 12th Podolski Lancers, was asked to send a patrol to the

135: Gurbiel's makeshift flag was later accompanied by a Union flag. (NARA)

Abbey. Second Lieutenant Kazimierz Gurbiel, of 1 Squadron, led the ten-man patrol cautiously into the Abbey and found the only Germans present – thirty wounded men with some medical orderlies. Gurbiel accepted the surrender of the German commander and ordered a makeshift flag to be hoisted on a branch. Rather than the Polish national flag, Gurbiel's 'flag' was an improvised regimental pennant, made from a Red Cross flag and a blue handkerchief. The flag raising was followed by Section-leader Czech playing the Kraków *Hejnal* on a bugle.[62] Shortly afterwards a Union flag was also raised alongside the Podolski Lancers' pennant to 'complement the Tricolour on the opposite entrance pillar of the Liri valley'.[63]

136: Section Leader Czech played the Kraków *Hejnal* when the flag had been raised on the Abbey. (NARA)

137: One of the most poignant inscriptions on any war memorial is this tribute to Polish soldiers who died at Monte Cassino. It appears on the obelisk on Point 593 in English, Italian, Polish and Latin. (Author's photo)

Also on that morning of 18 May a formal junction between XIII and II Polish Corps occurred when a patrol of three MM-holding corporals from 2nd Lancashire Fusiliers of 78th Division crossed Highway 6 'to convey the compliments of the 78th to the Poles'. It was more a formal ceremony than a military feat.[64] However, the Polish Corps' work was not finished: it had to pursue the retreating Germans, a task in which both XIII Corps and I Canadian Corps would also participate.

Chapter Twelve

As Heidrich's soldiers retreated to the Hitler Line, Fifth Army was pushing hard on the Allied left flank. Keyes' II Corps formed the army's left flank, with Coulter's 85th Division the closer to the sea; Sloan's 88th was on the corps' right and Juin's corps continued Fifth Army's line to the inter-army boundary. The two corps were attacking on diverging axes, II Corps to the west, its main weight falling on the north-south hills between Minturno and Monte Bracchi, while Juin's force was striking through the Aurunci mountains, using the mountain-fighting skills of its African soldiers; II Corps was also conducting some minor operations along the coastal strip.[1] All had waited anxiously for the order to attack, knowing that the Germans, although surprised, would react ferociously. Fifth Army had an advantage over Eighth in that it did not have to cross a deep, swift-flowing river to engage the enemy and, while the French had to attack into mountains, they set out from positions overlooking the German lines, a 'favourable state of affairs …[due to] the success of the British divisions' of X Corps in establishing a bridgehead across the Garigliano in January.[2]

The Custermen encountered almost instantaneous German reaction: 'a continuous band of machine-gun fire' met the attacking GIs while

> mortar and artillery fire began falling on forward positions of the Custer Division. The advance outposts in Tremensuoli were subjected to exceptionally heavy enemy artillery concentrations. There was no doubt that the enemy would not easily surrender his positions. The 85th had been well trained and had been battle-tested in a stabilized line, but this was something it had never before encountered. Now it was necessary for it to move forward over open ground in the face of fierce fire from all of the enemy's many weapons.[3]

Particularly tough resistance was encountered on the left by Colonel Brookner W. Brady's 339th Infantry (The Polar Bears)* advancing towards Point 79 and

---

* The regiment had taken part in the north Russian expedition during the First World War and a polar bear was adopted as the regimental symbol.

San Martino, the latter including Points 66 and 69. Heavily-mined ground caused many casualties amongst the attackers, with Pfc Anthony Tozzo among the first to die. Moving towards San Martino, 3rd/339th Regiment found a complicated obstacle in the Capo d'Acqua, a small steep-banked stream, supplemented by minefields and barbed-wire entanglements and covered by both mortar and enfilading machine-gun fire. Starr's comment that 'Successes had been reported in the first hours of the attack, as our infantry drove forward swiftly under cover of the artillery concentrations' belies the difficulties those infantrymen faced.[4] In contrast, Fisher noted that the artillery 'had little effect on the German infantry, [who were] deeply dug in'.[5]

Brady's regiment, with three battalions in line, found mines and machine-gun fire slowing their advance towards San Martino and Domenico ridge. The best they could achieve 'was to win tenuous footholds on the lower slopes of their objectives'. During this phase Lieutenant Robert T. Waugh (1st Platoon, Company G, 2nd/339th) carried out the first of two actions that earned him the Medal of Honor, the first awarded to 85th Division.

> In the course of an attack upon an enemy-held hill … Waugh personally reconnoitered a heavily-mined area before entering it with his platoon. Directing his men to deliver fire on six bunkers guarding this hill, Lieutenant Waugh advanced alone against them, reached the first bunker, threw phosphorous grenades into it and as the defenders emerged, killed them with a burst from his tommy-gun. He repeated this process on the five remaining bunkers, killing or capturing the occupants.[6]

Over the following three days Company G was engaged in operations that led to many casualties but also to success. Waugh had led his platoon down the slopes of Point 79, along the Capo d'Acqua and up the reverse slope of Point 79 to make the attack that contributed to his Medal of Honor. Following a similar tactic, 2nd Platoon took its objective against stubborn resistance while Fifth Army artillery was still bombarding it. Although casualties were heavy, the Germans were shocked by the loss of Point 79, a piece of vital terrain. Meanwhile 3rd Platoon, all but wiped out in minefields and by vicious machine-gun fire, had been forced to withdraw. However, 1st and 2nd Platoons held Point 79 against all efforts to dislodge them. Such was their tenacity that Company G was awarded a Distinguished Unit Citation

> For outstanding performance of duty in action from 11 to 14 May 1944 … . Taking advantage of the preparatory artillery barrage, the company moved into the attack and seized a large portion of the

objective before the barrage ceased falling. The two assault platoons, closing rapidly with the enemy before he could recover, killed 60 and captured 40 of the defenders, demolished 8 bunkers, reduced 7 pillboxes and captured 25 automatic weapons. The objective taken, Company G immediately emplaced and employed captured enemy weapons to assist the assaults of adjacent companies on two nearby hills and an intermediate ridge. After the enemy recovered from his initial confusion, Company G positions were pounded incessantly for 48 hours by artillery and mortar fire and were subjected to three determined counter-attacks. The company suffered heavy casualties, and because of its isolated positions went without food and water for over 36 hours. ... The fighting aggressiveness, courage, and devotion to duty displayed by members of Company G are worthy of emulation and reflect honor upon the armed forces of the United States.[7]

On the 14th Robert Waugh performed the second act that led to the Medal of Honor award when he

ordered his platoon to lay a base of fire on two enemy pillboxes located on a knoll which commanded the only trail up the hill. He then ran to the first pillbox, threw several grenades into it, drove the defenders into the open, and killed them. The second pillbox was next taken by this intrepid officer by similar methods. The fearless actions of Lieutenant Waugh broke the Gustav Line at that point, neutralizing six bunkers and two pillboxes and he was personally responsible for the death of thirty of the enemy and the capture of twenty-five others.[8]

Robert Waugh was killed leading his platoon in an attack in Itri five days later. He is buried in the US cemetery at Anzio.

Coulter's men continued against determined opposition. On its left the division held Colonel Oliver W. Hughes' 337th Regiment, less its 3rd Battalion (deployed under 339th Regiment's command), in reserve to assist the other two regiments if necessary. On the division's left Lieutenant Colonel Alfred A. Safay's 338th Regiment attacked towards the S Ridge, 'a long nose running in sinuous form southwest from the main hill mass at Tame down to the valley of Solacciano', a feature rising to 430 feet (131 metres) covered with terraced fields, olive groves, vineyards and stone farm buildings, ideal for defence. The only option was to send two battalions in a frontal assault towards Point 131 on the right and south of that point, 1st Battalion making the former attack and 3rd Battalion the latter. Both had difficult experiences, initially gaining only tenuous footholds on the ridge and making little progress the following day so that, by midnight on the 12th/13th, 1st Battalion had been reduced to 350 men, some on the slopes of Point 131, with others holding Points 109 and 103 to the north; 3rd Battalion, reduced to about 200 men, was dug in at Solacciano. Further attempts to advance on the afternoon of the 13th, aided by 1st/351st, and supported by tanks of 756th Tank Battalion, gained little other than Point 85.

Meanwhile Safay's 2nd Battalion had moved through 339th Regiment across Capo d'Acqua to Cave d'Argilla and Point 60, where a series of determined counter-attacks was fought off. By nightfall 338th Regiment had secured some positions but was still under effective fire from Points 131 and 126. Although the Germans had suffered badly from Allied artillery and air strikes, 'this fact was hardly discernible to the Americans' on the ground at the end of that day.[9]

The effects of artillery and air strikes were very obvious to German commanders. Steinmetz attempted to reinforce the defenders of San Martino Hill with a company from his reserves but, as that company assembled to move off, American guns bombarded the assembly area and all but wiped out the company. Constant gunfire also disrupted 94th Division's communications, cutting front-line troops off from the rear area, an isolation increased by Allied aircraft attacks. In spite of all this the Germans remained in place, proving 'remarkably tough' in the face of renewed assaults.[10]

However, by the end of the day on 13 May, II Corps had made some important gains with the Spigno road junction threatened, heavy losses inflicted on the foe and denial to him of reinforcements. With the French advance also having its effect, a nighttime withdrawal to the Dora Line was ordered.

II Corps had fought hard with considerable loss. As well as Robert Waugh's Medal of Honor and the Distinguished Unit Citation awarded to his company, Company C of 337th Regiment received a citation for its part in taking a strategically important hill, which another battalion had attacked but had failed to hold due to heavy casualties. Fighting through heavy enemy fire that stopped two other companies of the battalion, the company reached the crest, having suffered heavy casualties and was then subjected to determined counter-attacks.

> Surrounded on three sides, the Company received heavy and continuous machine-gun and small arms fire from strong enemy forces. With only 18 men and remnants of two other companies and with no heavy weapons support, the courageous infantrymen … held their positions against determined enemy attempts to recapture the hill. On the night of 13 May, relief arrived … and a final enemy assault was repulsed successfully. Pressure was relieved by units attacking on both flanks …and Company C was able to give supporting fire to both attacking elements.[11]

138: In the Aurunci mountains the *Monumente per la Pace* (Peace Memorial) is to be found in the Corena-Ausonia sector. (© Damiano Parravano, Chairman, Associazione Linea Gustav)

The experiences of 88th Division in the opening days of II Corps' advance were similar to those of the Custermen with a Blue Devils' NCO also earning the Medal of Honor. The division's initial objectives were Santa Maria Infante and Point 413, the first phase being assigned to Colonel J.C. Fry's 350th Regiment and Colonel Arthur S. Champeny's 351st. Sloan's third regiment, Lieutenant Colonel Joseph B. Crawford's 349th, was to establish itself on hills north-east of Tufo to support Champeny's attack but with no active part until the attackers had secured their first objectives.[12]

In less than an hour Fry's 350th Regiment had taken Monte Damiano, thus protecting the left flank of Juin's corps, allowing the French to fight through the bottleneck of Castelforte, which they dubbed 'Little Cassino'. The regiment was going over the crest of Monte Damiano just after dawn when the action that resulted in 88th Division's first Medal of Honor occurred. Staff Sergeant Charles W. (Red) Shea, who had sold iced drinks and peanuts at New York's Yankee Stadium,[13] was advancing with his company toward a hill when three machine guns engaged them, causing many casualties and stopping the advance. Shea's platoon commander was killed and the sergeant wounded. Taking cover from enemy fire, Shea noticed two trip wires at his head and feet, realized that he was in a minefield, but charged forward to engage the machine guns. Although pinned down he was able to crawl to the first nest which he overcame with hand grenades before engaging the second post which he also subdued.

> At this time the third machine gun fired at him, and while deadly small-arms fire pitted the earth around him Sergeant Shea crawled toward the nest. Suddenly he stood up and rushed the emplacement and with well-directed fire from his rifle he killed all three of the enemy machine gunners. Sergeant Shea's display of personal valour was an inspiration to the officers and men of his company.[14]

Shea's company continued its advance and achieved its objective. As well as receiving the Medal of Honor, Shea was also commissioned in the field.

Meanwhile 351st Regiment, with armour support, was attacking Santa Maria Infante, 2nd Battalion leading. However, the infantry climbing to the objective were caught in a 'hell of small-arms, machine-gun and mortar fire'. Company E was on the right with F on the left and G in reserve. Overcoming resistance from Point 130, F continued its advance and came up level with E on Points 146 and 150, the features known as the 'Tits'. Company E, its commander wounded, was held up and the battalion's commanding officer, Lieutenant Colonel Raymond E. Kendall, took charge, leading several attacks that allowed the advance to resume before it was again stopped by machine-gun fire. Once more Kendall

139: Staff Sergeant (later Lieutenant Colonel) Charles 'Red' Shea of Company F 350th Regiment in 88th Division, the Blue Devils, earned his division's first Medal of Honor on the Damiano ridge in the opening phase of II US Corps' advance. (Courtesy John Griffith, California)

took off, this time with a squad from the 2nd Platoon, and started for a gun … firing from a position in a stone house to the right. First building up all the firepower possible and joining in the fire fight himself with a carbine, bazooka, BAR and M1 with anti-tank grenades, Kendall then led the final assault …. As he pulled the pin on a hand grenade … he was hit by machine-gun bullets from the left flank, receiving mortal wounds. Unable to throw the grenade, he held it to his stomach and fell with it to prevent injury to his men. The first of the original 88th battalion commanders was gone.[15]

Raymond Kendall was posthumously awarded the Distinguished Service Cross. His sacrifice gave his regiment a precarious lodgement that, under the temporary command of Lieutenant Pat G. Coombs, an artillery liaison officer from 913th Field Artillery Battalion, they began expanding. Maintaining wireless contact with his guns, thus ensuring supporting fire, Coombs led his Doughboys to the spur, silencing three machine guns before ordering some of the company to dig in while he took the remainder to seize the feature. Aware that reinforcements were coming forward, Coombs stood up so that the new troops could identify his men and their position.[16]

The thrust towards Santa Maria Infante by Champeny's men was supported by tanks of 760th Tank Battalion that afternoon but still failed. Next day the attack was renewed with 85th Division ordered to hold fast, allowing 88th to use a wider frontage into which 349th Regiment moved to take over 1st/351st's sector. Another

140: Near Santa Maria Infante a US M1 57mm anti-tank gun is ready to deal with any enemy AFVs that might appear. The gun was a US-manufactured version of the British 6-pounder. (NARA)

day of heavy fighting saw more setbacks as determined resistance continued. Late in the day came some progress and, on the 14th, an attack on Point 109 by Champeny's men was successful, the small group of defenders proving keen to surrender. Point 131 also fell with little resistance.[17]

***

Although the Doughboys of 1st/351st Regiment were unaware of it, the 'unexpected ease with which [they] finally captured [Points] 109 and 131' had been a direct result of the breakthrough by Juin's divisions in the Monte Maio sector during the afternoon of the 13th. With the French expanding their breach, von Senger's deputy, Hartmann, ordered Steinmetz to re-establish contact with 71st Division by withdrawing his left flank by about a mile, anchoring it on Monte Civita, some two miles north-west of Santa Maria Infante.[18]

Juin's corps had, as already noted, been switched from the Allied right flank, where it had fought in the first battle, to the left, causing Kesselring to wonder where it was and in what strength it would attack.[19] Answer was provided by Fifth Army and the French general with the opening of DIADEM. The CEF was much stronger than in January, having been reinforced in February by *4e division de montagne marocaine* (4th Moroccan Mountain Division), under General François Sevez, which had arrived from occupation duty on Corsica, and the equivalent of another division of Moroccan *goumiers*. (Moroccan irregular soldiers, usually recruited from the Berber people of the Atlas mountains.) *Goumiers* served in company-sized groups, or *goums* (from the Arabic *qum*, a band, or troop) of which three, plus a heavy-weapons *goum* and an HQ, formed a *Tabor*, equating to a battalion. A brigade-equivalent formation created from three *Tabors* was a *Groupe de tabors marocain*. General Augustin Guillaume commanded the *goumiers*.[20] For DIADEM, Juin had grouped Sevez and Guillaume's commands as a mountain corps within the CEF under Sevez.[21]

Juin had persuaded Clark to make best use of the French soldiers' mountain-fighting abilities. Clark's final plan placed the CEF on Fifth Army's right flank, thus 'wisely [giving] the stiffest mountain country to the mountain-trained French and the slightly less difficult country to the American divisions ... [which] had trained as much as time and circumstances allowed for mountain warfare but had much to learn, and moreover had not yet experienced battle'.[22] In the first phase the CEF was to take Monte Maio and the Ausonia defile before striking north-westwards between Maio and the Garigliano into the Liri valley. Within this plan the Moroccan Mountain Corps 'had a separate and specially arduous task': infiltrate the Aurunci mountains via Monte Fammera and Monte Petrella, both roadless heights, to take Monte Revole, some four miles from the Pico-Itri

141: A *Goumier* of 4th Moroccan Division prepares his weapons for battle, sharpening his bayonet on a whetstone. (NARA)

road, Fifth Army's objective in the third phase. En route to Monte Revole the Moroccans were to liberate Esperia and Monte d'Oro. In the next phase II Corps and the CEF would advance across the Pico-Itri road, the French from the Monte Revole area and II Corps via the coastal strip.[23] Clark had also to plan for Truscott's

VI Corps' breakout from the bridgehead and, on 5 April, his field order to Fifth Army advised Truscott to 'be prepared to attack within forty-eight hours of receipt of Army Order in any of the following directions', of which four were listed: 1. Ardea; 2. Albano; 3. Cisterna-Cori; and 4. Littoria-Sezze.[24]

**

Juin planned three phased battles 'all aimed at turning the enemy's second major defensive line south of Rome, the Hitler Line'. His first, Monte Maio, was to be seized within five hours of the battle opening but, to protect the right flank, the CEF would first have to clear the high ground rising from the Massa di Ruggero, overlooking the axis of attack, on which the Germans were emplaced: Monte Cerasola, Point 739 and Monte Girofano.[25]

The opposition was Raapke's 71st Division, a formation of about 10,000 men holding an attenuated line with little artillery and no armour, although von Senger had deployed about forty tanks, part of XIV Panzerkorps reserve, some thirty miles behind the line. Raapke's infantry were well dispersed in covered dug-outs and so close to the French lines that they suffered little from the artillery bombardment, the main effect of which, on Fifth Army's front, was to disrupt landline communications and isolate infantry positions. Moreover, Raapke had moved most of his artillery in the week before the attack, recognizing that earlier Allied artillery fire had been intended to register his guns' positions. Thus resistance to the CEF was much stronger than anticipated. Juin's estimate of taking Monte Maio within the first five hours proved too optimistic.[26]

By mid-morning a regiment of 2nd Moroccan Division was atop Monte Faito with light losses but still more than a mile from Monte Maio while the defenders had repelled a supporting attack on Cerasola, Point 739 and Girofano. Nonetheless, General Dody decided to renew the advance but his plans were brought to naught by German resistance followed by a counter-attack. The Moroccans beat off the attackers, with artillery support, although their momentum had been disrupted and re-organization was necessary. While this was a setback to the CEF, the Germans had been surprised by the strength of the French attack; however, Kesselring considered it to be only a support for Eighth Army's assault in the Liri valley and this, plus his fear of an Allied landing on the Tyrrhenian coast, ensured that he did not deploy reserves into 71st Division's sector.[27]

Dody and Juin planned a fresh attack in the small hours of the 13th, with Dody's reserve regiment attacking the high ground above Massa di Ruggero after a heavy artillery bombardment on Cerasola, 739 and Girofano in that order. Sappers with Bangalore torpedoes blew gaps in barbed-wire barriers before the infantry attacked against little opposition. One by one the three heights fell to the Moroccans who took 150 prisoners and moved on to take high ground overlooking Vallemaio village below Monte Maio. On the divisional left the advance was checked but the Moroccans rebuffed several counter-attacks before advancing on Monte Feuci. The last German counter-attack had been made in daylight, the attackers breaking in the face of French artillery fire. This had a domino effect since Raapke had no reserves with which to defend Monte Maio. A withdrawal was ordered, the wireless message bearing that instruction being intercepted. A Moroccan patrol probed forward to find Maio deserted. That afternoon a battalion moved onto the mountain. A Tricolour was hoisted, 'large enough to be seen from Monte Cassino to the Tyrrhenian Sea'.[28]

Among those distinguishing themselves in the operation to take Monte Faito was Commandant de Foucaucourt, *1er Batallion* of *8ème Régiment de Tirailleurs Marocains*. A cavalry officer who had transferred to the infantry and had escaped France via Spain, de Foucaucourt was described as extraordinary. Tall, lean and muscular, he treated war as if it were a sport and sport as if it were war. The journalist and writer Pierre Ichac commented that the outcome of that first night, from Cassino to the sea, was in de Foucaucourt's hands. Against a ferocious defence, he led his men resolutely and, guided by a deserter (who approached, hands held high, calling 'Je suis alsacien!') passed safely through a minefield of which they had been unaware and deployed Lieutenant Lecomte's company to take Monte Faito. This prompted another commandant to exclaim: 'Bravo, mon vieux Fouc, tu es un lion!'[29] De Foucaucourt had undoubtedly played a major role in this action which led to the seizure of Monte Maio. Whether it was as important as Ichac opined is another matter, but de Foucaucourt was one of many Frenchmen who did much to restore the military reputation of France and its army.

Seizing Monte Maio proved pivotal. Dody's mountaineers had broken through the Gustav Line at one of its weakest points, splitting 71st Division and unhinging XIV Panzerkorps' front. As well as unlocking that front for advances north-westwards along parallel ridges towards Ausonia, San Giorgio and Esperia, and an attack towards Monte Fammera via the Ausonia defile, success at Monte Maio opened a much greater opportunity operationally, leaving the French poised to strike German defences in the Liri valley from the right. We have already noted how the CEF had eased II Corps' progress. Now awakened to the threat to Tenth Army's right flank in the Liri, Kesselring switched his concern from the Tyrrhenian flank, releasing 90th Panzergrenadier Division from its coastal defence role between Rome and Civitavecchia to augment Tenth Army's front. The first element of the division to arrive – 200th Grenadier Regiment – was deployed on 71st Division's left in the path of the CEF advance towards San Giorgio.[30] Other elements were inserted elsewhere in the line as indicated by those prisoners from 90th Panzergrenadiers taken by 38 Irish Brigade at Casa Sinagoga.

***

With the Gustav Line crumbling, Juin expanded the breach as his other divisions accomplished their tasks. Dody had removed the keystone of the defences while,

142: An M8 75mm howitzer motor carriage supporting French troops who are also relying on mule transport as they move onto higher ground. (NARA)

north-east of Monte Maio, Général de Brigade Brosset's *1ère Division* had engaged the enemy in the Garigliano bend. On the first night the division filled an anti-tank ditch to permit an attack with armour and infantry by 4 Brigade,* 757th US Tank Battalion and *8è Chasseurs d'Afrique* (a tank-destroyer battalion) against stout resistance, supported by German troops on Monte Girofano. However, once 2nd Moroccan Division took the mountain, Brosset's men made good progress. By midnight on the 13th/14th they had overcome all resistance, taken hundreds of prisoners and held Sant'Ambrogio, Sant'Apollinare and La Guardia hill.[31]

Castelforte had also fallen on the 12th to 4th Tunisians, supported by 755th Tank Battalion, the tank destroyers of *7è Chasseurs d'Afrique* and *3è Spahis Algériens*, the battlegroup having fought a hard battle with 94th Division throughout most of that day; the last Germans were expelled next day.[32]

The Tunisian battlegroup's success at Castelforte made an advance to Coreno possible once the hills on either side of the road between the two towns had been secured and the gap expanded. On the afternoon of 13 May the Blue Devils' 350th Regiment took Monte Rotondo to the south while 2nd Moroccans, 6th Moroccans and 4th Tunisians evicted the Germans from Monte Ceschito north of the road 'in a brilliant encircling attack which netted over 700 prisoners'.[33]

Thus on that evening of 13 May Juin's troops had broken through the German lines everywhere they had attacked, grinding down Raapke's 71st Division. The CEF's rapid success opened the way for exploitation to Esperia and Monte Revole, providing a jumping-off area for the *Corps de Montagne* to set off across the Ausonia valley and over the mountains to the Pico-Itri road. The corps included some 12,000 men and 4,000 pack animals of three Groups of Tabors (1st, 3rd and 4th) 1st Moroccan Infantry Regiment of 4th Mountain Division and 2nd Battalion 69th Artillery Regiment. Guillaume formed three task forces or *groupements*, linking tabors with infantry battalions.[34]

With Monte Ceschito in French hands the *groupements* moved out during the night of 13/14 May. Showing the high level of flexibility exhibited by the CEF, Guillaume formed his command into two columns, northern and southern: the southern column he commanded himself as *Groupement* Guillaume, consisting of *1er* and *4ème Groupes de Tabors*, *2ème* and *3ème Batallions* of *1er Régiment de Tirailleurs Marocains*, an artillery group from *69ème Régiment d'Artillerie* (69 RAM) and a section of engineers; the northern column, *Groupement* Bondis, commanded by Colonel Bondis, who commanded 4th Division's infantry, included *3ème Groupe de Tabors* and two infantry battalions, one each from *1er* and

---

* Unlike the other divisions of the CEF, which were organized, American style, in regiments, Brosset's division was structured on British lines with brigades.

2ème Régiments de Tirailleurs Marocains, a mountain artillery group from 69 RAM and a half-section of engineers. A reserve *groupement* under General Louchet was held until the 16th when its units were assigned to the other columns. Although *Groupement* Guillaume's units were held up for a time late on the 14th, they made good progress, *1er Groupement* fighting off some opposition to cross the Ausente and, passing Spigno, which 351st US Regiment held, take Monte Castello north of there. *Groupement* Bondis passed Ausonia and reached its objective, Monte Fammera, while *Groupement* Guillaume was making for the Petrella massif. The CEF was making its rapid push into the mountains, onto the massif, in the drive for Esperia.[35]

The soldiers of the *Corps de Montagne* were used to moving through untamed mountainous terrain:

> As the drive to Esperia got under way on the north, General Guillaume pressed west along the miserable trails of the mountains. During the night of 15/16 May the *goumiers* of the 1st and 4th Groups kept steadily on the march, except for a brief halt every four hours. Passing below Rave Grande and along La Valle, they crossed the basin of the Fraile by dawn, and at 0600, 16 May, the advance guard had reached the crest of Monte Revole (1,283 metres) – a gain of 12 miles from the old bridgehead line in four and one-half days. Opposition was paltry during this last push, for there were almost no Germans to meet our troops. Once again the daring of our plan, to strike the enemy where he least expected an attack, was proving justified.[36]

That 'daring' was Juin's rather than Clark's. Perhaps the latter had cause to consider how a breakthrough might have been achieved on the northern flank during the first battle had he not ordered Juin to change his axis of advance?

Groupement Guillaume's advance took the *goumiers* and Moroccan tirailleurs over terrain the Germans had considered impassable. Using goat tracks, Guillaume's soldiers scaled first one height, then another, lightly equipped and carrying the minimum of food and water. They marched on determinedly and at a speed no other soldiers on either side could have matched. Since the ground was so difficult the Germans were defending only lightly. Those positioned in the Moroccans' path were amazed and terrified to find knife-wielding *goumiers* among them. Flight was the sole option, the ensuing retreat being described by Notin in the words of a German cavalry officer, Rittmeister von der Borch.

> The French crushed everything. 'You can have no idea of the harshness and horror of this retreat,' wrote captain of cavalry der Borch in a letter to

his wife. '... the men were exhausted, not having had anything to eat for three days .... Our Free French and Moroccan foes were remarkably good. My heart bleeds when I consider my beautiful battalion after five days: 150 men lost .... The train was already far behind, three reconnaissance vehicles are in pieces, my armoured command vehicle and all the radio equipment and wires have been destroyed by a French armoured vehicle .... Arms, food, papers, all completely lacking since 26 April .... Until we meet again, I hope, in better days.[38]

It seems that von der Borch was not to see his wife again as his letter was found on the battlefield. The French moved on remorselessly towards Monte Revole with a brief halt to allow men and mules to recuperate. However, the two tirailleur battalions pressed on northward. By noon a battery of 75mm mountain guns of 69 RAM was emplaced on the Polleca stream, slightly over a mile east of Monte Revole, from where the *goumiers* could see the Germans retreating into Itri before II Corps.[39]

On the 17th thirty-six Douglas A-20 Havocs dropped some forty tons of supplies along the Spigno-Monte Strampaduro-La Valle track, of which about 60 per cent was recovered, enabling the leading troops to continue operations until pack-mule columns could bring up further supplies. By that stage the *Corps de Montagne* had two objectives: cut the Pico-Itri road and 'bring its full weight against the rear of Pico to smash the expected enemy stand on the Hitler Line'. To do so the *goumiers* moved west from Revole in three columns, one due west for Monte Calvo, three miles away, the second north-west towards Monte Faggeto and the third passing beyond that for Serra del Lago. All three faced long marches but were in position late that afternoon. The first group reached Monte Calvo without incident but met doughty opposition from a German rearguard covering the retreat into Itri. En route the other two groups encountered Germans building a road in the Valle Piana but the Moroccans deployed to high ground to either side, entrapped the enemy work parties and separated to make for their separate objectives. Meanwhile the battery of 69 RAM was moving its guns to Il Colle, where they could fire on the Pico-Itri road, which they did that afternoon.[40]

***

Juin was deploying his forces with skill and a keen instinct for battle, using the strengths of various elements of the CEF in the best possible manner. Lightly-equipped infantry was moving quickly along mountain ridges while armoured (some of them American) and motorized formations advanced along the available roads on the low ground. As Molony summarized it (page 236) the French were giving a master class in mountain warfare in all its simplicity and subtlety, by seizing tactically important summits, exploiting along high ridges with light infantry, and pushing mixed columns of armour and lorried infantry along the roads. Moreover, Juin had harmonized beautifully both forms of manoeuvre so that the Germans found that they simply had too few soldiers to defend the region. The end result was that the *goumiers*' penetration through the mountains split XIV Panzerkorps in two, leaving part to reel up the Ausente valley before the French mechanized formations while the other retreated along Highway 7, pursued by II Corps.

By the morning of 17 May 'French thrusts were moving so rapidly and were so numerous that the German command south of the Liri found itself completely unable to cope with the situation.' The previous two days had seen rapid advances, including an armoured thrust by elements of Monsabert's 3rd Algerian Division to Castelnuovo on the 15th, although a push towards the San Giorgio-Esperia road junction had been delayed by strong resistance at La Bastia Hill. However, the anti-tank guns on the slopes of the hill were knocked out early next morning, allowing armour to reach the junction by 8 o'clock. That afternoon III/200th Grenadiers launched an attack on *3ème Tirailleurs Algériens*, only to be rebuffed firmly; the Germans were fresh troops deployed to defend Esperia whose efforts were in vain, as were those of II/104th Panzergrenadier Regiment, sent from Fondi to Esperia, who suffered heavy losses, especially from Allied artillery.[41]

Meanwhile the *goumiers* deepened their penetration of the mountains so that by dawn on the 17th *Groupement* Bondis was 2,000 yards south of Esperia, ready to join 3rd Algerians in encircling the town; additional armour had joined the Algerians, having finished mopping-up in the Ausonia valley. Defence of Esperia was entrusted to elements of 71st Division but Kesselring and von Vietinghoff had agreed that withdrawal to the Hitler Line by XIV Panzerkorps was essential. Steinmetz's 94th Division would prevent the French reaching Highway 82, the Itri-Campodimele road, while Raapke's men held the Monte del Lago-Esperia-Casa Chiaia line.[42]

A plan to take Esperia by 3rd Algerian Division with one armoured and two infantry groups proved redundant when the Germans withdrew; the Algerians entered Esperia unopposed in the late morning. For the people of the Esperia district what followed the German departure must have seemed like images of hell as Juin's troops ignored discipline and respect for civilians and set about the mass rape of women, girls and boys. (One German veteran told the author that German prisoners were also raped as were animals, although his story could only be hearsay as he was a *Fallschirmjäger*.) Some 200 people were murdered by the North Africans, a figure that may be conservative as local people believe as many as 600 lost their lives. The French government has never accepted responsibility for this war crime. Esperia has not forgotten and a poignant monument, 'La Mamma Ciociara', commemorates the victims while a new verb was added to the Italian language: *marocchinate*, meaning 'those given the Moroccan treatment'.[43]

Advancing from Esperia, anti-tank guns in the defile between Monte d'Oro and Monte del Lago forced the armour to withdraw behind high ground to the west. Meanwhile, Brosset's 1st Division had also met stiff resistance, plus minefields, halting its advance. Although resistance continued next day, the 18th, *Groupement* Bondis, which had advanced from Monte Fammera to the hills south of Monte del Lago on the 17th, had moved by noon to the heights overlooking Sant'Oliva and south of that feature, on the lower slopes of which some German anti-tank guns were emplaced. A concerted attack by 1st Division and elements of 3rd Algerian, who had scaled Monte d'Oro while Brosset's men attacked the two hills to the north, had cleared the way for the advance. Other elements of Monsabert's division cleared Monticelli where they overcame a company of I/9th Panzergrenadier Regiment from 26th Panzer Division, the appearance of which indicated for the first time the strong reinforcements committed to stopping the French advance towards Pico.[44]

143: *La Mamma*, the memorial to the women and children raped and murdered by soldiers of the French corps in the Esperia area. (© Damiano Parravano, Chairman, Associazione Linea Gustav)

Further advance was made against continuing resistance designed to allow the enemy to fall back. By this stage Kesselring had ordered his strategic reserves into the line, 26th Panzer Division following 90th into Tenth Army's sector on the 16th, although he maintained control over the division rather than ceding command to von Vietinghoff. The following days saw additional formations being warned of moves to Tenth Army, including 8th and 1027th Grenadier Regiments of 3rd Panzergrenadier Division, while von Vietinghoff moved 305th and 334th Divisions from the Adriatic sector to the Liri valley. Hitler also ordered 16th Panzergrenadier Division to move from Germany to join the reserves in northern Italy, held against the possibility of Allied landings along the Ligurian coast. German uncertainty was proving an aid to the Allied advance.[45]

The French advance had unbalanced the Germans with the flexibility of Juin's command allowing formations and units to work so closely that some took objectives assigned to others. Kesselring noted how the French exploited success in contrast to the more methodical operational practice of their British and American allies, commenting that 'the French, particularly the Moroccans, fought with great *élan*, and exploited each local success by concentrating immediately all available forces at the weakened point'.[46]

***

On 19 May, the day after the Poles entered the Abbey, the CEF was aligned from Monte Calvo to Campodimele, along the eastern side of the Itri-Pico road, and through the mountains to the heights about Sant'Oliva and the east bank of the Forma Quesa to the Liri. Two *groupements* of *Corps de Montagne* tabors with two infantry battalions held the left flank; *Groupement* Bondis, with a group of tabors and two infantry battalions, and another group with five infantry battalions plus most of 3rd Algerian Division, held the centre. The right was held by Brosset's division; that flank swept around the western and northern slopes of Monte d'Oro. Since Eighth Army's advance had fallen behind the CEF's, 1st Division had to deploy much of its strength to cover the south bank of the Liri where German harassing fire was a constant factor.[47] However, the Allies could consider the Gustav Line as broken, allowing both armies to focus on the Hitler Line. Eighth Army was ready to advance to Pontecorvo, Aquino and Piedimonte San Germano, while Fifth Army had begun its move towards that line.

II Corps had continued its advance: Santa Maria Infante was in American hands on the afternoon of 14 May while the Germans had retreated across the Ausente. Spigno followed next day, after which Clark ordered Keyes 'to send 88th Division with all possible speed from Spigno directly across the mountains to Itri, nine miles away, and the road junction on the second of the enemy's two lateral communications routes, while Coulter's 85th Division followed the withdrawal of that part of 94th Division on the seaward side of the Aurunci mountains'.[48] Steinmetz's division had suffered heavy losses in nearly three days of infantry probes, bombardment by artillery and fighter-bombers, so that he had lost some 40 per cent of his infantry.[49] Although American formations had also suffered considerable losses these could be made good, even as the advance continued.

With Clark's eyes still on an advance through the Aurunci mountains to reach Anzio, 85th Division was to make for Castellonorato where an infantry and armour attack by 2nd/337th Regiment was successful after initial setbacks. At the same time 338th Regiment took Monte Penitro, the village of the same name and Santa Croce with its road junction. Thus II Corps had pushed through the Gustav Line on the seaward side of the mountains, making the German defences of Highway 7 on the coastal plain redundant.[50] Vietinghoff refused to assent to Hartmann's request to withdraw to the Dora Line, but before long such a withdrawal was inevitable. In spite of Steinmetz's best efforts, American pressure could not be repelled. Keyes' success led him to conclude that II Corps' best avenue of exploitation lay not through the Aurunci mountains but along the coastal slopes and he shifted the balance of his attack, with what had been intended as a secondary operation becoming the main effort. The force of II Corps' advance was applied along the Castellonorato–Maranola road to outflank Formia, which was critical to the Germans' use of Highway 82, their second lateral communications line.[51]

Eighty-fifth Division took Formia on the 17th and Gaeta two days later while on the 19th Monte Grande (2,513 feet/778 metres) was in American hands. Itri was then taken after a very short rearguard action by a mixture of German troops, including 620th Ost Battalion, which broke quickly, thus compelling withdrawal towards Fondi. 'In eight days II Corps had completed the mission assigned to it by the Fifth Army order.' On the 20th a probe by 91st Cavalry Squadron found Fondi defended only weakly.[52]

The information from 91st Cavalry Squadron encouraged Clark to 'disregard Alexander's operational concept' which was that, due to German resistance to Eighth Army in the Liri valley, Fifth Army should be ready to shift its axis of advance to the north with II Corps and the CEF making for the junction of Highways 6 and 82 in the valley to threaten the German lines of communication. However, Clark, more concerned with breaking through to the Anzio bridgehead, had been formulating a plan to send 36th Division, Fifth Army's reserve, and much of Coulter's 85th Division by sea to Anzio. He chose instead to take advantage of enemy weakness along the coast by pushing II Corps along the narrow corridor of Highway 7 to link with Truscott's VI Corps while allowing the CEF advance to continue and threaten the German flank as Alexander desired. When Clark advised Alexander of this decision the Army Group commander did not object. Interestingly the US official history noted:

> He [Alexander] had held as loose a rein on Montgomery in the Western Desert. This was the Allied commander's style of command. It had brought success to the Alexander-Montgomery team in North Africa, and Alexander expected that it would work in Italy with an equally independent subordinate.[53]

Thus the overall situation within Allied Armies in Italy was that Eighth Army was preparing for a major assault on the Hitler Line as Fifth Army advanced towards a junction with VI Corps. Alexander had decided that Eighth Army's attack would begin on the night of 21 May, or early on the 22nd, at which time he expected VI Corps to begin its breakout. In Eighth Army's sector Leese had brought I Canadian Corps into the Liri valley to make the main effort against the Hitler Line in Operation CHESTERFIELD. At the same time XIII Corps would maintain pressure at Aquino and be prepared to advance alongside the Canadians when the line was ruptured. The Polish II Corps had advanced four miles from Monte Cassino to take Villa Santa Lucia, a key German position, from which the defenders of the heights had been supplied, and were ready to continue to Piedimonte San Germano, the Hitler Line's northern anchor.[54]

In some respects the Hitler Line was more impressive than the Gustav with twenty-foot-deep steel shelters, concrete emplacements for anti-tank guns and machine guns with 360-degree fields of fire. Mobile steel cylindrical cells, or 'crabs',

> could be inserted in pits above which their steel domes rose to a height of only 30 inches; and the turrets of new Panther tanks, … mounting 75mm guns with all-round traverse, which also made barely visible intrusions above their concrete emplacements. All were sited and camouflaged with great skill, and since installation they had received an extra layer of covering from the great sproutings of spring.[55]

The attack on the Hitler Line was initiated by 78th Division, still reinforced by elements of 6th Armoured, with 1st Derbyshire Yeomanry and 10th Rifle Brigade making the first probe, followed by 36 Brigade supported by Ontarios' tanks. All the Ontario Shermans were hit, thirteen being lost. The Canadians followed 78th Division, their 1st Division, commanded by Major General Chris Vokes, running head-on into the leading elements of 90th Division. As the battle developed, 5th Canadian Armoured Division would also become embroiled but in the initial clashes the Canadian infantry were supported by Churchills of 25 Tank Brigade

144: The remains of a *Pantherturm* in the Hitler Line/Senger Line. It would have been surmounted by a Panther tank turret with its 75mm gun. Camouflaged by the growth of spring, these were difficult to spot and took a heavy toll of Allied tanks. (Author's photo)

since 1 Canadian Armoured Brigade was still attached to 8th Indian Division. This, the Churchills' operational debut in Italy, was a chastening experience. The terrain favoured the defenders with vineyards, cornfields and coppices offering excellent cover for infantry armed with *panzerfausten* anti-tank weapons.[56]

The main Canadian assault was launched on the night of 21/22 May. XIII Corps maintained pressure on Aquino, and was ready to exploit, while II Polish Corps engaged Heidrich's men at Piedimonte. Thus, on a relatively narrow front of little more than six miles, Leese had committed three corps. Having experienced the results of Montgomery's deployment of two overlapping corps at El Alamein, he should have foreseen the outcome but the pressures of coalition warfare bore on him and, whereas a single corps would have sufficed, national sensibilities had to be considered.

> Leese would himself have replied that the commander of an international army is clothed in the straitjacket of national pride, and just as the Poles had to fight as a corps on their own, so did the 1st Canadian Infantry and 5th Canadian Armoured Divisions.[57]

145: Also included in the Hitler Line defences were machine-gun positions; many are still visible. (Author's photo)

146: An armoured machine-gun post being removed by US Army engineers. This factory-made structure illustrates the ingenuity displayed in the defensive lines that faced the soldiers of Allied Armies in Italy. (NARA)

147: Soldiers of 78th Division, probably from 2nd Irish Rifles, patrol towards Aquino airfield. (Author's collection)

Problems arising from deploying three corps included additional strain on Eighth Army's already overloaded wireless network and traffic congestion that slowed artillery deploying to support the Canadian attack, which was delayed until 6.00am on the 23rd. Before then Vokes attacked Pontecorvo, believing that the speedy CEF advance might have loosened the German grip on the line but the attack proved only that that grip remained firm and, between Pontecorvo and Piedimonte, was applied by two of von Vietinghoff's best commanders, Baade of 90th Panzergrenadiers and Heidrich of 1st *Fallschirmjäger*.[58]

The Canadian main attack was launched as planned, half an hour before VI Corps began Operation BUFFALO, its breakout from Anzio. In spite of a storm of artillery fire the defenders fought back viciously, inflicting heavy losses on the attackers; in its first action in Italy, the North Irish Horse, supporting 2 Canadian Brigade, sustained its worst day's casualties in two world wars. Although a squadron of the Horse's tanks had breached the Hitler Line to reach the Pontecorvo-Highway 6 road, the Phase II line of Operation CHESTERFIELD, without infantry support they had to withdraw.[59]

As the battle continued, the line was breached by infantry of 3 Brigade, supported by Three Rivers Regiment tanks, who advanced to the Phase II line. The breach was expanded and on the 24th the Royal Canadian Regiment entered Pontecorvo.[60] However, the cost had been high: on the 23rd the Canadian 2 Brigade had suffered the highest single day's casualties of any brigade in the Italian campaign while Eighth Army's gunners had responded to a call from Brigadier Ziegler, CRA 1st Canadian Division, for a 'William Target', a concentration from all the army's guns in which 3,500 shells were dropped on German positions in two minutes by 600 guns.[61]

Fifth Armoured Division then advanced through the breach to clash with German armour and for several hours on the 24th Canadian Shermans fought Panthers and Mark IVs, four Shermans and three Panthers being disabled. By midday Canadian armour was at Mancici, north-west of Aquino, or over the Melfa river, forming a new bridgehead. As resistance hardened, one regiment, Lord Strathcona's Horse, lost seventeen Shermans.[62]

Elsewhere the XIII Corps' front was static until the 25th when patrols of 78th Division discovered that the Germans had quit Aquino. At much the same time the Poles found that Piedimonte had also been abandoned overnight. In two weeks' fighting the Polish Corps had suffered 3,784 casualties, including 860 dead, one of them Colonel Wincenty Kurek, commander of 5 Wileńska Brigade, killed while directing an attack at Sant'Angelo.[63]

Eighth Army began a pursuit that brought 2nd New Zealand Division back into the picture. While 4 New Zealand Armoured Brigade joined 8th Indian Division in pursuing the Germans along the valley sides, Freyberg's infantry probed into the mountains north of Cassino before setting off around Monte Cáiro to pursue the foe.[64]

148: Soldiers of the modern North Irish Horse visit the graves of their forebears killed in the Hitler Line battle, the bloodiest day in the regiment's history. (Author's photo)

Although the New Zealanders had been part of McCreery's X Corps on the Adriatic flank, this was not the insertion of another corps into the operation but the transfer of the division from X Corps. The Battleaxe Division also committed infantry to the pursuit, but with tanks of 9 Armoured Brigade relieving those of 6th Armoured Division. Nine Armoured Brigade had not been in action since El Alamein where its regiments had suffered horrendous losses along the Trigh el Rahman. It had crossed Italy on 18 and 19 May to wait five days at Triflisco before joining the pursuit.[65]

Sixth Armoured Division was also deployed with 26 Armoured Brigade ordered to break out through the Canadian sector. However, this increased congestion in the valley and not until late in the afternoon did the Derbyshire Yeomanry reach the Melfa river where some tanks crossed but, with no infantry support and determined opposition, the crews were told to leave their tanks and return across the river; the order was obeyed but with twenty-one German prisoners included in the party.[66]

On the Melfa on 24 May the final Victoria Cross of the Cassino battles was earned by a Canadian officer. Major John Keefer Mahony commanded A Company of the Westminster Regiment which crossed against strong opposition to join Lieutenant E.J. Perkins' Reconnaissance Troop which had crossed earlier, captured a house with its eight German occupants and placed its tanks in hull-down positions to await reinforcements.

149: The memorial to all who died in the Hitler Line battle, situated at I Canadian Corps' start line. (Author's photo)

150: 'Vancouver' moving forward with Major General B.M., 'Bert', Hoffmeister, GOC of 5th Canadian Armoured Division in the turret, near Castrocielo. (Strathy Smith/Library and Archives Canada/PA204155)

The crossing was made and a small bridgehead was established … where it was only possible to dig shallow weapon pits. From 1530 hours the company maintained itself in the face of enemy fire and attack until 2030 hours, when the remaining companies and supporting weapons were able to cross … and reinforce them.

151: The Polish Cemetery in the shadow of the Abbey. Over 1,000 Polish soldiers are buried here, as is General Anders and other prominent members of II Corps who died during the Soviet era when this piece of ground in Italy represented 'Free Poland'. (© Damiano Parravano, Chairman, Associazione Linea Gustav)

152: Second New Zealand Division also returned to the battle. A trio of New Zealand soldiers study a divisional axis sign. (Public domain)

A Company's bridgehead was overlooked on three sides by enemy artillery, machine guns and mortars, including two 88mm self-propelled guns and four 20mm AA guns, and an estimated company of infantry. The company was constantly under fire until it knocked out the self-propelled equipment and infantry on the left flank. Not long after the bridgehead had been established, the Germans counter-attacked unsuccessfully with infantry, tanks and StuGs; A Company used PIATs, 2-inch mortars and grenades to defeat them. Mahony, who had organized his defences with great skill, showed complete fearlessness, personally directing the fire of the PIATs while encouraging and exhorting his soldiers.

The counter-attack whittled A Company's strength down to sixty men; all but one platoon officer had been wounded. Less than an hour later German tanks formed up about 500 yards away and, with about a company of infantry, counter-attacked again, during which Mahony, 'determined to hold the position at all costs, went from section to section with words of encouragement, personally directing fire of mortars and other weapons'. When one section was pinned down by accurate intense machine-gun fire in the open, he crawled to their position and, with smoke grenades, extricated them with the loss of only one man. The second counter-attack was also beaten off, the Germans losing three StuGs and a Panther.

Although wounded in the head and twice in the leg at an early stage, Mahony refused medical aid and directed the defence in spite of extreme pain. Only when the Westminsters' other companies had crossed the Melfa to support A Company did he allow his wounds to be dressed. Even then he refused to be evacuated.

> The forming and holding of a bridgehead across the river was vital to the whole Canadian Corps action and failure would have meant delay, a repetition of the attack, probably involving heavy losses in men, material and time, and would have given the enemy a breathing space which might have broken the impetus of the Corps advance.
>
> Major Mahony ... never allowed the thought of failure or withdrawal to enter his mind and infused his spirit and determination into all his men. At the first sign of hesitation or faltering Major Mahony was there to encourage, by his own example, those who were feeling the strain of battle. The enemy perceived that this officer was the soul of the defence and consequently fired at him constantly with all weapons, from rifles to 88mm guns. Major Mahony completely ignored the enemy fire and with great courage and absolute disregard for personal danger commanded his company with such great confidence, energy and skill that the enemy's efforts ... were all defeated.[67]

Mahony's actions saved the bridgehead, hastening the departure of the Germans whom he may also have distracted sufficiently to have enabled 11 Canadian Lorried Infantry Brigade's assault crossing and subsequent advance of a thousand yards beyond the river, which further disrupted the enemy. Another German withdrawal that night was followed next day by a Canadian advance.

Chapter Thirteen

We left the CEF on 19 May, the day Juin reviewed the progress of the battle and enlarged his intentions while directing the *Corps de Montagne* to amend its axis by moving more to the west on the line Lenola-Vallecorsa-Amaseno.[1] He also calculated that Allied efforts thus far had 'destroyed about five German divisions and the equivalent of another two regiments' while 26th Panzer Division, having been thrown into the maelstrom, had suffered heavily. Juin believed that the Hitler Line was no longer a realistic rallying position for the enemy since the CEF was about to turn its flank and I Canadian Corps was ready to push through it between Aquino and Pontecorvo. That left the Germans with the line Valmontone-Velletri-Anzio perimeter on which to rally. Believing the Allies were on the cusp of a major success, with his corps the principal contributor, Juin considered his best course of action was to continue through the Aurunci and Ausoni mountains, coupled with a Canadian advance north of Pontecorvo while II Corps, advancing along the axis Itri-Fondi-Terracina, covered his flank. Truscott's VI Corps was scheduled to break out from Anzio on the 23rd.[2]

Juin ordered Monsabert's 3rd Algerian Division to make for Ceprano and the *Corps de Montagne* for Castro dei Volsci with Brosset's 1st Division moving into reserve when Burns' Canadians reached the Melfa. Monsabert continued his relentless advance, using the same proven flexible operational doctrine. Thus, on 20 May, Monsabert's Algerians cleared Monte Leucio, penetrating the defences to some 3,000 yards. However, elements of the *Corps de Montagne* were stopped by I/134th Grenadier Regiment on their advance to Montecelli di San Onofrio while an armoured group, commanded by Commandant Dodelier, was halted by anti-tank guns on the Itri-Pico road. The loss of Monte Leucio had prompted von Senger to order 26th Panzer Division to occupy a line from Campo di Morti to the Matrice stream, from which he hoped to recapture the mountain.[3]

Even as they retreated with numbers much depleted, the Germans retained a strong fighting spirit, which they demonstrated on 21 May, described by one French officer as 'a very hard day'. On that day the *Corps de Montagne* fought for Monte Appiolo, held by the 3rd Alpine Battalion. The mountain changed hands several times before the French secured it, allowing Dodelier's armoured group to advance along the Itri-Pico road, harrying II/104th Panzergrenadier Regiment northwards. That advance came to a standstill near Montecelli di San Onofrio

153: Kesselring and von Senger confer, although the latter had not returned to the battlefield from Germany until 20 May. (NARA)

but other elements of the CEF continued, *Groupement* Guillaume pushing for Lenola; companies of Monsabert's division established themselves in Pico's southern outskirts and on Point 270, west of there. However, a counter-attack by 67th Panzergrenadier Regiment of 26th Panzer Division, supported by a Panther company, later that day evicted the two companies from Pico, but a series of counter-attacks on Point 270 led to furious fighting, with the French pushed off the feature three times and regaining it three times. A fourth German assault seemed to have settled ownership but then 'with unbreakable spirit, the survivors attacked for the fourth time, won back the hilltop and this time held it'. Brosset's 1st Division had taken Monte Morrone but, while advancing towards San Giovanni, the division was counter-attacked by I/104th Panzergrenadier and 26th Panzer Regiments and withdrew to positions between Monte Morrone and Monte Leucio. Nonetheless, pressure on the Germans remained relentless over the following days.[4]

By 22 May most of the CEF's artillery, including the US 13 Artillery Brigade, had been re-positioned in the area of Sant'Oliva, Montecelli and the ground east of Monte d'Oro to support the next phase of Monsabert's advance. Those elements of XIV Panzerkorps, namely 26th Panzer Regiment and what was left of 15th Panzergrenadier Division, holding, respectively, Pico, Campo di Morto and the Matrice stream and the defences west of the Itri-Pico road on the line Monte Trella-Monte Schierano-Monte Cimale, suffered the weight of those guns as Monsabert thrust against Pico and its flanks with most of his division. Although the Germans fought hard as always, Pico was taken by the Algerians while the *Corps de Montagne* cleared both Monte Trella and Monte Schierano before heading northwards for Cima Alta. *Groupement* Guillaume took Lenola with only about a hundred men of 276th Grenadier Regiment escaping. Juin had broken through his sector of the Hitler Line. The CEF stood ready for the next phase of operations.[5]

Juin had criticized Eighth Army for failing to keep pace with his own corps but the CEF had advanced through very difficult mountainous terrain that the Germans had considered impassable and therefore had not fortified as they had the Cassino massif or the valley and approaches to Cassino. Nor had XIV Panzerkorps deployed troops in sufficient numbers. The rush to reinforce 94th and 71st Divisions often led to piecemeal insertion of units and formations. In contrast, Eighth Army had encountered the toughest German divisions. Deploying five divisions, including armour, Leese depended very much on roads and bridges but demolitions of the latter slowed the advance. However, sappers were able to build replacements quickly, even when under enemy fire as with 577 Field Company, under Major Donald Booth, which bridged the Melfa in twenty-four hours and subsequently excelled themselves by erecting a bridge at Arce in five hours, then a record.[6]

As Eighth Army advanced, XIII and I Canadian Corps were in close company, which led to one notable incident some five miles from Ceprano when the Irish Regiment of Canada was relieved by 38 (Irish) Brigade's 1st Royal Irish Fusiliers and a Canadian soldier was heard to shout directions: 'Canadian Irish this way; English Irish that way.' No offence was taken by the Faughs, however, and the story became part of regimental lore.[7]

Many actions were being fought as the Germans retreated at their own pace, forcing the Allies to fight whenever they pressed too closely. Alongside Highway 6, 1 Guards Brigade, the infantry of 6th Armoured Division, suffered many casualties advancing through the hills and 17 Indian Brigade also met determined opposition while fighting for yet more mountains. *Fallschirmjäger* forced 1st/5th Gurkhas to fight hard for Rocca d'Arce on the 29th although, that same day, 3rd Grenadier Guards took Monte Grande unopposed, the Germans having slipped away during the night; 3rd Welsh Guards were thus enabled to ride into Arce on Lothian tanks.[8]

Eighth Army's advance continued, not helped by the mass of troops and vehicles committed to the Liri valley. In the six days after the breaking of the Hitler Line XIII Corps advanced only eleven miles and although I Canadian Corps increased their speed they still lagged behind the CEF. By the 30th the Canadians were in the valley of the Sacco, a tributary of the Liri, where progress was difficult due to 'wooded ridges, sunken, twisted lanes, gullies, brooks, and riverlets' in addition to the usual demolitions and booby traps. In XIII Corps, 78th Division was advancing on Frosinone while 8th Indian Division pursued the retreating Germans through the mountains.[9]

That same day 78th Division took Ripi and the Canadians cut Highway 6 when Corporal J.B. Matthews, a Sherman commander, dashed along the road from Arnara, knocking out a StuG and two 26th Panzer Division tanks before holding his ground until it could be consolidated. Matthews was awarded the DCM, the second-highest gallantry award for an 'other rank', for a deed that proved yet again how a small group, or even one man, can shape a battle's outcome.[10] Next day the Edmontons secured Frosinone while the Maoris joined 4 New Zealand Armoured Brigade in Sora, some twelve miles north-east of Frosinone where the New Zealand armour, having supported the Indians, rejoined 2nd New Zealand Division, then deploying to cut Highway 82 and block the retreat of LI Mountain Corps.

***

The Gustav Line had been smashed as had the Hitler Line. Alexander's armies were on their road to Rome. Truscott's VI Corps had begun the breakout from Anzio in Operation BUFFALO on 23 May, threatening the Germans with being trapped in a pincer movement leading to a major defeat and heavy losses; such was the strategic imperative of Alexander's plan. VI Corps had been strengthened for BUFFALO by a complete 1st Armored Division, Combat Command B having arrived, and 36th Division. Harmon's 1st Armored, 'Old Ironsides', included three US armoured regiments, with two US tank battalions and the British 46th Royal Tank Regiment attached. US infantry included 3rd Division, under Major General John W. O'Daniel, Ryder's 34th Division, Walker's 36th and Major General William W. Eagles' 45th, plus 1st Special Service Force, still commanded by Frederick. The British element of VI Corps included 1st Division, commanded by Brigadier C.E. Loewen, and Gregson-Ellis' 5th Division. Corps artillery included a US battery of 240mm howitzers, an 8-inch howitzer battalion, seven field artillery battalions of 155mm howitzers, three of 155mm guns, eighteen of 105mm howitzers and two batteries of 75mm howitzers, plus two British medium regiments (one with 5.5-inch guns, the other with 4.5s) and seven 25-pounder field regiments; there were also British and US anti-aircraft and anti-tank regiments.[11]

Truscott, consulting with Clark, had drawn up the plans for BUFFALO, a breakout directed on Valmontone, but both believed that circumstances might occur that made other options possible. Should the Germans withdraw rapidly to the Alban hills before Fifth and Eight Armies' advance, VI Corps might be able to strike farther west, either on the axis Carroceto-Campoleone-Rome or Ardea-Rome. Plans were laid for both eventualities, codenamed TURTLE and CRAWDAD respectively. Another plan, GRASSHOPPER, envisaged an attack to join Fifth Army's main force as it advanced north-westward, if support was needed.[12] Alexander visited Truscott on 5 May to discuss the operation, advising VI Corps' commander that there 'was only one direction in which the attack should or would be launched, … from Cisterna to cut Highway 6 in the vicinity of Valmontone in the rear of the German main forces'.[13] Learning this, Clark told Truscott that nothing was more important than Rome. Determined to be in the city before the British, he thought Alexander was conspiring to ensure Eighth Army arrived first.[14]

***

The breakout began on the morning of 23 May, American divisions making the main attack; the two under-strength British divisions had a holding role, although British units were involved in the breakout. Both British divisions would create a diversion, Operation HIPPO, a distraction from the offensive's true direction. Most of VI Corps' artillery fired as part of the supporting bombardment, including three battalions of 155mm howitzers, one of 8-inch howitzers and a battery of 240mm howitzers, with three 90mm anti-aircraft battalions available to engage ground targets. Two British artillery regiments lent support; only one battalion of 105mm howitzers assigned to 1st Armored Division was not included in the corps fireplan. Prior to D Day for BUFFALO, aircraft of XII Tactical Air Command increased attacks on enemy communications, artillery positions and supply dumps. Throughout D Day they flew twenty-eight planned missions

154: Generals Alexander and Truscott confer on the break-out of VI Corps from the Anzio beach-head. (NARA)

against ground targets and provided cover against Luftwaffe attacks. Two US Navy cruisers' firepower reinforced that of the artillery.[15]

Although Truscott had asked for three days' warning for D Day, he received only two. This proved no problem. Since he had anticipated events, having begun preparations for a possible D Day on 21 May, on the 18th, the

> shortness of notice proved no problem to [his] staff. 36 (US) Division was arriving in the beachhead and would be concentrated in time to back up the offensive. Moreover, the weather forecasts …were now sufficiently promising to give a fair chance of full air support over the beachhead on 23 May.[16]

Leading VI Corps' attack were, from right to left, 3rd Division, Special Service Force, 1st Armored and 45th Divisions; 135th Regiment of 34th Division reinforced 1st Armored. Truscott intended 3rd Division to take Cisterna and La Villa and advance about two miles to the north. While 1st Special Service Force advanced north-eastwards towards Highway 7, and guarded against counter-attack, 1st Armored was to strike towards Highway 7, cut the road north-west of Cisterna and reconnoitre towards Giulianello, Velletri and Campoleone. Forty-fifth Division would expand the armour's penetration by advancing along the Carano 'wadi' to the railway line. This was BUFFALO's phase one.[17]

In phase two 36th Division was to pass through 3rd Division towards Cori while 1st Armored advanced to a line between Giulianello and Velletri and Special Service Force made for Monte Arrestino, south-east of Cori. Thereafter those formations were to take Artena, at which stage the final thrust for Valmontone would be decided.[18]

Fourteenth Army's I *Fallschirmjäger* Corps and LXXVI Panzerkorps deployed five divisions, von Mackensen having lost four divisions after the failed March offensive. In Schlemm's I *Fallschirmjäger* Corps were 4th *Fallschirmjäger*, 65th Infantry and 3rd Panzergrenadier Divisions. Only the parachute division had three three-battalion regiments, the others having two-battalion regiments although 65th had 1027th Regiment of two battalions under command and 3rd Panzergrenadier had the three-battalion Infantry Lehr Regiment. Two regiments had been withdrawn from Schlemm's corps to combat II Corps in the Lepini mountains. Nor did Fourteenth Army have defences as solid as those of the Gustav and Hitler Lines; there were no embedded tank turrets, factory-made steel bunkers, or concrete works, other than a few of the last-mentioned in the Lanuvio-Velletri sector.[19]

> There were several belts of mutually supporting strongpoints, each large enough to hold a platoon and four machine guns, and smaller posts had been dug ahead of the platoon strongpoints. Most ... strongpoints were protected by wire and anti-personnel mines. All likely tank-runs were sown with anti-tank mines. The belts of strongpoints were not very deep although the final defences formed part of the Cäsar Line ... .[20]

The defenders' inherent strength rested on holding higher ground, from where observers could see all possible Allied axes of advance, generally well-prepared field defences, and those belts of mines and wire. From the outset opposition was strong, but yet again there came demonstrations of how individuals or small groups can influence a battle's course. That no fewer than seven Medals of Honor were earned on D Day indicates the fight US forces faced. In 34th Division two

NCOs, Technical Sergeant Ernest H. Dervishian and Staff Sergeant George J. Hall, earned their country's highest gallantry award, as did three privates first class from 3rd Division, John Dutko, Patrick L. Kessler and Henry Schauer, a young officer of 1st Armored, Second Lieutenant Thomas W. Fowler, and another NCO of 45th Division, Technical Sergeant Van T. Barfoot.

Ahead of his company with four others of his platoon while attacking enemy positions, Technical Sergeant Dervishian charged the enemy alone, his four comrades covering him. With another four soldiers he engaged enemy posts under heavy fire, at one point feigning death before assaulting a position and capturing its occupants. Although one of his men was killed and another wounded, Dervishian continued, finally clearing all the Germans he could find before returning with more prisoners. He was later commissioned as well as receiving the Medal of Honor.[21]

Staff Sergeant George J. Hall, also of Dervishian's company, survived too, but with serious injuries that probably contributed to his early death in 1946. Pinned down by three machine guns and riflemen, Hall crawled along a furrow, engaged the first German position with four grenades before taking possession of the post and then, with German grenades, duelled successfully with another position. Crawling closer to a third post, splinters from shellfire severed his right leg but his company, outflanking the position, continued its advance.[22]

Third Division's three Pfc Medal of Honor laureates showed similar qualities of courage and leadership. During an artillery concentration, John Dutko attacked three machine guns and a mobile 88, running for 100 yards through intense fire, sheltering briefly in a shell hole and resuming his assault. He knocked out the first machine gun and, although wounded by the second, advanced on the 88, shooting its team with his Browning automatic rifle (BAR) before dealing with the third machine-gun team. He shot both gunners but was hit by return fire and fell dead over the Germans.[23] Patrick Kessler also made a suicidal attack on a machine gun before, seeing two comrades killed assaulting a strongpoint, seizing a BAR and ammunition and attacking the strongpoint, overcoming the defenders and another two riflemen whom he captured. His actions allowed his company to continue its advance. Kessler was killed in action two days later.[24] The sole survivor of the trio, Henry Schauer, also used a BAR in several engagements, at one point walking 'deliberately thirty yards toward the enemy'. He ignored enemy fire, knocked out two machine guns and continued his actions next day, engaging another machine-gun position, again defying sustained fire, and shelling from a tank. Schauer was later promoted to technical sergeant.[25]

With his platoon pinned down by enemy troops on higher ground, Technical Sergeant Van Barfoot, of 45th Division's 3rd/157th Regiment, made a solo flanking attack on two machine-gun posts, one with a grenade, the other with his SMG, prompting the crew of a third post to surrender. Barfoot continued his foray, eventually gathering seventeen prisoners. After re-organizing his men, and coming under attack by tanks and infantry, he engaged three tanks with a bazooka, knocking out one, which forced the others to withdraw. After a fire fight with the disabled tank's crew, Barfoot destroyed a field gun and, returning to his platoon, assisted two badly wounded men to safety over a distance of almost a mile. In addition to receiving the Medal of Honor, Barfoot was commissioned.[26]

Second Lieutenant Thomas W. Fowler was a tank officer on foot who encountered two 'completely disorganized infantry platoons' held up by a minefield. Taking charge and re-organizing them, Fowler reconnoitred the minefield, clearing a path by hand through which he led the infantry before guiding supporting tanks through to overcome German infantry. Deciding to close the gap between his company and the unit to the right, he deployed the infantry into suitable positions to achieve this. When one of his battalion's tanks was set ablaze in a counter-attack, he raced to save the crew's lives. Only when almost overrun by enemy tanks did he withdraw. He then tended to nine wounded infantrymen 'in the midst of the relentless incoming fire'.[27]

***

VI Corps was making steady progress. Enemy defences seemed strongest around Cisterna, extending in depth back to the railway line; there were also strong defences on the Lanuvio-Velletri-Valmontone line. However, advancing units found that 'though the enemy had done enough work to make our progress costly he had nowhere finished his labors' as shown by dummy communication trenches. Complete surprise had been gained and German command and control disrupted to the extent that the enemy never recovered fully. The most stubborn resistance was encountered by O'Daniel's 3rd Division, as evidenced by the three Medal of Honor awards.[28]

The first day of BUFFALO proved 'extremely successful', first objectives being gained everywhere except the extreme right. Almost 1,500 prisoners were taken, half of them by 3rd Division, but O'Daniel's men had also suffered the highest losses – 950 dead, wounded or missing. About a hundred US tanks or tank-destroyers had been knocked out, but most were repairable.[29]

On the 24th two more Medals of Honor were gained by O'Daniel's division as the advance continued, preceded by a half-hour artillery bombardment. Sergeant Sylvester Antolak, 15th Regiment, died earning the Medal of Honor, having charged 200 yards over flat terrain to destroy a machine-gun nest. Wounded three times, he rushed the enemy with a submachine gun and, less than fifteen yards from the foe, opened fire, killing two Germans and forcing ten to surrender. Re-organizing his squad, he advanced on another strongpoint some 100 yards away, having refused treatment for his wounds. Again he charged into a hail of bullets and fell to that fire.[30]

Also in 15th Infantry was America's most decorated soldier of the war, the future film star Audie Murphy. His platoon was following Antolak's.

> A sergeant in the first platoon senses the predicament. If his men are isolated, they will likely be destroyed. ... Motioning his men to follow, he rises and with a submachine gun charges head-on toward one of the enemy positions ....
>
> On the flat, coverless terrain, his body is a perfect target. A blast of automatic fire knocks him down. He springs to his feet with a bleeding shoulder and continues his charge. The guns rattle. Again he goes down.
>
> Fascinated, we watch as he gets up for the third time and dashes straight into the enemy fire. The Germans throw everything they have at him. He falls to the earth; and when he again pulls himself to his feet, we see that his right arm is shattered. But wedging his gun under his left armpit, he continues firing and staggers forward. Ten horrified Germans throw down their guns and yell 'Kamerad'.
>
> That is all I see. But later I learn that the sergeant ... charged the second enemy strongpoint. ... he advanced sixty yards before being stopped by a final concentration of enemy fire. He reeled, then tottered forward another few yards before falling.
>
> Inspired by his valor and half-insane with rage, his men took over, stormed the kraut emplacement, and captured it. When they returned to their leader, he was dead.[31]

Private James H. Mills was the second 3rd Division soldier to earn the Medal of Honor that day, his first in action. When his platoon was engaged by a machine gun, Mills killed the gunner with a single shot and forced the other gunner to surrender. Fired on by a machine gun, machine pistols and rifles some fifty feet away, he charged the Germans, firing his M1 from the hip, demoralizing them so much that they surrendered. Engaging more Germans, he took a further prisoner and feinted an attack on his platoon's objective: standing up and shouting at the enemy, he fired in their direction while his platoon closed on the strongpoint, overwhelmed the defenders and took twenty-two prisoners with no casualties.[32]

The defenders around Cisterna proved more stubborn but both 30th and 15th Regiments, to the north and south respectively, closed in, with 2nd/30th gaining Highway 7. As a gap developed between 1st Armored and 3rd Divisions, Ryder's Red Bulls, less 133rd Regiment, filled it to protect against the threat of counter-attack and allow Harmon's armour more freedom to exploit the collapse below

Cori. Other than elements of 362nd Division in the rubble of Cisterna and some paratroopers near Velletri, Fourteenth Army's left flank was falling back. However, von Mackensen's headquarters was deploying 1060th Grenadier Regiment and the Hermann Göring Reconnaissance Battalion to block the drive on Valmontone. Both units were making for Cori past Giulianello against the flow of retreating traffic in spite of the attentions of Allied aircraft, so desperate was the German situation.[33]

Under pressure from the air – it was calculated that aircraft had destroyed 645 vehicles and damaged 446 – the defence of Cisterna collapsed on the 25th; 1st Armored exploited by driving north while 3rd Division's 30th and 15th Regiments completed encircling Cisterna before advancing to Cori. A battalion of each remained to guard the eastern exits from Cisterna while their main elements engaged 1060th Grenadiers and the Hermann Göring Recce Battalion, badly-battered units that proved no hindrance to O'Daniel's men; 'the survivors reeled back in complete defeat with the rest of the fleeing enemy.'[34]

By nightfall on the 25th Cisterna, Cori and Monte Arrestino were in American hands. First Armored and 3rd Divisions remained in good shape, in spite of their losses, having taken the objectives for both phases. The opposing German divisions, 362nd and 715th, had suffered heavily and were disorganized; 2,640 prisoners were taken.[35]

***

Clark had been impressed by the D Day success and, on the 25th, decided to broaden the front, ordering VI Corps to attack towards the line Lanuvio-Campoleone, the planned axis for Operation TURTLE, by noon on the 26th. That meant moving substantial elements of two divisions on foot or in transport between four and fifteen miles and relocating the artillery but Clark's deadline was met by excellent staff work at VI Corps HQ: 34th and 45th Divisions attacked at 11.00am. In 34th Division, 133rd and 168th Regiments attacked through 135th west of Highway 7. A shift in 1st Armored's axis of advance created another gap which was filled by 36th Division.[36] However, this departed from Alexander's strategy.

The Red Bulls' new task led to another Medal of Honor award. Lieutenant Beryl R. Newman, Company F, 2nd/133rd Regiment, with his platoon under fire from two machine guns on higher ground, remained standing to locate the guns. Leading a squad forward, deploying another to the right and with one squad pinned down, Newman attacked alone. Armed with a Thompson SMG, he wounded a German in each machine-gun post. The others fled. Newman eliminated a third post before attacking a house held by German troops, calling on them to surrender. He kicked in the door and eleven Germans capitulated. Singlehanded, Newman had silenced three machine guns, wounded two Germans, killed two more and taken eleven prisoners, a 'demonstration of sheer courage, bravery, and willingness to close with the enemy even in the face of such heavy odds'.[37]

In its advance 45th Division crossed the area close to the 'Factory', the Allied troops' name for the modern town of Aprilia. On the 27th Pfc Salvador Lara, a squad leader in Company L, 180th Regiment, and three other soldiers, in a fight to neutralize enemy positions, killed four Germans, forced fifteen to surrender, and prompted two mortar crews to abandon their weapons. Next morning Lara was wounded badly in the leg but, despite his pain and the extreme danger, requested permission to attack a machine-gun post that had caused heavy casualties in his company. Armed only with a BAR, 'Lara crawled towards the nearest enemy position, charged the machine-gun nest, and killed the crew members. Unwavering in his bravery, he then opened fire on another enemy position, killing three others. His aggressive attacks then forced two other crews to flee.'[38] Lara was awarded the Distinguished Service Cross. However, a review of Jewish-American and Spanish-American awards considered that there had been prejudice in Lara's case and he was posthumously awarded the Medal of Honor by President Obama who presented it to Lara's brother Alfonzo on 18 March 2014; Staff Sergeant Lara died in Germany in September 1945.[39]

Third Division continued its advance but encountered stiff opposition that stopped it between 27 and 30 May – two well-executed counter-attacks by the Hermann Göring Division, which deployed to slow the Americans and allow the German forces in the Liri valley to withdraw through Subiaco and Palestrina. Also committed around Valmontone were 'the scraps of 715th Grenadier Division and other units retreating before the French'.[40] Thus 3rd Division faced a tough task.

On 28 May, near Artena, Staff Sergeant Rudolph B. Davila, Company H, 7th Regiment, distinguished himself when caught on an exposed hillside by heavy fire. With his machine gunners reluctant to go into action, Davila risked death to provide heavy weapons support to a beleaguered rifle company. Crawling fifty yards to the nearest machine gun, he brought it into action. Ignoring return fire, including rounds passing between his legs, he ordered a gunner to relieve him and crawled forward for better observation where, with hand and arm signals, he directed the duel until both German guns were silenced. Bringing his three remaining guns into action he drove the enemy back. Although wounded, he mounted a disabled tank and, under fire, engaged another enemy group from the turret before singlehandedly attacking an enemy-held house, engaging the occupants through the attic and destroying another two machine guns.[41]

In contrast, the drive towards Lanuvio by 34th and 45th Divisions met much lighter resistance during the first two days, usually from rearguards, tanks and

155: Pfc Salvador Lara, of Company L 180th Regiment in 45th Division, was awarded the Distinguished Service Cross but this was upgraded to the Medal of Honor following a review of Jewish-American and Spanish-American awards and his brother Alfonzo received the Medal from President Obama in 2014. (Courtesy John Griffith, California)

StuGs, plus some long-range machine-gun fire. With the Americans less than two miles from their objectives at Lanuvio and Campoleone station, German resistance toughened, with battlegroups and 'alarm companies', as well as weak spots reinforced with some paratroopers released from their right flank. Starr wrote that the 'ingenuity and craft of the Germans in defence were rarely better demonstrated than in the battle of Lanuvio'. The American right-flank 168th Regiment faced two 'extremely nasty strongpoints', San Gennaro hill and Monte Crocetta, on the crest of Point 209, which, over three days, defied the regiment's efforts, even supported by tanks and tank destroyers.[42] On the 29th, after two unsuccessful attacks, Captain William W. Galt, a staff officer at 1st Battalion HQ, went forward to assess the situation and volunteered to lead another attack. When the crew of the only surviving tank destroyer assigned to support 1st/168th refused to advance, Galt climbed on the AFV and ordered it forward, manning the turret machine gun himself. The tank destroyer led a rifle company as Galt located and engaged enemy positions, directing fire on and knocking out an anti-tank gun. Closing on the Germans, he stood up, firing the machine gun and hurling grenades into trenches in spite of rifle and machine-gun fire before manoeuvring the tank destroyer to trap forty Germans in a trench. When they refused to surrender he opened fire. Shortly afterwards an anti-tank round struck his vehicle. Galt was mortally wounded and received a posthumous Medal of Honor.[43]

With the Germans remaining obstinate, it seemed that Fifth Army's drive had been stopped. On the 30th 1st Armored and 45th Divisions had fought fiercely on the Albano road making no progress while 34th had been stopped near Lanuvio the day before and 36th, although encircling Velletri, faced a determined garrison. On the right flank, where II and VI Corps had linked up, 85th Division was moving to support O'Daniel's 3rd near Valmontone. The Germans were determined to stall the Allies until their own troops cleared the Liri and Sacco valleys. Juin's CEF forces continued their advance, Sevez's division on the axis of the Amaseno-Carpineto road and Dody's on the Sacco's south bank. In the Liri valley Eighth Army was pursuing the enemy towards Avezzano. Before Fifth Army, German numbers were diminishing and would not be reinforced. In spite of the spirited defence, the Allies were in the ascendant.[44]

On the 31st progress was made that would lead to the final breakthrough at Colli Laziali. This resulted from advances begun by elements of 36th Division the day before, leading to the nocturnal seizure of high ground around Monte Artesimo and a rapid advance towards the Velletri-Nemi road. The Hermann Göring Division counter-attacked but without effect, and the Velletri-Valmontone line had been pierced.[45] As the American thrust continued, Private Furman L. Smith, 3rd/135th Regiment of Ryder's Red Bulls, earned the Medal of Honor when Company L's attack on a strongpoint was held up by heavy fire and Smith's squad, which was leading, was attacked by eighty Germans. When the squad leader and another soldier suffered serious wounds and the others retreated to the company position, Smith refused to abandon the wounded, taking them to shelter in small craters before engaging a counter-attack. Although his accurate rifle fire reduced the attack's momentum, he could not hope to beat them off but stood his ground, firing until he was killed.[46]

On 1 June German resistance was still strong but Allied overall strength was having its effect and progress was made: 1st Special Service Force gained its objective and 15th Regiment reached Highway 6 by the evening. The Hermann Göring

Division's armoured regiment pulled back from Valmontone towards Tivoli and its infantry also withdrew, as did other elements under its command. Valmontone was unoccupied when 15th Regiment entered and then moved forward, supported by 751st Tank Battalion. Further bitter fighting lay ahead during which another two soldiers of 15th Regiment earned the Medal of Honor, as did two 34th Division Nisei (Japanese-American) soldiers, although they were originally awarded the Distinguished Service Cross which was upgraded after a review in 2000.

The Nisei Medal of Honor laureates were Technical Sergeant Yeiki Kobashigawa and Private Shinyei Nakamine, both of 100th Battalion, which had earned the soubriquet 'Purple Heart Battalion' in the first battle for Cassino. Yeiki Kobashigawa served in Company F while Shinyei Nakamine was in Company B; both earned the Medal of Honor on 2 June. During an attack near Lanuvio Kobashigawa's platoon encountered strong resistance from several machine guns. With one other man, Kobashigawa crawled forward, threw a grenade and charged one post with his sub-machine gun, the other soldier providing covering fire. He killed one German and captured two but was fired on by a machine gun some fifty yards ahead. Deploying a squad to his first position, he attacked that position with grenades and provided supporting fire as a fellow soldier charged and took four prisoners. Kobashigawa discovered four more machine-gun posts and skilfully led a squad to neutralize two of them. Near La Torreto, when Private Shinyei Nakamine's platoon was pinned down by machine-gun fire from a small knoll 200 yards away, he crawled towards one hostile weapon and, from twenty-five yards, charged the post, firing his SMG, killing three enemy troops and capturing two. Later he discovered an enemy soldier on his platoon's right flank whom he shot and killed, having crawled twenty-five yards from his position. Leading a BAR team team towards another post he crawled close to it under covering fire to lob grenades at the enemy, wounding one and capturing four before leading his team towards another hostile position where a burst of machine-gun fire killed him.[47]

On 2 June 15th Regiment had advanced in column of battalions to relieve 1st Special Service Force of its right-flank protection duties. Early on the 3rd a German ambush threatened to overrun a patrol but Private Herbert F. Christian sacrificed himself to allow his comrades to escape. Braving close-range machine-gun fire and some sixty riflemen and three tanks, he stood up, signalled the patrol to withdraw and fired his SMG. Lit up by flares and badly wounded, his right leg severed above the knee, his attempt to advance distracted the enemy and allowed his twelve comrades to escape. He closed on the Germans, firing until their bullets killed him.[48] Private Eldon H. Johnson also sacrificed his life in similar fashion, advancing in the face of machine-gun, rifle and shell fire from tanks. Firing his BAR from the hip, he walked slowly and steadily towards the Germans, knocked out a machine gun from only fifteen feet, reloaded and engaged a small infantry group,

156: Japanese-Americans, or Nisei, were also the subject of prejudice in the award of the Medal of Honor. Pte Shinyei Yakamine, of 100th Battalion in 34th Division, was awarded the Distinguished Service Cross which was upgraded to the Medal of Honor in 2000. (Public domain)

of whom he killed or wounded four, before being brought down by machine-gun fire. Even on his knees he continued firing, hitting another German before falling dead. As with Private Christian he had enabled twelve men to escape an ambush.[49]

That day saw Fifth Army holding a continuous line from the Moletta river around the slopes of Colli Laziali and on to the Sacco. II Corps was pivoting west, its wheeling manoeuvre placing it in front of the CEF and Eighth Army's main force, threatening a massive traffic jam below Palestrina. AAI HQ temporarily changed the inter-army boundary to allow II Corps more freedom to move, a change that was to be reversed when Eighth Army drew level. However, Leese's command did not reach there until II Corps had entered Rome for, by the evening of the 3rd, Keyes' corps was poised to reach the Eternal City in a further bound.[50]

VI Corps owed its success not only to the courage of its soldiers but also to the ingenuity of its engineers who developed some new devices to assist armour and infantry penetrate the enemy defences. These included the 'snake', a giant Bangalore torpedo, pushed by a tank: of six-inch-diameter iron tubing extending up to 400 feet long, the device had a rounded head to negotiate obstacles and, except for the ten feet closest to the pusher tank, was filled with explosive. That final ten-foot length was sand-filled to protect the tank. Once the 'snake' had been pushed through a mine belt, the tank released it before reversing to a safe distance to detonate it by machine-gun fire aimed at a target detonator on the end of the device. The resulting explosion cleared any wire and most mines, allowing a passage for tanks. Infantry had a similar but lighter device, fired by mortar to clear a path for soldiers to advance in single file; in this case explosive was contained in a hose, or a rope of detonating cord was used. Finally, infantry could also be carried in armoured 'battle sledges', towed behind tanks. Although an uncomfortable way of entering battle, the sledges reduced the infantrymen's vulnerability; up to six could be coupled together behind a tank.[51]

***

Anxious to be seen as the liberator of Rome, Clark had ordered Truscott to change VI Corps' axis of advance on the 25th. His order was delivered by Brigadier General Donald W. Brann, Fifth Army's operations officer. Although Truscott tried contacting Clark to confirm the order, Clark was unavailable, leaving Truscott no choice but to execute the order.* As a result the opportunity to sever at least

---

* Clark was at Borgo Grappa, re-enacting for the cameras the meeting of leading elements of II and VI Corps. He was included in the images although he had not been present at the original event.

one of von Vietinghoff's lines of retreat had to be abandoned – only the Hermann Göring reconnaissance elements were between 3rd Division and Highway 6 – as VI Corps turned north-west towards a less tired foe. Alexander accepted Clark's change of plan on the assurance that the advance towards Valmontone would be maintained.[52] Truscott's HQ made a superb re-alignment but Clark's decision removed the opportunity to destroy Tenth German Army. Rick Atkinson commented:

> Yet the harsh truth remains: with duplicity and in bad faith, Clark contravened an order from a superior officer. His assertion, to Keyes on May 28, that the British 'are scheming to get into Rome the easiest way' was predicated on no substantive evidence. His thirst 'for glory', as the official British history would later conclude, 'spoiled the fulfilment of Alexander's plan in order to obtain for himself and his army the triumph of being the first to enter Rome.'[53]

Clark wrote:

> Not only did we intend to become the first army in fifteen centuries to seize [sic] Rome from the south, but we intended to see that the people at home knew that it was the Fifth Army that did the job, and knew the price that had been paid for it. I think that these considerations are important to an understanding of the behind-the-scenes differences of opinion that occurred in this period.[54]

Blumenson accepted Clark's version of events, and his rationale, drawing from the latter's diary that most of his worries had nothing to do with the immediate battle but were 'political in nature', due to British intentions to have Eighth Army enter Rome 'notwithstanding Alexander's constant assurances to me that Rome is in the sector of the Fifth Army'. Clark maligned Eighth Army, stating that it had 'done little fighting', lacked aggression 'and failed in its part of the combined Allied effort'.[55]

Clark continued denigrating Eighth Army throughout the Italian campaign, writing to his wife that he could not expect British troops to 'carry the ball', even while British troops were fighting successfully in Fifth Army. Such was his ego that he ensured that Fifth Army was referred to as 'General Clark's Fifth Army' in the media rather than 'Fifth Army' or 'the US Fifth Army', nor were corps or divisional commanders to be mentioned. His fear that Alexander was plotting to allow Eighth Army to enter Rome before Fifth suggests that Clark believed Alexander to be devious, an accusation no one else has ever made about the Irishman. Arguably

Clark's obsession with identifying Fifth Army with himself, his unwillingness to give credit to subordinates and his distrust of Alexander say much more about his own trustworthiness. Be that as it may, on 4 June Clark entered Rome and ended up getting lost. However, he ensured that a Praetorian Guard of pressmen recorded his triumphal entry for the public in the United States and for posterity. On the 5th he was front-page news. On the 6th the Italian campaign was all but banished from the eyes of the world as Allied forces landed in Normandy in Operation OVERLORD.

157: Mark Clark's ambitions were centred on Rome and he was determined that Fifth Army should liberate the city as it did on 5 June. Romans greet tank destroyers at the Colosseum as the Americans drive into the Eternal City. (NARA)

Although Fifth and Eighth Armies would continue fighting in Italy, they would do so with reduced numbers. Operation OVERLORD was to have been accompanied with simultaneous landings in southern France, Operation ANVIL. However, representations from British commanders, supported by Churchill, had brought about a postponement of ANVIL until mid-August as Operation DRAGOON. To provide the force for DRAGOON, Fifth Army would lose much of its strength, including Juin's CEF, and VI Corps (3rd, 36th and 45th US Divisions). Of the redeployment of these forces to the delayed landings in southern France, Lord Ismay wrote that 'the heavy fighting at Anzio and Cassino had, to a large extent, accomplished the very purpose for which ANVIL had been designed, by drawing off some of the best German divisions from France'.[56] The opportunity to destroy a German army in Italy was lost by Clark's insubordination, but the diversion of experienced manpower, especially Juin's mountain fighters, also ensured that the weakened army group would not smash through the Gothic Line in the late summer, extending the Italian campaign into 1945.

Kesselring was frustrated with von Mackensen, Fourteenth Army's commander, who had 'been unable to rid himself of a preconceived fixation as to the way the breakout from the beachhead would go'. Although von Mackensen was removed, the damage had been done, according to Kesselring.

> After many disagreeable interviews, the inability of [von Mackensen] to close the gap led to a change in command. In fact, the gap, which at the beginning could have been closed by a single battalion, kept widening until 31 May, with the result that our flank was turned and the road to Rome finally opened to the enemy. It was a catastrophe that the divisions which fought with such exemplary bravery on the right flank and in the centre had no equal partner on the left. Meanwhile the Tenth Army fell back fighting stubbornly, effected a link-up with the Fourteenth and won fresh laurels by getting troops through to the mountain road to Subiaco and Tivoli.[57]

Senger's comments on the battle and subsequent retreat are critical of von Vietinghoff and Kesselring for several factors including: the altered chain of command which meant that XIV Panzerkorps could not fall back by swivelling on the pivot of Cassino as he had intended, thus reducing the usefulness of the Sengerriegel (Senger Barrier) or Hitler Line; failure to maintain 15th Panzergrenadier Division as a cohesive reserve behind XIV Panzerkorps' right wing, but splitting it into battalions and redeploying it piecemeal rather than inserting it between 71st and 94th Divisions where it might have stopped the Allied onslaught. There were other tactical opportunities to avert disaster, but the Allied

158 & 159: Heinz Laier, Erwin Griebel and Max Rosenberger all died on 24 May and are among the many dead who rest in the German cemetery at Cáira. (Author's photos)

advance and breakthrough led to Tenth Army's front wavering all along the line, leading to an 'acute danger of the enemy thrusting north-eastwards from Rome and driving a wedge between the two retreating German armies, which would probably seal the fate of both'.[58]

Clark's decision to switch VI Corps' main thrust undoubtedly helped both German armies to escape, although harassment by Allied tactical aircraft ensured they sustained heavy losses. Once VI Corps changed direction, the opportunity to destroy Tenth Army evaporated. Fifth Army was not moving fast enough to manoeuvre ahead of the retreating enemy while Eighth Army was encumbered by the commitment of too many troops, including three armoured divisions (the South Africans were entering the fray) with all their vehicles, in the Liri valley. Carrying out Alexander's original plan should have led to the destruction of Tenth Army. As it was, von Vietinghoff's command survived to fight again and again, as did Fourteenth Army but with von Mackensen replaced by Joachim Lemelsen.

***

The fourth battle of Cassino was over. Allied troops moved towards and around Rome to begin a pursuit along the Tiber valley. Clark's moment of glory was brief. The liberation of Rome passed into history as Alexander's armies pressed on towards their next major encounter with those of Kesselring.

The cost of the final battle had been high. Between 11 May and 4 June losses in Eighth Army included 2,263 British (including Canadian, Indian and New Zealand) troops killed, 8,978 wounded and 924 missing and 714 Polish dead, 2,846 wounded and 339 missing, an overall total of 2,977 dead, 11,824 wounded and 1,263 missing. In Fifth Army 3,160 Americans died, 13,870 were wounded and 1,088 missing as well as 1,634 French dead, 7,325 wounded and 605 missing, an army total of 4,794 dead, 21,195 wounded and 1,693 missing. German figures for the dead are not available; an estimate suggests about 5,820 which, added to known figures for wounded or captured (45,934) means that German casualties amounted to 51,754.[59]

Chapter Fourteen

The long struggle to liberate Rome was over. Mark Clark had his 'day' but the bulk of the Allied armies by-passed the city to pursue the retreating Germans through the Tiber valley, seeing along the roads hard evidence of the effectiveness of Operation STRANGLE in the shape of 'burnt-out German vehicles, varying from Tigers and seventy-ton Ferdinands down to volkswagens' littering the roads. On the roadsides, slit trenches every 400 or 500 yards provided 'funk holes from air strafing'. Of the Luftwaffe there was no sign. Allied airmen ruled the skies.[1]

While Allied soldiers may have expected the pursuit to continue and war in Italy to come to a rapid end, the plan for landings in southern France weakened ground and air forces in Italy. Alexander was to lose Juin's CEF and Truscott's VI Corps, stripping Fifth Army of seven divisions, most of its strength; losing Major General Lucian Truscott was another major blow to Fifth Army. Thus the Allies' next major operation, the attack on the Gothic, or Green, Line in August, would deliver a weaker punch than Alexander would have wished: the absence of the French mountain troops was felt sorely. None of that was known to the soldier on the ground in the early days of June. Instead he could reflect on success at the end of a battle that had raged since January and which had been the toughest fought by the western Allies in the course of the European campaigns. Success came at a very high price. We have already noted Allied and German casualty tolls in the final battle which have to be added to those from three earlier clashes.

It is difficult to provide full and accurate figures for Allied losses in the earlier battles but in the first battle the US II Corps had sustained over 4,000 casualties, the majority in 34th Division during twenty days in combat; 36th Division had suffered 1,681 casualties in its three-day attempt to cross the Gari. CEF losses were also heavy at almost 8,000 between December 1943 and mid-February 1944. To these may be added the losses of X Corps, totalling 4,145 between 23 January and 13 February. Thus Fifth Army casualties numbered over 16,000. In XIV Panzerkorps losses were lower with 6,444 casualties between 21 January and 10 February.[2]

The second battle lasted only four days, accounting for over 800 casualties in the New Zealand Corps, 590 in 4th Indian Division and 226 in 2nd New Zealand Division, although the British official historian puts New Zealand losses at 549.

Then came the third battle in which Freyberg's corps suffered over 2,100 casualties. XIV Panzerkorps losses in the second and third battles (the Germans regarded the second battle as a continuation of the first) were over 7,600, some sustained by divisions under von Senger's command on other areas of the front. (Molony indicates 3,218 between 15 and 24 March.) The cumulative effect of the struggle, including Allied air attacks, was diminishing German manpower so much that, had the front been on low ground rather than in mountains, Kesselring's forces would have been hard pressed to continue.[3] In the battle area there were at least 7,000 civilian casualties. (An elderly resident of Terelle told the author in 2016 that many more from the village were killed *after* the war by unexploded ordnance than during the conflict; Plowman and Rowe indicate that sixty villagers died during the wartime fighting.)[4]

***

What had the battles achieved? The road to Rome had been opened, leading to the liberation of that city, an Allied capital as distinct from Clark's impression that it was still an Axis capital, and allowing the Allies to advance beyond the Eternal City. The Cassino campaign had inflicted heavy casualties on the Germans and the loss of much equipment that could not easily be replaced; German industry was enduring the onslaught of Allied strategic bombers and, although many innovative measures were adopted, the capacity to maintain large armies in the field with all that they needed was being eroded. Nevertheless, the Germans established another defensive line across Italy, Rommel's Pisa-Rimini line, which would halt the weakened Allies yet again. In many ways smashing the Gustav and Hitler Lines led to another stalemate north of Rome, one that would last, in spite of Operation OLIVE, until Operation GRAPESHOT, the final Allied offensive in April 1945.[5] Had Clark obeyed Alexander's orders German losses might have been much greater, especially in Tenth Army. Thus, to recall Majdalany's definition of a modern battle, the end was not final and, indeed, is hard to define accurately.

Nonetheless, there had been positive effects including the way in which the Allies adapted operational tactics to the situation. In the final battle Polish II Corps prevented LI Mountain Corps from intervening significantly in XIII Corps' battle while the latter made excellent use of its engineers as its leading divisions fought across the Gari. With considerable experience already built up in dealing with all forms of obstacles and demolitions, the sappers excelled as they bridged a significant water obstacle. Part of that excellence was innovation in assault engineering, Plymouth Bridge clearly indicating innovative thinking. The sappers would continue developing new ideas as the campaign moved north of Rome so that, by spring 1945, an assault engineer brigade, with the skills of Hobart's 79th Armoured Division, but much fewer resources and locally-produced equipment, would play a critical part in the final offensive.[6]

Arguably, Amazon Bridge was the best-known of those built by the engineers. When 586 Field Company of Eighth Army Troops was sent to assist there, Major Colin Douglas Clark, its commander (later Sir Colin, 4th Baronet Dunlambert), had an important role in its completion, the second occasion on which he had shown 'great energy combined with the soundest Engineering knowledge and organizing ability', the first having been with 78th Division in April. Already Mentioned in Despatches, Clark was recommended for appointment as an MBE but this less than appropriate honour was amended to the Military Cross as the recommendation ascended the chain of command.[7]

There had been other innovations for the final battle. Alexander had a surfeit of armour and, even with 6th (South African) Armoured Division in reserve, could deploy his armour in close co-operation with the assaulting infantry, combined-arms battlegroups with close artillery support and integral support from machine-gun battalions marking a step away from infantry and armour fighting separately. However, in the Anzio bridgehead, Major General Harmon, commanding 1st Armored Division, did not accept Truscott's intention for his armour and O'Daniel's 3rd Division to work together, believing that the infantry should precede the armour. While Harmon was unhappy, commanders in Eighth Army welcomed the fact that armour and infantry would be working so closely. Comments from men such as John Horsfall about the training programme were positive; the friction that had existed between the two arms began to dissipate. While armour was seen as protection for the infantry by the latter, there were many instances of the reverse being true, the close presence of infantry proving invaluable to tanks, the sacrifice of Corporal Barnes of 2nd London Irish at Casa Sinagoga being perhaps the best example.

The decision not to fight through the ruins of Cassino in May was a wise one, since earlier attempts to do so had proved costly. No cognizance seems to have been taken of the Canadian experience in Ortona, the 'Stalingrad of the Abruzzi', in December 1943 when 1st Canadian Division, supported by tanks of 1 Canadian Armoured Brigade, fought street by street and building by building, creating a template for operations in a built-up area. The lessons of the Canadian experience at Ortona seem not to have been applied by New Zealand Corps HQ in Cassino, the bombing of the town making Ortona-style tactics impossible.[8]

Artillery arms across both armies were critical in all four battles, but especially in the final thrust. The guns that initially laid down the biggest bombardment of the war to date continued providing fireplans that were devised and implemented quickly, adding to the enemy's woes.

160: As Allied troops moved up through Cassino they found a scene of utter devastation as did this despatch rider of the Royal Artillery, Gnr J.J. Doherty, the author's father. (9th HAA Regiment Archive)

> The refinement of survey, communications and fire planning enabled any number [of guns] to be directed quickly onto a single target with devastating effect on the enemy. The added refinement of the Air OP … and a Counter-Mortar Organisation placed the enemy under continuous artillery attack. But always, on the high ground, overlooking the valleys, he had to be ejected by the infantry, supported by the artillery FOOs and OPs before the rivers below could be crossed and the way opened for the armoured follow-up.[9]

Mention of the counter-mortar organization cannot be made without noting the unexpected role of anti-aircraft gun-laying (GL) radar in the Anzio bridgehead. Designed and deployed to direct anti-aircraft fire on attacking aircraft, the realization that some targets appearing on GL screens were not aircraft but enemy shells proved an aid to the counter-mortar organization and a GL Mark II set was used to detect hostile artillery. Further experiments with GL sets, including the US SCR584, against captured German mortars and artillery led to specialized radar units to detect enemy artillery and mortar rounds; by early 1945

161: Those passing through Cassino were reminded of the dangers of mines and booby traps. (NARA)

a two-battery field artillery radar regiment was serving with Eighth Army with noteworthy results.[10]

Not only did the artillery provide support when needed, but Allied air arms had secured almost complete control of the air, leaving the Luftwaffe unable to react effectively. In the North African campaign the Desert Air Force* had devised and refined its close air support doctrine, including the development of fighter-bombers, first used at El Hamma in Tunisia in March 1943. Air Vice Marshal William Dickson, commanding DAF from late March 1944, had accompanied Air Marshal Leigh-Mallory on an inspection in Tunisia the previous year and had been so impressed by the fighter-bomber concept that he ordered more conversions of DAF fighters to the role upon assuming command. He also further intensified the use of the Rover David Cab-rank system, initiated by Group Captain David Heysom, the South African commander of DAF Operations, earlier in the campaign on mainland Italy, although its origins also dated back to El Hamma. Using RAF officers 'embedded' with ground troops, a 'cab-rank' of fighter-bombers already in the air could be deployed quickly to support ground operations. A MORU (Mobile Operations Room Unit), codenamed 'David' was the hub of such operations. MORU 'Rovers', codenamed 'Paddy', 'Jack', 'Joe', 'Tom' and 'Frank', were added to the system, each commanded by an RAF officer with experience of working with the army and who was in radio contact with the 'cab-rank' aircraft. Each 'Rover' included an armoured vehicle with the wireless link to the aircraft while observation officers also flew in light aircraft and could control operations. The USAAF had no equivalent until Fifth Army landed at Salerno but British doctrine was adopted quickly so that both armies had effective close air support, limited only by weather and ground conditions.[11]

Although medical services faced considerable difficulties, including the high number of head and eye injuries, the plans for the final battle proved more than adequate; in the case of Eighth Army the actual number of injuries, including sickness, was less than the 17,000 estimated by the medical planners. Casualty evacuation was critical, to ensure that wounded received treatment or were operated on as soon as possible. This included moving casualties from the front line to the main hospitals in the rear areas. Forward surgical and blood transfusion units (FSUs and FTUs) were part of the arrangements that ensured the highest possible chances of survival.[12] However, casualty evacuation from the Polish and CEF areas was beset by difficulties, many hours often being needed to bring a

---

*   Officially it had become 1st Tactical Air Force (1TAF) but retained the Desert Air Force title; 2TAF was formed for north-west Europe and 3TAF for Burma.

162: The medical services carried out sterling work in very difficult circumstances as did the men of this jeep ambulance ferrying lightly wounded men down from the mountains. (Author's collection)

casualty from the point of wounding to an aid post. Probably for that reason 6th Polish General Hospital, a 200-bed unit, was at Venafro, closer to the front than its British or Canadian equivalents.[13] In the first and fourth battles the French had also to cope with very difficult terrain but their arrangements, reflecting the US Army system, under General Hugonot, were designed to cope with such difficulties.[14]

The gallantry of medical personnel throughout the battles was exemplified by Major Francis O'Dowd, 26th Indian Field Ambulance, who received an immediate DSO during the second battle when he went to treat a wounded soldier, passing through a minefield to dress his wounds under intense enemy fire and then, with a stretcher-bearer, bringing the man to safety[15] and Captain John MacKay, also 26th Indian Field Ambulance, who received a periodic MC for actions that included his tending and evacuating wounded 'under heavy shell fire' during the fourth battle.[16] (At Ripi in June MacKay's ADS came under enemy fire but he continued his duties 'completely imperturbable as usual'.)

Of course there were many other elements contributing to Allied success, including the personnel of the transport units, including Sergeant Grenville Ford, 1801 (Bailey) Platoon, Royal Army Service Corps, attached to the Royal Engineers building Amazon bridge. Ford was 'responsible for ensuring the smooth feeding of bridging equipment' to the site and liaising with the officer commanding the operation and carried out his duties under mortar, shell and small-arms fire; on the second night he 'showed complete disregard for his personal safety and … encouraged and set an example to the drivers … delivering the equipment'. He received an immediate award of the Military Medal.[17] Other drivers and supply personnel ensured that essential supplies for front-line units were delivered when and where they were needed, irrespective of risk while military policemen controlled the movement of traffic.

Other corps in what today is known as combat service support also played their roles. The Royal Army Ordnance Corps not only helped maintain RASC vehicles (usually the task of the Corps of Royal Electrical and Mechanical Engineers, formed in 1942) by ordering 1,200 replacement engines which were stored in a new depot at Bari in October 1943, but also established Port Ordnance and Port Ammunition Detachments, and ensured supplies of ammunition. This was done effectively with the exception of the Anzio operation for which HQ Fifth Army was responsible but failed to include adequate British representation; there was no Ordnance staff officer until 26 January, four days after the SHINGLE landings.[18]

**

In London General Sir Alan Brooke had been watching events in Italy, although his main attention was on OVERLORD, planned for 5 June. His diary included a series of comments beginning with the frustrated note on 12 May that, although the attack had started as planned, he had received no news until late that evening and was waiting for a message to be deciphered at 11.30pm. Four days later he commented: 'Luckily the Italian news continues to be good.' On the 19th he wrote: 'Thank heaven the Italian attack is going well, and it should play its part in holding [German] formations in Italy and keeping them away from the Channel.' Monte Cassino had been taken and Brooke noted the following day that 'Alexander's news of Italian fighting continues to be excellent'. The next mention of Italy came on the 23rd: Alexander's offensives from Anzio and in the Liri valley had begun but had perhaps moved too soon to 'reap full benefits of favourable situation confronting him. However he alone can judge, being on the spot'. On the 25th: 'Just heard Anzio bridgehead and main front are joined up together. Thank heaven for it!!' Next day Brooke commented: 'The Italian offensive is going on well, [German] reserves are being drawn in, and it is performing just the function we wanted with reference to the cross Channel operation.' On 30 May Churchill was 'at his worst' with 'not a single word of praise' for Alexander but 'only threats of what he would think of him if he did not bring off a scoop!' at which point Brooke lost his temper. Then, on the 31st, he noted that the news 'continues to be very good' and hoped that Alexander would succeed 'in breaking through on the Vilitri-Valtone [sic] front'. Late on 4 June he received the news 'that we were in Rome'. Three days later, Alexander 'is all for dashing off to the Pisa-Rimini Line'.[19]

However, attention in London and Washington had switched to Normandy and Italy became a secondary theatre, a standing emphasized by the removal of formations for DRAGOON. Although the war in Europe would continue for another eleven months, the hardest and longest battle for the western Allies had been fought and won along the Gustav Line. The victory raised questions about Allied strategy and tactics, their operational art and the abilities of commanders.

Much ink and paper has been consumed over the decades since in trying to answer these questions so that a summary should suffice in this volume. Allied grand strategy was a result of Allied policy, on which the two principal western Allies, the UK and the USA, were not in harmony. The former considered a campaign in Italy a natural outworking of the North African campaign, opening a 'second front', as demanded by Stalin, earlier than could be achieved by launching an expeditionary force from Britain, and tightening the ring around Germany. The latter believed that maximum effort should be concentrated on the cross-Channel operation and had much less enthusiasm for continuing operations in the Mediterranean region, suspecting British motives for such operations. Thus, from the beginning, there was no clear Allied objective for the Italian campaign.

Operations and tactics were dictated by terrain but also influenced by the abilities of senior commanders. Again there were differences along national lines, some of which may be attributed to the personality of Mark Clark who guarded jealously what he may have described as US interests but which were really his own interests. His insistence that Fifth Army should be described as 'General Clark's Fifth Army', that no media mention should be made of corps or divisional commanders, his belief that Alexander was conspiring against Fifth Army (as in the break-out operation from Anzio) all suggest that Clark was a toxic commander unsuited to working with allies in a coalition army group. It is likely that a major part of Clark's problem stemmed from his lack of command experience at divisional and corps levels – the essence of Richardson's comment that Clark had never commanded a division, in the British Army an essential qualification for higher command. Although undoubtedly an excellent staff officer, his abilities as a commander were less impressive. Caddick-Adams' book on Montgomery and Rommel includes a comment on two other very good staff officers, Percival of Singapore and Paulus of Stalingrad, both remembered for their failures as commanders.[18] (Clark's letters to his wife, his memoirs, and even Blumenson's biography give some indications of his shortcomings.)

Clark was not the only commander with flaws although his were the most significant in the campaign. He failed to see the opportunities presented by the CEF advance in January and the importance of the Atina valley. His order to Juin to switch his axis of advance removed the threat to the valley, although that threat prompted von Senger to move his headquarters from Roccasecca. Senger also noted how, when 71st Division was ordered to counter-attack the French, he visited the attacking German regiment

> in the Belmonte valley, I was struck by the inadequacy of our infantry in comparison with the French colonial troops. The regimental battle HQ was located in a rock-cave. In the intense bombardment ... it was almost impossible to make oneself understood. These lowland troops, unaccustomed to the hills and unsuitably clad in overcoats, were expected to attack up the steep mountain slopes, passing through a barrage fire that was intensified by the rock splinters.[19]

Kesselring also noted the French ability to move quickly through the mountains. Clark's order to Juin, issued on 23 January, followed the rebuff of 36th Division on the Gari at Sant'Angelo. By the time Keyes' II Corps had been launched and Walker's division had begun its assault across the Gari, Juin's men had made good progress in the mountains which should have suggested to Clark that reinforcing Juin's effort would have been better than launching II Corps. Walker had recognized the risks but Clark had not. Moreover, McCreery's X Corps had also begun crossing the Garigliano and had achieved success that included a bridgehead that would play an important role in the final battle. Thus Clark had the further option of reinforcing X Corps, or indeed both the CEF and X Corps. That, however, would never have done for a commander who wanted to emphasize the Americanism of his army. Although the British 46th Division was unsuccessful in its part of X Corps' operation, a second attempt to cross, reinforced by US troops might have succeeded. While 36th Division expended itself on the Gari, 34th Division crossed the Rapido north of Cassino, making headway into the town and onto the heights at considerable cost. The entire II Corps operation might have been better set aside in favour of the CEF and X Corps attacks, but such a course of action was extremely unlikely from Clark.

When 34th Division's efforts were baulked on both axes of advance, Clark inserted Freyberg's newly-created New Zealand Corps into the battle. Since Freyberg's divisions relieved 34th Division and a regiment of 36th in their forward positions, the German narrative begins to differ from the Allied as the latter define the New Zealand experience as the second and third battles whereas the Germans see Freyberg's initial effort as a continuation of the American attack, and the March battle (the Allied third) as the second.

The defining moment of the second battle was the bombing of the Abbey, an event that demonstrated weaknesses in New Zealand Corps' command structure; the staff of 2nd New Zealand Division were 'double-hatting' at corps level. Freyberg had not excelled as a corps commander on previous occasions and did not do so at Cassino; he had probably reached the limit of his ability as a divisional commander. However, he was also commander of II New Zealand Expeditionary Force (II NZEF) with a direct line to the New Zealand government and thus the commander of a national army, albeit a small one. His greatest failure at Cassino was in continuing the baulked American advance rather than developing a new operational plan, although in part this was due to pressure from Clark (with ultimate sources of pressure in London and Washington). While Freyberg may be excused the continuation of a failed plan in the second battle, it is all but impossible to excuse his further continuation of that plan in the third battle, for there was little original thinking in the third battle. Of course, Freyberg had the disadvantages of losing two capable divisional commanders – Tuker of 4th Indian before the second battle, and Kippenberger of 2nd New Zealand before the third – but the effects of those losses emphasize the weaknesses of Freyberg's command. A very capable divisional commander and an exceptionally courageous officer, Freyberg may be judged to have failed as a corps commander. That neither Clark nor Alexander could remove him from his post, other than by disbanding the corps, was due to his position as the commander of II NZEF.

In retrospect there was little, if any, chance of either the second or third battles achieving the aim of breaking *through* the Gustav Line, although both did break *into* the line. The final battle stands in stark contrast as a masterpiece of planning at all levels, the work of Alexander's gifted chief of staff, John Harding, being evident throughout. As we have seen, on the strategic level Kesselring and his generals were fooled about the timing, leaving Tenth Army and XIV Panzerkorps without commanders at a critical time, while they also 'lost' Juin's corps, whom they feared greatly, were unaware of the presence of Anders' II Corps and believed the Canadians were part of a plan for another seaborne landing. Operationally, the use of all-arms battlegroups was innovative and successful with engineers proving their worth time and again. With X Corps holding the Adriatic sector, the army group's right wing was the Polish Corps which demonstrated great courage and tenacity during Operation HONKER. If there were flaws in the plan, they were at the operational level and the responsibility of the army commanders. We have already noted Clark's failings but Leese was also guilty of faults: was it really necessary to deploy three corps into the Liri valley? One could question the plan for II Polish Corps to attack into the mountains where earlier attacks had been rebuffed. They would have supported XIII Corps by drawing off possible reinforcement of XIV Panzerkorps in the valley by elements of LI Mountain Corps simply by maintaining pressure in the Cassino massif without expending blood and lives in efforts to capture features that had already eluded Americans and Indians. Was the cost in Polish lives justified when the enemy still held out on Point 593 and elsewhere, only withdrawing when pressure elsewhere, from the CEF and XIII Corps, made it inevitable?

Throughout the campaign, from January to June, Allied Armies in Italy fought as a multi-national coalition. Alexander estimated that he had over twenty different nationalities under his command and several, Canadians, French, New Zealanders and Poles especially, representing different national interests, were effectively national armies. Thus he had to deal with differing national aspirations, which were not always compatible. It would have been impossible not to give the Poles a major role in the final battle; they had waited too long for revenge on the Germans. Although they did not succeed as they had hoped, yet the battle was one in which Polish pride was upheld and remains to this day a vibrant symbol of that pride. (The author has visited the battlefield many times but has never once been at the Polish cemetery when there were no Polish visitors present.)

Alexander may have had problems with Clark but his handling of the army group was masterly. Even though Clark had shifted the axis of Truscott's VI Corps in defiance of his orders, he did not take umbrage. Clark was fortunate in that patrols from VI Corps found a gap in the Caesar Line through which a division moved onto the Alban hills. Eighth Army, enmeshed in a traffic jam in the Liri valley, was in no position to push towards Rome; Fifth Army was better poised to do so. What mattered to Alexander was that Rome should be liberated, not which army did the liberating.[22] Alexander's great skill was his ability to work with such a disparate array of commanders and get the best from them. He was the ideal commander for such a coalition and few could have commanded it so well. Arguably the only other man who could have done so was Eisenhower, but Ike, for all his skills with people, lacked the battle experience of Alexander, although it is interesting to speculate what *his* reaction to Clark's insubordination might have been.

For as long as the Second World War is discussed the Italian campaign and the battles for Cassino will be subjects for debate. However, with little time to reflect, in June 1944 the Allies were more concerned with pursuing and trying to destroy the enemy's armies than discussing the intricacies of battles they had fought over the previous six months. There was relief that the long hard struggle was over, the Germans were retreating and victory in Italy might soon be within their grasp. Above all there was that sense of joy that comes from victory.

The ground had been won. More battles might lie ahead but Rome had been liberated, the Allies had landed in France and hope beckoned. Of his Allied Armies in Italy, Alexander wrote:

> I now have two highly organized and skilful armies capable of carrying out large scale attacks and mobile operations in closest co-operation. Morale is irresistibly high as a result of recent successes and the whole forms one closely articulated machine capable of carrying out assaults and rapid exploitations in the most difficult terrain. Neither the Apennines nor even the Alps should prove a serious obstacle to their enthusiasm and skill.[23]

Alexander's confidence was justified. The professionalism honed in the battles of Cassino would permeate and drive the Allied armies in Italy, taking them to victory in April 1945 in what was arguably the western Allies' finest example of manoeuvre warfare.

Endnotes

Preface

1. *Catholic Encyclopedia*, www.newadvent.org/cathen/02467b.htm, accessed 25 August 2016
2. Ibid.
3. See Hapgood and Richardson, *Monte Cassino*. Most accounts of the Cassino battles credit Oberstleutnant Julius Schlegel of the Hermann Göring Division with initiating and organizing the removal of the Abbey's treasures to Rome and safety but the authors make a forensically strong case for the prime mover being Dr Maximilian Becker, a medical officer in the same division, who, for his efforts, was transferred out of Italy. On Schlegel's death, his former home in Vienna was marked with a plaque proclaiming him to be the saviour of the Abbey of Monte Cassino's art treasures.
4. Senger und Etterlin, *Neither Fear Nor Hope*, p.208

Thanks are also due to the Reverend Michael Fava CF for his kind assistance and advice with the preface.

Chapter One

1. Majdalany, *Cassino*, p.13
2. Molony, *The Mediterranean and the Middle East*, Vol. V, p.238
3. Ibid., p.2
4. Churchill, *The Second World War*, Vol. VIII, *The Hinge of Fate*, p.356
5. Molony, p.191
6. Alexander, *Despatch*, p.2879
7. Doherty, *Victory in Italy*, pp.2–5. Summarized from Doherty, *Ireland's Generals in the Second World War*, pp.48–61, Nicolson, *Alex*, and Alexander, *Memoirs*
8. Molony, pp.191–2
9. Ibid.
10. Ibid., p.193
11. Ibid., p.196
12. Quoted in ibid., p.196
13. Blumenson, *Mediterranean Theater of Operations: Salerno to the Alps* (hereafter 'Salerno'), p.16

14. Ibid.,pp.16-17
15. Alexander, p.2880
16. Graham and Bidwell, *Tug of War*, pp.47-52
17. Alexander, p.2886
18. Forty, *The Armies of Rommel*, p.182
19. Ibid., pp.182-3
20. Molony, pp.208-9
21. Senger, op. cit., p.181
22. Graham and Bidwell, p.50
23. NA Kew, WO169/8520, war diary Eighth Army HQ, GS I, Sep-Dec 1943, IntSum 544
24. Kesselring, *Memoirs*, pp.186-7
25. Ibid., pp.17-18
26. Ibid., p.19
27. Macksey in ibid., pp.9-10
28. Mitcham, *Hitler's Field Marshals*, pp.358-9
29. Kesselring, p.104
30. Blumenson, *Salerno*, p.21
31. Graham and Bidwell, pp.47-52
32. Molony, p.243
33. Graham and Bidwell, p.39; Jackson, *The Battle for Italy*, p.111
34. Molony, p.256; see also Starr, *Salerno to the Alps*, p.11; Blumenson, *Mark Clark* (hereafter *Clark*), pp.131-2
35. Starr, p.11; Blumenson, *Salerno*, pp.43-4
36. Molony, pp.302-7
37. Alexander, p.2880
38. Ibid.
39. Blumenson, *Salerno* pp.166-7
40. Doherty, *Clear The Way!* (hereafter *CTW*), p.84
41. Brooks, *Montgomery and The Eighth Army*, p.348
42. NA Kew, CAB44/135, Cabinet Office war histories draft chapters, Section IV Chapter N: 'Italy operations winter 1943–44; part I, introduction and summary', by Major F. Jones, p.1
43. Molony, p.430
44. Blumenson, *Salerno*, pp.207-8
45. Molony, p.430
46. Blumenson, *Salerno*, p.208; refers to Vietinghoff MSS, 15 AG IntSum 22, 27 Oct 1943, Fifth Army G-3 Journal
47. Senger, p.181
48. Linklater, *The Campaign in Italy*, p.126

49. Blumenson, *Salerno*, p.166
50. Senger, p.181

Chapter Two

1. Majdalany, op. cit., p.8
2. Blumenson, *Clark*, op. cit., pp.115-16
3. Ibid., p.11
4. Ibid., pp.16-42
5. Ibid., pp.56-68
6. Richardson, *Flashback*, p.158
7. Blumenson, *Clark*, p.107
8. Danchev & Todman, *War Diaries 1939-1945: Field Marshal Lord Alanbrooke*, p.363n
9. D'Este, *Eisenhower*, pp.455-6
10. Summarized from Mead, *The Last Great Cavalryman*, pp.22-108
11. Strawson, *The Italian Campaign*, pp.183-4
12. Senger, p.183
13. Ibid., p.184
14. Ibid., p.185
15. Oliva, *Soldati e Ufficili*, p.266; Dapino was referred to by Clark as a brigadier general
16. Starr, op. cit., pp.61-6
17. Senger, p.187
18. Fraser, *Knight's Cross*, p.451
19. Ibid.
20. Mitcham, op. cit., p.355
21. Blumenson, *Clark*, p.151
22. D'Este, *Eisenhower*, pp.453-4
23. Wilson, *Report by the Supreme Allied Commander Mediterranean to the Combined Chiefs of Staff on the Italian Campaign, 8th January 1944 to 10th May 1944*, pp.1-3
24. Ibid., p.6
25. Blumenson, *Salerno*, pp.254-5
26. Ibid., pp.253-4
27. Ibid., p.255
28. Wilson, p.7
29. Ibid.
30. Blumenson, *Clark*, p.154
31. Ibid., p.162
32. Clark, *Calculated Risk*, p.247
33. Ibid., p.249

34. Senger, pp.188-9
35. Forty, *Battle for Monte Cassino*, p.67
36. Senger, p.189
37. Ibid., p.179
38. Liddell Hart, Foreword to *Neither Fear Nor Hope*, p.5
39. Senger, p.45
40. Summarized from *Neither Fear Nor Hope*, passim
41. Forty, p.52
42. Notin, *La Campagne d'Italie*, pp.173-5 & 181-7; Starr, pp.71-2; Molony, pp.519-20; Shepperd, *The Italian Campaign*, p.169; Blumenson, *Salerno*, pp.288-9; Böhmler, *Monte Cassino. A German View*, pp.131-2
43. Notin, pp.191-200
44. Shepperd, pp.169 & 189; Starr, pp.72-3; Blumenson, *Salerno*, pp.305-13
45. Böhmler, p.133; Hougen, *The Story of the Famous 34th Division*. Unfortunately, the pages in this book are not numbered.
46. www.themedalofhonor.com, accessed 24 January 2017
47. Böhmler, p.133
48. Horsfall, *Fling Our Banner to The Wind*, p.42
49. Böhmler, pp.133-4
50. Nicolson, p.243
51. Blumenson, *Salerno*, p.288
52. Kesselring, op. cit., p.191
53. Ibid.; Senger, p.190
54. Blumenson, *Salerno*, p.288

Chapter Three

1. Senger, op. cit., p.190
2. Ibid., p.192
3. Ibid., p.190
4. Ibid., p.190; Starr, op. cit., p.82
5. Senger, p.190
6. Starr, pp.79-82; Blumenson, *Salerno*, pp.310-12; Molony, op. cit., pp.516-17; Böhmler, op. cit., pp.69-70; Kesselring, op. cit., pp.198-9
7. Caddick-Adams, *Cassino*, pp.27-8
8. Böhmler, p.70
9. Blumenson, *Salerno*, pp.311-12
10. Ibid., p.313
11. Notin, op. cit, p.211
12. Ibid., p.225
13. Ford, *Cassino: The Four Battles*, p.22

14. Blumenson, *Salerno*, p.315
15. Ibid.
16. Ibid.
17. Molony, p.606; Caddick-Adams, pp.74-5
18. Starr, p.84
19. Ibid., p.85
20. Ibid., pp.85-7
21. Aris, *The Fifth British Division*, pp.179-80
22. Fox, *The Royal Inniskilling Fusiliers in the Second World War, 1939-45* p.109; NA Kew, WO170/302, X Corps G Report on 46th Division crossing of the Garigliano; WO170/1403, war diary 2 Innisks, 1 Feb-31 Dec 1944
23. Aris, p.184
24. Ibid., pp.185-9; Molony, p.615; Starr, p.87
25. Starr, pp.87-9; Molony, pp.615-16
26. Messenger, *The Commandos*, pp.320-1; Starr, p.89
27. Starr, p.88
28. Ibid.; Molony, p.616
29. Senger, p.190
30. Ibid.
31. Ibid., p.191
32. Ibid., p.192
33. Starr, pp.88-9
34. Ibid., p.89
35. *London Gazette*, 10 August 1944
36. Starr, p.89
37. Ibid. p.89
38. Ibid., pp.89-90; Mead, op. cit., pp.146-7; NA Kew, WO170/310, war diary HQ X Corps AG, 1 January-31 May 1944
39. Blumenson, *Clark*, p.165

Chapter Four

1. Blumenson, *Clark*, p.164
2. Starr, op. cit., pp.91-2
3. Ibid., p.92
4. Ibid., pp.93-4; Blumenson, *Salerno*, p.322
5. Starr, p.93
6. Majdalany, op. cit., p.60
7. Richardson, p.160
8. Blumenson, *Clark*, p.165
9. Molony, op. cit., p.619

10. Ibid.
11. Starr, p.98
12. Molony, pp,619–20
13. Senger, op. cit., p.193
14. www.themedalofhonor.com, accessed 24 January 2017
15. Bond, *Return to Cassino*, p.47
16. Ibid., p.45
17. Clark, op. cit., p.265
18. Böhmler, op. cit., pp.147–8
19. Clark, *Anzio*, p.83
20. Molony, p.620
21. Starr, p.98
22. Ibid., pp.98–9
23. Atkinson, *The Day of Battle*, p.402
24. Hougen, op. cit.
25. Blumenson, *Salerno*, p.369
26. Ibid., p.367
27. Ibid., p.370
28. Ibid.
29. Neither Blumenson nor Starr offer this as a reason
30. Blumenson, *Salerno*, pp.371–5; Starr, pp.101–3
31. Blumenson, *Salerno*, p.371
32. Quoted in Molony, p.624n
33. Notin, op. cit., p.245
34. Molony, p.626
35. Notin, p.247
36. Molony, p.624
37. Notin, pp.246–7
38. Blumenson, *Salerno*, p.372
39. Böhmler, p.150
40. Ibid.
41. Notin, pp.249–51; Starr, pp.103–4; Molony, pp.623–6; Blumenson, *Salerno*, pp.371–2
42. Notin, pp.246–9
43. Ibid.; Molony, p.627
44. Böhmler, p.150
45. Molony, pp.625–7; Blumenson, *Salerno*, p.372; Notin, pp.250–5
46. Böhmler, p.151
47. Senger, p.195
48. Blumenson, *Salerno*, pp.372–3. Point 156 is described wrongly as Point 56.

49. Hougen, op. cit.

50. Blumenson, *Salerno*, p.373; Starr, p.103

51. Blumenson, *Salerno*, pp.373-4

52. Ibid., p.373; Starr, p.104

53. Clark Diary, 30 Jan 44, quoted in Blumenson, *Salerno*, p.374 & Clark, *Calculated Risk*, p.282

54. Blumenson, *Salerno*, p.375

55. Clark, *Anzio*, op. cit., pp.132-3

56. Ibid., p.146; The unit was 2nd Sherwood Foresters (from 35 officers & 786 other ranks, it was reduced to 8 & 250)

57. Blumenson, *Clark*, p.297

58. Blumenson, *Salerno*, p.375

59. Senger, p.195

60. Blumenson, *Salerno*, p.376

61. Molony, pp.696-7

62. Blumenson, *Salerno*, p.376

Chapter Five

1. Hougen, op. cit.

2. Ibid.

3. Blumenson, *Salerno*, op. cit., pp.376-7; Starr, op. cit., p.106

4. Hougen; Starr, p.104; Blumenson, *Salerno*, pp.376-7

5. Starr, pp.106-8; Blumenson, *Salerno*, p.377

6. Blumenson, *Salerno*, pp.378-9; Starr, p.108

7. www.themedalofhonor.com, accessed 24 January 2017

8. www.themedalofhonor.com, accessed 24 January 2017

9. Blumenson, *Salerno*, pp.378-9; Starr, p.109

10. Böhmler, op. cit., p.154

11. Starr, p.108

12. Blumenson, *Salerno*, pp.379-80

13. Böhmler, p.154

14. Blumenson, *Salerno*, pp.379-81

15. Starr, p.109; Hougen.

16. Böhmler, p.153

17. Hougen.

18. Ibid.

19. Starr, p.110

20. Ibid.

21. Ibid.

22. Molony, pp.697-9

23. Ibid., pp.635-6
24. Starr, p.110
25. Ibid., p.111; Blumenson, *Salerno*, pp.382-3
26. Ibid., p.381
27. Ibid., pp.381-2
28. www.themedalofhonor.com, accessed 24 January 2017
29. Blumenson, *Salerno*, pp.382-3
30. Ibid., p.383
31. Stevens, *Fourth Indian Division*, p.275
32. Starr, pp.129-32 & 141-4; Blumenson, *Salerno*, pp.388-91 & 394-6; Clark, *Anzio*, pp.136-52 & 158-70
33. *London Gazette*, 30 March 1944; Clark, *Anzio*, pp.166-7
34. Molony, p.707; Stevens, pp.282-3
35. Phillips, *The Sangro to Cassino*, p.198
36. Ibid., pp.198-9
37. Stevens, pp.280-2
38. Molony, pp.710-13
39. Stevens, p.282
40. Ibid.
41. Ibid., p.283

Chapter Six

1. Phillips, op. cit., p.181
2. Ibid.; Stevens, op. cit., p.280; Molony, op. cit., pp.706-7
3. Blumenson, *Salerno*, p.402
4. Blaxland, *Alexander's Generals*, pp.24-5
5. Ibid., p.24
6. Mead, *Churchill's Lions*, p.149
7. Ibid., pp.149-50
8. Ibid., p.150; Doherty, *British Armoured Divisions and Their Commanders*, pp.106-8
9. Blaxland, p.25
10. Mead, pp.460-5. Mead notes that Leese, XXX Corps' commander at El Alamein 'did not regard [4th Indian Division] as capable of offensive action'.
11. Ibid.
12. Blaxland, p.52
13. Forty, op. cit., p.88
14. Molony, p.707
15. Majdalany, *The Monastery*, p.12
16. Harpur, *The Impossible Victory*, p.65 – a conversation between Harpur and Majdalany in 1955; the words are Majdalany's.

17. Clark, notes in author's possession
18. Bond, p.113
19. Phillips, p.205
20. The diary is quoted in Hapgood & Richardson, op. cit., p.102
21. Ibid.
22. Molony, pp.708-9
23. Majdalany, *Cassino*, op. cit., pp.114-15
24. Webster and Frankland, *The Strategic Air Offensive*, Vol I, pp.388-9
25. *Advertiser*, Adelaide, SA, 8 Jan 1944, accessed 14 April 2017
26. Blumenson, *Salerno*, p.403
27. Blaxland, p.53
28. Buckley, *Road to Rome*, p.294
29. Smith, *The Battles for Cassino*, p.68
30. Blumenson, *Salerno*, p.408
31. Hapgood & Richardson, op. cit., p.185
32. Ibid., p.169
33. Caddick-Adams, op. cit., p.145
34. Blumenson, *Salerno*, p.409
35. Ibid., p.411n
36. Hapgood & Richardson, p.199
37. Ibid., p.191
38. Kippenberger, *Infantry Brigadier*, p.356
39. Quoted in Hapgood & Richardson, p.200
40. Buckley, p.296
41. John Lardner, *Newsweek*, 28 February 1944, p.77
42. Hapgood & Richardson, p.202
43. Bond, op. cit., p.115
44. Blumenson, *Salerno*, p.413
45. Hapgood & Richardson, p.203
46. Clark, *Calculated Risk*, p.302
47. Stevens, op. cit., p.283
48. Joe Robinson, 2 LIR, Londonderry, 1968, and Hans Teske, 5 *FJR*, Lich, Germany, 1990
49. Smith, p.79; Majdalany, *Cassino*, p.135
50. Blumenson, *Salerno*, p.411
51. Starr, p.114
52. Blumenson, *Salerno*, p.411
53. Ibid., p.413
54. Ibid., p.416
55. Ibid., p.417
56. Phillips, p.223

57. Ibid.
58. Clark, p.303
59. Smith, pp.82-3
60. Majdalany, p.143
61. Stevens, p.287
62. Molony, p.714. Stevens noted twenty casualties.
63. Majdalany, pp.146-9; Molony, p.714
64. Phillips, p.223
65. Majdalany, p.153; Stevens, pp.288-90; Molony, pp.714-18
66. Phillips, p.223
67. Stevens, p.288
68. Majdalany, p.154
69. Ibid.
70. Ibid., pp.154-5
71. Smith, p.92
72. Stevens, p.289
73. Ibid., pp.289-90
74. Smith, p.90; Stevens, p.290
75. Stevens, pp.289-90
76. Phillips, p.240
77. Ibid., p.229
78. Ibid., pp.229-30
79. Ibid., pp.230-4
80. Smith, p.87
81. Phillips, p.237
82. Majdalany, p.161
83. Ibid.
84. Blumenson, *Salerno*, p.419
85. Alexander, *Despatch*, p.2915
86. Blumenson, *Salerno*, p.424
87. Majdalany, p.165
88. Stevens, p.291
89. Senger, op. cit., p.206
90. Stevens, p.291
91. Ibid.

Chapter Seven

1. Quoted in Blumenson, *Salerno*, p.433
2. Phillips, op. cit., p.229
3. Quoted in Alexander, *Despatch*, p.2916

 4. Danchev & Todman, op. cit., p.548

 5. Alexander, pp.2915-16

 6. Ibid., p.2916

 7. Blumenson, *Salerno*, p.434

 8. Majdalany, op. cit., p.166

 9. Ibid., pp.166-7

10. Quoted in Blumenson, *Salerno*, p.434

11. Ibid., p.434.

12. Ibid., pp.434-5; Starr, op. cit., p.116

13. Kippenberger, op. cit., p.358

14. Blumenson, *Salerno*, p.435

15. Ibid.

16. Ibid., p.436

17. Ibid., p.437

18. Ibid., p.438

19. Ibid., pp.438-9

20. Stevens, op. cit., p.295

21. Ibid., pp.296-7; NA Kew, WO373/68/472; *London Gazette*, 30 June 1944

22. NA Kew, WO373/68/472, op. cit.

23. Stevens, p.296

24. Ibid., p.297

25. Phillips, p.248

26. Ibid., pp.249-50

27. Ibid., p.251

28. Ray, *Algiers to Austria*, p.111

29. Phillips, p.251

30. Ray, p.113

31. Molony, p.780

32. Phillips, p.252; Blumenson, *Salerno*, p.439

33. Smith, op. cit., p.101

34. Clark, *Calculated Risk*, p.312; Blumenson, *Salerno*, p.439

35. Blumenson, *Salerno*, p.439

36. Molony, p.785

37. Phillips, p.268

38. Smith, p.103

39. Ibid.

40. Blumenson, *Salerno*, p.441

41. Ryder, *Oliver Leese*, pp.159-60

42. Blumenson, *Salerno*, p.441

43. Starr, p.117

44. Senger, op. cit., pp.213-14
45. Böhmler, op. cit., pp.212-13
46. Ibid., p.214
47. Ibid., p.216
48. Senger, p.215
49. Ibid.
50. Quoted in Böhmler, p.216
51. Phillips, pp.269-70
52. Ibid., p.253
53. Ibid., p.270
54. Böhmler, p.215
55. Molony, p.789
56. Phillips, p.272
57. Ibid.
58. Böhmler, p.213
59. Phillips, p.270; Molony, pp.786-7
60. Molony, p.787
61. Böhmler, p.215; Molony, p.787; Phillips, p.274
62. Phillips, pp.272-3
63. Ibid., p.273
64. Smith, p.109
65. Molony, p.788; Stevens, pp.298-9; Böhmler, p.217
66. Smith, p.111
67. Molony, pp.787-8; Stevens, p.298
68. Molony, p.788; Stevens, pp.298-9
69. Stevens, p.299
70. Ibid., pp.299-300; Molony, p.788; Smith, p.113
71. Stevens, p.299. Stevens describes Morris as a sergeant of 19th Armoured Regiment
72. Phillips, p.287
73. Stevens, pp.299-300

Chapter Eight

1. Stevens, op. cit., p.299
2. Ibid., p.300
3. Blumenson, *Salerno*, pp.443-4. Blumenson's source was the Steiger MS, written by Alfred G. Steiger of the Canadian Army Historical Section.
4. Molony, op. cit., p.790
5. Smith, op. cit., p.116
6. Ibid., p.117
7. Ibid.

8. Stevens, p.301; Molony, pp.794-5

9. Stevens, p.301

10. Ibid., pp.301-2; Molony, p.795; Phillips, op. cit., p.305

11. Molony, p.789

12. Ibid.

13. Ibid.

14. Senger, op. cit., p.216

15. Ibid., pp.216-17

16. Ibid., p.215

17. Molony, p.791

18. Ibid., p.792

19. Phillips, pp.293-4

20. Ibid., pp.294-8

21. Böhmler, op. cit., p.217

22. Ibid.

23. Molony, p.793

24. Ibid., pp.792-3

25. Ibid., p.795; Phillips, p.298

26. Phillips, p.298

27. Ibid.

28. Ibid., pp.303-4; Molony, p.795

29. Phillips, p.304; Molony, p.796

30. Molony, p.795

31. Phillips, p.304

32. Molony, p.796

33. Stevens, p.293; Majdalany, op. cit., p.187

34. Majdalany, p.187

35. NA Kew, WO169/18780, war diary 4th Indian Division RE; *Engineers in the Italian Campaign*, pp.62-3

36. Molony, p.796; Böhmler, p.236

37. Smith, p.126; Phillips, p.309

38. Smith, p.126; Stevens, p.303; Molony, p.797

39. Stevens, pp.303-4

40. Ibid.

41. Ibid., p.304

42. Ibid.

43. Ibid.

44. Ibid., p.305

45. Ibid.

46. Ibid., p.306; Phillips, p.311

47. Phillips, p.310
48. Plowman and Rowe, *The Battles for Monte Cassino*, p.182
49. Stevens, p.306; Phillips, p.311
50. Phillips, p.311
51. Ibid., pp.311-12
52. Ibid., p.312
53. Molony, pp.798-9
54. Ibid., pp.796-7
55. Phillips, p.314
56. Böhmler, p.220
57. Ibid.
58. Majdalany, p.209
59. Senger, p.217
60. Phillips, p.314
61. Ibid., p.315
62. Senger, p.218
63. Ibid., pp.218-19
64. Böhmler, p.220
65. Smith, p.134
66. Ibid., p.134; Molony, p.800; Stevens, p.307; Phillips, p.321
67. Molony, p.800; Stevens, pp.307-8
68. Molony, p.800
69. Phillips, p.319
70. Ibid., pp.322-3
71. Ibid., p.324
72. Ibid., pp.325-6; Böhmler, p.222; Stevens, p.308
73. Phillips, pp.325-6; Böhmler, p.222
74. Molony, p.802
75. NA Kew, WO170/1128, war diary 9th HAA Regiment, 1944; WO170/1161 war diary 25 HAA Bty, 1944; L/Bdr M. Stott. The author's father was one of a group who had climbed Vesuvius just a few days before the eruption: John Ormsby, 'Journal'
76. Phillips, p.326
77. Ibid., p.329
78. Ibid., p.330
79. Molony, pp.801-2; Senger, p.218
80. Molony, p.801
81. Stevens, p.311; Phillips, p.333
82. Majdalany, p.209
83. Stevens, p.311
84. Gaylor, *Sons of John Company*, p.151

85. Stevens, p.311; NA Kew, WO169/18970, war diary, 4th/16th Punjab Regiment, 1944
86. Wilson, op. cit., p.40; Ray, op. cit., p.116

Chapter Nine

1. Churchill, *The Second World War*, Vol. V, p.448
2. Majdalany, op. cit., p.171
3. Danchev & Todman, op. cit., p.533
4. Ibid., p.535
5. Ibid.
6. Ibid.
7. Churchill, p.450
8. Alexander, op. cit., p.2916
9. Ibid.
10. Ibid., p.2918
11. Starr, op. cit., pp.176-7
12. Alexander, p.2916
13. Molony, *The Mediterranean and the Middle East*, Vol. VI, Part I, p.36
14. Mead, *Churchill's Lions*, pp.241-4; Ryder, op. cit., passim
15. Alexander, p.2916
16. Molony, *The Mediterranean and the Middle East*, Vol. V, op. cit., pp.594-6
17. Schultz, *The 85th Infantry Division in World War II*, pp.7-68; Fisher, *Cassino to the Alps*, pp.23-4
18. Delaney, *The Blue Devils in Italy*, pp.8-45
19. Fisher, pp.23-4
20. Molony, *The Mediterranean and the Middle East*, Vol. VI, Part I, pp.14–16; Gaujac, *Le Corps Expeditionnaire Français en Italie*, passim
21. Gaujac provides detailed orders of battle for each division of the CEF.
22. Molony, pp.14–15; Williams, *From Warsaw to Rome*, pp.242-7
23. Ibid., pp.12–16; NA, Kew, WO170/151, war diary, Main HQ Eighth Army, March 1944; WO170/156, war diary, Main HQ, Eighth Army, April 1944
24. Molony, p.30n
25. Ibid., pp.29–31
26. Ibid., pp.30-1
27. Ibid., table II, following p.53
28. Ibid., pp.36-7
29. Ibid., p.40
30. Ibid., pp.42-3
31. Alexander, *Memoirs*, p.44
32. Williamson, *The Fourth Division*, p.108; www.cwgc.org, Brigadier Ivan Victor Russell Smith was 47.

33. Williamson, pp.109-11
34. Ford, *Battleaxe Division* (*BD*), p.151. This account refers to 5th Northamptons in 11 Brigade but the process was the same for all units.
35. Doherty, *CTW*, p.123; Captain Norman Bass, Transport Officer, 1 RIrF, interview with author, May 1992
36. Hingston, *The Tiger Triumphs*, pp.67-8
37. Ford, *BD*, pp.149-50
38. Ray, op. cit., p.118
39. Ibid., p.116
40. Ibid., p.118
41. Ibid.
42. Majdalany, p.200
43. Scott, 'Account of the Irish Brigade'
44. Bredin, interview with author, February 1989; NA Kew, war diary 6 Innisks, 1 Jan-30 April 1944
45. Bredin, interview with author, February 1989
46. Ibid.
47. Horsfall, *Fling Our Banner To The Wind*, pp.31-2
48. Gunner, *Front of the Line*, p.81
49. Majdalany, p. 207; Crew, *The Army Medical Services: Campaigns* Vol. III pp.183 & 263
50. Williamson, p.112
51. Ford, *Mailed Fist*, p.130
52. Ibid., p.131; Williamson, p.114
53. Williamson, p.117
54. Ibid., p.121
55. Ibid., p.116
56. Pite, letter to author, 1992
57. *Faugh A Ballagh! Gazette*, No.159, p.227; *LG*, 24 Aug 1944; NA Kew, WO373/7/185
58. Carver, *Harding of Petherton*, pp.134-5
59. Kesselring, op. cit., p.200; Molony, p.22
60. Ellis, *Cassino: The Hollow Victory*, p.276
61. Molony, pp.22-3
62. Scott. op. cit.
63. Molony, pp.68-75 provide the German order of battle prior to DIADEM
64. Ibid., pp.29-31
65. Ray, pp.122-3; Doherty, *CTW*, p.126; Ford, *Mailed Fist*, pp.131-2
66. Comment attributed to John Horsfall by Brian Clark during an interview with the author, August 1990
67. Ray, p.123

68. My thanks to my young Californian cousin, Kiel Ireland, for the explanation of the origin of 'Americano'.
69. Fisher, p.23
70. Schultz, p.61
71. Ibid.
72. Delaney, p.60
73. Starr, op. cit., pp.178-9
74. Fisher, p.24
75. Ibid., p.26
76. Horsfall, p.33
77. Ibid., NA, WO170/606, war diary HQ 38 (Ir) Bde, April-June 1944; Lt Col B.D.H. Clark MC GM, interview with author, August 1990
78. Summarized from Anders, *An Army in Exile* and Williams, *From Warsaw to Rome*. I am grateful to Dr Tomasz Piesakowski, a survivor of a Soviet camp in Siberia, for information on the treatment of prisoners by the Soviets. (Interview in London in January 2013)
79. Williams, p.69
80. Orr, *Wojtek the Bear*, pp.24-8
81. Ibid., p.47
82. Williams, p.195
83. Horsfall, p.32-3
84. Ibid., p.29; Scott, op. cit.

Chapter Ten

1. NA Kew, WO204/10402, HQ 15 AG (AAI), Operational orders & instructions, 1 Aug 1943-31 Jul 1944
2. Ibid., AAI Operation Order 1
3. Molony, op. cit., p.58
4. NA Kew, WO204/10402
5. Molony, pp.58-9
6. NA Kew, CAB106/418, 'Campaign in Central Italy, 26 Mar-10 Aug 1944', p.11
7. Molony, p.59
8. Ibid.
9. Ibid., p.60; NA Kew WO204/10416, HQ 8 Army G Plans
10. Molony, p.60
11. Ibid., p.141
12. Blaxland, op. cit., p.76
13. Starr, op. cit., p.181
14. Senger, op. cit., pp.243-4; Molony, p.70
15. Molony, pp.70-1

16. Ibid., p.68

17. Ibid., pp.69 & 72

18. Ibid., pp.69-73

19. Ibid., pp.68-75

20. Kesselring, op. cit., p.199

21. Ellis, op. cit., pp.276-7

22. Senger, p.244

23. Ibid., p.244

24. Danchev & Todman, op. cit., p.546

25. Molony, p.71: the figures relate to 23 April for Tenth Army and 10 May for Fourteenth

26. Fisher, op. cit., p.39

27. Scott, op. cit.

28. Fisher, p.29

29. Molony, p.32n

30. Fisher, p.43; p.36 re the naval gunfire, from 8-inch guns of a heavy cruiser

31. NA Kew, CAB106/418, op. cit., p.12

32. Starr, p.185

33. NA Kew, CAB106/418, p.12; WO170/929, war diary 17 Fd Regt, 1944; Molony, p.99; Williamson, pp.12-14

34. NA Kew, CAB106/418, p.12; Molony, p.105; Williamson, op. cit., pp.124-5

35. Molony, pp.105-7; Williamson, p.125; NA Kew, WO170/407, war diary, HQ 4 Div G Br, Jan-Jun 1944

36. Williamson, p.125; NA Kew, WO170/407

37. Williamson, p.130

38. Evans, *With the East Surreys*, pp.149-50

39. Williamson, p.130

40. Ibid., p.131; Squire & Hill, *The Surreys in Italy*, p.36

41. Williamson, p.131

42. Ibid., pp.132-3; NA Kew, WO170/1358, war diary 2 Beds & Herts, Jan-Jul 1944

43. Williamson, pp.132-3

44. NA Kew, WO170/407

45. Williamson, pp.132-3; NA Kew, WO170/1418, war diary 2 King's Apr-Dec 1944; WO170/596, war diary, 28 Bde, Jan-Aug 1944

46. NA Kew, WO170/596; Williamson, pp.134-5; Mead, op. cit., pp.469-72

47. Joslen, *Orders of Battle Second World War 1939-1945*, p.448

48. Hingston, op. cit., p.69

49. Ibid.

50. Parkinson, *Always a Fusilier*, pp.186-7

51. Hingston, p.70

52. Ibid.

53. *London Gazette*, 27 July 1944; NA Kew, WO98/8/810

54. Hingston, pp.72-3; Molony, p.108; NA Kew, WO170/1365, war diary 1 A&S Hldrs, 1944

55. Hingston, p.73

56. *Engineers in the Italian Campaign*, p.34

57. Ibid., p.35; Pal, *The Campaign in Italy*, p.166; Plowman & Rowe, op. cit., pp.286-7. The RCEME was formed in February 1944 on the model of REME, combining elements of the Royal Canadian Army Service Corps and Royal Canadian Ordnance Corps.

58. Plowman & Rowe, p.287

59. Nicholson, *The Canadians in Italy*, p.405; Hingston, p.75

60. Hingston, p.75

61. Ibid.; ffrench-Blake, *A History of the 17th/21st Lancers 1922-1959*, p.102; Williamson, pp.139-40

62. Williamson, pp.139-41; NA Kew, WO170/558, war diary 12 Bde, 1944

63. *London Gazette*, 13 Jul 1944

64. Molony, pp.117-18; Williamson, pp.141-2

65. Molony, pp.116-17; Doherty, *Eighth Army in Italy*, p.92

66. *London Gazette*, 13 July 1944

67. Ibid.

68. Hingston, p.78

69. Williamson, pp.145-8; NA Kew, WO170/1366, war diary 6 BW, Mar-Dec 1944

70. NA Kew, WO170/829, war diary, 17/21L, 1944

71. ffrench-Blake, p.103

Chapter Eleven

1. Anders, *An Army in Exile*, p.174

2. Molony, op. cit., p.109

3. Anders, op. cit., p.172

4. Ibid., p.171

5. Molony, p.109

6. Anders, p.172

7. 'Polish artillery in Italy' in *The Royal Artillery Commemoration Book 1939-1945*, Duncan et al, p.313. Major General R.W. Odzierzynski CBE was Commander II Polish Corps Artillery. His command included 3rd Carpathian Division Artillery (1st, 2nd and 3rd Carpathian Field Regiments, 3rd Anti-Tank and 3rd LAA Regiments) and 5th Kresowa Division Artillery (4th, 5th and 6th Kresowa Field Regiments, 5th Anti-Tank and 5th LAA Regiments). Corps Artillery included 1st Polish Survey Regiment, 7th Anti-Tank and 7th and 8th LAA Regiments.

8. Connell, *Monte Cassino*, p.167. The comment about the spoons and sandbags was from Major Offenkowski.
9. Williams, op. cit., p.185
10. Ibid., pp.110-11
11. Ibid.; Williams, pp.186-7
12. Anders, p.175
13. Ibid., pp.176-7
14. Ibid., p.177
15. Ibid.; Molony, p.111; Ryder, op. cit., pp.166-7
16. Anders, p.177
17. Molony, pp.129-31
18. *Engineers in the Italian Campaign*, p.35
19. Ibid., p.36
20. Ray, op. cit., pp.124-5
21. Doherty, *CTW*, p.126
22. Col P.J.C. Trousdell, letter and notes to author
23. Scott, op. cit.
24. This account is based on the war diaries of 6th Inniskillings and 38 Bde, as well as Fox, *The Royal Inniskilling Fusiliers in the Second World War*, Scott's 'Account of the Irish Brigade' and interviews with a number of veterans.
25. Horsfall, op. cit., p.49; NA Kew, WO170/1433, war diary 2 LIR; WO170/606, war diary 38 Bde, April-June 1944
26. Horsfall, pp.49-51; Doherty, *CTW*, pp.136-8; Scott.
27. Holland, *Italy's Sorrow*, pp.107-9; Caddick-Adams, op. cit., pp.244-5
28. Horsfall, p.55
29. Woods, personal account, copy in author's possession
30. Ibid.
31. Ibid. Woods told the author that he never forgot Jimmy Barnes's courage and felt that he was unjustly deprived of the VC.
32. Horsfall, p.59
33. Davies, personal account, copy in author's possession
34. Ibid.
35. Horsfall, pp.60-2
36. Ray, p.128. The P-40s were probably DAF machines, 'astray from their target'.
37. Blaxland, op. cit., p.99
38. Ibid., p.100
39. *London Gazette*, 13 July 1944
40. Doherty, *CTW*, p.140; Ray, pp.131-2
41. Col P.J.C. Trousdell to author
42. Horsfall, p.67

43. Doherty, *CTW*, pp.140-2

44. Ibid., pp.142-4; Horsfall, pp.67-9; Fox, p.101, plus interviews with veterans, including Bredin, Clark and Horsfall

45. Blaxland, p.101

46. Molony, pp.126-7

47. Kesselring, op. cit., p.202

48. Blaxland, p.101. The quotation is from the Grenadier Guards' regimental history.

49. Anders, p.177

50. Ibid., p.178; Williams, pp.193-4

51. Williams, p.201

52. Anders, p.178

53. Williams, p.201

54. Ibid., p.202

55. Ibid.

56. Ibid., p.204

57. Böhmler, op. cit., p.268

58. Williams, pp.204-6

59. Ibid., pp.205-6

60. Ibid.; Molony, p.133; Blaxland, p.101; Kesselring, p.202; Böhmler, p.268

61. Böhmler, pp.268-9

62. Piekalkiewicz, *Cassino: Anatomy of the Battle*, p.181; Fisher, op. cit., p.78

63. Blaxland, p.102

64. Majdalany, op. cit., pp.250-1; Ray, p.132

Chapter Twelve

1. Starr, op. cit., pp.198-9

2. Fisher, op. cit., p.45

3. Schultz, op. cit., p.74

4. Starr, p.186

5. Fisher, p.47

6. www.themedalofhonor.com, accessed 12 February 2017

7. General Orders No.81, War Department, 14 October 1944

8. www.themedalofhonor.com, accessed 12 February 2017

9. Fisher, p.55

10. Ibid., pp.55-6

11. General Orders No.81, op. cit.

12. Delaney, op. cit., pp.62-3; Fisher, pp.46-7

13. Obituary, *New York Times*, 26 April 1994

14. www.themedalofhonor.com, accessed 12 February 2017

15. Delaney, p.67; Fisher, pp.51-2

16. Delaney, p.69; See *Small Unit Actions*, pp.119-70, for a detailed account
17. Delaney, pp.71-3; Fisher, pp.68-9; Plowman & Rowe, op. cit., pp.252-3
18. Fisher, p.69
19. Kesselring, op. cit., p.200
20. Molony, op. cit., p.62n; Fisher, p.57; Gaujac, op. cit., pp.11, 14 & 33
21. Molony, p.63n
22. Ibid.
23. Ibid.; Starr, pp.179-81; Fisher, pp.32-5
24. Molony, p.62
25. Fisher, p.56
26. Ibid., pp.59-60
27. Ibid., p.60
28. Ibid., pp.60-2
29. Notin, op. cit., pp.359-60
30. Fisher, p.62
31. Starr, p.188; Plowman & Rowe, pp.266-7
32. Starr, p.188; Plowman and Rowe, p.267
33. Starr, p.189; Plowman & Rowe, p.266
34. Starr, p.189-92
35. Ibid., pp.192-3; Plowman and Rowe, p.269; Notin, p.382n
36. Starr, p.193
37. Notin, p.382
38. Starr, p.193
39. Ibid., pp.193-4
40. Ibid., p.195
41. Ibid., p.196; Plowman & Rowe, p.280
42. Starr, p.197
43. In *Reconquérir: 1944-1945* (pp.32-3), Marshal de Lattre de Tassigny argued that there were only (sic) isolated cases of rape that were exaggerated by German propaganda. However, de Lattre de Tassigny did not serve in Italy. In the Esperia area and elsewhere there is no doubt that an atrocity did occur. It has been the subject of books and other publications, including Alberto Moravia's 1957 novel *La Ciociara*, upon which the film *Two Women*, starring Sophia Loren, who won the Academy Award for Best Actress, was based. The author is aware that the reputation of the French colonial soldiers was such that they were feared by Italian civilians generally and women especially.
44. Ibid., p.198; Fisher, pp.79-81
45. Quoted in Starr, p.198
46. Starr, p.198
47. Ibid.

48. Fisher, p.73

49. Ibid.

50. Ibid., p.75

51. Ibid., p.76

52. Ibid., pp.83-9; Starr, pp.208-9

53. Fisher, p.90

54. Ibid., p.90; Starr, pp.213-16; Molony, pp.176-9; Nicholson, *The Canadians in Italy*, pp.411-16

55. Blaxland, op. cit., p.103

56. Molony, pp.188-9; Nicholson, pp.411, 413-14

57. Blaxland, p.106

58. Molony, p.189; Blaxland, p.119; Doherty, *A Noble Crusade*, p.216

59. Nicholson, p.419

60. Ibid., p.425

61. Molony, p.193; Mead, *Gunners at War*, p.90

62. Nicholson, pp.428-31

63. Anders, op. cit., p.181; Blaxland, p.106

64. Molony, pp.200-1 & 241-2; Blaxland, pp.121-2

65. Platt, *The Royal Wiltshire Yeomanry*, p.161; NA Kew, WO170/838, war diary, Warwick Yeo, 1944

66. Molony, p.200; Blaxland, p.122

67. *London Gazette*, 13 July 1944; Nicholson, pp.431-3

Chapter Thirteen

 1. Molony, p.167

 2. Ibid., pp.173-4

 3. Ibid., pp.174-5

 4. Ibid., pp.175-6

 5. Ibid., p.176

 6. Doherty, *A Noble Crusade*, p.220

 7. Scott; Doherty, *CTW*, p.148

 8. Blaxland, p.124

 9. Ibid., pp.124-5

10. Ibid., p.127; Nicholson, p.445

11. Molony, pp.219-20

12. Ibid., p.221; Fisher, pp.105-6

13. Molony, p.221

14. Jeffers, *Command of Honor*, pp.184-5

15. Fisher, pp.114-15

16. Jackson, *The Battle for Rome*, p.173

17. Molony, p.222
18. Ibid.
19. Ibid., pp.224–5
20. Ibid., p.225
21. www.themedalofhonor.com, accessed 10 March 2017; St John, *Thirty-fourth Infantry Division*, p.30
22. www.themedalofhonor.com, accessed 10 March 2017; St John, p.30
23. Ibid.
24. Ibid.
25. Ibid.
26. Ibid.
27. Ibid.
28. Starr, pp.232–3
29. Ibid., p.235
30. www.themedalofhonor.com, accessed 10 March 2017
31. Murphy, *To Hell and Back*, pp.152–3
32. www.themedalofhonor.com, accessed 10 March 2017
33. Starr, p.237
34. Ibid., p.239
35. Ibid.
36. Ibid., p.240; Jackson, p.186
37. www.themedalofhonor.com, accessed 10 March 2017
38. Ibid.: www.abmc.gov/news
39. www.abmc.gov/news
40. Starr, pp.243–4
41. www.themedalofhonor.com, accessed 10 March 2017
42. Starr, pp.246–7
43. www.themedalofhonor.com, accessed 10 March 2017
44. Starr, pp.250–1
45. Ibid., pp.252–3
46. Ibid.
47. Ibid.
48. Ibid.
49. Ibid.
50. Starr, p.257
51. Jackson, p.174
52. Jackson, *The Battle for Italy*, pp.242–3; Atkinson, op. cit., pp.546–7
53. Atkinson, p.549
54. Clark, *Calculated Risk*, p.332
55. Blumenson, *Clark*, p.210

56. Ismay, *Memoirs*, p.361
57. Kesselring, p.203
58. Senger, op. cit., pp.248-9
59. Molony, p.284

Chapter Fourteen

1. Scott.
2. Plowman & Rowe, op. cit., p.380; Molony, Vol.V, op. cit., p.636
3. Plowman & Rowe, p.384; Molony, pp.803 & 807
4. Plowman & Rowe, p.385
5. See the author's *Victory in Italy: 15th Army Group's Final Campaign 1945* (Pen & Sword Books, 2014)
6. This was 25 Armoured Engineer Brigade
7. NA Kew, WO373/11
8. Nicholson, *The Canadians in Italy*, pp.325, 328-32; Doherty, *Eighth Army in Italy*, pp.53-5
9. Roberts, *31st Field Regiment RA*, p.52
10. Routledge, *Anti-Aircraft Artillery*, p.292
11. Evans, *Decisive Campaigns of the Desert Air Force*, pp.158-9
12. Crew, op. cit., pp.243-90
13. Ibid., p.263
14. Gaujac, op. cit., pp.150-61
15. NA Kew, WO373/7
16. Ibid., WO373/11
17. Ibid., WO373/7
18. Steer, *To The Warrior His Arms*, pp.99-100
19. Danchev & Todman, op. cit., pp.546-55
20. Caddick-Adams, *Monty and Rommel*, pp.510-11
21. Senger, op. cit., p.195
22. Clarke, *With Alex at War*, p.149
23. Quoted in Wilson, *Report*, Pt II, p.29

Bibliography

Adleman, Robert and Walton, Colonel George, *Rome Fell Today* (Leslie Frewin, London, 1969)

Alexander, Field Marshal Sir Harold, *Despatch* (on the Allied Armies in Italy during the period from 3 September 1943 to 12 December 1944) (HMSO, Supplement to *The London Gazette*, London, 6 June 1950)

——, *Memoirs*, John North (Ed.) (Cassell, London, 1962)

Anders, Lt Gen W., CB, *An Army in Exile. The Story of the Second Polish Corps* (Macmillan, London, 1949)

Anon, *The London Irish at War* (Old Comrades Assn, London, 1948)

Aris, George, *The Fifth British Division 1939 to 1945* (The Fifth Division Benevolent Fund, London, 1959)

Arthur, Max, *Symbol of Courage: A History of the Victoria Cross* (Sidgwick and Jackson, London, 2004)

Ascoli, David, *A Companion to the British Army 1660-1983* (Harrap, London, 1983)

Atkinson, Rick, *The Day of Battle: The War in Sicily and Italy 1943-1944* (Little, Brown, London, 2007)

Badoglio, Pietro, *Italy in the Second World War* (Oxford University Press, London, 1948)

Bailey, Lt Col D.E., *Engineers in the Italian Campaign 1943-1945* (Central Mediterranean Force, np, 1945)

Barber, Laurie and Tonkin-Covell, John, *Freyberg: Churchill's Salamander* (Hutchinson, London, 1990)

Barclay, C.N., *The History of The Royal Northumberland Fusiliers in the Second World War* (William Clowes and Son, London, 1952)

——, *History of the 16th/5th Queen's Royal Lancers 1925-1961* (Gale and Polden, Aldershot, 1963)

Barzini, Luigi, *The Italians* (Hamish Hamilton, London, 1964)

Bateson, Henry, *First into Italy* (Jarrolds, London, 1944)

Baynes, John, *The Forgotten Victor: General Sir Richard O'Connor* (Brassey's, London, 1989)

Bidwell, Shelford, *Gunners at War: A Tactical Study of the Royal Artillery in the Twentieth Century* (Arms & Armour Press, London, 1970)

Bidwell, Shelford and Graham, Dominick, *Tug of War. The Battle for Italy 1943-45* (Hodder & Stoughton, London, 1979)

——, *Fire-Power. British Army Weapons and Theories of War, 1904-1945* (HarperCollins, London, 1982)

Blackwell, Ian, *Battleground Europe: Cassino* (Pen & Sword, Barnsley, 2005)

——, *Fifth Army in Italy: Battleground Europe: Anzio* (Pen & Sword, Barnsley, 2006)

——, *Fifth Army in Italy: A Coalition at War* (Pen & Sword, Barnsley, 2012)

Blaxland, Gregory, *Alexander's Generals: The Italian Campaign 1944-45* (William Kimber, London, 1979)

Blumenson, Martin, *United States Army in World War II: The Mediterranean Theater of Operations: Salerno to Cassino* (Office of the Chief of Military History, US Army, Washington DC, 1969)

——, *Bloody River: Prelude to the Battle of Cassino* (George Allen & Unwin, London, 1970)

——, *Mark Clark* (Jonathan Cape, London, 1984)

Böhmler, Rudolf, *Monte Cassino: A German View* (first published in German in 1956; UK edition, Pen & Sword, Barnsley, 2015)

Bond, Harold L., *Return to Cassino. A Memoir of the Fight for Rome* (J. M. Dent, London, 1964)

Bourhill, James, *Come Back to Portofino: Through Italy with the 6th South African Armoured Division* (30° South Publishers, Johannesburg, 2011)

Bowlby, Alex, *Countdown to Cassino. The Battle of Mignano Gap, 1943* (Pen & Sword, Barnsley, 1995)

Bowman, Martin W., *USAAF Handbook 1939-1945* (Sutton Publishing, Stroud, 1997)

Bowyer, Chaz & Shores, Christopher, *Desert Air Force at War* (Ian Allan Ltd, Shepperton, 1981)

Bryant, Sir Arthur, *Triumph in the West. Completing the War Diaries of Field Marshal Viscount Alanbrooke* (Collins, London, 1959)

Bullen, Roy, *History of the 2/7th Battalion The Queen's Royal Regiment 1939-1946* (np, 1958)

Burns, E.L.M., *General Mud* (Clark and Irwin, Toronto, 1984)

Caddick-Adams, Peter, *Monty and Rommel: Parallel Lives* (Preface Publishing, London, 2011)

——, *Monte Cassino: Ten Armies in Hell* (Preface Publishing, London, 2012)

Carpentier, General Marcel, *Les Forces Alliées en Italie: La Campagne d'Italie* (Éditions Berger-Levrault, Paris, 1949)

Carver, Field Marshal Lord, *Harding of Petherton: Field Marshal* (Weidenfeld and Nicolson, London, 1978)

——, *The Imperial War Museum Book of the War in Italy 1943-1945* (Sidgwick & Jackson, London, 2001)

Churchill, Winston S., *The Second World War*, Vols VII & VIII, *The Hinge of Fate*; Vol. IX, *Closing the Ring*; Vol. XI, *Triumph and Tragedy* (Cassell, London, 1951, 1952, 1954)

Clark, Lloyd, *Anzio: Italy and the Battle for Rome – 1944* (Headline, London, 2006)

Clark, Mark, *Calculated Risk* (Harrap, London, 1951)

Clarke, Rupert, *With Alex at War from the Irrawaddy to the Po 1941-1945* (Leo Cooper, Barnsley, 2000)

Cole, David, *Rough Road to Rome: A Foot-soldier in Italy 1943-44* (William Kimber, London, 1983)

Connell, Charles, *Monte Cassino: The Historic Battle* (Elek Books, London, 1963)

Cooper, Matthew, *The German Army 1933-1945. Its Political and Military Failure* (Macdonald and Jane's, London, 1978)

Crew, F.A.E, FRS, *The Army Medical Services: Campaigns Vol. III, Sicily, Italy, Greece (1944-45)* (History of the Second World War: United Kingdom Medical Services) (HMSO, London, 1957)

Cunliffe, Marcus, *The Royal Irish Fusiliers* (Oxford University Press, Oxford, 1952)

Danchev, Alex and Todman, Daniel, *War Diaries 1939-1945 Field Marshal Lord Alanbrooke* (Weidenfeld & Nicolson, London, 2001)

Daniell, D.S., *History of the East Surrey Regiment* (Ernest Benn, London, 1957)

Davies, Norman, *Trail of Hope: The Anders Army, An Odyssey across three continents* (Osprey Publishing, Oxford, 2015)

Delaney, John P. and Sloan, John E., *The Blue Devils in Italy: A History of the 88th Infantry Division in World War II* (Infantry Journal Press, Washington DC, 1947)

D'Este, Carlo, *Eisenhower: Allied Supreme Commander* (Weidenfeld & Nicolson, London, 2002)

——, *Fatal Decision: Anzio and the Battle for Rome* (HarperCollins, London, 2008)

——, *World War II in the Mediterranean, 1942-1945* (Workman Publishing, New York, 1990)

Doherty, Richard, *Clear the Way! A History of 38 (Irish) Brigade, 1941-47* (Irish Academic Press, Dublin, 1993)

——, *Only the Enemy in Front: The Recce Corps at War 1940-1946* (Tom Donovan Publishing, London, 1994)

——, *A Noble Crusade. The History of Eighth Army 1941-45* (Spellmount, Staplehurst, 1999)

——, *The North Irish Horse. A Hundred Years of Service* (Spellmount, Staplehurst, 2002)

——, *Ireland's Generals in the Second World War* (Four Courts Press, Dublin, 2004)

——, *Eighth Army in Italy 1943-45: The Long Hard Slog* (Pen and Sword, Barnsley, 2007)

——, *Ubique: The Royal Artillery in the Second World War* (The History Press, Stroud, 2008)

——, *In the Ranks of Death: The Irish in the Second World War* (Pen and Sword, Barnsley, 2010)

——, *British Armoured Divisions and Their Commanders, 1939-1945* (Pen & Sword, Barnsley, 2013)

Duncan, W.E. et al (Eds), *The Royal Artillery Commemoration Book 1939-1945* (G. Bell & Sons, London, 1950)

Durnford-Slater, John, *Commando* (William Kimber, London, 1953)

Ellis, John, *Cassino, The Hollow Victory: The Battle for Rome January-June 1944* (Andre Deutsch, London, 1984)

Ellwood, David W., *Italy 1943-1945* (*The Politics of Liberation* series) (Leicester University Press, Leicester, 1985)

Evans, Bryn, *With the East Surreys in Tunisia and Italy 1942-1945: Fighting for Every River and Mountain* (Pen & Sword, Barnsley, 2012)

——, *The Decisive Campaigns of the Desert Air Force 1942-1945* (Pen & Sword, Barnsley, 2014)

Fergusson, Bernard, *The Black Watch and the King's Enemies* (Collins, London, 1950)

Fisher, Ernest F., Jnr, *United States Army in World War II: The Mediterranean Theater of Operations: Cassino to the Alps* (US Army Center of Military History, Washington DC, 1977)

ffrench-Blake, R.L.V., *A History of the 17th/21st Lancers 1922-1959* (Macmillan, London, 1962)

——, *The 17th/21st Lancers 1759-1993* (Leo Cooper, London, 1993)

Ford, Ken, *Battleaxe Division. From Africa to Austria with the 78th Division 1942-45* (Sutton, Stroud, 1999)

——, *Cassino: The Four Battles January - May 1944* (Crowood Press, Marlborough, 2001)

——, *Cassino. Breaking the Gustav Line* (Osprey, Botley, 2004)

——, *Mailed Fist. 6th Armoured Division at War 1940-1945* (Sutton, Stroud, 2005)

Forman, Sir Denis, *To Reason Why* (Andre Deutsch, London, 1991)

Forty, George, *The Armies of Rommel* (Arms and Armour, London, 1997)

——, *Battle for Monte Cassino* (Ian Allan, Hersham, 2004)

Fox, Sir Frank, *The Royal Inniskilling Fusiliers in the Second World War, 1939-45* (Gale & Polden, Aldershot, 1951)

Fraser, David, *Alanbrooke* (Collins, London, 1982)

——, *And We Shall Shock Them: The British Army in the Second World War* (Hodder & Stoughton, London, 1983)

——, *Knight's Cross. A Life of Field Marshal Erwin Rommel* (HarperCollins, London, 1993)

Frederick, J.B.M., *Lineage Book of British Land Forces 1660-1978* (Microform Academic Publishers, Wakefield, 1984)

French, David, *Raising Churchill's Army. The British Army and the War against Germany 1919-1945* (Oxford University Press, Oxford, 2000)

Freyberg, Paul, *Bernard Freyberg VC: Soldier of Two Nations* (Hodder & Stoughton, London, 1991)

Gaujac, Paul, *Le Corps expéditionnaire français en Italie* (Histoire et collections, 2003)

Gaylor, John, *Sons of John Company: The Indian and Pakistan Armies 1903-1991* (Spellmount, Staplehurst, 1992)

Gellhorn, Martha, *The Face of War: Writings from the Front Line 1938-1985* (Sphere Books, London, 1967)

Gore, Enid, *This Was The Way It Was. Adrian Clements Gore* (privately produced, 1977)

Graham, Dominick and Bidwell, Shelford, *Coalitions, Politicians & Generals: Some Aspects of Command in Two World Wars* (Brassey's (UK), London, 1993)

Graves, Charles, *The History of the Royal Ulster Rifles*, Vol.III (Regimental Committee, Belfast, 1950)

Gunner, Colin, *Front of the Line: Adventures with The Irish Brigade* (Greystone Books, Antrim, 1991)

Hallam, John, *The History of The Lancashire Fusiliers 1939-1944* (Sutton, Stroud, 1993)

Hapgood, David and Richardson, David, *Monte Cassino* (Angus & Robertson, London, 1984)

Hingston, W.G., *The Tiger Triumphs: The Story of Three Great Divisions in Italy* (HMSO, London, 1946)

Hinsley, F.H., *British Intelligence in the Second World War (Official History of the Second World War)* (Abridged Edition) HMSO, London, 1993)

Historical Division, US War Department, *Small Unit Actions (American Forces in Action Series)* (War Department, Washington DC, 1946)

Hogg, Ian V., and Weeks, John, *The Illustrated Encyclopedia of Military Vehicles* (Quarto, London, 1980)

Holland, James, *Italy's Sorrow: A Year of War 1944-45* (Harper Press, London, 2008)

Horsfall, John, *Fling Our Banner to the Wind* (Kineton Press, Kineton, 1978)

Hougen, John H., *The Story of the Famous 34th Infantry Division* (np, 1949; re-published Literary Licensing.com, Whitefish, MT, nd)

Howard, Michael, *Grand Strategy*, Vol. IV (Official History of the Second World War) (HMSO, London, 1972)

——, *Grand Strategy*, Vol. V, *Strategic Deception* (Official History of the Second World War) (HMSO, London, 1990)

——, *The Mediterranean Strategy in the Second World War* (Greenhill Books, London, 1993)

Howarth, Patrick, *My God, Soldiers. From Alamein to Vienna* (Hutchinson, London, 1989)

Jackson, Robert, *Army Wings: A History of Army Air Observation Flying 1914-1960* (Pen & Sword, Barnsley, 2006)

Jackson, W.G.F., *The Battle for Italy* (Batsford, London, 1967)

——, *The Battle for Rome* (Batsford, London, 1969)

——, *The Mediterranean and the Middle East*, Vol. VI, *Victory in the Mediterranean, Part II – June to October 1944* (Official History of the Second World War) (HMSO, London, 1973)

Jeffers, H. Paul, *Command of Honor: General Lucian Truscott's Path to Victory in World War II* (NAL Caliber, New York, 2008)

Joslen, Lt Col H.F., *Orders of Battle Second World War 1939-1945* (HMSO, London, 1960)

Kay, Robin, *From Cassino to Trieste*, Vol. II of *Italy: History of New Zealand in the Second World War* (Department of Internal Affairs, Wellington, 1967)

Keegan, John (Ed.), *Churchill's Generals* (Weidenfeld & Nicolson, London, 1991)

Kesselring, Field Marshal Albert, *Memoirs* (William Kimber, London, 1953; Greenhill Books, London, 1988)

Kippenberger, Maj Gen Sir Howard, *Infantry Brigadier* (OUP, London, 1949)

Koskodan, Kenneth K., *No Greater Ally: The Untold Story of Poland's Forces in World War II* (Osprey Publishing, Oxford, 2011)

Kossakowski, Irena, *A Homeland Denied: In the Footsteps of a Polish PoW* (Whittles Publishing, Dunbeath, 2016)

Lamb, Richard, *War in Italy 1943-1945. A Brutal Story* (John Murray, London, 1993)

Liddell Hart, B.H., *The Other Side of the Hill* (Cassell, London, 1948 and 1951)

——, *The Rommel Papers* (Da Capo Press, New York, 1953)

Linklater, Eric, *The Campaign in Italy* (HMSO, London, 1959)

Lord, Cliff, and Watson, Graham, *The Royal Corps of Signals: Unit Histories of the Corps (1920-2001) and its Antecedents* (Helion, Solihull, 2003)

Lucas, James, *Storming Eagles: German Airborne Forces in World War Two* (Arms & Armour Press, London, 1988)

Lunt, James, *The Scarlet Lancers. The Story of 16th/5th The Queen's Royal Lancers 1689-1992* (Leo Cooper, London, 1993)

McLaughlin, Redmond, *The Royal Army Medical Corps* (Leo Cooper, London, 1972)

Macksey, Kenneth, *Kesselring. German Master Strategist of the Second World War* (Greenhill Books, London, 1996)

Majdalany, Fred, *The Monastery* (John Lane, The Bodley Head, London, 1945)

——, *Cassino. Portrait of a Battle* (Longmans, Green & Co., London, 1957)

Martel, Lt Gen Sir Giffard Le Q., *Our Armoured Forces* (Faber and Faber, London, 1945)

Mead, Peter, *Gunners at War 1939-1945* (Ian Allan, London, 1982)

Mead, Richard, *Churchill's Lions: A biographical guide to the key British generals of World War II* (Spellmount, Stroud, 2007)

——, *The Last Great Cavalryman: The Life of General Sir Richard McCreery, Commander Eighth Army* (Pen & Sword, Barnsley, 2012)

Merewood, Jack, *To War with The Bays. A Tank Gunner Remembers 1939-1945* (1st The Queen's Dragoon Guards, Cardiff, 1996)

Messenger, Charles, *The Commandos, 1940-1946* (William Kimber, London, 1985)

Mitcham, Samuel W., Jr, *Hitler's Field Marshals and their Battles* (William Heinemann, London, 1988)

Molony, C.J.C., *The Mediterranean and the Middle East*, Vol. V, *The Campaign in Sicily 1943 and the Campaign in Italy 3rd September 1943 to 31st March 1944* (*Official History of the Second World War*) (HMSO, London, 1973)

——, *The Mediterranean and the Middle East*, Vol. VI, *Victory in the Mediterranean – Part I – 1st April to 4th June 1944* (*Official History of the Second World War*) (HMSO, London, 1974)

Mowat, Farley, *And No Birds Sang* (Stackpole Books, Mechanicsburg PA, 1973)

Murphy, Audie (with David McClure), *To Hell and Back* (St Martin's Press, New York, 2002)

Neillands, Robin, *Eighth Army: from the Western Desert to the Alps, 1939-1945* (John Murray, London, 2005)

Nicholson, Lt Col G.W.L., *Official History of the Canadian Army in the Second World War*, Vol. II, *The Canadians in Italy 1943-1945* (Queen's Printers, Ottawa, 1956)

Nicolson, Nigel, *Alex: The Life of Field Marshal The Earl Alexander of Tunis* (Weidenfeld & Nicolson, London, 1973)

Notin, Jean-Christophe, *La Campagne d'Italie; Les victoires oubliées de la France* (Librairie Académique Perrin, Paris, 2002)

Oliva, Gianni, *Soldati e Ufficiale: L'Escerito Italiano del Risorgimento a Oggi* (Arnalolo Mondadori editore S.p.A., Milano, 2009)

Orpen, Neil, *Victory in Italy* (*Official History of South Africa in the Second World War*) (Purnell, Cape Town, 1975)

Orr, Aileen, *Wojtek The Bear: Polish War Hero* (Birlinn, Edinburgh, 2010)

O'Hara, Vincent, *Struggle for the Middle Sea. The Great Navies at War in the Mediterranean, 1940-1945* (Conway, London, 2009)

O'Sullivan, Edmund, *All my brothers: A London Irish family at war* (privately published, London, 2007)

Pakenham-Walsh, Maj. Gen. R.P., *The History of the Corps of Royal Engineers, Vol. IX, 1938-1948* (The Institution of Royal Engineers, Chatham, 1958)

Pal, Dharm, *The Campaign in Italy: Official History of the Indian Armed Forces in the Second World War* (Orient Longmans, 1960)

Parker, Matthew, *Monte Cassino: The Story of the Hardest-Fought Battle of World War Two* (Headline, London, 2003)

Parkinson, C. Northcote, *Always a Fusilier* (Sampson Low, London, 1949)

Piekalkiewicz, Janusz, *Cassino. Anatomy of the Battle* (Orbis, London, 1980)

Phillips, N.C., *The Sangro to Cassino*, Vol. I of *Italy: The History of New Zealand in the Second World War* (Department of Internal Affairs, Wellington, 1957)

Place, Timothy Harrison, *Military Training in the British Army, 1940-1944. From Dunkirk to D-Day* (Frank Cass, London, 2000)

Platt, Brigadier J.R.I., *The Royal Wiltshire 1907-1967: Britain's Oldest Yeomanry Regiment* (Garnstone Press, London, 1972)

Plowman, Jeffrey, and Rowe, Perry, *The Battles for Monte Cassino: Then and Now* (After the Battle Publications, Old Harlow, Essex, 2011)

Prince, A.R., *Wheeled Odyssey: The Story of the Fifth Reconnaissance Regt, Royal Armoured Corps* (np, nd)

Raghavan, Srinath, *India's War: The Making of South Asia 1939-1945* (Allen Lane, London, 2016)

Ray, Cyril, *Algiers to Austria. The History of 78 Division 1942-1946* (Eyre & Spottiswoode, London, 1952)

Rhodes-Wood, E.H., *A War History of the Royal Pioneer Corps 1939-1945* (Gale & Polden, Aldershot, 1960)

Richardson, General Sir Charles, *Flashback: A Soldier's Story* (William Kimber, London, 1985)

Roberts, Owen N., *31st Field Regiment RA. A Record* (31st Field Regiment Old Comrades Association, Bristol, 1994)

Rosignoli, Guido, *The Allied Forces in Italy 1943-45* (David & Charles, Newton Abbot, 1989)

Ross, Alexander, *Slow March to a Regiment* (Vanwell, Ontario, 1993)

Routledge, Brigadier N.W., *Anti-Aircraft Artillery, 1914-55* (Brassey's, London, 1994)

Ryder, Rowland, *Oliver Leese* (Hamish Hamilton, London, 1987)

St John, Philip A., *Thirty-fourth Infantry Division* (Turner Publishing. Paducah, KY, 1989)

Saunders, Hilary St G., *The Green Beret: The Story of the Commandos 1940-1945* (Michael Joseph, London, 1949)

Schultz, Paul L., *The 85th Infantry Division in World War II* (Infantry Journal Press, Washington DC, 1949)

Senger und Etterlin, General Frido von, *Neither Fear Nor Hope: the wartime career of General Frido von Senger und Etterlin, defender of Cassino* (Macdonald, London, 1963)

Shepperd, G.A., *The Italian Campaign 1943-45. A political and military re-assessment* (Arthur Barker, London, 1968)

Short, Neil, *German Defences in Italy in World War II* (Osprey, Botley, 2006)

Smart, Nick, *Biographical Dictionary of British Generals of the Second World War* (Pen & Sword, Barnsley, 2005)

Smith, E.D., *The Battles for Cassino* (Ian Allan, London, 1975)

——, *Even the Brave Falter* (Robert Hale, London, 1978)

Smyth, Sir John, *The Story of the Victoria Cross 1856-1963* (Frederick Muller, London, 1963)

Squire, Lt Col G.L.A. and Hill, Maj P.G.E., *The Surreys in Italy* (Queen's Royal Surrey Regiment Museum, Guildford, 1992)

Starr, Lt Col Chester G., *From Salerno to the Alps. A History of Fifth Army 1943-1945* (Infantry Journal Press, Washington DC, 1948)

Steer, Frank, *To The Warrior His Arms* (Pen & Sword, Barnsley, 2005)

Stevens, Lt Col G.R., OBE, *Fourth Indian Division* (McLaren & Son, Ontario, 1948)

Strawson, John, *General Sir Richard McCreery* (Published privately by Lady McCreery, 1973)

——, *The Italian Campaign* (Secker & Warburg, London, 1987)

Trevelyan, Raleigh, *Rome '44* (Secker & Warburg, London, 1981)

Truscott, Lucian K., Jr, *Command Missions* (E.P. Dutton, New York, 1954)

Tuker, Francis, *The Pattern of War* (Cassell, London, 1948)

——, *Approach to Battle: A Commentary. Eighth Army, November 1941 to May 1943* (Cassell, London, 1963)

Vokes, Maj Gen Chris, CB CBE DSO CD, *My Story* (Gallery Books, Ottawa, 1985)

Wake, Sir Hereward and Deedes, W.F., *Swift and Bold: The Story of the King's Royal Rifle Corps in the Second World War 1939-1945* (Gale & Polden, Aldershot, 1949)

Wallace, Sir Christopher, *The King's Royal Rifle Corps … the 60th Rifles. A Brief History: 1755 to 1965* (The Royal Green Jackets Museum Trust, Winchester, 2005)

Ward, Robin (Ed.), *The Mirror of Monte Cavallara: An Eighth Army Story by Ray Ward* (Birlinn, Edinburgh, 2006)

Webster, Sir Charles, and Frankland, Noble, *The Strategic Air Offensive Against Germany*, *Vol. I*, *Preparation* (HMSO, London, 1961)

Whiting, Charles, *The Long March on Rome: The Forgotten War* (Century Hutchinson, London, 1987)

Williams, David, *The Black Cats at War. The Story of the 56th (London) Division TA, 1939-1945* (Imperial War Museum, London, 1995)

Williams, Martin, *From Warsaw to Rome. General Anders' Exiled Polish Army in the Second World War* (Pen & Sword, Barnsley, 2017)

Williams, Jeffery, *Princess Patricia's Canadian Light Infantry 1914-1984; Seventy Years' Service* (Leo Cooper with Secker and Warburg, London, 1985)

Williamson, Hugh, *The Fourth Division 1939 to 1945* (Newman Neame, London, 1951)

Wilson, Field Marshal Sir Henry Maitland, *Report by the Supreme Allied Commander Mediterranean to the Combined Chiefs of Staff on the Italian Campaign 8th January 1944 to 10th May 1944* (HMSO, London, 1946)

——, *Report by the Supreme Allied Commander Mediterranean to the Combined Chiefs of Staff on the Italian Campaign, Pt II – 10th May 1944 to 12th August 1944* and *Report by the Supreme Allied Commander Mediterranean to the Combined Chiefs of Staff on the Italian Campaign, Pt III – 13th August 1944 to 12th December 1944* (HMSO, London, 1948)

Wilson, Lt Gen Sir James, *Unusual Undertakings. A Military Memoir* (Pen & Sword, Barnsley, 2002)

Unpublished

Chavasse, Col K.G.F., DSO*, 'Some Memories of My Life'

——, 'Some Memories of 56th Reconnaissance Regiment'

Clark, Lt Col B.D.H., MC GM, Notes on a lecture on the final battle of Cassino given to the Military History Society of Ireland

Davies, Maj. Sir Mervyn, MC, 'An Account of E Company, 2nd London Irish Rifles in Italy'

ffrench–Blake, Col R.L. Valentine, DSO, 'Italian War Diary 1944-45'

Ledwidge, John, Notes on his service with 2nd London Irish Rifles

Lipinski, Romuald, 'My Story' (Memoir: Monte Cassino - 30 April-23 May)

Ormsby, John J., Personal Journal (25 HAA Bty, 9th (Londonderry) HAA Regiment RA (SR)

Parsons, Capt. Alan, MC, 17th Field Regiment RA, extracts from wartime letters to his parents

Scott, Brig T.P.D., DSO, 'Account of the Service of the Irish Brigade' (Feb 1944–May 1945)

Skellorn, John, 'What Did You Do in the War, Grandpa?' (An account of his service with 16th/5th Lancers)

Trousdell, Col P.J.C., notes on his service with 1st Royal Irish Fusiliers in Italy

Woods, Col A.D., MC*, A personal account of his service with 2nd London Irish Rifles in Italy

Newspapers etc.

Advertiser, Adelaide, South Australia
Belfast Telegraph
Daily Telegraph
Faugh A Ballagh Gazette   Regimental Journal of the Royal Irish Fusiliers
London Gazette
New York Times
The Sprig of Shillelagh   Regimental Journal of the Royal Inniskilling Fusiliers
The Times
Crusader   Eighth Army newspaper
Stars and Stripes   US Armed Forces newspaper

Journal of the Society for Army Historical Research
The Journal of Military History

Britain at War Magazine

National Archives Kew

Including a list of all files consulted at the National Archives would consume too much space and so I list only those that were most important.

AIR23/1750 – Photo reconnaissance for the Mediterranean Allied Tactical Air Force and Allied Armies in Italy.

CAB106/361 – Italy: Digest of United States combat experience and battle lessons 1 February-30 September 1944.

CAB106/362 – Italy: 8th Indian Division newsletter on operations March 1944–April 1945.

CAB106/366 – Italy: Account of operations of New Zealand Corps at Cassino 3 February–26 March 1944.

CAB106/369 – Italy: Report on the campaign in Southern Italy 3 September–1 October 1943: includes maps.

CAB106/393 – Italy: Report on operation SHINGLE, the amphibious landing south of Rome, by Colonel A.G. Young, Commander 3rd Beach Group.

CAB106/407 – Italy: Operations of British, Indian and Dominion forces 3 September 1943–2 May 1945; part I, the conquest of southern Italy 3 September 1943–26 March 1944. Section A, chapter I: allied strategy; planning and operations to 21 September 1943.

CAB106/408 – Italy: Operations of British, Indian and Dominion forces 3 September 1943–2 May 1945; part I, the conquest of southern Italy 3 September 1943–26 March 1944. Section A, chapter II: allied strategy; operations 21 September 1943–26 March 1944.

CAB 106/410 – Italy: Operations of British, Indian and Dominion forces 3 September 1943–2 May 1945; part I, the conquest of southern Italy 3 September 1943–26 March 1944. Section C, appendices.

CAB106/411 – Italy: Operations of British, Indian and Dominion forces 3 September 1943–2 May 1945; part I, the conquest of southern Italy 3 September 1943–26 March 1944. Section C, X Corps operations, Salerno to the Garigliano.

CAB106/412 – Italy: Operations of British, Indian and Dominion forces 3 September 1943–2 May 1945; part I, the conquest of southern Italy 3 September 1943–26 March 1944. Section C, appendices.

CAB106/413 – Italy: Operations of British, Indian and Dominion forces 3 September 1943–2 May 1945; part I, the conquest of southern Italy 3 September 1943–26 March 1944. Section D, British forces at Anzio.

CAB106/414 – Italy: Operations of British, Indian and Dominion forces 3 September 1943–2 May 1945; part I, the conquest of southern Italy 3 September 1943–26 March 1944. Section E, New Zealand Corps at Cassino.

CAB106/415 – Italy: Operations of British, Indian and Dominion forces 3 September 1943–2 May 1945; part I, the conquest of southern Italy 3 September 1943–26 March 1944. Section F, German strategy.

CAB106/416 – Italy: operations of British, Indian and Dominion forces 3 September 1943–2 May 1945; part I, the conquest of southern Italy 3 September 1943–26 March 1944. Section G, principal administrative aspects.

CAB106/417 – Italy: Operations of British, Indian and Dominion forces 3 September 1943-2 May 1945; part I, the conquest of southern Italy 3 September 1943-26 March 1944. Section G, appendices.

CAB106/418 – Italy: Operations of British, Indian and Dominion forces 3 September 1943-2 May 1945: part II, the campaign in central Italy 26 March-10 August 1944. Section A, allied strategy.

CAB106/419 – Italy: Operations of British, Indian and Dominion forces 3 Sep. 1943-2 May 1945: part II, the campaign in central Italy 26 March -10 August 1944. Section B, Eighth Army advance to Rome.

CAB106/420 – Italy: Operations of British, Indian and Dominion forces 3 September 1943-2 May 1945: part II, the campaign in central Italy 26 March-10 August 1944; appendices A-B.

CAB106/421 – Italy: Operations of British, Indian and Dominion forces 3 September 1943-2 May 1945: part II, the campaign in central Italy 26 March-10 August 1944; appendices C-F.

CAB106/422 – Italy: Operations of British, Indian and Dominion forces 3 September 1943-2 May 1945: part II, the campaign in central Italy 26 March-10 August 1944. Section C, British forces in the advance from Anzio; Section E, V Corps on the Adriatic coast.

CAB106/423 – Italy: Operations of British, Indian and Dominion forces 3 September 1943-2 May 1945: part II, the campaign in central Italy 26 March-10 August 1944. Section D, Eighth Army advance to Florence.

CAB106/424 – Italy: Operations of British, Indian and Dominion forces 3 Sep. 1943-2 May 1945: part II, the campaign in central Italy 26 March-10 August 1944, appendices.

CAB106/425 – Italy: Operations of British, Indian and Dominion forces 3 September 1943-2 May 1945; part II, the campaign in central Italy 26 March-10 August 1944. Section F, German strategy.

CAB106/467 – Italy: Brief outline of the campaign 3 September 1943-2 May 1945, with illustrations, compiled by Royal Armoured Corps.

CAB106/476 – Italy: History of the United States Fifth Army; part III, 16 November 1943-15 January 1944; the Winter Line.

CAB106/477 – Italy: History of the United States Fifth Army; part IV, 16 January-31 March 1944; Cassino and Anzio.

CAB106/478 – Italy: History of the United States Fifth Army; part V, 1 April-4 June 1944; the drive to Rome.

CAB106/645 – Italy: Despatch on the campaign 10 May-12 August 1944, by General Sir H. Maitland Wilson, Supreme Allied Commander-in-Chief, Mediterranean Theatre.

CAB106/667 – Italy: Despatch on the campaign 3 September 1943-8 January 1944, by General Dwight D. Eisenhower, Supreme Allied Commander, Mediterranean Theatre; copy of original.

CAB106/683 – North Africa & Italy: History of the United States Fifth Army Engineering Section, Vol. II.

CAB106/699 – Italy: Report on the events leading to the bombing of the Abbey of Monte Cassino 15 February 1944, by Major F. Jones.

CAB106/768 – Sicily & Italy: 'The Guns of 6th Army Group, Royal Artillery', account of operations 1943-1945; illustrated.

WO169/18776: war diary 4th Indian Division: App. 1 – Report on Operation REVENGE

WO169/18851: war diary 7 Indian Brigade Recce Squadron, Jan-Jun 1944

WO169/18780: war diary 4th Indian Division RE war diary: Appendices on Cavendish Road, construction of Cavendish Road and Roorkee Track

WO169/18970: war diary 4th/6th Rajputana Rifles 1 Jan-31 Aug 1944

WO169/19006: war diary 1st/9th Gurkha Rifles 1944

WO170/302: war diary X Corps G, Jan 1944 (Report on 46th Division crossing of Garigliano river) Jan 1944

WO170/555: war diary 11 Bde, Jan-Jun 1944

WO170/605: war diary 38 (Ir) Bde, Jan-Mar 1944

WO170/606: war diary 38 (Ir) Bde, Apr-Jun 1944

WO170/825: war diary 16th/5th Lancers, 1944

WO170/829: war diary 17th/21st Lancers, 1944

WO170/836: war diary 1st Derbyshire Yeomanry, Jan-Jun 1944

WO170/841: war diary 2nd Lothians & Border Horse, 1944

WO170/1386: war diary 1/4th Essex Regt, 1944

WO170/1395: war diary 2nd Hampshire Regt, 1944; App. – Account of Y Coy's crossing of Garigliano river

WO170/1399: war diary 2/4th Hampshire Regt, 1944

WO170/1406:   war diary 1st Royal Irish Fusiliers, 1944

WO170/1419: war diary 1st Royal West Kent Regt, Feb-Dec 1944

WO170/1424: war diary 2nd Lancashire Fusiliers, Jan-Aug 1944

WO170/1433: war diary 2nd London Irish Rifles , May 1944

WO170/1479: war diary 2nd Somerset LI, Mar-Dec 1944

WO170/1485: war diary 1/6th East Surrey Regt, Jan-Aug 1944

WO204/8222: Operations at Cassino: II Polish Corps, May 1944

WO204/8196: Assault crossing of the River Liri: employment of Bailey bridges, May 1944

Websites

http://aad.archives.gov

http://www.defensemedianetwork.com/stories The First Special Service Force and Operation RAINCOAT

http://www.studicassinati/db1/jupgrade/index La battaglia di S. Angelo in Theodice e la confusion traifiumi Rapido e Gari (The battle of S. Angelo in Theodice and the confusion between the Rapido and Gari rivers.) by G. Petrucci

http://www.abmc.gov/news

http://www.history.army.mil/medalofhonor US Army Center of Military History, Medal of Honor website

http://www.history.army.mil/brochures US Army Center of Military History/ brochures on campaign histories

http://www.custermen.com/History85htm US Army divisional histories/85th Infantry Division

http://minnesotanationalguard.org History of the 34th Infantry Division

http://www.themedalofhonor.com

http://www.irishbrigade.co.uk History of 38 (Irish) Brigade in the Second World War

http://www.historynet.com/rage-over-the-rapido by Duane Schultz. An account of 36th (Texas) Division's failed attempt to cross the Gari river.

http://www.historynet.com/mark-w-clark-a-general-reappraisal by Robert M. Citino

https://www.nationalarchives.gov.uk/

Index

Formations, units etc.

Allied:

Army Groups

    15 Army Gp/Allied Armies in Italy xxviii, 3, 5, 7, 15, 22

    18 Army Gp, 1, 5, 21

    21 Army Gp, 200

Armies

British:

    First, 21, 207

    Eighth, 22–3, 25, 27, 39, 46, 58, 78, 103, 140, 143–4, 190, 199, 202–203, 205–206, 211, 223–4, 226–7, 230, 234–6, 241, 243–4, 252, 256, 260–1, 264, 271, 273, 287, 307, 315–17, 321, 330–2, 341, 344–5, 349, 352, 355, 361

French:

    Détachement d'armée A, 28

United States:

    Fifth, xxv, xxxvii, xxxix, xl, xliv, 5–7, 12–14, 17–28, 30–1, 33–4, 39, 44–5, 54, 58, 63–4, 71, 76–8, 80, 86, 88–9, 95, 108–10, 114, 116, 118, 129, 133, 140, 192, 194, 198–200, 203–204, 206, 208, 226–7, 235–6, 243, 273, 287, 297–8, 305–307, 315–17, 332, 341, 344–7, 349, 350, 355, 357–8, 361

    Seventh, 2, 7, 30

Corps

British:

    I, 4

    V, 7, 11, 196–7, 205, 211, 226, 234–5, 241

    X, xxxvii, xxxix, 6–7, 13, 22–4, 26, 31, 38, 45–7, 50–1, 53–4, 57, 64, 77–8, 89–90, 103, 131, 145, 199, 205, 219, 297, 322, 350, 359–60

    XIII, xxxviii, xxxix, xl, 7, 11, 104, 193, 196–7, 205, 211, 219, 221–4, 226, 235–6, 242–4, 251, 253–4, 260, 262, 271, 273, 286, 288, 292, 296, 317–18, 321, 331, 351, 361

    XXX, 103, 200–202

Canadian:

    I Cdn Corps, x, 78, 222, 227, 242, 296, 317, 326, 328, 331

French:

    Corps expéditionnaire français (CEF), xxxvii, xxxviii, 28–9, 31, 35, 39, 44–5, 71–4, 76, 78, 90, 145, 200, 203, 287, 305–308, 310–12, 315–16, 321, 328–31, 341, 344, 347, 350, 355, 359, 361

    Corps de montagne, xxxviii, 310

New Zealand:

    Creforce, 104

    New Zealand Corps, xxxviii, xxxix, 89, 95, 100–101, 103–104, 107, 111, 115, 120, 133, 140, 142, 145, 168, 192, 196, 199, 205, 211, 350, 352, 359–60

Polish:

    I, 229

    II, xxiv, xl, 140, 205, 223, 227, 230–1, 235–6, 243–4, 260–1, 264, 271, 273, 288, 292, 296, 317–18, 321, 351, 360–1

United States:

    II, xxxvii, xxxviii, xl, xliv, 7, 22, 28, 31, 35, 45, 47, 50, 53, 55, 58, 60–1, 64, 76, 78, 86, 89–91, 95, 97, 99–100, 102, 118, 145, 200, 203–204, 225–6, 273, 287, 297, 300, 302, 306, 308, 312–13, 315–16, 328, 334, 344, 350, 359

    VI, xxxix, 7, 13, 23, 28–9, 31, 35, 44, 54, 56, 76–7, 92, 131, 193, 199, 203–204, 226–7, 234, 237, 307, 316–17, 321, 328, 331–2, 334, 336, 338, 341, 344–5, 347, 349–50, 361

Divisions

British:

    Gds Armd, 202

    1st Armd, 23, 103–104

    6th Armd, xxxix, 205, 219, 224, 253–4, 317, 322, 331

    7th Armd, 14, 23

8th Armd, 24

1st Inf, 3, 23–4, 80, 92, 332

4th Inf, xxxix, 208, 211, 219, 221, 224, 244, 247, 254, 257, 273, 286, 288

5th Inf, 46–8, 53, 204, 221, 332

15th (Sc), 202

50th (Northumbrian), 14

51st (H'ld), 14

56th (London), 23, 46–8, 50–1, 53–4, 89, 131

78th (Battleaxe), xxxviii, xxxix, 89, 107–108, 133–4, 136, 140–1, 169, 188, 191, 194, 196, 205, 211, 213, 222, 224, 233, 253, 260, 271–3, 279, 281n, 283, 296, 317, 321–2, 331, 352

1st A/b, 14

Canadian:

5th Armd, 203, 205, 317–18

1st Inf, 205

Canadian/US:

1st Special Service Force, 26, 36, 204, 332, 334, 341–2

French:

1st Free French/Motorized, 204, 314, 328, 330

2nd Moroccan, 28–9, 31, 35, 39, 44–5, 76, 226, 307–308, 310

3rd Algerian, 29, 44, 71–2, 74, 76, 214, 226, 313–15, 328

4th Moroccan, 226, 305

Groupement de Tabors Marocains, 204

Groupement Guillaume, 310–11, 329–30

Groupement Bondis, 310–11, 313–15

Groupement Louchet, 311

Indian:

4th Inf, xxxviii, 78, 80, 89, 95, 97, 99, 101–105, 108, 114–16, 132–4, 136, 138, 142–4, 154–7, 159, 165, 169, 174–5, 183, 188, 194, 196, 241, 350, 360

8th Inf, 205, 211, 219, 221, 224, 227, 244, 247–8, 251, 253–4, 256, 318, 321, 331

10th Inf, 241

34th Inf, 105

44th A/b, 196

Italian:

Legnano, 26

Mantova, 26

Piceno, 26

New Zealand:

2nd NZ, xxxviii, 58, 78, 80, 89, 102–104, 115, 123, 126, 134, 136, 141–2, 150, 169n,

174, 188, 194, 196, 205, 219, 227, 321, 331, 350, 360

Polish:

3rd Carpathian, xxxix, 140, 205, 230–1, 261, 288, 290, 294

5th Kresowa, xxiv, 205, 227, 231, 261, 288, 294

South African:

6th Armd, 205, 352

1st Inf, 205

United States:

1st Armd (Old Ironsides), 23, 36, 55, 131, 138, 203–204, 331–2, 334–5, 337–8, 341, 352

2nd Armd, 14

1st Inf, 14

3rd Inf, 22–3, 35, 63, 131, 204, 331, 334–9, 345, 347, 352

5th Inf, 21

9th Inf, 14

15th Inf, 337

34th Inf (Red Bulls), xxxvii, 35–6, 38, 42, 45, 51, 53, 55, 64–5, 70–1, 74, 76, 80–1, 86, 88–9, 91, 105, 116, 118, 123, 140, 149, 203–204, 227, 332, 334, 337–9, 341–2, 350, 359

36th Inf (Texas), xxxvii, xl, 13, 23, 35, 38, 42–3, 45, 50, 53, 55–60, 63, 65, 67, 72, 74, 89, 91, 97, 136, 203–204, 222, 226, 247, 251, 316, 331–4, 338, 341, 347, 350, 359

45th Inf, 13, 23, 35, 55–6, 203–204, 332, 334–5, 338–9, 341, 347

82nd (A/b), 14

85th Inf (Custer), 203–204, 225, 297–8, 302, 304, 316, 341

88th Inf (Blue Devils), 203–204, 225–6, 297, 302–304, 315

Other:

81st (West African), 126n

Brigades/Regiments

British:

2 Armd, 23

8 Armd, 103

9 Armd, 322

23 Armd, 46, 53, 241

25 Tk, 205, 317

26 Armd, 219, 224, 322

1 Gds, 205, 221

10, 208, 221, 244–5, 247, 256–7

11, 188, 190, 196, 213, 278, 281
12, 208, 221, 224, 247, 254, 256, 258, 286–7, 331
13, 47
15, 48
17, 47–8, 53
24 Gds, 92, 205
28, 221, 247, 256
29, 202
36, 141, 211, 317
38 (Ir), 108, 213–14, 217, 222, 224, 227, 233, 273, 274n, 277–9, 281, 284–6, 309, 330
128 (Hants), 50
138, 50–1, 53, 89
167, 50
168, 50–1, 89
169, 50
201 Gds, 38, 47–8
2 Special Service, 54, 89
2 Ind Para, 205, 211
Prestonforce, 208
Canadian:
1 Armd, xxxix, 205, 211, 219, 236, 248, 318, 352
2 Inf, 321
3 Inf, 321
11 Lorried Inf, 327
French:
1 Inf Bde, 204
2 Inf Bde, 204
4 Inf Bde, 204
1st Moroccan Rifle Regt, 204, 310
2nd Moroccan Rifle Regt, 204, 310–11
3rd Algerian Rifle Regt, 204
4th Moroccan Rifle Regt, 35, 204
4th Tunisian Rifle Regt, 204, 310
5th Moroccan Rifle Regt, 35, 44, 204
6th Moroccan Rifle Regt, 204, 310
7th Algerian Rifle Regt, 45, 204
8th Moroccan Rifle Regt, 35, 204
1st *Groupe de Tabors*, 310–11
3rd *Groupe de Tabors*, 310
4th *Groupe de Tabors*, 310
Indian:
5 Inf, 97, 124, 154, 164, 168–9, 196
7 Inf, 97, 112, 124, 174–5, 196
11 Inf, 97, 141, 190, 196
17 Inf, 211, 248, 331
19 Inf, 211, 248–9, 251
21 Inf, 211

Italian:
1° Raggruppamento Motorizzato, 25–6, 205
New Zealand:
4 Armd, 136, 138, 321, 331
5 Inf, 126, 140, 168
6 Inf, 136, 140, 149–51, 164–5, 169, 174
Polish:
Nowogródska Cavalry, 229
2 (Warsaw) Armd, 205, 231, 292
Highland, 229
Carpathian Rifle, 229–30
1 Carpathian Rifle, 230–1, 261, 265
2 Carpathian Rifle, 230–1, 261
5 Wileńska, 231, 261, 263, 321
6 Lwów (Lwówska), 227, 231, 261, 263
United States:
Combat Comd B/1st Armd, 55–6, 89, 134, 175, 331
5 Bde, 22
13 Fd Arty, 71
1108th Engr Gp, 75
7th Inf, 339
11th Inf, 21
15th Inf, 336–8, 341–2
30th Inf, 337–8
133rd Inf, 67–8, 75, 81, 83, 86, 90–1, 140, 337–8
135th Inf, 36, 67–8, 81–2, 86, 88–91, 334, 338
141st Inf, 55, 57, 59, 63, 91, 204
142nd Inf, 25–6, 56, 72, 74–6, 81
143rd Inf, 55, 57, 59, 62
168th Inf, 36, 67–8, 75–6, 81, 88, 90–1, 116, 338, 340
179th Inf, 131
180th Inf, 339–40
337th Inf, 299–300, 316
338th Inf, 299–300, 316
339th Inf, 203, 297–300
349th Inf, 302, 304
350th Inf, 302–303, 310
351st Inf, 204, 300, 302, 304–305, 311

Units (Regiments/Battalions)
British:
5th (R. Ir.) Lncrs, 224
12th Lncrs, 23
16th/5th Lncrs, 224, 273, 276–7, 279, 281, 284–5
17th/21st Lncrs, xxxiv, 244, 254, 256, 259, 281

North Irish Horse, 321
1st Derby Yeo, 317, 322
2nd Lothians & Border Yeo, 221, 254, 256, 258, 284–5
40th R. Tanks, xxxv, 47
46th R. Tanks, 331
4th Recce Regt, 208, 221
56th Recce Regt, 191
1st Fd Regt, 178
11th Fd Regt, 139, 162
17th Fd Regt, 273, 287
31st Fd Regt, 139
98th Fd Regt, 151
138th Fd Regt, 211
102nd Med. Regt, 264
140th Med. Regt, 264
57th LAA Regt, 100, 132
14th A/Tk Regt, 257
64th A/Tk Regt, 281
149th A/Tk Regt, 132
3rd Gren Gds, 287, 331
5th Gren Gds, 95
1st Cldsm Gds, 202
3rd Cldsm Gds, 38
2nd Scots Gds, 38
3rd Welsh Gds, 331
2/5th Queen's, 50
2/6th Queen's, 50
2/7th Queen's, 50
5th Buffs, 191, 211
1st R. Fus., 248, 254, 257, 288
2nd R. Fus., 254
8th R. Fus., 50–1
9th R. Fus., 50
2nd King's (L'pool), 247
2nd Somerset LI, 208, 247
2nd Beds & Herts, 208, 245–6
2/5th Leicester, 53
1st Green Howards, 48, 51
2nd R. Scots Fus., 48
2nd Lancs Fus., 1, 141, 196, 213, 278, 281–2, 296
2nd Cameronians, 51
2nd R. Innisk. Fus., 47–8
6th R. Innisk. Fus., 213–14, 217, 273–4, 276–7, 285
1st E. Surrey, 141
1/6th E. Surrey, 245–6
1st R. Sussex, 99, 112, 118–19, 122–4, 139, 196

2nd Duke of Cornwall's LI, 247, 256
2nd Hampshire, 50
2/4th Hampshire, 247, 256, 274
6th Black Watch, 254, 256, 258
7th Ox. & Bucks. LI, 50
1/4th Essex, xxxv, 123, 154–5, 157, 162, 174, 176, 178–9, 181–2, 190, 195, 211
2/4th Essex, xxxv
2nd Sherwood Foresters, 369n
1st Loyals, 131
2nd Northamptons, 48
5th Northamptons, 141, 196, 281
10th R. Berkshire, 50
1st R. West Kent, 256, 258, 276, 288
6th R. West Kent, 188, 190, 192, 211, 274
1st King's Own Yorks LI, 48
2nd Wiltshire, 47–8
16th Durham LI, 54
6th Seaforth Hldrs, 47–8
2nd Cameron Hldrs, 123, 132
2nd R. Ulster Rifles, 214, 274n
1st R. Ir. Fus, xxxvi, 108, 213–14, 222, 228, 273, 274n, 283–5, 330
1st A. & S. Hldrs, 248, 251, 254
8th A. & S. Hldrs, 196, 211
10th Rifle Bde, 317
1st Kensington, 108, 281
1st London Scottish, 51
1st London Irish, 50
2nd London Irish, xxv, xxvi, 117, 213, 273, 276, 281, 352
No.9 (Army) Cdo, 38, 54, 89
No.10 (Inter-Allied) Cdo, 54, 288
40 (RM) Cdo, 47, 50–1
43rd (RM) Cdo, 54
6th Para Bn, 11
65th Gen. Hosp., 219
92nd Gen. Hosp., 219
152nd Fd Amb., 224
Hood Bn, 102
Misc:
358 Fd Bty, 211
392 SP Bty, 151
25 HAA Bty, 193
214 Fd Coy RE, 224, 273
7 Fd Coy RE, 254
59 Fd Coy RE, 254
225 Fd Coy RE, 254
577 Fd Coy RE, 330
578 Fd Coy RE, 254

586 Fd Coy RE, 254
8 Fd Sqn RE, 254
Force II, 50
No. 2 Spt Gp, 208
A Tp 40 Cdo, 50
P Tp 40 Cdo, 50
X Tp 40 Cdo, 50
1801 (Bailey) Pln RASC, 356
Special Night Squads, 214, 274n
Canadian:
  Lord Strathcona's Horse, 321
  11th (Ontario) Armd, 211, 254, 317
  12th (Three Rivers) Armd, 321
  14th (Calgary) Armd, 211, 253
  R. Cdn Regt, 321
  Westminster Regt, 322, 326
  Irish Regt of Canada, 330
Misc:
  Recce Tp Westminster Regt, 322
French:
  3rd Algerian Spahis, 72, 310
  7th African Chasseurs, 71, 310
  8th African Chasseurs, 310
  63rd Arty, 71
  64th Arty, 71
  67th Arty, 71
  69th Arty, 310, 312
  1st/4th Tunisian Rifle Regt, 72
  2nd/4th Tunisian Rifle Regt, 72
  3rd/4th Tunisian Rifle Regt, 72
  2nd/1st Moroccan Rifle Regt, 310
  3rd/1st Moroccan Rifle Regt, 310
  1st/8th Moroccan Rifle Regt, 308
Misc:
  9 Coy, 3rd/4th Tunisian Rifle Regt, 72–3
  11 Coy, 3rd/4th Tunisian Rifle Regt, 72–3
Indian:
  Bengal Sappers & Miners, 162
  Madras Sappers & Miners, 138, 174
  1st/6th Rajput Rifles, 123–4, 154, 156–62,
    165, 173–4, 178
  4th/6th Rajput Rifles, 100, 123, 132, 162–3,
    174, 178–9, 196
  4th (Outram's) Bn, 196
  3rd/8th Punjab Regt, 248–50, 252, 254
  4th/16th Punjab Regt, xxxv, 120, 139, 196
  1st/12th Frontier Force Regt, 248–9
  6th/13th Frontier Force Rifles, 251, 257
  1st/2nd Gurkha (Goorkha) Rifles, 100,
    104–105, 123, 139, 154, 156–7, 159–63,

  165–7, 169, 173–4, 176, 182, 188, 194–6
  1st/5th Gurkha Rifles, 249, 254, 275, 331
  6th Gurkha Rifles, 126n
  2nd/7th Gurkha Rifles, 100, 123, 132, 179,
    190
  1st/9th Gurkha Rifles, xxxv, 123-5, 132
  26th Fd Amb., 356
Misc:
  7 Bde Recce Sqn, 175, 184
  11 Fd Pk Coy RIE, 138
  12 Fd Coy RIE, 100
New Zealand:
  Divisional Cavalry, 128, 141, 191
  4th Fd Regt, 193, 263–4
  19th Armd Regt, 128, 149, 151, 164, 166, 188
  20th Armd Regt, 156, 182
  23rd Bn, 140–1, 188, 191
  24th Bn, 140, 164, 173, 195
  25th Bn, 140, 149, 151, 153, 164, 166–7, 186,
    188, 191
  26th Bn, 150–1, 153, 166–7, 174, 191
  27th Bn, 140
  28th (Maori) Bn, 124, 128–9, 140, 174, 186,
    188
Misc:
  4 Fd Coy NZ Engrs, 156
  5 Fd Pk Coy NZ Engrs, 186
  6 Fd Coy NZ Engrs, 175
Polish:
  1st Krechowiecki Armd Regt, 231
  4th Skorpion Armd Regt, 231, 264, 289, 294
  6th Children of Lwów Armd Regt, 231
  12th Podolski Lncrs, 231, 294, 295
  15th Poznanski Lncrs (Poznan Uhlans), 231,
    288, 289
  7th Reserve Tank Bn, 231
  7th Horse Arty Regt, 263
  1st Carpathian Fd Regt, 381n
  2nd Carpathian Fd Regt, 381n
  3rd Carpathian Fd Regt, 381n
  4th Kresowa Fd Regt, 381n
  5th Kresowa Fd Regt, 381n
  5th Lt Arty Regt, 289, 381n
  6th Kresowa Fd Regt, 381n
  3rd LAA Regt, 381n
  5th LAA Regt, 381n
  7th LAA Regt, 381n
  8th LAA Regt, 381n
  3rd A/Tk Regt, 381n
  5th A/Tk Regt, 381n

7th A/Tk Regt, 289, 381n
1st Survey Regt, 381n
1st Carpathian Bn, 265, 267
2nd Carpathian Bn, 265, 267
4th Carpathian Bn, 290–1, 292, 294
5th Carpathian Bn, 290
6th Carpathian Bn, 290, 292
13th Wileńska Bn, xxiv, 263
15th Wileńska Bn, 263, 290
16th Lwowski Bn, 289, 290
17th Lwowski Bn, 265, 289–90, 292
18th Lwowski Bn, 263, 289
6th Gen. Hosp., 356
Misc:
  Army Gp Polish Arty, 263
  22 Supply Coy, 231, 233
United States:
  751st Tank Bn, 342
  753rd Tank Bn, 81
  755th Lt Tank Bn, 205, 310
  756th Tank Bn, 67, 75, 81, 83, 300
  757th Tank Bn, 205, 310
  760th Tank Bn, 75, 81, 85, 175, 304
  151st Fd Arty Bn, 86
  175th Fd Arty Bn, 75
  913th Fd Arty Bn, 304
  48th Combat Engr Bn, 84, 164
  235th Engr Bn, 75
  2nd/30th Inf, 337
  1st/133rd Inf, 86, 88
  2nd/133rd Inf, 338
  3rd/133rd Inf, xxxiv, 83, 86, 88, 91
  1st/135th Inf, 68, 86, 88
  2nd/135th Inf, 81, 86–8
  3rd/135th Inf, 81, 86, 341
  1st/141st Inf, 59
  1st/143rd Inf, 59
  2nd/143rd Inf, 59
  3rd/143rd Inf, 59
  3rd/157th Inf, 335
  1st/168th Inf, 90, 341
  3rd/168th Inf, 81, 82
  1st/337th Inf, 300
  2nd/337th Inf, 316
  3rd/337th Inf, 299
  1st/338th Inf, 299–300
  3rd/338th Inf, 299–300
  1st/351st Inf, 204, 300, 304–305
  2nd/351st Inf, 302
  100th Inf Bn, 67–8, 90, 227, 342

Misc:
  Coy B 756th Tank Bn, 83
  Coy C 760th Tank Bn, 69, 85
  Coy I 133rd Inf Regt, 86, 91
  Coy K 133rd Inf Regt, 88, 91
  Coy L 133rd Inf Regt, 88, 91
  Coy L 168th Inf Regt, 88
  91st Cav Recce Sqn, 55, 140, 316

Axis
Army Groups
  Heeresgruppe B 8, 11, 27
  Heeresgruppe C 8, 38
  Heeresgruppe North, 10
  Heeresgruppe von Zangen, 241
Armies
German:
  Sixth, 7, 34
  Tenth, xxxiv, 241–2, 287, 308, 315, 347, 349,
    351–60
  Fourteenth, 76–8, 92, 123, 131, 234, 241–2,
    334, 338, 347, 349
  Panzerarmee Afrika, 8, 24
Italian:
  Eighth, 3
Corps
  XIV Panzerkorps, 9, 17, 26, 32, 34–5, 44–5,
    51, 61, 63, 74, 77, 166–7, 189, 237–9, 242,
    273, 307–308, 313, 330, 347, 350–1, 360–1
  LI Mountain, 34, 237, 239, 241, 287, 331,
    351, 361
  LXXVI Panzerkorps, 8, 77, 334
  Korpsgruppe Hauck, 241
Divisions
  3rd PzGren, 39, 78, 315, 334
  7th Pz, 34
  15th PzGren, 9, 39, 57, 61, 74, 78, 116, 184,
    237, 240, 330, 347
  16th Pz, 9
  16th PzGren, 315
  17th Pz, 34
  3rd PzGren, 39, 78, 315, 334
  5th Gebirgs, 31, 39, 78, 237, 241–2
  21st Pz, 103
  26th Pz, 8, 11, 223, 241, 314–15, 328–9, 331
  29th PzGren, 8, 11, 27, 36, 39, 64, 67, 78,
    223, 241–2
  44th *Hoch-und-Deutschmeister*, 27, 35–6, 39,
    65, 73–4, 78, 237, 241
  65th Inf, 334

71st Inf, 39, 74, 78, 237, 240, 273, 305,
    307–308, 310, 313, 330, 347, 359
90th Gren/PzGren, 39, 51, 64, 74, 78,
    88, 103, 129, 141, 223, 241–2, 280, 287,
    308–309, 315, 317, 321
92nd PzGren, 223, 241, 347
94th Inf, 39, 48, 50–1, 77, 237, 240, 273, 300,
    310, 313, 316, 330, 347
114th *Jäger*, 131, 237, 240–1
305th Gren., 31, 35, 241, 315
334th Inf, 241, 315
362nd Inf, 131, 338
715th Gren, 338, 339
1st *Fallschirmjäger*, 8, 78, 82, 141, 239, 241,
    321
4th *Fallschirmjäger*, 334
Hermann Göring, 9, 36, 39, 67, 223, 241,
    339, 341–2
Regiments/Brigades
    3rd Cav Regt, 34
    8th Gren Regt, 315
    26th Pz Regt, 330
    67th PzGren Regt, 329
    85th *G-jgr* Regt, 45, 241
    100th Mtn Regt, 35
    104th PzGren Regt, 56, 237
    115th PzGren Regt, 35, 256
    129th PzGren Regt, 56
    131st Gren Regt, 66, 240
    132nd Gren Regt, 66, 241
    132nd PzGren Regt, 36
    134th Gren Regt, 66, 241
    191st Gren Regt, 74
    200th Gren Regt, 97, 308
    211th Gren Regt, 57, 86, 142
    276th Gren Regt, 330
    576th Gren Regt, 241
    721st *Jgr* Regt, 237, 241
    724th *Jgr* Regt, 237
    741st *Jgr* Regt, 241
    1027th Gren Regt, 315, 334
    1060th Gren Regt, 338
    Infantry Lehr Regt, 334
    3rd *F-jgr* Regt, 142, 261, 289
    5th *F-jgr* Regt, 117
Battalions
    3rd Alpine, 241, 328
    4th Alpine, 241
    44th Recce, 240
    94th Füsilier, 240

I/9th PzGren, 314
II/100th Mtn, 241
I/104th PzGren, 330
II/104th PzGren, 313
115th Recce, 56, 240
I/115th PzGren, 241
II/115th PzGren, 241
III/115th PzGren, 241
I/129th PzGren, 57
I/134th Gren, 328
305th Füsilier, 241
III/361st PzGren, 128
620th Ost Bn, 316
II/1st *F-jgr*, 186
I/3rd *F-jgr*, 142, 167
II/3rd *F-jgr*, 142, 146
III/3rd *F-jgr*, 82
I/4th *F-jgr*, 177, 185
II/4th *F-jgr*, 185–6
III/4th *F-jgr*, 183–6
F-jgr MG Bn, 174, 256
HG Recce Bn, 338, 345
Misc:
    K/gp Gräser, 92
    K/gp Pfeiffer, 92
    71st *Werfer* Regt, 141, 148, 158
    Bode Blocking Gp, 241

Naval:
    12th Cruiser Sqn, 11

Air:
    Bomber Comd, 114
    Coastal Air Force, 137
    Desert Air Force, xxxix, 103, 110, 111, 144,
        158, 231, 355
        see also 1st Tactical AF
    Luftflotte I, 10
    Luftflotte II, 10, 27
    Mediterranean Air Comd (MAC), 111
    Mediterranean Allied Air Forces (MAAF),
        111, 116, 142, 207
    Mediterranean Allied Strategic AF
        (MASAF), 111, 137, 200, 207
    XII Air Support Comd, 57, 137, 144
    Twelfth Air Force, 111–12, 158
    Fifteenth Air Force, 111–12
    XV AF Service Comd, 111
    1st Tactical AF, 355n
        see also Desert AF

2nd Tactical AF, 355n
3rd Tactical AF, 355n
No.205 Gp RAF, 111
5th Bombardment Wing, 113–14
2nd Bombardment Gp, 113
92nd Bombardment Gp, 113
97th Bombardment Gp, 113
301st Bombardment Gp, 113
No.651 Sqn RAF, 264

Allied Central Mediterranean Force (ACMF),
   133
Allied Forces HQ (AFHQ), London, 22

Bavarian War Academy, 9
British Expeditionary Force, 3, 202

Coldstream Guards, 201
Combined Chiefs of Staff (Allied), 2, 6–7
Commandos, 13, 23, 38
Creforce, 104

'Desert Rats', 14, 23
Dorsetshire Regiment, 247

Forward Surgical Units, 355
Forward Transfusion Units, 355

General Staff (German), 39
Grenadier Guards, 103

Indian Army, xxxiv, 105, 250
Indian Army Staff College, 202

King's Regiment, 221

Labour Aux. Service (Polish), 231
Lancashire Fusiliers, 1
Luftwaffe, xxxix, 6, 10, 12, 22, 39, 76, 115, 118,
   166, 169, 174, 189, 192–3, 223, 241, 333,
   350, 355

Middle East Staff College, 202n
Mobile Ops Room Unit (MORU), 355

New Zealand Expeditionary Force, 360

OKW Auffrisschungstab München, 7

Panzerjäger, 76

Pestki, 231
'Polar Bears', 297
Polish Women's Aux. Service (PSK), 231
Port Ammunition Detachments, 357
Port Ordnance Detachments, 257

Rangers (US Army), 13, 23
Red Army, 3, 228-30
'Red Eagles', 105
Reichswehr, 10, 44
Rover David system, 355
Royal Army Ordnance Corps (RAOC), 357
Royal Army Service Corps (RASC), xxxvii,
   356–7
Royal Canadian Army Service Corps, 381n
Royal Canadian Electrical & Mechanical Engrs,
   253
Royal Canadian Engineers, 254
Royal Canadian Ordnance Corps, 381n
Royal Corps of Signals, xxvi, 204
Royal Electrical & Mechanical, 357
Royal Engineers, 356
Royal Indian Engineers, 100, 254
Royal Navy, 11
Royal Ulster Rifles, 274n

Staff College, 23
Ships:
   HMS *Abdiel*, 11
   MS *Batory*, 230
   USS *Boise*, 11

Southern Command, 4

Territorial Army (TA), xxxv, 23
Todt Organization, 44, 208

United States Army Air Forces (USAAF),
   xxxiii, 45, 71, 110–11, 163, 193, 355
United States Navy, 7, 11, 243, 333

West Point, 21

Individuals
Adye, Lt Col John, 183
Aldinger, Capt., 183
Alexander, Gen. Sir Harold, xxxviii, xl, 1, 3,
   5–7, 14–15, 22–4, 28, 31, 38, 58–9, 77–8, 80,
   86, 89, 91, 105, 108–109, 111, 131, 133–4,
   142, 190, 192, 198–200, 203, 205–206, 208,

222–5, 237, 242–4, 316–17, 331–2, 338, 345–6, 349, 350–2, 357–8, 360–2
Allen, Gen., 138
Allfrey, Lt Gen. Charles, 205, 241
Allkin, L/Cpl, 281
Anders, Lt Gen. Władysław, xxiv, xl, 205, 227, 229–30, 233, 236, 260–2, 264, 267, 271, 273, 286, 288–90, 292, 360
Andrae, Lt Col, 149
Antolak, Sgt Sylvester MoH, 336–7
Arkwright, Brig. R.H.E., 46
Arnold, Gen. Henry H. 'Hap', 137
Atkinson, Rick, 345
Auchinleck, Gen Sir Claude, 5, 24

Baade, Maj. Gen. Ernst-Günther, 88, 129, 141–2, 287, 321
Bacqué, Cmdt, 72–3
Badoglio, Marshal Pietro, 3
Baduila, 20
Baker, Lt Jimmy, 285
Barfoot, T/Sgt Van T. MoH, 335–6
Barnes, Cpl J.A. 'Jimmy', 280, 282, 352, 382n
Barton, Maj. Patrick, 182, 184
Basil the Great, St, xliii
Bastaïe, Col Radiguet de la, 44, 71
Bastico, Marshal Ettore, 11
Bateman, Brig., 154, 165
Becker, Dr Maximilian, 363n
Beckett, Maj. D.A., 155, 178–9, 181
Behr, Col, 74
Belisarius, 20
Benedict of Nursia/ Benedetto da Norcia, St, xli–xlvi, xlviii, 9
Benedict XVI, Pope, xlvi
Berne, Cmdt, 72–3
Bertharius, Abbot, xlv
Bessel, Maj. Gen. Hans, 15, 40–1, 44
Białecki, Lt, 267
Blaxland, Gregory, 103, 105, 112
Blumenson, 22, 54, 78, 102, 158, 345, 358
Boatner, Col. Mark, 67, 116–17
Bode, Col, 241
Bock, 10
Böhmler, Rudolph, 16, 36, 39, 44, 63–4, 86–7, 146, 150, 152–3, 167, 175, 186, 190
Bohusz-Szyszko, Maj. Gen, Zigmunt, 229–30
Bonaparte, Napoleon, xlvi
Bond, Capt. Arthur, 125
Bond, Lt Harold L., 63, 108, 116

Bondis, Col, 310–11
Bonifant, Lt Col, 150–1, 167, 169
Bonin, von, Col, 8
Borch, Rittmeister von der, 311–12
Böttcher, Cpl, 8
Boucher, Brig. Charles, 248–9
Bourquin, Maj. Gen. Alexander, 237, 241
Bouscary, Capt., 45
Brady, Col Brookner W., 297–8
Brann, Brig. Gen. Donald W., 344
Bredin, Lt Col H.E.N. 'Bala' DSO MC*, 214, 274, 276–8, 285
Brooke, FM Sir Alan, 133, 198, 242, 357
Brookes, Albert Cecil MBE (Mr Blockbuster), 110
Brosset, Gen.de Brig., 204, 310, 314–15, 328, 330
Buckley, Christopher, 110
Burns, Lt Gen. E.L.M. 'Tommy', 205, 328
Butler, Brig. Gen. Frederick B., 72, 76

Caddick-Adams, Peter, 112, 358
Caledon, Earl of, 3
Cannon, Maj. Gen. John K., 111, 134, 200
Carey, Lt, 153
Champeny, Col Arthur S., 302, 304–305
Chapell, Maj. L.W.A. MC, 182
Chol, Lt, 73
Christian, Pte Herbert F. MoH, 342, 344
Churchill, Winston, xxxiv, xxxvii, 1–6, 27, 30, 103, 192, 198–9, 213n, 230, 347, 357
Clark, Capt. (later Lt Col) Brian MC GM, xxiii, xxxvi, 108, 228, 285
Clark, Maj. Colin Douglas MC, 352
Clark, Lloyd, 64
Clark, Lt Gen Mark W., xxxvii–xxxix, xl, 5, 13–14, 20–4, 27–8, 30–1, 33, 54, 57–9, 61, 63, 65, 71–4, 76–8, 89–91, 103, 108–10, 116, 119–20, 131, 134–6, 142, 144, 190, 192, 200, 305, 306, 311, 315, 316, 332, 338, 344–7, 349–50, 351, 358–61
Clarke, Maj. Jimmy MC*, xxiii, 285
Constantine the African, xlv
Cook, Maj. Reggie, 281
Coombs, Lt Pat G., 304
Córdoba, Gen. Gonzalo Fernández, 20
Coulter, Maj. Gen. John B., 203, 297, 299, 316
Crawford, Lt Col Joseph B. 302
Crowder, Lt Herbert, 183

Cruickshank, Maj. Malcolm, 183
Cunningham, Adm. Sir Andrew, 5–6
Czech, Sect. Ldr, 295
Dapino, Gen. Vincenzo, 26
Darlan, Adm. François, 22
Davies, Maj. Mervyn MC, xxiii, 279–80
Davila, S/Sgt Rudolph B. MoH, 339
Dawley, Maj. Gen. Ernest, 13–14, 23
Dervishian, T/Sgt Ernest H. MoH, 335
Desiderius, Abbot, xlv
D'Este, Carlo, 27
Devers, Gen. Jacob, 111, 113, 116, 142
Diamare, Abbot Gregorio, 114
Dickson, AVM William, 355
Dimoline, Brig. Harry K. 'Ken', 101–102, 104,
   115, 118, 123, 133, 165
Dobree, Brig. Thomas, 249
Dodelier, Cmdt, 328
Dody, Maj. Gen. André, 28, 35, 44, 204,
   307–309, 341
Drayton, Maj. Denis, 179
Drinkall, Capt. Michael, 156–7, 159
Duch, Maj. Gen. Bronisław, 205
Dutko, Pfc John MoH, 335

Eagles, Maj. Gen. William W., 204, 332
Eaker, Lt Gen. Ira C., 111–13, 116, 137, 142
Eisenhower, Gen. Dwight D., xl, 2, 5–6, 12, 14,
   23, 27–8, 111, 361
Engs, Ruth Clifford, xlv
Esson, 2/Lt, 140
Evans, Maj. Bradford E. (USAAF), 114–16
Evans, Maj. (Gurkhas), 160
Evelegh, Maj. Gen. Vyvyan, 205

Fabius, 20
Fanslau, Lt Col, 290–1
Feurstein, Gen. Valentin, 237, 271
Foltin, Maj, 147
Forty, George, 34
Fowler, 2/Lt Thomas W. MoH, 335–6
Franek, Lt Gen. Fritz, 39
Franklyn-Vaile, Maj. Laurie, 285
French, Lt J.R.M., MC, 162
ffrench-Blake, Lt Col Val DSO, 221
Ford, Sgt Grenville MM, 356
Foucaucourt, Cmdt de, 308
Fowler-Esson, Lt Col, 256–7
Freyberg, Lt Gen. Sir Bernard 'Tiny', xxxviii,
   xl, 58, 95, 97, 101–105, 108–11, 113–15,

118, 123, 131–8, 141–2, 145, 150, 153, 163,
   165–9, 174–5, 184, 186, 188, 190, 192–3,
   205, 211, 229, 321, 351, 359–60
Fridolin, St, 34
Fry, Col J.C., 302

Galloway, Maj. Gen. Sandy, 165, 169, 179, 182,
   184, 188, 194, 202n
Galt, Capt. William W. MoH, 341
Gandoët, Cmdt Paul, 72–3
Gause, Maj Gen Alfred, 8
George VI, King, 139, 251
Gill, Maj. Robert P., 224, 274, 285
Glennie, Lt Col, 119–20, 122–3
Glinski, Col, 292
Gobillot, Capt., 45
Goff, Lt Col Ion, 227, 277
Gort, FM Lord VC, 202
Grannell, Maj. Peter, 279–80
Gregory the Great, xlv
Gregson-Ellis, Maj. Gen. P., 46, 204, 332
Gruenther, Gen. Al, 57, 76, 108–10, 142
Guillaume, Gen. Augustin, 204, 305, 310–11
Gurbiel, 2/Lt Kazimierz, 295

Haislip, Maj. Gen. Wade H., 203
Hall, S/Sgt George J. MoH, 335
Haller, Gen, 230
Hannibal, 20, 175
Hanson, Col, 186
Harding, Maj. Gen. John, xxxviii, 108–109,
   199, 222–3, 360
Harmon, Maj. Gen. Ernest, 36, 59, 138, 331,
   337, 352
Harris, ACM Sir Arthur, 114
Harris, Lt H.G., 245
Hartmann, Gen. Otto, 242, 305, 316
Hauck, Maj. Gen. Friedrich-Wilhelm, 241
Hawkesworth, Maj. Gen. John, 46–7
Hayman-Joyce, Maj. Gen. John, 208
Heber-Percy, Brig. A.G.W., 254
Heidrich, Lt Gen. Richard, 88, 141, 146–7,
   149, 153, 158, 166–8, 184, 192, 237, 241–2,
   256, 262, 287, 292, 297, 318, 321
Heilmann, Col, 146, 149–50, 166
Herr, Gen. Traugott, 8
Heysom, Gp Capt. David, 355
Hillian, Lt MC, 281
Hitler, Adolf, 5, 7–8, 11–12, 17–18, 27, 131,
   149, 228–9, 242, 315

Hoffmeister, Maj. Gen. B.M. 'Bert', 205
Holworthy, Maj. Gen. A.W.W. DSO MC, 196
Hopkinson, Maj. Gen., 11
Horrocks, Lt Gen. Brian, 22, 24, 103–104
Horsfall, Lt Col John, xxiii, xxv, 216, 224, 227,
    277–81, 352
Hoth, Gen., 34
Hougen, Lt Col John H., 81, 88
Hube, Lt Gen. Hans-Valentin, 9, 17, 32
Hughes, Col Oliver W., 299
Hugonot, Gen, 356

Ichac, Pierre, 308
Inwood, Maj. P.R., 158
Ireland, Kiel, 379n

Jamrowski, Lt, 186
Jefferson, Fus. Francis VC, 282–3
Jennings, Lt, 195
John the Baptist, St, xliv
John XXII Pope, xlvi
Johnson, Pte Eldon H. MoH, 342
Jordy, Lt, 73
Juin, Gen. Alphonse, xxxvii, 28–31, 35,
    39, 44–5, 64, 66, 71–4, 76, 90, 182, 200,
    203–204, 206, 226–7, 236, 242, 273, 287,
    297, 302, 305, 307, 309–13, 315, 328, 330,
    341, 347, 350, 359–60

Keightley, Maj. Gen. Charles, xl, 140, 194, 233,
    272–3, 278, 281, 285
Kelleher, Father Dan MC, 222
Kendall, Lt Col Raymond E., 302–304
Kendrew, Brig. Douglas 'Joe', 50
Kerr, Maj. John MC, 285
Kesselring, FM Albrecht (Albert), 7–10, 12–15,
    17–18, 20, 27, 38, 40, 51, 71, 76–8, 129, 166,
    207, 222–3, 241–2, 287, 292, 305, 307–308,
    313, 315, 347, 349, 351, 359–60
Kessler, Pfc Patrick L. MoH, 335
Ketteley, Maj. Frank MC, 178
Keyes, Maj. Gen. Geoffrey, xl, xliv, 59, 65, 68,
    70, 72, 74–6, 97, 111, 200, 226, 287, 297,
    315–16, 344–5, 359
Kingsmill, Capt. Tony, 253
Kippenberger, Brig. Howard, 101, 115, 124,
    126, 128, 134, 136, 140, 150, 360
Kirkman, Lt Gen. Sidney, 193, 196, 205, 236,
    271, 273, 292
Klaus, 2/Lt Charles MM, 173

Klein, Lt Jupp, xxxvi, 278–9, 281, 284
Kleist, FM von, 242
Kobashigawa, T/Sgt Yeiki MoH, 342
Kurek, Col Wincenty, 321

La Ciociara, 384n
Lara, Alfonzo, 339
Lara, Pfc Salvador MoH, 339
Lattre, Gen. Jean de Lattre de Tassigny *see*
    Tassigny
Leclerc, Gen. Philippe, 103
Lecomte, Lt, 308
Leeks, Maj., 152–3
Leese, Lt Gen. Sir Oliver Bt, xl, 22, 24, 58, 78,
    80, 103, 144, 200–202, 205, 235–6, 261–2,
    271, 273, 286, 288, 317–18, 330, 344, 360
Leigh-Mallory, AM Sir Trafford, 355
Lemelsen, Gen Joachim, 349
Lemnitzer, Gen., 22, 91
Loewen, Brig. C.E., 332
Loftus-Tottenham, Maj. Gen. Freddie, 126n
Loftus-Tottenham, Lt John, 126n
Loftus-Tottenham, Lt Ralph, 126
Loren, Sophia, 384n
Louchet, Gen., 311
Lovatt, Lt Ken, 277
Loveday, Lt Col John, 277
Lovett, Brig. Oscar de T., 97, 100, 112, 116–18,
    120, 122–3
Lucas, Maj. Gen. John P., 14, 28, 30, 35, 44, 55,
    63–4, 76
Lunn-Rockcliffe, Maj. Paul, 278

MacDuff, Lt Col, 149
MacKay, Capt. John MC, 356
McCall, S/Sgt Thomas E. MoH, 62–3
McCreery, Lt Gen. Richard, xxxvii, 13, 22–6,
    31, 38, 45–6, 53–4, 58, 89, 199, 205, 322,
    359
McGaffin, Lt Col, 151
McGill, Pte, 281
McInnes, Maj., 153
McNair, Lt Gen. Leslie, 116
Mack, Col Stephen B., 137
Mackensen, Col Gen. Eberhard von, 92, 123,
    131, 287, 334, 338, 347, 349
Madden, Lt Col, 258
Mahony, Maj. John Keefer VC, 322, 326–7
Majdalany, Maj. Fred, 1, 20, 107–109, 112, 129,
    175, 184, 187, 198, 213, 351

Mallinson, Lt, 195
'Marcus Aurelius Clarkus', 22
Marshall, Col. Carley L., 67
Marshall, Gen. George, 2–3, 6–7, 21–2, 27–8, 225
Marshall, Maj., 158
Mason-MacFarlane, Maj. Gen. Noel, 230
Massey, Frank, 150
Matthews, Cpl J.B. DCM, 331
Maurus, St, xliii
Mayo, Sgt Eddie MM, 280
Michel, Capt., 45
Middleton, Maj. Gen. Troy H., 35
Mills, Pte James H. MoH, 337
Mitchell, Pte George Allan VC, 51–3
Molony, C.J.C., 153, 174, 236, 240, 312, 351
Monsabert, Gen. Aimé de Goislard de, 44, 71, 204–205, 208, 313–14, 328–30
Montgomery, Gen. Bernard L., 2, 5–6, 15, 22, 24, 27, 103–105, 200–202, 235, 317–18, 358
Moravia, Albert, 384n
Morris, Sgt Alan, 156–7
Murat, Joachim, xlvi
Murphy, Audie, 337
Murphy, Brig. W.C., 205
Murray, Lt Angus, 156–7
Mussolini, Benito, 3, 7–8, 20

Nakamine, Pte Shinyei MoH, 342
Nangle, Lt Col, 156
Napoleon *see* Bonaparte
Nelson, Adm. Lord, 203
Neuhoff, Oberfeldwebel, 150–1
Newman, Lt Beryl R. MoH, 338
Noble, Lt Col Arthur, 154, 182
Normand, Lt, 195
Nowina-Sawicki, Col Witold, 227
Nugent von Westmeath, Laval Graf, xlvi

O'Daniel, Maj. Gen. John W. 'Iron Mike', 204, 332, 336, 338, 341, 352
O'Dowd, Maj. Francis DSO, 356
O'Reilly, Cpl Edward MM, 280
Obama, President, 339
Odzierzynski, Maj. Gen. R.W. CBE, 381n
Offenkowski, Maj., 264, 382n
Oswald, Maj. Ronald, 178

Pachomius, St, xliii
Parfitt, Sgt, 162

Parker, Cpl Edwin, 178
Parkinson, Brig., 150, 163–4, 166, 169, 192, 194
Patton, Gen. George, 2, 5, 226
Paulus, FM Friedrich, 34, 358
Penney, Maj. Gen. Ronald, 204
Percival, Lt Gen, 358
Perkins, Lt E.J., 322
Peter, St, xlii
Phillips, Maj. Geoffrey, 277
Phillips, N.C., 150, 153, 182, 184, 191
Piesakowski, Dr Tomasz, xxiv, 379n
Pius XII, Pope, 105
Placidus/Placid, St, xliii
Poole, Maj. Gen Evered, 205
Porter, Col Robert, 111
Powers, Pfc Leo J. MoH, 84–5
Prendys, L/Cpl Peter, 231
Preston, Lt Col, 208

Queree, Brig. R.C., 102

Raapke, Lt Gen. Wilhelm, 39, 74, 85, 237, 240, 307–308, 310, 313
Rakowski, Brig. Gen. Bronisław, 205
Ram, Sepoy Kamal VC, 250–1, 282
Ram, Subedar Sumera, 250
Renall, Lt Harold, 184
Richardson, Gen. Sir Charles, 22, 57–8, 358
Richtofen, Lothar von, 27
Richtofen, Manfred von, 27
Richtofen, FM Wolfram von, 27
Ringel, Lt Gen. Julius, 31–2, 35, 241n
Riordan, 2/Lt Paul F. MoH, 85, 90–1
Rodt, Lt Gen. Eberhard, 39, 74, 237
Romanus, xlii
Rommel, FM Erwin, 7–8, 11, 24, 27, 34, 351, 358
Roosevelt, Pres. Franklin D., 2–3, 30, 105
Rose, WOI DCM, 178
Roux, Col. Jacques, 72–4
Rudnicki, Col, 289
Russell, Maj. Gen. Dudley 'Pasha', 205, 211, 253
Ryder, Maj. Gen. Charles W. 'Doc', 36, 38, 64, 66–70, 74–5, 80, 82, 86, 89, 140, 204, 332, 337, 341

Safay, Lt Col Alfred A., 299–300
Sans, Lt, 45
Schauer, Pfc Henry MoH, 335

Schlegel, Oberstleutnant Julius, 363n
Scholastica, St, xlv
Schrank, Lt Gen. Hans-Günther, 241
Scott, Brig. C.A.Montagu-Douglas, 244, 247
Scott, Brig. Pat, 227, 233, 243, 273, 277, 285
Senger und Etterlin, Lt Gen. Fridolin von,
    xxxvii, xliv, xlviii, 2, 17, 25–6, 31–4, 38–40,
    50–1, 53, 61, 63, 71, 74, 77–8, 82, 88, 131,
    147, 149, 165–7, 186–9, 237, 239, 242, 244,
    305, 307, 328, 347, 351, 359
Sevez, Gen. François, 204, 305, 341
Shea, S/Sgt Charles W. 'Red' MoH, 302
Sheehy, Capt. Jack, 88
Shoosmith, Brig., 244
Showers, Lt Col, 125
Sidney, Maj. Philip VC, 95
Sikorski, Gen. Władysław, 230
Singh, Maj. Amar, 249
Singh, Maj. Gardhari, 250
Singh, Maj. Sujan, 250
Slessor, AM Sir John, 111
Sloan, Maj. Gen. John E., 204, 297, 302
Smith, Lt E.D. 'Birdie', xxiii, 125, 144, 155,
    177
Smith, Pte Furman L. MoH, 341
Smith, Brig. Ivan, 208
Specker, Sgt Joe MoH, 36
Spencer, Capt. W.G., 245
Stalin, Joseph, 2, 230, 358
Starr, Lt Col Chester G., 86, 89, 118, 143n,
    298, 340
Steiger, Alfred G., 374n
Steinmetz, Lt Gen. Bernard, 39, 51, 77, 237,
    300, 305, 313, 316
Steinmuller, Hauptfeldwebel, 167
Stevens, Lt Col G.R., 125, 138, 146, 175, 176,
    178, 182, 192
Strawson, John, 25
Streuli, Sgt William A., 204
Strong, Maj. Gen. George V., 6
Subramanyan, Subedar GC, 138–9
Sulik-Sarnowski, Maj. Gen. Nikodem, 205

Tassigny, Gen. Jean de Lattre de, 384n
Tedder, ACM Sir Arthur, 6, 111
Templer, Maj. Gen. Gerald, 46, 50
Tetley, Brig. J.N., 205
Thapa, Naik Birbahadur, 126
Thapa, S/Bearer Sherbahadur, 126

Thomas of Aquino/Thomas Aquinas, St,
    xlv–xlvi
Thomazo, Cmdt, 45
Thompson, Lt Col R.O.V., 245–6
Totila, 20
    see also Baduila
Tozzo, Pfc Anthony, 298
Treman, Capt. Douglas MC, 250
Trousdell, Lt Jim, xxiii–xxvi, 273, 284–5
Truscott, Lt Gen. Lucian K. Jr, xxxix–xl, 35,
    131, 226, 237, 306–307, 316, 328, 331–4,
    344–5, 350, 352, 361
Tuker, Maj. Gen. Francis 'Gertie', 101,
    103–105, 109–10, 114–15, 196, 236, 360
Tumelaire, Lt, 73
Twining, Maj. Gen. Nathan E., 137

Utili, Gen. Umberto, 205

Victor III, Pope, xlv
Victor Emmanuel III, King, 3
Vietinghoff-Scheel, Gen. Heinrich von, 8–9,
    19, 34, 45, 77–8, 129, 166–7, 239, 242, 244,
    287, 313, 315–16, 321, 345, 347, 349
Vokes, Maj. Gen. Christopher, 205, 317, 321

Wakeford, Capt. Richard VC, 256–7
Walker, Maj. Gen. Fred L., 38, 59, 63, 91, 97,
    118, 332, 359
Ward, Col., 67
Ward, Maj. Gen. Dudley, 205, 221, 244, 247,
    254
Waugh, Lt Robert T., 298–300
Wavell, FM Lord, 251
Wayne, Lt, 254
Wenninger, Gen., 208
West, Lt Col, 154, 158
Westphal, Gen. Siegfried, 166
Wilson, Gen. Sir Henry Maitland 'Jumbo', 30,
    109, 113, 133, 136, 200, 230
Woods, Maj. Desmond MC*, 277, 279–80
Wright, Maj., 249–50

Young, Lt Col, 128

Zangen, Gen. Von, 241
Ziegler, Brig., 321

General

Abbey of St Benedict, xxxviii–xxxix, xli–xlii, xliv–xlviii, 9, 81, 87–8, 90, 99–100, 105, 107–11, 113–14, 116–18, 120, 123–5, 131, 133–4, 136–7, 139, 142, 143n, 145, 154, 156, 160, 162, 164, 167, 169, 173–4, 176–7, 182–6, 190, 194–5, 205, 213, 233, 236, 262, 266–7, 287, 292, 294–5, 315, 360

Abruzzi mountains, 16, 25, 27, 31, 35, 237, 352

Ace track, 272

Adriatic plain, 15

Adriatic sea, 9, 41, 82

Aegean islands, 8

Affile, xlii

Alam el Halfa, Battle of, 5

Alban Hills, 332, 361

Albaneta Farm (Massa Albaneta), 64, 67, 90–1, 174–5, 183–4, 241, 261–2, 265, 267, 289–92, 294

Albania, 3

Albano, 307, 341

Alfedena, 16

Algeria, 22

Algiers, 6

Alpine passes, 8

Alps, the, 15, 362

Amalfi, 224

Amazon bridge, xxv, 244, 254, 272, 352, 356

Amaseno, 328, 341

'Americano' coffee, 225

Ancina valley, 208

Ancona, 235

Anzio, xxvi, xxxvii–xxxix, 1, 5, 27–8, 30–1, 35, 39, 44, 51, 54–6, 58, 63–4, 76–8, 80, 89, 92, 95, 108, 112, 114, 122–3, 131, 133, 138, 142, 193, 199, 203–205, 221, 223, 226–7, 234–5, 237–8, 242, 287, 299, 316, 321, 328, 331, 347, 352–3, 357–8

Apennine mountains, xxxviii, 17, 19, 25, 41, 58–9, 80, 140, 199, 202, 362

Aprilia, 76, 339

Aquino, xlv, 55–6, 149, 158, 242, 315, 317–18, 321, 328

Arce, 330–1

Ardea, 307, 332

Armistice, 3, 12, 23, 179

Army List, the, xxxiv, 121n

Artena, 334, 339

Ascensione stream, 244

Atina, 35, 45, 64, 71, 159, 236

Atina valley, 359

Aurunci mountains, xxxvii, xxxix, 20, 199, 273, 297, 305, 316, 328

Ausente river, 45, 235, 311, 313, 315

Ausonia, 46, 308, 311

Ausoni mountains, 328

Ausonia valley/defile, 54, 235, 242, 305, 308, 313

Avellino, 226

Avezzano, 27, 234, 243, 341

Badajos, 126

Baden-Württemberg, 33

Bailey bridges, 124, 253, 356

Balkans, 5–6

'Bank' objective, 249

Barbara Line, 17–19, 23

Bari, 14, 357

Baron's Palace, 164, 221–2

Belmonte, 158, 208, 241

Belmonte valley, 74, 359

Benedictine Order/Rule, xliii, 34

Berber, 305

Berlin, 10

Bernhardt Line, 15–19, 23, 25, 27, 30, 34, 41

Biferno river, 17

Billancourt, 110

Blackwater bridge, 244, 257

Blitzkrieg, 228

Blockbuster bombs, 105, 110, 114

Blue Line, Gari crossing, 244, 247

Bofors guns, 245

Bologna, 207–208

Borgo Grappa, 344n

Botanical Gardens, 164, 166, 169, 195

'Bradman', 142

Britain, 6, 23, 110, 114, 358

Britain, Battle of, 10

Brown Line, Gari crossing, 244

Buonriposa ridge, 92

Buzuluk, 230

Burma, 4, 126n, 355n

C Line, 243

Caesar Line, 18, 234, 243, 361

Cáira, xxxvi, 39, 67, 70, 76, 81, 97, 175, 183, 209, 213, 222, 227, 233, 262

Cairo conference, 30

Calabria, 7–8, 11, 14

Campo di Morti, 328

Campodimele, 313, 315
Campofiore, 50
Campoleone, 332, 334, 338, 340
Camp Gruber, 204
Camp Shelby, 203
Capo d'Acqua stream, 48, 298, 300
Cape of Good Hope, 2
Capri, 12, 224
Carano 'wadi', 334
Carabinieri barracks, 67–8, 75–6, 81, 83, 140
Cardiff bridge, 248
Carmelite Church, 152
Carpineto, 341
Carroceto, 92, 95, 332
Carroceto bridge, 95
Carthaginian army, 141
Caruso Road, 149, 151
Casablanca, 1
Casa Chiaia, 313
Casa Petracone, 256
Casa Sinagoga, xxvi, 277, 279, 309, 352
Caserta, 28, 30
Casinum Acropolis, xliv
Cassino, 321–2, 330, 342, 347, 349, 351–2, 359–62
Cassino jail, 90, 150, 194
Cassino massif, 330
Castel di Sangro, 16
Castelforte, 46, 50–1, 53–4, 89, 302, 310
Castellonorato, 316
Castelnuovo, 313
Castle Hill, xxxviii, 85, 86, 88–9, 136, 140–1, 150–4, 155–6, 158, 161–2, 164, 169, 174, 182, 186, 188, 190–1, 194–6
Castrocielo, 168
Castro dei Volsci 328
Catanzaro narrows, 9
Cave d'Argilla, 300
Cavendish Road, xxxviii, 174–6, 182–3, 262
Cenobitic lifestyle, xliii
Ceprano, 328, 330
Cerasola, 89, 307
Cerreto, 71
Cervaro, 36, 142, 204
Cesa Martino, 56–7
Channel, the, 133, 357–8
Cherbourg, 34
Chiesa del Carmine, 152
Cima Alta, 330
Cisterna, 76, 307, 332, 334, 336–8

Civitavecchia, 223, 235, 241, 308
Club track, 272
Colle Abate, 71–4, 76
Colle Belvedere, 16, 71, 74–6
Colle Monache, 277, 281
Colle San Magno, 241
Colle Sant'Angelo, 64, 67, 81, 86, 141, 261, 263, 289–90
Colli Laziali, 341, 344
Colosseum, 144, 164, 167
Congo bridge, 244, 257
Continental Hotel, 150–1, 160, 162, 166–7, 169, 173–4, 186, 191
contrails, 116, 143
Convent, 152–3, 164, 166–7, 191
Coreno, 243, 310
Cori, 235, 307, 334, 338
Corsica, 5–7, 32, 138, 241, 305
Crete, 8, 80, 103–104
Crotone, 7

Daily Telegraph, 110
Damiano ridge, 51
Dead Man's Gully, 292
Dead Mule Corner, 217
Dialogues, xlv
Diamond track, 272
Distinguished Service Cross (US), 66, 304, 339, 342
Distinguished Service Order (DSO), xxix, 103
Domenico ridge, 298
D'Onofrio ridge, 261, 289
Dora Line, 18, 242–3, 300, 316
Dunkirk, 4, 202

East Africa, 80
Eastern Front, 3, 9, 31, 34
Edenbridge bridge, 248
Egypt, 23–4, 103, 230
El Alamein, Battles of, xxiv, 5, 24, 103–5, 158, 201, 206, 235, 318, 322
El Hamma, 355
Enfide, xlii
England, 102, 200–1
Eritrea, 104
Esperia, xxxix, 242, 306, 308, 310–11, 313–14, 384n
'Eternal City', 27, 235, 344, 351
Europe, xxxvi, xxxix, xlii, xlviii, 1–3, 6, 34, 36, 41, 111, 116, 355n, 358

Excelsior Hotel, 147

Factory, the, 92
Fernie reporting line, 279, 283, 285
Ferrara, 207
First World War, xxxiv, xxxvi, 3, 9, 27, 33–4,
    40, 66, 102–104, 108, 201, 229, 297n
Flers Courcelette, 202
Florence, 235
Foggia, 6, 14, 114, 138, 142
Foggia Plain, 5, 138, 142
Fondi, 242, 313, 316, 328
Forma Quesa, 315
Formia, 46, 287, 316
Fort Leavenworth, 21
Fraile river, 311
France, xliii, 2–3, 7–8, 10–11, 20–1, 23, 27–8,
    30, 34, 76, 116, 200, 202, 206, 214, 229,
    241–2, 274n, 308, 347, 350, 362
French North-West Africa, 22
Frosinone, 27, 58, 223, 242, 331

Gaeta, 17, 20, 237, 242, 316
Gaeta, Gulf of, 31n, 237–8
Gaeta-Ortona line, 17
Gari river, xxv, xxxvi–xxxvii, xl, 31n, 42–3, 53,
    55–8, 60–1, 65, 74, 77, 128, 136, 195, 211,
    223, 235–6, 243–5, 248, 251, 253–4, 256,
    260, 271–3, 282, 350–1, 359
Garigliano river, xxxvi–xxxvii, 9, 15–16, 31,
    38–9, 44–8, 50, 53–4, 77–8, 200, 204, 208,
    237, 248, 297, 305, 310
Garigliano sluice, 16
George Cross, 139
German Cross in Gold, 34
'gibbet platform', 156
Giulianello, 334, 338
Gleiwitz, 228
Gliwice, 228
Gothic Line/Green Line, 234, 347, 350
Goths, xlv, 20
Goums, 204
Goumiers, 305, 311–13
Grafton reporting line, 274, 276
Great War, 103
Greece, 3, 8, 76, 80, 103
Greek islands, 3
Green Line, Gari crossing, 244
Green Line/Gothic Line, 234, 347, 350
Gustav Line, xxxvii, xxxix, 5, 9, 15–19, 27–30,
    34–6, 38–40, 43–6, 48, 51, 54, 63, 76–7, 80,
    86, 100, 118, 137, 198, 202, 204, 206, 208,
    223, 225, 243, 262, 299, 308–309, 315–16,
    331, 358, 360

Haifa, 202n
Hangman's Hill, xxxviii, 77, 154, 156–7,
    159–63, 165–9, 173–4, 176, 181–2, 184, 188,
    190–1, 193–5
Heart track, 272
Herculaneum, 193
Highway 6, 20, 56, 82, 86, 88–9, 91, 97, 102,
    105, 134, 136, 140, 149–51, 153, 158, 164,
    166–7, 169, 173, 183, 186, 188, 190–1, 193,
    199, 234–7, 257, 260, 271, 273, 283, 285,
    287–8, 292, 296, 316, 321, 331–2, 341, 345
Highway 7, 19, 45, 48, 313, 316, 334, 337–8
Highway 82, 313, 316
Hitler Line, xxxix, 18, 234, 236, 242, 262,
    286–7, 292, 297, 307, 312–13, 315, 317, 321,
    328, 330–1, 334, 347, 351
Hotel des Roses, 169, 173–4, 186, 191
Hummocks, 128–9, 151, 164–5, 167, 174, 195

Ides of March, 142
Il Colle, 312
India, xxviii, xxxii, 5, 20, 104–105, 196, 251
Italy, xxiii, xxv–xxvii, xxxix, xli, xliii, xlv–xlvi,
    2–3, 5–9, 11, 14–15, 19–20, 22, 27, 31, 34, 41,
    44, 48, 76–7, 104–105, 115, 131, 133–4, 137,
    189–90, 199–200, 202–208, 213, 227, 230,
    235, 240–2, 251, 259, 274, 276, 315, 317–18,
    320–2, 325, 347, 350–1, 355, 357–8, 361–2
Itri, 287, 299, 305–6, 310, 312, 315–16, 328, 330
Itri-Campodimele road, 313

Jesionka Stasiowa, 229
    see also Yasenka Stets'ova
'Jumelles', les, 45

Katyń forest, 229
Keren, 104
Knight's Cross, 34
Korean War, 50, 110
Kraków *Hejnal*, 295
K-ration, xxx, 73, 116
Kuki expedition, 104

La Bastia Hill, 313
Lagone, 35

La Guardia, 310
La Mamma Ciociara, 314
Lake District, English, 36
La Propoia, 76
La Torreto, 342
La Valle, 311–12
La Villa, 334
Lazio, 20
Leghorn, 235, 241
    see also Livorno
Lenola, 328–30
Lepini mountains, 334
Libya, 2, 11, 103, 201
Ligurian coast, 315
Liri Appendix, 211, 251, 257
Liri river, 20, 31n, 34, 46–7, 57, 211, 235,
    237, 241
Liri valley, xxxvii, xxxix, 15, 27, 30–1, 42, 44–5,
    55, 58, 67–8, 71, 74, 76, 86, 89, 91, 102, 123,
    128–9, 134–6, 138, 141, 159, 184, 190, 192,
    198–9, 206, 222–3, 226, 234–6
'Little Cassino', 302
Littoria, 307
Livorno, 235
    see also Leghorn
l'Olivella, 71
Lombards, xlv
Lombardy Plain, 5
London, 22–3, 230, 248, 357–8, 360
London bridge, 248
London Gazette, 139n
Lorenzo, 50
Low Countries, 10
Lubianka prison, 229
Lwów, 229

'Mad Mile', the, 210
Madras Circus, 183–4
Maiella massif, 15–16
Maiola ridge, 81, 91, 132, 175, 183, 261, 265
Maiori, 224
Mancici, 321
Manna Farm, 76
Maoris, 124, 128–9, 131, 180, 186, 192, 331
Maranola, 316
Mareth Line, 103
Marina di Minturno, 48
Massa Albaneta *see* Albaneta Farm
Massa di Ruggero, 307
Massa de Vivo, 256

Massa Tamburrini, 274
Massa Vendittis, 274
Matese mountains, 17
Matrice stream, 328, 330
Meath, County, 224
Medal of Honor, xxv, 36, 62, 85, 90, 298–300,
    302, 335–9, 341–2
Mediterranean, 2–3, 5, 10–11, 30, 34, 111, 200,
    206, 358
Melfa river, 321–2, 326, 328, 330
Melfa valley, 236
Mesopotamia, 104
Messina, Strait of, 2, 11
Mestre, 207–208
Michele, 35
Middle East, 228, 230–1
Mignano, 38
Mignano Gap, 25–7
Military Cross (MC), 23, 281, 352
Military History Society of Ireland, 108
Military Medal (MM), 357
Minturno, 16, 46, 48, 51, 203, 237, 297
Minturno ridge, 48
Mississippi, 203
Molotov-Ribbentrop Pact, 228
Monaghan, County, 280
Monastery Hill, xxxix, 77, 81, 87–90, 100, 105,
    108–109, 125, 129, 143–4, 147, 158, 169,
    198, 211, 221, 236, 287, 289
Mondragone, 17, 48
Monna Acquafondata, 45
Monna Casale, 44–5
Montaquila, 143
Monte Appiola, 328
Monte Aquilone, 36
Monte Arrestino, 334, 338
Monte Artesimo, 341
Monte Belvedere, 16, 71–6, 81, 208
Monte Bracchi, 297
Monte Cáiro, 15, 42, 74, 103, 141, 182, 213,
    237, 242, 264, 267, 321
Monte Calvario, 118, 261, 292
Monte Calvo, 312, 315
Monte Camino, 16, 25–6
Monte Capraro, 36
Monte Casale, 35, 44–5
Monte Castellone, xxvi, 64–5, 67–8, 74–6,
    81–2, 89, 97, 99, 105, 158, 213, 216–17, 227,
    233, 262
Monte Cassino, xxxiii, xli, xliii–xlvi, 15, 31,

77–8, 81, 91, 107, 111, 114–16, 118, 128–9, 134, 136, 141, 144, 149–50, 157, 159, 175, 217, 237, 241, 244, 262–4, 287, 292, 308, 317, 357
Monte Cavallo, 35
Monte Cerasola, 307
Monte Ceschito, 310
Monte Cifalco, 72
Monte Cimale, 330
Monte Crocetta, 340
Monte Damiano, 50, 302
Monte d'Argento, 48
Monte del Lago, 313–14
Monte d'Oro, 306, 314–15, 330
Monte Faggeto, 242, 312
Monte Faito, 54, 89, 307–308
Monte Fammera, 242, 305, 311, 314
Monte Fuga, 53, 204
Monte Girofano, 307, 310
Monte Grande, 316, 331
Monte la Civita, 243
Monte la Difensa, 16, 25–6
Monte Leucio, 328, 330
Monte Lungo, 25
Monte Maggiore, 16, 25–6
Monte Maio, 15, 36, 46, 305, 307–308, 310
Monte Marrone, 76
Monte Massico, 17
Monte Mignano, 9
Monte Natale, 48, 51, 53
Monte Ornito, 89
Monte Penitro, 316
Monte Petrella, 305
Monte Porchia, 36, 45
Monte Purgatorio, 53
Monte Revole, 305–306, 310–12
Monte Rotondo, 51, 310
Monte Sammucro, 16
Monte Santa Croce, 45, 64
Monte Scauri, 48
Monte Schierano, 330
Monte Strampaduro, 312
Monte Trella, 330
Monte Trócchio, 36, 45, 56, 75, 116, 124, 150
Monte Valle Martina, 16, 50
Monte Venere, 77n
    see also Hangman's Hill
Monte Vesuvio (Vesuvius), 193
Monte Villa, 67
Montecelli si San Onofrio, 328

Morocco, French, 21
Morocco, Spanish, 21
Moscow, 229
Munich, 8

Naples, xxxvii, xlvi, 5-9, 14, 17, 19, 20, 23, 27, 45, 76, 109, 113, 116, 138, 203, 222, 224
Naples, Bay of, 15, 42, 115
Nemi, 341
Nepal, 20
New Jersey, 204
New York, 302
New Zealand, 102-3
Normandy, xxxix, 23, 30, 131, 346, 358
Normandy landings, 27, 111
North Africa, 2-3, 5, 7-8, 10-11, 25, 104, 138, 204, 206, 229, 235, 317
North African campaign, 1, 105, 355, 358
North Midlands, 23
Norcia/Nursia, xli

Oblates, xliii–xliv, xlviii
OED, xli
Oklahoma, 23, 204
Operations:
    ACHSE, 8, 12
    ALARICH, 8, 12
    ANVIL, 30, 206, 347
    AVALANCHE, 7, 11-12, 17, 24
    AVENGER, 126, 134
    BARBAROSSA, 229
    BAYTOWN, 7, 11, 13
    BUFFALO, 234, 237, 321, 331–2, 334, 336
    CHESTERFIELD, 317, 321
    CRAWDAD, 332
    DIADEM, 207, 223–4, 234, 239, 242–3, 256, 261, 305
    DICKENS, 142
    DRAGOON, 206, 347, 358
    FISCHFANG, 131
    GRAPESHOT, 351
    GRASSHOPPER, 332
    HECTOR, 176
    HIPPO, 332
    HONKER, 235, 241, 243, 261, 273, 360
    HUSKY, 2, 6–7, 201
    LIGHTFOOT, 105
    MUSKETEER, 274n
    NUNTON, 222–3, 242
    OLIVE, 24, 351

OVERLORD, 30, 133, 200, 203, 346–7, 357
PANTHER, 46, 50, 54
RAINCOAT, 26
REVENGE, xxxviii, 176, 182
SHINGLE, 28, 30, 51, 357
SLAPSTICK, 7
STRANGLE, 137, 159, 200, 207–208, 223, 243, 350
SUPERCHARGE, 24
SUPERCHARGE II, 103
TURTLE, 332, 338
Orange Line, 242
'Orinoco' crossing, Gari river, 244
Orsogna, 104
Ortona, xxxviii, 17, 25, 352
Ostia, 39
Ostrogoths, xlv
Oujda, 21
Oxford, 33
Oxford bridge, 248, 253-4, 272

Paestum, 13
Pakistan, 202
Palestine, 214, 229–30, 274n
Palestrina, 339, 344
Panaccioni, 254
Pasquale road, 140, 152
Pantano massif, 35
Pantelleria, 2-3
Panzernester, 42, 44
Parallel Road, 140, 151
Paris, 110, 202
Passo Corno, 263, 290
Paterson, 204
Pathans, 217
Pearl Harbor, 22, 57
Peccia stream, 50
Peninsular War, 126
Penitro, 316
Persia, 104, 230–1
Pescara, 15, 27
Petrella massif, 311
Phantom Ridge, 184, 263, 267, 288–90
PIAT, 48, 281–2, 326
Pico, 287, 305, 312, 314, 329–30
Pico-Itri road, 287, 305–306, 310, 312, 315, 328, 330
Piedimonte San Germano, 315, 317
pigeons – Saints Andrew, David & George, 195
Pignataro, 55, 159, 257–8, 274

Piopetto stream, 245, 256, 274
Pisa-Rimini line, 200, 207, 234, 351, 358
Pittsburgh, 117
Piumarola, xlv, 284–5
Platform knoll, 248, 257
Plymouth bridge, 248, 253–4, 271–2, 351
Point 31, 254
Point 33, 254, 256
Point 36, 245
Point 41, 256
Point 46, 256
Point 50, 256
Point 60, 300
Point 63, 245–6, 250, 256
Point 66, 298
Point 69, 256 298
Point 79, 297–8
Point 85, 300
Point 86, 276
Point 103, 300
Point 109, 300, 305
Point 126, 300
Point 130, 302
Point 131, 299–300, 305
Point 146, 302
Point 150, 302
Point 156, 67, 75, 83
Point 165, 154–5, 157, 160–2, 173–4, 188, 190
Point 175, 83, 85, 88, 90, 140, 155, 191, 194–6
Point 193, 140, 153, 186, 188
Point 201, 51
Point 202, 162, 164, 173–4, 188, 190–1, 195
Point 209, 340
Point 213, 67–9, 75, 81
Point 236, 154, 156, 158–60, 162, 164–5
Point 270, 329–30, 340
Point 324, 81
Point 342, 51
Point 411, 50
Point 413, 46, 50–1, 54, 302
Point 435, 88, 154, 188
Point 444, 90, 123–4
Point 445, 86, 88, 90, 97, 132, 136, 186, 190
Point 450, 97, 125, 132
Point 468, 241
Point 470, 71–3
Point 479, 183
Point 505, 289
Point 569, 88, 125, 131, 261, 265, 267, 289, 294
Point 575, 131, 133, 175, 263, 267, 289–90, 292

Point 593, 82, 86, 88–90, 97, 99–100, 118, 120, 122–5, 131–2, 139, 141, 143, 175, 183–4, 194–6, 237, 261, 267, 289–92, 294, 361
Point 596, 265
Point 681, 73
Point 700, 72
Point 706, 82, 86, 204, 289–90
Point 711, 89
Point 721, 16
Point 739, 307
Point 771, 72
Point 862, 73–4
Point 1029, 44
Poland, 10, 34, 228–30, 261
Polish Government in Exile, 230
Polish Sappers Road, 265
Polleca stream, 312
Pompeii, 193, 224
Pontecorvo, 47, 158, 234, 242, 315, 321, 328
Pontine marshes, 20
Portella, 97
Pozzilli, 143
Presenzano, 17, 116
Puglia, 8, 14
Purple Heart, 66
'Purple Heart Alley', 225
'Purple Heart Battalion', 342
Pytchley reporting line, 277, 279, 281

QUADRANT conference, 230
Quebec, 230
Quebec bridge, 248
'Queen Street', 237, 245, 249, 254, 256
Quetta, 202
Quisling objective, 151

Railway station, 124, 128–9, 140, 144, 149, 151, 164–6, 169, 195
Rapido river, xxxvi–xxxvii, 15–16, 31, 42, 44–5, 50, 53, 55, 63–5, 67–72, 75, 77, 97, 123–4, 128–9, 131–2, 134, 140–1, 143, 157–8, 162, 164, 169, 190, 192, 195–6, 199, 208, 235, 359
Ravello, 224
Rave Grande, 311
Ravin Gandoët, 73
Red Line, Gari crossing, 244
Reggio di Calabria, 7, 11
Reichswehr Ministry, 10
Reinhard Line, 9, 16
'Rhine' crossing, Gari river, 244

Rhodes Scholar, 33
Rimini, 137, 200, 207, 234, 351, 358
Ripi, 331, 356
Rocca d'Arce, 331
Rocca Janula, xlv
Roccasecca, xxxviii, 71, 241, 359
Roman Empire, xlv–xlvi
Romania, 229
Rome, xxvi, xxxvi, xxxix, xlii, xlv–xlvi, 5-9, 11, 13–15, 18–20, 22, 27–8, 39, 44–5, 51, 63, 77, 128, 137, 141, 190, 199–200, 203, 223, 234–5, 242–3, 307–309, 331–2, 344–7, 349–51, 358, 361–2
Round House, 128, 174
Royal Palace, Caserta, 28
Rule, The Benedictine, xliii–xlvii
Russia, 10, 229–30, 261, 297n

S ridge, 299
Sacco river, 235, 331, 341, 344
St John's College, Oxford, 33
St Lô, 116
St Patrick's Day, 168
St Peter's Square, xlvi
Salerno, 5, 7, 9, 12–14, 23, 28, 76, 222, 226, 355
Salerno, Gulf of, 12
Salvatito Hill, 50–1
San Biagio (Saracinisco), 16, 35
San Carlo Opera House, 224–5
San Gennaro hill, 340
San Germano (& Battle of), xlv–xlvi, 315
San Giorgio, 46–7, 64, 308, 313
San Giorgio Dragoni, 219
San Giovanni, 330
San Giuseppe, 330
San Martino, 298
San Martino hill, 300
San Pasquale, 140
San Salvo, 17
San Vittore, 36
Sangro river, 9, 15–16, 25, 27
Sant'Ambrogio sul Garigliano, 47, 50, 237, 310
Sant'Angelo in Theodice, 42–3, 55–7, 65, 74, 126, 136, 245, 248–9, 254, 256–7, 359
Sant'Apollinare, 242, 310
Sant'Elia Fiumerapido, 31, 35, 45, 72, 208
Sant'Oliva, 242, 314–15, 330
Santa Maria Infante, 302, 304–305, 315
Sardinia, 2–3, 5–7, 32, 118, 138, 240, 242
Saracens, xlv

Scotland, 229
Scottish Highlands, 216
Secco stream, 72, 76
Secco valley, 74, 208
Second World War, xxvi–xxxvii, xl, xli, xlviii,
    1, 34, 66, 228, 252, 361
Seine river, 23
Sengerriegel (Senger Barrier), 347
Serra del Lago, 312
Sezze, 307
Sicilian campaign, 3, 6–7
Sicily, 2–3, 5–6, 25, 30, 32, 34, 201, 226, 276
Sinagoga wood, 280
Singapore, 358
Smolensk, 229
Snakeshead ridge, 120, 123–4, 261, 265, 290
Solacciano, 299–300
Somme, battle, 102, 149
Somme river, 23
Sora, 331
Soviet Union, 6, 34, 229–30
    see also USSR
Spade track, 272
Spigno, 300, 311–12, 315
Spoleto, xlii
Square Wood, 245
Stalingrad, xxxvi, 2, 7, 34, 358
'Stalingrad of the Abruzzi', 25, 352
Stretcher-bearers, 37, 128, 132, 138, 174, 179,
    191, 222, 257, 356
Subiaco, xlii–xliii, 339, 347
Suez canal, 2
Suio, 50
Swindon bridge, 248
SYMBOL conference, 2
Syria, 80, 229

Tabor, 204, 305, 310, 315
Tame, 299
Taranto, 7, 11
Teano, 17
Tebaga Gap, 103
Tehran conference, 30
Terelle, 66, 71–4, 97, 209, 241, 351
Termoli, 17, 214, 274n
Terracina, 20, 237, 242, 328
Tertiaries, xliii
Texas, 23
Tiber valley, 349–50
'Tits', the, 302

Tivoli, 342, 347
Tonbridge bridge, 248
Torre Annunziata, 193
Torre del Greco, 193
Travertine limestone, 43, 218
Tremensuoli, 48, 225, 297
Treviso, 207
TRIDENT conference, 3
Trieste, 39
Triflisco, 322
Trigh el Rahman, 322
Trigno river, 17
Tripoli, 2
Tufo, 48, 51, 302
Tunisia, xxiv, 1–2, 5, 21, 80, 103, 105, 201, 214,
    226, 276, 355
Tunisian campaign, 5, 21, 117, 208
Tunnels, 186, 200
Two Women, 384n
Tyrrhenian coast, 9, 14, 16, 19, 34, 203, 237,
    307
Tyrrhenian sea, 41, 45, 203, 308

Ultra decrypts, 114
Ulverston, 282
United Kingdom (UK), 2, 14, 23, 33, 111,
    143n, 200, 206, 228–30, 358
United States of America (USA), xxiv–xxv,
    xxxix, 21, 206n, 225, 299, 346, 358
Upper Silesia, 228
US Congressional enquiry, 61
USSR, 228–30
    see also Soviet Union
Uzbekistan, 230

Vallecorsa, 328
Vallemaio, 243, 308
Valle Piana, 312
Vallerotonda, 208
Valmontone, 135, 199, 234–5, 237, 243, 328,
    332, 334, 336, 338–9, 341–2, 345
Valvori, 208
Vandra, 50
Vasto, 144, 205
Vatican, the, 105, 107
Velletri, 234, 243, 328, 334, 336, 338, 341
Venafro, 25, 35, 143–4, 204–205, 356
Venice, 207
Ventosa, 50
Verdun, 108

Vesuvius, xxxvii, 115, 193, 207
Via Anziate, 131
Via Appia, 199
Via Casilina, 186
Viale Dante, 128
Vicenza, 207
Vichy, 22
Vichy French, 22
Victoria Cross, 51, 92, 102, 251, 256, 280, 322
Vienna, 363n
Viktor Line, 17, 19
Villa Santa Lucia, 173, 213, 216, 290, 317
Viterbo, 235
Viticuso, 35–6, 219
Volturno river, 15, 17, 23, 41, 116, 211, 219, 221

Wadi Akarit, 104
Wadi Zigzaou, 103

Waldshut, 33
Washington DC, 3, 358, 360
Waterloo, Battle of, xlvi
Waziristan, 105
West Riding of Yorkshire, 23
Western Desert, 80, 317
Western Front, 34
Wild geese, 261
Winter Line, 9, 15, 17, 25, 30

X crossing, Gari river, 244

Y crossing, Gari river, 244
Yankee Stadium, 302
Yasenka Stets'ova, 229
    see also Jesionka Stasiowa
Yorkshire, 23, 205
Yugoslavia, 3, 131